the cinema of GEORGE A. ROMERO

DIRECTORS' CUTS

the cinema of

GEORGE A. ROMERO

knight of the living dead

tony williams

 **WALLFLOWER PRESS** LONDON & NEW YORK

A Wallflower Press Book
Published by
Columbia University Press
Publishers Since 1893
New York • Chichester, West Sussex
cup.columbia.edu

A complete CIP record is available from the Library of Congress

ISBN 978-1-903364-62-8 (cloth : alk. paper)
ISBN 978-1-903364-73-4 (pbk. : alk. paper)
ISBN 978-0-231-85030-8 (e-book)

Series design by Rob Bowden Design

Columbia University Press books are printed on permanent
and durable acid-free paper.
This book is printed on paper with recycled content.

Printed in the United States of America

c 10 9 8 7 6 5 4 3 2
p 10 9 8 7 6 5 4 3 2

CONTENTS

ACKNOWLEDGEMENTS

I wish to thank Southern Illinois University for providing me with a sabbatical to undertake this work; graduate student Chris Costello for his valuable preliminary research in investigating certain leads into naturalism, the grotesque, Stephen King and the comic strip; Chris Hauserman for alerting me towards Romero's use of new technology; Robert Singer for insights into the complex and diverse operations of twentieth-century cinematic naturalism; Steve Bissette for research material; the Humanities and Inter-Library loan staff of the Morris Library of Southern Illinois University for their valuable efforts in obtaining key material; Steven Schneider for encouragment; Anna Gural-Migdal, Monique Fol, Vincent Lacey, Director of CAIRL Laboratory for his generous help with technical problems; The Latent Image for their kind hospitality granted me during my 1979 visit to Pittsburgh, especially George A. Romero, Christine Forrest, Michael Gornick, Tony Buba and Vince Survinski; and Dean Shirley Clay Scott of the College of Liberal Arts for providing me with travel funding for further interviews in Chicago with George A. Romero and Christine Forrest. Finally, I wish to acknowledge Del Cullen of Wallflower Press for his copy-editing work.

INTRODUCTION

This book aims to introduce the reader to the films of George A. Romero along the lines of the Wallflower Press *Directors' Cuts* series. By concentrating upon the features Romero has directed it will analyse them in the light of the social and historical circumstances affecting cinema from the late 1960s to the present day. However, this book differs from many of its predecessors in attempting to outline some relevant, but neglected, cultural and literary factors influencing the work of this director. As my previous studies concerning the American family horror film and the work of Larry Cohen have revealed, no cinematic work can really be understood apart from significant aspects of a highly influential national cultural tradition. Such features often operate as salient unconscious factors influencing the work of any innovative director. Until recently, Romero had not directed a film since *The Dark Half* (1993); his relative inactivity resulted from a deliberate policy of withdrawal from the dehumanising conservatism infecting the film industry since the Reagan era. However, I wish to argue that the specific nature of his work is not entirely comprehensible because of what Robin Wood has elsewhere described as those powerful radical elements rooted in the Vietnam/Watergate syndrome of disillusionment, protest and subversion (1986: 133, 189–91) which evaporated during the 1980s. Romero's films have always been characterised by a lack of false optimism, a willingness to look objectively at the hard facts of reality, and a recognition that any victories may be tentative (or even unlikely) in grim situations. Rather than seeing his work as entirely symptomatic of a specific era, I would argue that its particular vision is more appropriately related to certain neglected factors in the American cultural tradition such as the apparently outdated tradition of literary naturalism. Although naturalism is one of those 'master narratives' supposedly rendered obsolescent by fashionable late-capitalistic discourses such as postmodernism, it is relevant to an era hysterically attempting to forget important historical lessons. Although naturalism has suffered from its associations with Emile Zola's dogmatic theories expressed in his essay 'The Experimental Novel', the author's fiction often operates in a creatively different and dynamic manner, which refutes any attempts to classify it into conveniently rigid theoretical parameters. Zola's work was not just influential in Europe but also America. It stimulated not only diverse American literary explorations by writers such as Stephen Crane, Theodore Dreiser, Jack London and Frank Norris, but also achievements in early silent and sound cinema. The movement includes such diverse works as *Greed* (1924), *The Salvation Hunters* (1925) and *Last Exit to Brooklyn* (1989).

The American cultural tradition developed its own version of naturalism. It also recognised the diversity of a movement where aspects of the grotesque and fantasy appeared within its terrain. Gothic features also characterised certain works of European and American naturalism. They developed in specific literary and cinematic incarnations during the later years of the nineteenth and the early decades of the twentieth century. Literary features characteristic of 'New American Gothic' also appear in films as diverse as *The Texas Chainsaw Massacre* (1974) and *Wise Blood* (1979), the fiction of Stephen King, as well as another neglected cultural phenomenon relevant to both past and present American cinema – the comic strip.

During the 1950s, Romero was influenced by the visual style of EC Comics. Although castigated by conservative forces, McCarthy-era hysteria and academic experts such as psychiatrist Dr Frederic Wertham, who claimed to find a link between comic books and juvenile delinquency in *The Seduction of the Innocents* (1954), these examples of 'trash culture' were often more visually and thematically subversive of institutional values than the politically motivated work of those unfortunate victims of the witch hunt. Such visual features have always influenced Romero's work; they appear explicitly in *Creepshow* (1982). Although the film is not one of the director's major achievements, it by no means deserves the comparison made by Robin Wood with British Amicus horror films of the 1970s involving 'the same pointlessness, the same moral squalor: nasty people doing nasty things to other nasty people' (1986: 191). Despite its appropriations by an artistically bankrupt and decadently redundant Hollywood system, the role of the comic strip as a purveyor of serious messages, particularly in historically repressive eras such as the 1950s, still needs serious re-evaluation as an alternative mode of expression.

The sub-title of this book, 'Knight of the Living Dead', accidentally occurred before my realisation of its use in Tom Allen's article on the director. But it is not entirely coincidental or gimmicky. Romero's best work has always operated as a wake-up call to those dominated by a materialistic culture that promises life but actually delivers a living-dead philosophy. As Wood notes, Romero's zombies differ little from their living counterparts who are programmed into consumerist products of a decadent, late-capitalist civilisation and need desperate re-awakening before they supplement the former's ranks. The title of Ibsen's play *When We Dead Awaken* also operates as an unconscious, but relevant, parallel to the situations encountered by Romero's characters. Like all key artists, Romero never makes the message overtly didactic; but it exists within the text for those willing to discover it. His vision directly opposes those debased Hollywood values of the last twenty years. Rather than capitulate to market forces, Romero has decided to maintain his independence as an outsider by articulating an eloquent silence which is also oppositional in nature. This study thus attempts to trace the source of the director's oppositional directions. Previous studies of his work by R. H. W. Dillard and Gregory Waller relate Romero to the traditions of the classical horror film. Steven Shaviro sees the zombie films as a critique of the capitalist logic of production as well as noticing Romero's debt to the EC Comics tradition of the 1950s. Steve Beard regards the zombies as an allegorical representation of 'the disenfranchised underclass of the material world' and 'a projection of post-modern capitalism's worst anxieties about itself' (1993: 30). However, the films of George Romero deal with other issues also and should not be limited to zombies. As we shall see, they owe much to the tradition of literary naturalism derived from the work of Zola which entered the American mainstream and developed accordingly. Romero's films represent an intuitive appropriation of a discourse which has often been denied and rejected by the status quo. Although the director has never read Zola, his films intuitively reflect themes which originally appeared in the French writer's work and which infiltrated the American appropriation of naturalism in both literature and film. Artists are often influenced by relevant discourses, whether consciously or not. This book thus attempts to place George Romero within a particular cultural context and argues for seeing his work against a much broader background, rather than limiting him to the creator of the modern cinematic zombie.

Chapter one, 'A Director and his Traditions', is an extensive account of Romero in relation to relevant cultural, historical and industrial influences affecting his films. Chapter two examines his creative breakthrough as a director in *Night of the Living Dead* (1968). Chapter three reveals connections his recently released 'lost' film, *There's Always Vanilla* (1972), has to the concerns of his so-called 'horror' movies. Chapters four and five relate Romero's two neglected 1973 independent commercial films, *Jack's Wife* and *The Crazies*, to the developing conservative climate of Nixon's America. Chapter six investigates the relationship of *Martin* (1977) to both traditional Gothic fantasy and the New American Gothic explorations of writers such as Stephen King. Chapter seven examines the second part of his zombie trilogy, *Dawn of the Dead*, while chapter eight interrogates *Knightriders* (1981) as a dark allegory of compromise and contamination affecting both Romero and his fellow Americans confronting developing Reaganite cultural hegemony. Chapter nine examines *Creepshow* in terms of its relationship to naturalism and EC Comics influences. Chapter ten investigates the final part of his zombie trilogy, *Day of the Dead* (1985) and the cultural and industrial reasons for its neglect. Chapters eleven and twelve examine the unjustly neglected *Monkey Shines* (1988), his contribution to the Dario Argento production *Two Evil Eyes*, and *The Dark Half* (both 1990). The book concludes with an examination of his most recent film, *Bruiser* (2000), in terms of Romero's overall career.

CHAPTER ONE

A Director and his Traditions

Although hailed as the director of *Night of the Living Dead* (1968), a film popularly associated with initiating the gore and special effects syndrome affecting contemporary horror films such as *Scream* (1997) and *I Know What You Did Last Summer* (1998), the name of George A. Romero really owes much to that relatively brief moment of independent commercial cinema of the 1960s and 1970s. Stimulated by the success of *Easy Rider* (1969), many major studios invested and distributed early works of newcomers such as Dennis Hopper, George Lucas and Steven Spielberg. The era also saw the emergence of a renaissance in the American horror film characterised by significant works by directors Larry Cohen, Wes Craven, Brian De Palma and Tobe Hooper, which promised revitalisation of the Hollywood film industry. However, despite the appearance of early 1970s works including the *Godfather* films (1972, 1974), *Chinatown* (1974) and the films of Robert Altman, Hollywood cinema soon deteriorated into a complicit alliance of corporate conglomerates. Studios became dominated by multinational firms eager to include cinema as one item in a profit-sheet agenda.[1] Although making money had always been part of the pre- and classical Hollywood cinema, the profit motive had not exclusively interfered with the production of quality films, several of which involved some degree of thought and even challenge to contemporary patterns of life. The mid-to-late 1970s saw the appearance of two blockbusters, adolescently regressive films which would sadly herald the decline of a formerly great Hollywood industry – *Jaws* (1975) and *Star Wars* (1977). Among several other critics, Andrew Britton and Robin Wood have analysed the ideology determining these artistically impoverished works whose box-office success and dumbing down tendencies have contaminated the Hollywood film industry to the present day.[2]

Although elements of visual excess, horror and special effects characterised earlier horror films, the success of *Jaws* and the creatively bankrupt cycles of films in the

Halloween, *Friday the 13th* and *Nightmare on Elm Street* series led to the horror genre's change into a reductive series of roller-coaster experiences submerging the sporadic expression of intermittently interesting ideas within the narratives (see Williams 1996). This industrial late-capitalist movement led to the decline and debasement of talents who showed great promise in the 1970s. While Larry Cohen, Tobe Hooper, and George Romero became marginalised in the following decade, others like Brian De Palma and Wes Craven continued to work within the system but their later films never displayed the radical potentials and dynamic creativity that characterised the achievements of their 1970s work.

Apart from *Monkey Shines* and *The Dark Half,* Romero experienced inactivity during the late 1980s and early 1990s. These last two films differ visually from his previous work. On the surface, the formal nature of their respective styles appears to resemble an average Hollywood production as opposed to the independent film-making styles he employed in his earlier films. However, despite these differences, Romero was following a different type of style which moved away from his earlier visually 'excessive' type of direction. Yet his concerns in these later films remained the same as those contained in his earlier work. Most critics associate Romero with major achievements within the horror genre of the late 1960s and 1970s such as *Night of the Living Dead* and *Dawn of the Dead.* But they often neglect his other diverse films such as *There's Always Vanilla, Jack's Wife* and *The Crazies,* made during the same period. Internet web pages and journalistic discourses usually connect Romero's *Night of the Living Dead* to the gore and special effects operating within the contemporary horror genre. Most Hollywood mainstream horror films now indulge in sensationalism and special effects to the detriment of character portrayal and stimulating thought. They are actually debased heirs of an early film form commonly known as the 'cinema of attractions'.[3] Romero is often linked with the horror genre's emphasis on sensationalism and violence, but such associations are far from the truth and are less important in understanding the specific nature of his films. Although *Night of the Living Dead* and *Dawn of the Dead* are associated with the horror genre, their links and implications are far broader.

Romero's role as director is far more complex than it initially appears. Despite convenient application of generic labels such as 'horror' to his diverse output, Romero's works resemble Larry Cohen's. Like Cohen, Romero often engages in satirical attack on American society and employs comic strip imagery within certain films (see Williams 1997). But, unlike Cohen, Romero also unconsciously uses distinctive cinematic techniques derived from American literary naturalism, New American Gothic, grotesque realism, and cartoon imagery borrowed from EC Comics of the 1950s. Romero has also expressed his debt to the work of the British team, the Archers (Michael Powell and Emeric Pressburger), and has specifically mentioned their cinematic opera *Tales of Hoffman* (1951) in several interviews. As with other major artists, Romero often operates intuitively. He tends to be surprised at critical comments exploring his work, but significant cultural and historical structures of meaning are by no means absent from his films. While Romero may consciously employ the visual style of EC Comics in certain films, others exhibit patterns which belong to the American literary naturalist tradition and represent its cinematic development.

Zola's Influence

The naturalist connection appears an arbitrary connection. Does Romero not operate within the excessive generic realms of horror cinema, a world apart from literary naturalism's associations with factors of heredity and environment? However, naturalism is a complex cultural phenomenon. It is associated with Zola's literary and theoretical explorations contained in the Rougon-Macquart series of novels as well as his essay 'The Experimental Novel'. The Rougon-Macquart series emphasised genetic factors such as heredity and the wider realm of environment as key influences affecting the historical roles of individual characters. Many critics and readers believed that these factors operated in a rigid manner trapping many of Zola's fictional characters into behavioural patterns they had no control over. But such influences often *appeared* deterministic. Zola's nineteenth-century interpretations of certain hereditary and environmental factors affecting his characters involved *potential*, rather than rigidly deterministic, features. Such hereditary and environmental factors within Zola's fiction are capable of other, more flexible, interpretations. Modern reformulations would place these factors in a wider context, such as how genetic-family-induced features in the human personality interact with outside, environmental forces, themselves influenced by historical and ideological factors. In Zola's novels characters such as Gervaise Macquart, Jacques Lantier, Claude Lantier, and others appear to suffer from factors stemming from biological and environmental predestination when faced with overwhelming circumstances. However, although certain characters such as Jean Macquart and Etienne Lantier often encounter overwhelming odds and temporarily succumb to forces beyond their individual control, the novels in which they appear such as *Le Débâcle* and *Germinal* frequently conclude with hopes for a better future. Circumstances may change at any time. Zola never predicted any false optimistic solutions for future struggles facing his characters. Several of his works suggest possible alternatives, such as *Dr. Pascal*, but others, such as *L'Assommoir*, *Nana* and *La Bête Humaine*, end pessimistically. In these works, the main characters find that any alternatives are impossible due to the presence of overwhelming personal and social factors which cannot be overcome in specific circumstances.

Zola, however, was never entirely pessimistic. His utopian philosophy appears explicitly in his city trilogy, *Lourdes*, *Rome* and *Paris*. They involve Pierre Fremont's struggle to articulate a new religious and social order for those unhappy individuals caught within negative historical forces. Although these features characterise his less significant novels, they do reveal optimistic currents which often struggle for expression throughout most of his work. Like naturalism itself, Zola's work is a complex entity.

At its best, naturalism is never static but creative and dynamic. In his exploration of the contemporary urban film, Robert Singer notes that Zola's 'The Experimental Novel' makes a metaphorical comparison between the biological circulus, an organic solidarity, with its 'perpetual movement, until ... *dérangement* ... has broken the solidarity or brought about some trouble or stoppage', and a social circulus. For Zola, 'in society, as in human beings, a solidarity exists which unites ... members ...

in such a way that if one becomes rotten many others are tainted'.[4] Singer sees the concept of the social circulus often involving such 'dérangements' when heredity and environmental factors interact in specific and complicated ways. Such interactions appear in literary and cinematic naturalist texts. These texts often analyse and document individually damaging movements within the social circulus resulting from either hereditary or environmental factors or a specific combination of both. Despite the reductive nature of Zola's theoretical definition in 'The Experimental Novel', his fiction supplies empirical testing grounds for the operation of such formulas. Fortunately, his novels reveal more creative and dynamic modes of interaction than the more static philosophy contained in his theoretical formulations.

Certain objections may arise at this point, especially concerning the biological nature of Zola's ideas. They appear anachronistic and irrelevant within the concerns of a more modern historical era. But, as Richard Lehan has pointed out, despite the emphasis of recent studies upon naturalist associations with linguistic and institutional features, biological factors have always been common within the realm of literary naturalism (1995: 50).[5] However, we need not think of these factors within now anachronistic concepts of nineteenth-century genetic determinism. They are better understood in terms of Michel Schneider and Robin Wood's socially relevant reinterpretations of Freud's dubious metaphysical definition of an eternal 'repetition compulsion' affecting human nature. Quoting Schneider, Wood comments, 'like decadent bourgeois philosophers, he (Freud) mistook the "death instinct" of a murderous and suicidal class, the imperialist bourgeoisie, for the instinctive nature of man *as such*' (1998: 16). By understanding Zola's original genetic formula in this manner, greater insights into the author's fiction become possible. Already trapped by biological and environmental factors, Zola's fictional characters symbiotically exist within a dehumanising and materialistic Second Empire, moving towards its final apocalyptic descent in *Le Débâcle*. This situation also foreshadows Romero's deadly cinematic symbiotic relationships that feature contaminating social structures and negative behavioural patterns leading everyone towards the path of mass destruction.

Robin Wood and Sumiko Higashi are two critics aware of the relationship of Romero's films to their social and historical conditions of production. Such relationships also parallel June Howard's understanding of the naturalistic discourse as a 'form that struggles to accommodate that sense of discomfort and danger, a form that unremittingly attends to the large social questions of its period' (1985: ix). Howard further notes that any investigation of naturalism 'thus doubly entails an investigation of its historical moment – as the condition of its production and as the source of discourses embedded within the works ... It is a way of imagining the world and the relation of the self to the world, a way of making sense – and making narrative – out of the comforts and discomforts of the historical moment' (xi). Whether literary or cinematic, naturalism is no museum exhibit. In Howard's words, it is 'a dynamic solution to the problem of generating narrative out of the particular historical and cultural materials' (xi) available to any artist at any particular time.

Although many Zola novels end pessimistically, naturalism also has utopian possibilities. It informs the reader, as Howard states, of the 'discovery that our own history is contingent, that our world was not a foregone conclusion. That discovery may *perhaps* produce not only a renewed sense of historical difference but a renewed sense of historical possibility' (xi). For example, both *Germinal* and *Le Débâcle* end on a note of total defeat for the vast majority of characters. But they conclude with their main characters leaving the respective scenes of their personal failures and deciding to build a new future. In *Germinal*, the new season inspires Etienne Lantier with a renewed and reinvigorating sense of new possibilities. *Le Débâcle* does conclude pessimistically in one sense when Jean Macquart accepts the fact that his chance of a romantic relationship with Maurice's sister is now impossible since he has accidentally killed him during the military assault on the Paris Commune. But it also ends on an optimistic note with Jean's desire to rebuild his country after its defeat in the Franco-Prussian war. However, Zola's optimism always faces challenge by any changing factors which may occur in the future. Despite his relative freedom from contamination by the deterministic nature of hereditary and environmental factors affecting the rest of his family, Jean is not an entirely convincing hero whom the reader may expect to overcome satisfactorily any later obstacles. Any progress is provisional and liable to reversal at any time. Similarly, the concluding novel of the Rougon-Macquart series also reveals that little has changed since the Fall of the Second Empire in Zola's rural community of Plassans. As in the opening novel of the series, *La Fortune des Rougon* (1871), *Dr. Pascal* sees Félicité Rougon still exercising control over her extended family. Although she succeeds in destroying her deceased son's incriminating family history, fragments still remain for his surviving lover to begin his work anew. The obstacles will be great. But success is not entirely impossible. Similar thematic constraints also affect characters in the films of George Romero.

These literary references suggest that naturalism is not entirely deterministic or pessimistic as the endings of other Rougon-Macquart novels such as *L'Assommoir*, *La Bête Humaine* and *Nana* also appear to suggest. Howard notes that naturalist determinism may be neither pessimistic nor rigid in nature. It may operate according to a desire to place characters in situations of temptation from which they may or may not emerge successfully.[6] Furthermore Zola's 'scandalous' observations on the sordid aspects of certain facts of everyday existence do not result from either 'bad taste' or a perverse desire to provide sensationalism as his detractors argue. They result from drawing attention to unpalatable facts of human existence which readers ignore at their peril. This certainly occurs in the opening chapters of *Paris*. Affluent urban inhabitants ignore the plight of the dying, aged worker Laveuve. But their ignorance leads to apocalyptic consequences in this *fin-de-siècle* novel written near the beginning of a new century.

The naturalist movement soon crossed the Atlantic. American literary naturalism developed along chosen cultural and historical paths in the New World. But it also owed much to its British and French predecessors. As Jacqueline Tavernier-Courbin notes, 'Interest in contemporary French literature was a striking feature of cultural life in the United States during the last decade of the nineteenth century, and Zola's popularity is evidenced by the numerous translations of his works and by the fact that even novels he had not written were published under his name'.[7] Pre-World

War One cinema produced many films influenced by both European and American literary naturalism. These included not only literary adaptations by Jack London, often filmed in a distinctively naturalist cinematic style but even some works of Zola himself![8] Even the different consumerist Jazz Age of the 1920s saw the appearance of naturalist films such as Erich von Stroheim's *Greed* (1924) and Josef von Sternberg's *The Salvation Hunters* (1925). But the very idea of a naturalist horror film appears to contradict what most people generally understand by the term 'naturalism' if we understand it reductively as a slice of life representation.

However, elements of horror and excess typical of this cinematic genre are not entirely foreign to literary naturalism. In *Thérèse Raquin* (1868), the work he designated as his first naturalistic novel, Zola depicts his guilty lovers tormented by images of a dead husband returning from the grave to haunt them. His descriptions operate on a realistic level so that the hallucinations depicted take on material form very similar to the appearances of Freddy Krueger in the everyday world of his victims in the *Nightmare on Elm Street* series. Thérèse and Laurent are also under surveillance by the castrating gaze of a mother-in-law. Despite suffering from a stroke she still condemns them with her eyes. The imagery anticipates the castrating gaze of the dead Mrs Bates in Hitchcock's *Psycho* (1960), whose gaze encompasses guilty son Norman, intruder Lila Crane, and the cinema audience itself. *La Fortune des Rougon* opens with tragic young lovers Silvère and Miette meeting near a now disused, old Plassans cemetery where bone fragments are often scattered in the damp turf. Zola introduces significant grotesque and metaphorical imagery into the opening paragraphs framing the meeting of his doomed Romeo and Juliet figures. They become the first youthful sacrificial victims of a political strategy which leads both to the restoration of the Monarchy and the imposition of the dead hand of the past. These factors dominate the lives of future victims of the Second Empire during the entire Rougon-Macquart series. Both young lovers die separately in the novel. But their deaths leave a void throughout the remainder of the series. The dead past destroys any possibility of youthful potential and development. It is almost as if the dead rise from the graveyard to consume their youthful descendants in much the same manner as those living-dead elders of the Rougons and Macquarts destroy the lives of their children. Romero's zombies attack the living in the same manner. Although the final novel, *Dr. Pascal* (1893), concludes after the fall of the monarchy, the repressive patriarchal forces which initially led to its victory are still in control as symbolised by the dominating figure of Félicité Rougon who attempts to control past history. The book ends with the deceased Dr. Pascal's lover facing the huge task of opposing a life-denying authoritarian order. This climax resembles those tentative endings of *Dawn of the Dead* and *Day of the Dead* with the surviving heroines facing an uncertain future.

It is not surprising that Zola opens his first Rougon-Macquart novel with images of death and putrefaction closely linked with the future victory of a repressive order associated with patriarchal control (*La Conquête du Plassans, Son Excellence Euguene Rougon*), sexual repression (*La Faute du l'Abbé Mouret, La Joie du Vivre, Un Page d'Amour*), social decadence (*La Curée, Nana, Pot-Bouille*), consumer capitalism (*Au Bonheur des Dames*), economic excess (*L'Argent*), working-class misery (*L'Assommoir*,

Germinal, Paris), rural oppression (*La Terre*), marital infidelity (*L'Assommoir, La Bête Humaine*) and, finally, the collapse of French civilisation (*Le Débâcle*). Although no Marxist, Zola is critical of impossible utopian solutions (as witnessed by his satire of the dying, young Marxist in *L'Argent*), and sceptical about human development, and his work contains strong, moralistic messages criticising a familial, political and societal system that causes great injury to its unfortunate victims. Despite Zola's philosophical attachment to certain outmoded nineteenth-century theories concerning heredity and environment, his Rougon-Macquart series anticipates the American family horror film by revealing key relationships between the microcosmic and macrocosmic forms of social life. Zola's creative works belong to a particularly turbulent period of French history; similarly Romero's major achievements belong to another significantly influential historical period a century after Zola.

As many of Zola's readers know, qualities of literary excess often characterise his fiction, as novels such as *Le Ventre du Paris* and *La Faute du l'Abbé Mouret* reveal. Passages in certain novels often collapse traditional divisions between reality and fantasy. Father Mouret's hyper-realistic vision of nature's restoration of its former power (the taking over a country church in an apocalyptic manner in *La Faute du l'Abbé Mouret*) is one of many instances. Grotesque and supernatural imagery erupt within the text in a manner akin to the return of the repressed in a horror film. Despite its rejection by the literary establishment for most of the twentieth century, naturalism is not the simplistic dogma parodied by its opponents. Like all innovative ideas, naturalism's complexity suffered from distortion. But, as Raymond Williams commented in his re-evaluation of the term, 'actual positions and practices are very much more diverse than their subsequent ideological presentations and ... we shall misunderstand and betray a century of remarkable experiments if we go on trying to flatten them to contemporary theoretical and quasi-theoretical positions' (1989: 66). Williams also noted that very little historical support exists for divisions generally made between supposedly formally different artistic movements such as naturalism and modernism. Naturalism and modernism share a common aim of criticising society. Although naturalism ironically later came to be popularly understood in terms of the very things it attempted to challenge, such as the static reproduction of everyday life via theatre and television set design or mere grotesque spectacle, it was never reductive. It also contained several unexplored potentials for future development. Williams notices neglected opportunities inherent within naturalism which horror films might generically develop culturally and historically:

> In the same sense there is a crisis at that point in Naturalist theatre where someone stares from the window at a world he or she is shut off from. Dissident bourgeois art, including much of great interest and value, often stops at that point, in a moment of exquisite nostalgia or longing. But the more significant development is the growing conviction that all that can really be seen in that window is a reflection: a screen, one might say for indefinite projections; all the crucial actions of the world in a play of psyche or of mind. The powerful images which result will of course not be Naturalist, naturalistic, or classically realist either. When Strindberg, at just that point of crisis, changed his mind

about what made people unhappy, he began writing plays of great power which there, in the 1890s, were contemporary with the first films and in fact, as we read them now, are effectively *film* scripts involving the fission and fusion of identities and characters; the alteration of objects and landscapes by the psychological pressures of the observer; symbolic projections of obsessive states of mind: all, as material processes beyond the reach of even his experimental theatre, but all, as processes of art, eventually to be realised in film: at first, as in expressionism, in an exploratory cinema; later as available techniques in routine horror and murder films and in the kind of anti-science fiction commercially presented as SF. (1989: 115)[9]

Williams notes how naturalism extends in different directions and uses various forms to realise its goals. It is a tradition Romero intuitively appropriates. Although popular audience response to his zombie trilogy often remains at gratuitously spectacular levels, the films actually contain deeper levels of meaning.

One such meaning linking both Zola and Romero involves the concept of the crowd. Although more mobile than their zombie counterparts, Zola's fictional crowds often occupy terrifying roles. They can be also as mindless and violent as Romero's zombies. *La Fortune des Rougon* depicts both national guard and insurgent forces acting in an uncontrolled manner. In *Germinal*, female rioters castrate a butcher who has been sexually exploiting them for years and proudly display their trophy! Etienne Lantier gets carried away by the crowds in his self-appointed role as political leader. Everyone descends into irrational mass hysteria that harms their respective causes. Etienne's actions foreshadow Scottie's male bravado in *Dawn of the Dead*, which leads to his downfall. David's 'debacle' in the same film occurs after he, too, succumbs to the consumer greed linking both the marauding bikers and shuffling zombies returning to reclaim their commodified mall kingdom.

Crowds in naturalist fiction embody both literal and symbolic consuming qualities.[10] In *Au Bonheur des Dames*, Zola's female consumers in search of commodities in the new Parisian grandstore resemble those frenzied activities characterising both the living and the dead in Romero's *Dawn*. Mob imagery also occurs in American naturalist novels such as Frank Norris' *The Octopus* where events finally move out of control and disaster affects everyone. Norris' novel also contains a penultimate chapter anticipating the type of cinematic montage used by D. W. Griffith in *A Corner in Wheat* (1909). It contrasts the death by starvation of a helpless foreign immigrant with the cannibalistic feasting undertaken by members of the upper classes. Norris does not need to emphasise the metaphorical associations linking these two events. Very little difference exists between humans and zombies in Romero's films. The human vigilantes in *Night of the Living Dead* and *Dawn of the Dead* act in as mindless a manner as their zombie counterparts. Tom Savini's remake of *Night of the Living Dead* concludes with Barbara watching the human posse apprehensively and fully aware of the relationship they have with their zombie quarry. The living and dead also belong to a particular culture of consumption which Richard Fox and T. Jackson Lears regard as indicative of twentieth-century America, a connection which explicitly appears in *Dawn of the Dead*. Ironically, Romero's zombie trilogy views consumerist behaviour as literally, rather than metaphorically, devouring everyone in its path.[11]

Most of Romero's films emerge from a particular geographical location – Pittsburgh. Once a thriving industrial centre, it has now become an example of post-capitalist decline in American society. Naturalist literature and cinema often deal with issues of human deprivation resulting from the decay of a once-thriving inner-city environment. Romero's *Martin* and Tony Buba's documentary films *Sweet Sal* (1979) and *Lightning over Braddock* (1988) depict an environment whose decline not only expresses the collapse of American heavy industry but also that of human development and potential. Romero displays this important social message by using cinematic forms of narration. He deliberately selects the horror genre for his purposes, but concentrating particularly on its zombie aspect. The choice is not accidental.

Zombie Cinema

Zombies existed in cinema long before *Night of the Living Dead*. They are a generic feature of horror in the sound era but are surprisingly absent from silent cinema. Romero's films not only revitalised their cinematic treatment but also developed significant links with previous elements within the horror genre. *Night of the Living Dead* introduced cannibalistic features into 'living dead' representation, which later films such as *I Eat Your Skin* (1971), *The Living Dead at the Manchester Morgue* (1974), *Zombie Flesh Eaters* (1979), *Zombie Holocaust* (1979) and countless (forgettable) imitators all reinforced. Before *Night of the Living Dead*, zombies bore little relationship to their more visceral screen descendants. Originally zombies were creatures based on Haitian folklore who were supposedly corpses brought back to life as a result of supernatural voodoo practices.[12] The revived zombie was usually black and existed in a somnambulistic fashion resembling Conrad Veidt's Cesare from *The Cabinet of Dr. Caligari* (1919). Usually, the zombie supposedly provided cheap labour for sugar-cane plantations.

However, screen zombies differed from their mythical counterparts in several respects. Although the first sound zombie film *White Zombie* (1932), directed by Victor Halperin, depicts black Haitian zombies grinding wheat in Legendre's mill, the film is notoriously vague about what they actually did. The film opens with a scene of Haitian blacks performing a funeral rite over the grave of one of their number at a roadside to prevent its appropriation into the realm of the living dead. Audiences assume that the black workers seen later are actually dead. But Legendre's methods appear to have little to do with actually reviving corpses in the instances we see him functioning. In two cases he uses a poisoned flower and doctored drink to overpower his white victims as well as long-distance hypnosis. Once Legendre loses control, the victim recovers unless it is too late. In *White Zombie*, Legendre's zombie entourage includes key representatives of Haiti's governing classes.[13] In Halperin's *Revolt of the Zombies* (1936), the villain (Dean Jagger) also uses intoxicating fumes, as well as hypnosis, to dominate his victims. He never resorts to reviving the dead. Other films draw clear distinctions between white and black zombies and usually reserve traditional Haitian methods of resuscitation for the latter. *The Ghost Breakers*

(1940), *King of the Zombies* (1941) and *I Walked with a Zombie* (1943) follow this pattern. Although the black community in the last film clearly regard the white Christine as one of their own, the nature of her ailment is ambiguous and left open to suggested causes such as fever and a mother-in-law's wish-fulfilment desire for an obedient, dutiful zombie daughter rather than a live adulterous one. The film ends with Christine's lover killing her and both drowning. Bob Hope's zombie assailant in *The Ghost Breakers* is clearly black and decomposing but his counterpart in *Scared Stiff* (1953), a remake starring Dean Martin and Jerry Lewis, is played by caucasian heavy Jack Lambert. Both these films have zombies functioning as scary subordinate players, as in *Zombies on Broadway* (1945) where Bela Lugosi helps press agents find new acts for jaded Manhattan theatregoers.

However, prior to 1968, zombies were generally black rather than white in American cinema. Apart from Halperin's films, the rare appearances of white zombies differed from their Haitian counterparts. Boris Karloff's character in *The Walking Dead* (1936) is an unjustly executed convict brought back to life by medical means and who exercises limited powers of rationality and thought. Both *King of the Zombies* (1941) and *Revenge of the Zombies* (1943) depicted mad scientists unsuccessfully attempting to enlist zombies for world conquest by Axis powers. In *Voodoo Man* (1944), Lugosi turned pretty white females into zombies to keep his dead wife alive. However, during the 1940s the zombie soon became reduced to the type of Universal caricature depicted in *Abbot and Costello Meet Frankenstein* (1946). Romero's zombies are much more threatening. He reworks the figure similarly to naturalism's reinvention of the human being as a wild man and savage brute. Howard comments that in literary naturalism 'the creature who defines humanity by negation and represents a problematical area of existence is imagined as living not outside the bounds of human society, not in the wilderness (where images of the American Indian as savage placed it) but within the very walls of the civilized city' (1985: 80). Romero belongs to a 1970s horror tradition where the threat becomes internal rather than external. He thus depicts his zombies as progressively encroaching on the boundaries of civilised society in a similar manner to the savage crowds in naturalist fiction.

British horror cinema differed little from its American counterpart. The zombie in an episode of *Dr. Terror's House of Horrors* (1964) is clearly black and dead while the humans controlled by alien invaders in *Quatermass II* (1957) are white. Although termed 'zombies' by the local population they are actually alive since the aliens use methods similar to those of Lugosi and Jagger in controlling their human servants. Once the threat dissipates, they recover like Madge Bellamy in *White Zombie* and the white colonials and Cambodians in *Revolt of the Zombies*. In John Gilling's *Plague of the Zombies* (1965), the victims are all white and almost exclusively working-class male inhabitants of a Cornwall community used by the local squire (John Carson) as unpaid slave labour in his tin mine. This racial difference results from an English class system which regards the proletariat as little better than savages. Carson's villain in *Plague of the Zombies* puts into practice the suggestion Legendre made to Beaumont in *White Zombie* about using the living dead as unpaid labour on his Haitian plantation. Although Gilling's zombies resemble Romero's white prowling living dead crowds they are not cannibals.

Post-1968 representations generally discard class and racial distinctions between white and black zombies in classical films. In Romero's zombie trilogy, his living dead include male and female, diverse ethnic groups and members of different classes. His zombies also became explicitly cannibalistic, desiring both living and dead flesh. *Day of the Dead* (1985) shows attempts by the scientific establishment to control zombies in ways similar to methods used in earlier films like *Plague of the Zombies*. Dr. Logan (Richard Liberty) actually follows up a suggestion made by Richard France's scientist in *Dawn of the Dead* concerning the control of this new population. Various methods employed seek to render dangerous threats harmless to the body politic similar to Roland Barthes' concept of ideological inoculation described in *Mythologies*. Class factors condition attempts at controlling this new multitude who threaten the very precarious status quo existing in Romero's trilogy. Minority humans and the majority zombie population co-exist in an uneasy situation.

Naturalist Associations

The methods used by human survivors in Romero's films differ little from those within naturalistic novels where the upper classes attempt to control a growing agrarian and industrial proletariat. Such ideas also apply to Romero's zombies. According to the director, 'Zombies are the real lower-class citizens of the monster world and that's why I like them' (quoted in Beard 1993: 30). Both *Night of the Living Dead* and *Dawn of the Dead* see zombies as dangerous others while *Day of the Dead* features Dr. Logan training his pliable zombie Bub by using traditional child rearing methods. Whatever method employed, zombies become a new proletariat who threaten a hierarchically ordained 'order of things' as much as their living working-class counterparts in *Germinal* and George Gissing's *Demos* who are also characterised by cannibalistic imagery.[14] By dying from a zombie bite, humans fall into a deterministic mode of being whereby they fall into a 'living dead' existence, becoming zombies often little different from their everyday lives. They have no control over this process in much the same manner as Beauty Smith and Jim Hall have no control over the respective forces of heredity and environment which have molded them into human beasts in Jack London's *White Fang*.

But other human beings have a choice. They may succumb like Roger and Dave or decide to live on and fight another day like Fran and Peter in *Dawn of the Dead* and the small multi-ethnic community in *Day of the Dead*. Although odds against survival appear limited, the fate of human survivors is never totally deterministic. Some form of survival is also possible. Although Peter and Fran and the small community of *Day of the Dead* eventually leave the specific confines of cinematic narration and face overwhelming odds which threaten their survival, they still live at the climax of each film and may even continue to do so after the final credits.

Romero's *Night of the Living Dead, Dawn of the Dead* and *Day of the Dead* trilogy features imagery owing much to the naturalist tradition of class insecurity as well as the horror genre's special effects, the latter now having little social relevance in contemporary examples operating on purely sensational and exploitative levels. Like his other films, *Jack's Wife* and *Martin*, Romero's zombie films are usually classified as horror films devoid of social meaning. But, as Robin Wood demonstrates, all cinema genres are never rigidly discrete but fluidly interact with one another. Many naturalist novels also use features from many other genres.[15] In both *Night of the Living Dead* and *Dawn of the Dead*, as well as *Jack's Wife* and *The Crazies*, domestic and family issues occupy key narrative segments within the films which resemble scenes from naturalist novels. The naturalist scenario is never absent from a Romero zombie film. June Howard's observations are pertinent in this regard:

> In the degraded world of *McTeague* and *Maggie* the family is no safe enclave in which humanity, affection, and virtue can assert themselves; instead brutality, passion, and indifferent causality predominate. The family itself becomes a nightmare; the bonds between family members are not only ambivalent, as in *Seth's Brother's Wife*, but manifestly burdened with sexual and aggressive impulses. Both *McTeague* and *Maggie* comment ironically on the courtship plot and the image of the family as represented in sentimental formulas and the domestic novel, revealing life as it 'really' is – at least in another part of the city ... In the slums the family is not a haven but only the most intimate arena for the forces of destruction. (1985: 180)

This imagery evokes the bland romantic interlude between Tom and Judy in *Night of the Living Dead* before their destruction. It also parallels images of the Coopers whose mutual domestic antagonism parallels the devouring activities of the zombies outside the farmhouse. Like the American family horror film of the 1970s, naturalist novels and Romero's films both contain different versions of what Howard aptly describes as 'a potentially disruptive fissure in the text' (1985: 180). An unusual element which initially appears contradictory may actually embody a different means of expressing the core features of the discourse. Similarly, naturalism may also employ zombie imagery in horror films associated with contemporary twentieth-century cinema.

As one of a group of critics who convincingly argues that naturalism also extends into twentieth-century literature, Donald Pizer frequently argues against any rigid understanding of the entire naturalist discourse. He also relates it to other forms such as realism, the extraordinary and the excessive. Pizer points out that a 'naturalistic novel is thus an extension of realism only in the sense that both modes often deal with the local and contemporary. The naturalist, however, discovers in this material the extraordinary and the excessive in nature.'[16] If naturalism is really fluid in nature and capable of modification and development during different historical eras, certain horror films may also contain features associated with this movement.

As Howard notes, naturalism may also contain melodramatic action and 'unrealistic' animal imagery as seen in its fascination with the 'brute' side of human nature. She cites Frank Norris' first completed novel *Vandover and the Brute* (1894–95) for its representation of the dark side of human nature. The imagery occurring within this early work has many associations with Robin Wood's definition of the horror film as representing 'the return of the repressed'. The brute of the novel is actually Vandover's 'secret self', which eventually grows and devours him: 'As the brute grows, it devours Vandover – it is a carnivore, indeed a cannibal within him.'[17]

Romero's characters are often dominated by repressed desires that they cannot acknowledge. Eventually, they either free themselves from the carnivore within themselves or literally become carnivorous living dead creatures preying on others. *Vandover and the Beast* ends with its title character becoming an animal in all but name.

Howard's reference to brute imagery in naturalistic novels parallels excessive motifs occurring within horror films. These elements represent part of a text's productive meaning within which messages are inscribed. As Howard notes, the moral and formal aspects of a certain type of production often co-exist in the text. She does not see Vandover as explicity becoming a werewolf since the causes invoked to explain his transformation are natural and never supernatural. Furthermore, not only do the moral and medical systems of explanation coexist in *Vandover and the Brute.* But 'the moral is inscribed *as* the medical, the energies and events of melodrama are rewritten though the conventions of causality' (1985: 67). The same is also true of Romero's use of horror effects, which are never employed merely for their own sake. They are intrinsically related to logical and scientific explanations often supplied in each part of the trilogy.

Romero's various screen characters also embody certain particular features peculiar to the naturalist tradition. Howard quotes Warren French's observations concerning differences between characters in the novels of Dreiser and Henry James. French comments that:

> the former are not represented as being conscious of what they are doing or capable of any self-analysis of their motivations; whereas the latter are almost obsessively preoccupied with self-conscious analysis ... A useful distinction may thus be made between fictions that deal essentially with characters presented by their creators as aware of what they are doing and of the potential consequences of these actions, and fictions that deal essentially with characters envisioned by their creators as altogether at the mercy of such forces as environment, heredity, instinct, and chance. (in Howard 1985: 104)

Howard correctly notes that this distinction neglects the role of a self-conscious agent operating in the text whether it be a fictional character or narrator who operates to provide a particular perspective on the various events.

Various characters in *Night of the Living Dead* are victims of blind forces beyond their control and express no consciousness about the implications affecting their dilemma. Like a literary narrator, Romero provides a cinematic perspective and opportunity for audiences to draw their own conclusions but he does not intrude them into the text. Although his films often echo themes of naturalist determination, certain sections contain characters who are moving closer to the Jamesian tradition of self-consciousness. In *Dawn of the Dead*, Peter's character parallels Ames in *Sister Carrie*; he expresses a self-awareness concerning the zombies relationship to human beings. In the same film, Fran is often both apprehensive and fully aware of the dangers facing her group inside the consumerist Mall environment. In *Day of the Dead*, Sarah (Lorie Cardille) and her multi-ethnic community distance themselves from an increasingly ugly civilised status quo represented by the military and scientific establishment. They attempt to find some form of utopian escape. However, both characters and audience may find themselves trapped into a situation of paralysis represented by the spectacular nature of an overpowering threat threatening their humanity as in naturalist novels. Towards the end of *Dawn of the Dead*, Peter and Fran fall into a temporary form of paralysis by masochistically submitting to the zombie onslaught before deciding to escape. In the original screenplay and novelisation, they both commit suicide. Peter shoots himself and Fran allows the helicopter blades to decapitate her. Sarah and her companions magically escape from the zombies at the climax of *Day of the Dead* while Barbara in Tom Savini's *Night of the Living Dead* makes self-aware decisions almost immediately, unlike her predecessor in Romero's original.[18] Although they escape from the outer darkness like Humphrey Van Weyden in *The Sea Wolf* and Jack London himself in *The People of the Abyss*, thus avoiding the fates of Hurstwood and Vandover, their freedom is only temporary. They still have to face unknown challenges after the conclusion of each film. Similarly, screen spectators may choose to become passive spectators by consuming the fetishistic nature of special effects. But they are also in danger of becoming consumed by the spectacle itself, like a literary naturalistic mob rather than moving beyond the seductively narcotic dominance of cinematic voyeurism.

Like Hitchcock, Romero offers his spectators the opportunity of moving beyond spectacle to consider the actual nature of relevant social meanings concealed within such excessive displays. Similarly, both literary naturalism and Zola's fiction offer spectators a choice between remaining shocked at the grotesque aspects of the narrative or understanding the circumstances which have initiated them and moving forward towards changing such conditions. Readers who remain appalled at Zola's supposedly 'sordid' discourse, Hitchcock's 'bad taste', and the gory spectacles of Romero's zombie trilogy remain as trapped as those characters caught within naturalism's supposedly deterministic framework. As Howard notes, although aspects of voyeuristic enclosure and paralysis appear in Zola's *Thérèse Raquin* and London's *The Sea Wolf* these are not exclusive features within each text. We may also experience 'both the radical disjuncture between understanding and action and the obsessive inscription of the observer into the narrative' (1985: 114). Like Romero, both authors offer readers the possibility of choice in appealing to 'a magical transformation of society by the will signified in and by a work of art' (116). However, in all cases, tensions between determinism and change remain fully operational challenging both fictional characters and cinema audiences.

EC Comic Naturalism

Romero's films involve particular stylistic choices. One visual tradition he employs is a comic book style, especially that relating to 1950s EC Comics condemned by so-called experts such as Frederic Wertham in *The Seduction of the Innocents*. The tradition was often misunderstood and still offends many critics. Vilified as negative influences on American children during the Cold War era, EC Comics were actually much more complex than their detractors admitted both then and now. Although condemned for graphic imagery and 'gleefully perverse transgressions of almost every imaginable cultural taboo, including thematic treatments of incest, bondage and sadomasochism, dismemberment and disembowelment, and family murders of every possible combination' (Witek 1989: 15),[19] these comics actually provided culturally satirical antidotes to the hypocritical conformism of an era, typified by *The Man in the Gray Flannel Suit*. While the title character of Sloan Wilson's novel represented a post-war veteran generation who sacrificed body and soul to corporate America, his comic strip contemporaries worked under publisher William Gaines in far less lucrative, but more satirically satisfying, conditions. They provided alternative and subversive imagery to a youthful world reacting against materialism and Cold War conformity.

Many EC Comics artists had either undergone military service or knew the difference between actual combat and officially sanitised visual representations.[20] The visual style contained in EC Comics was certainly graphic and 'un-American' for the times. But by continuing grotesque imagery characteristic of the American Gothic tradition in the works of writers such as Ambrose Bierce, Nathaniel Hawthorne and Edgar Allan Poe, EC Comics provided an antidote to a hypocritically sanitised world of American materialism. Bodies decayed after death. Violence caused bloodshed and pain. People were not always good and moral. Society contained a darker vision beyond those presented by comics sanctioned by the Comics Code Authority Seal of Approval and Walt Disney. Although EC Comics contained visually graphic details which offended 1950s sensibilities, the storylines often contained moral elements. They demonstrated the dangers of injustice and oppression to anyone considering such criminal paths. EC Comics suffered from similar judgements in condemning horror films. Criticism often focused upon the supposed unhealthy effects of sensational depictions rather than relating style to content. The EC Comics were not an early version of 1980s slasher films. They often contained plots paralleling the social justice aspects of literary naturalism and the moral vision of Rod Serling's *The Twilight Zone*. Robert M. Stewart has commented that during 1950–55 EC Comics exhibited the influence of three decades of popular culture such as film noir, radio drama, television, science fiction and detective pulps which combined tightly structured stories with diverse characterisations. As well as engaging in the media satire later developed by *Mad* magazine and occasional adaptations of writers such as Ray Bradbury, many non-horror EC Comics like *Shock Suspense* and *Crime Suspense* engaged in unAmerican social criticism – such as condemning blind patriotism and lynching. EC Comics often borrowed 'punch endings' from O. Henry while others echoed the ironic conclusions contained in the works of European writers of the Guy de Maupassant school. Stewart notes that Romero's films often reflect some of EC's 'more persistent images' involving corpses with decaying flesh rising from their graves and zombies, imagery Romero acknowledged in a 1978 interview. Finally, in view of their indebtedness to previous media discourses in American society, a case can also be made for understanding the EC Comics tradition as another form of that unstable, transitional modernism Michael Denning sees as characterising the proletarian grotesque associated with the cultural world of the 1930s popular front.[21] Several EC Comic stories may have influenced Romero's films. 'Living dead' themes were quite common: Al Feldstein's 'A Shocking Way to Die' dealt with a gangster returning from the electric chair to avenge himself on judge and jury while his body progressively decayed;[22] and the zombie motif occurs in Johnny Craig's 'Zombie' and 'Till Death', the latter dealing with a plantation owner's rotting zombie wife which Joseph Witek sees as a satire of 'America's obsession with hygienic commodities'.[23] Stewart also sees a relationship between Joe Orlando's 'Impressed by a Nightmare' about a woman who believes that occult forces guide her life and 'Jack's Wife' as well as the attack on the title character by the decaying corpses of the husbands she has murdered in Orlando's 'Madame Bluebeard'.[24] This graphic imagery must certainly have contributed to scenes in later Romero films. For example, the cover of *The Vault of Horror*'s 1953 issue contained a graphic depiction of a living corpse with a meat cleaver in its head which visually foreshadows the fate of one zombie under attack by Tom Savini's biker gang in *Dawn of the Dead*.[25] EC artists such as Jack Davis, Joe Orlando, and Johnny Craig deserve further study. They may not only be authors within their own domain but also key influences on the future work of Romero.

Although political and public pressure resulted in the demise of EC Comics, their satirical vision took on a new lease of life in the founding of *Mad* Magazine. Joseph Witek regards this as a major element in a cultural fusion which eventually resulted in the underground comics of the 1960s. This also stimulated the more widely accepted works of Harvey Pekar, Art Spiegelman and John Jackson in the 1980s. Many of the underground artists were just old enough to remember the pre-Comics Code EC comics and all grew up at a time when the sharpest satire of American culture was found each month in the pages of *Mad* (see Witek 1989: 45). Several obituaries of Gaines commented upon his cultural iconoclasm and influence on writers such as Stephen King and directors such as Wes Craven and George Romero.[26] EC Comic employment of frantic verbal pacing, compulsive simile-making and quick, disconcerting jumps in point of view to heighten cultural anxiety anticipate many prominent stylistic features characteristic of *Night of the Living Dead*, *The Crazies* and *Dawn of the Dead*.

Finally, the work of Stephen King occupies a central point of comparison with the films of George A. Romero. Both authors were influenced by EC Comics in their childhood and collaborated later. Although neglected by the critical literary establishment (unless condemned as a prolifically ungrammatical and unstylistic hack writer) or acclaimed solely for his horrific aspects, King's fiction is a fundamental part of an American cultural tradition that also influences Romero's films. As a chronicler of historical influences on American literature and cinema, King has frequently expressed acknowledgement of his country's neglected naturalistic tradition, aspects of which appear in his writing.[27] King's fiction echoes many themes characteristic of contemporary American horror films especially those involving those struggling to survive in the dark side of the American Dream and falling into the fantastic worlds of horror which symbolise their daily experiences. The supernatural aspects of King's novels are really secondary to the grim fictional realities of Americans attempting to survive in an uncaring materialist society. Indeed, King's horrific dimensions actually parallel the dark realms depicted within EC Comics which allegorically depict the deadly nature of a material everyday existence responsible for acts of paranoia and violence. Many of King's works complement consumerist critiques in Romero's films. In *The Shining*, supernatural elements are less important than the historical and materialist factors causing the downfall of Jack Torrance. *Salem's Lot* is King's darkly ironic version of Thornton Wilder's *Our Town*. *Carrie*, *Cujo* and *Pet Sematary* contain several examples of socially dysfunctional American families that rival Zola's Rougon-

Macquart group in the realms of neurosis and violence.[28] 'The Mist' forms an ideal companion piece to Romero's *Dawn of the Dead*. It is not surprising that King has not only appeared in several Romero films but has actively collaborated with him on the two *Creepshow* films.

The films of George A. Romero are not just exciting achievements in themselves. They also significantly relate to an important American cultural tradition, providing a relevant perspective for viewers to really appreciate the critical nature of his achievements in American cinema. Although prominently identified with the horror genre and a decade which saw many significant achievements within that field, Romero has real claims to be taken more seriously. Whether conscious or not, his films relate to key issues affecting American culture and society both past and present.

CHAPTER TWO

Night of the Living Dead

Night of the Living Dead has long been associated with the derogative term 'splatter movie'. It is now popularly regarded as the film which introduced gore and special effects into the contemporary horror film, a genre now almost entirely devoid of social meaning and dependent upon gratuitous sensationalism. However, *Night of the Living Dead* is much more than a mere horror film. As well as being a key work of independent low-budget cinema, it also combines several important cultural traditions such as the grotesque aspect of literary naturalism and the thematic traditions of 1950s EC Comics in terms of a devastating critique upon the deformations of human personality operating within a ruthless capitalist society.

The film's success took its creators by surprise; so much so that poor business and distribution deals resulted in the lack of economic returns to its original investors. It was a low-budget independent movie made over weekends by a group of enthusiasts who had little foreknowledge of their pioneering contribution to the contemporary horror film. Raw, unpolished in terms of eschewing the bland standards of media reproduction, lacking in Hollywood studio expertise, and shot on black-and-white stock, the film seemed destined for a limited life in drive-in theatres. But, on national release, the film caught the mood of an America in turmoil. It soon became a cult film which would endure over the years and lead to a 1990 remake. It also resulted in an unfortunate so-called direct-to-video 'director's cut' by John Russo in 1999 adding footage shot some thirty years later. Romero had no involvement with this 'version'.

Night of the Living Dead broke many taboos. It lacked a 'happy ending' and left none of its central characters alive at the climax. No hero and heroine walked into the sunset after the cessation of the monstrous threat. Also, well before the emergence of the so-called 'blaxploitation' genre, *Night of the Living Dead*'s leading character was black, a fact Romero still ascribes today to mere coincidence. However, the film's culturally-influential predecessors, such as *Mad* and 1950s EC Comics, also contained leading characters including Afro-Americans, Jews and even North Koreans, who were often depicted as victims of contemporary society. These ethnic figures also occasionally appeared in more heroic roles unlike their counterparts in more mainstream forms of representations who were conspicuous by their very cultural absence.[1] Unlike most of his heroic predecessors in horror films, *Night of the Living Dead*'s leading character, Ben, does not survive but dies a death which is absurd in nature.

Although some horror films did contain leading characters who never survived into the final reel, convention often demanded that the future of humanity continue in the form of two young lovers. Tom and Judy fit the bill in this film, so much so that one of its 'dead' sequences involves a lovey-dovey moment between them – a staple of previous genre movies. But Tom and Judy literally become 'dead meat'. Their flesh provides an unexpected barbecue meal for the marauding zombies. The human survivors never unite to defeat the zombies. They are constantly at each other's throats and attempt to devour each other in an ironically metaphorical version of the outside assault by their living dead opponents. Indeed, the dead appear more united than the living in terms of their concentrated focus upon a specific aim. The zombies often mobilise by silent, intuitive communication. In most contemporary films the traumatised heroine usually recovers at the climax to battle heroically against the enemy. Barbara certainly does this. But, ironically, her efforts are too little, too late, and futile against the living dead adversaries. The zombie host entering the farmhouse towards the end of the film even includes her formerly alive brother who will now devour her in place of the candy bar he desired at the beginning of the film. Furthermore, Hollywood's idealistic images of childhood become tarnished forever when young Karen begins to devour the dead body of her father and stabs her mother to death. Ironically, the conclusion shows that father really knows best. Ben finally takes refuge in the basement which aggressive patriarch Harry frequently asserted was the only safe place in the besieged farmhouse.

As in EC comic book narratives, family values are thrown into question. Johnny and Barbara and the Cooper family engage in different forms of verbal aggression. Their combative mental cannibalism eventually concludes in a grotesque literal manner which logically represents the only manner the verbal conflict inside the farmhouse may reach its logical culmination. *Night of the Living Dead* is a film dealing with domination and possession on many levels. An unseen mother manipulates Johnny and Barbara into performing a ritual neither of them shows any real feeling for. Johnny attempts to scare Barbara in revenge for making him join her on a long journey to their father's grave. Barbara's attitudes certainly duplicate the very same type of passive-aggressive family mechanisms which her mother used on her so often in the past. Ben and Harry later verbally and physically fight over possessive mastery of the farmhouse and its strategic territorial space. Their conflict echoes that of two Cold War nations struggling for supremacy over a colonised area. Harry attempts to dominate his wife like a 1950s authoritarian patriarch in a manner both forced and ridiculous and is clearly resented by a spouse who mostly submits to male control except when it explicitly appears futile. Eventually, Helen's possessive mother-love for her daughter (probably the only reason she stays with Harry) leads to her death in the victorious cannibal holocaust of the zombie aggressors. These figures also act out another logical result of a dysfunctional personal and social system which destroys everyone caught within its psychological traps.

Night of the Living Dead's monochromatic style has several connections with early literary and cinematic naturalism. As in works such as Frank Norris' *McTeague* (1900) and *Vandover and the Brute* (1894–95), human beings confront a threatening environmental situation which may devour them in more ways than one. Like Hurstwood in Dreiser's *Sister Carrie* (1998), who leaves his secure Chicago environment and descends into New York's hostile, unfamiliar urban landscape, *Night of the Living Dead*'s characters find themselves suddenly removed from their familiar surroundings and customary patterns of behaviour and thrust into a violent world that threatens their lives and securities. If they do not descend into the bestial, carnivore world of their zombie antagonists, they may find themselves reproducing the behaviour of their assailants on the verbal level by attempting to dominate (or consume) their conveniently designated opponents in a conquest for domination.

The film has several reasons to be regarded as a naturalistic horror film. It uses the violent and grotesque imagery of its literary predecessor and fuses it with several of the concerns of 1950s EC comics such as social malaise and arbitrary violence that is more often than not connected with the body politic. These dark images from the American cultural underground were often too radical in the Cold War to receive full expression in the Eisenhower era. However, they erupted into full expression during the following decade.

Night opens to reveal a bleak and deserted country road. The long shot shows the isolated terrain until viewers discern a car appearing microscopically in the background. Gradually it fills the image, moving from right to left into the foreground before leaving the frame. Romero then uses several successive shots cutting between different images depicting the car's journey until it reaches an old cemetery. This location is as abandoned as the country road. A sign is splattered over with mud. The area appears tidy but not overtly. It exhibits rudimentary state care of a landscape containing the dead and useless products of American society. Following shots show the car driving past tombstones. One shot reveals it passing an American flag as the camera pans right. Romero's director credit appears superimposed over this shot. It not only signifies cinematic authorship but also alerts the viewer to *Night of the Living Dead*'s examination of a culture characterised by death as well as life: 'Old Glory' will soon become an American landscape of 'Old Gory'.

A low-angle shot frames the car before we see the occupants. This angle emphasises a vision of the dominant technology which most Americans place their trust in. As twentieth-century successor to the covered wagon of pioneer days, the automobile promises easy transportation and accessibility as well as shelter from weather and possible attack. When pursued by the first zombie (Bill Hinzman), Barbara (Judith O'Dea) immediately seeks shelter inside only to find that the keys, which would activate her means of escape, are no longer there. The once-secure automobile becomes little better than a useless shell affording Barbara merely a temporary means of escape. Its redundant nature anticipates human reliance upon all forms of science and technology which will prove useless against the zombie assault in this film and the rest of the zombie trilogy. In fact, this significant 'structure of meaning' also appeared in the ECComic tradition as several illustrations affirm. For example, the cover of *The Vault of Horror* 26 contains an illustration of a late-model car threatened by the hands of the living dead breaking through the concrete.[2] Thus, it is not accidental that the anachronistic science fiction 'radiation' formula used to explain tentatively the zombie phenomenon in the film originates in this aspect of the American cultural experience. We must also remember that the failure of human reliance upon advanced technology formed an important trope of most 1950s science fiction films from *The Thing From Another World* (1951) and *The War of the Worlds* (1953) onwards. Significantly, Johnny and Barbara's car radio also appears to malfunction.

The next scene reveals the two occupants, Barbara and her brother Johnny (Russell Streiner). Johnny first appears searching for a candy bar before he joins his sister outside. This fact initially appears redundant until later in the film when Barbara mentions it to Ben (Duane Jones) when recalling the events which led her to the farmhouse. Johnny feels hungry and wishes to consume a candy bar. Ironically, he later fulfills his wish by feasting on the living dead body of his sister. Before he leaves the car he turns the dial of their car radio which has seemingly broken down, the first evidence of technological malfunction appearing in the film.

By the time they arrive it is 8pm. Expressing frustration against what he feels is an outmoded ritual, Johnny complains about his mother's rigid attitudes in making her children visit the grave of a father he barely remembers: 'We have to move mother out here or move the grave to Pittsburgh. We still *remember*! I don't even remember what the man looks like so we drive three hundred miles into the country and she stays home.'

They arrive on a Sunday during the first day of daylight saving time. As they move towards father's grave, the camera tilts down from the sky to reveal them at the right of the frame in a visually destabilising shot, suggesting the presence of ominous forces which will soon shatter their lives. Johnny also complains about the manufactured wreath he brings with him and suggests that the local graveyard officials remove the one they bring each year, repaint it, and sell it to them the following year (possibly making a profit over the transaction). If Johnny is correct, consumerism affects the dead as well as the living in American society. No longer active consumers, the dead now become profitable objects whose new value consists in making a buck from their still-living relatives.

As Barbara kneels at her father's graveside, Johnny becomes impatient, 'Come on, Barbara. Church was this morning.' The two siblings begin to argue over church attendance. A flash of lightning suddenly occurs followed by thunder ominously booming on the soundtrack, heralding both the beginning of Johnny's verbal aggression towards his sister as well as the forthcoming appearance of the first zombie. Johnny remembers a past incident from their childhood when he scared his sister by leaping at her from behind a tombstone, an act that drew the wrath of their grandfather. Deciding to profit from his sister's vulnerability to childhood fears, he begins to scare her by taking on a voice which parodies once-threatening Karloff-Lugosi imagery from classical horror films now rendered camp both by Halloween celebrations and pop songs such as 'The Monster Mash'. He intones the sentence which has now passed into horror film legend, 'They're coming to get you Barbara.' However, Johnny will soon find that his evocative imagery will be no joke. Although certain forms of horror now become harmless and parodic, new ones arise to take their place.

Johnny and Barbara revert to replaying features from an unhappy childhood experience never entirely distant from their more developed, supposedly adult, consciousness. In this sense, they fall into behavioural patterns reminiscent of those damaging forces of heredity and environment dominating the various members of Zola's Rougon-Macquart family tree. Barbara's passive-aggressive hold on her brother and her moralistic criticisms of his infrequent church attendance clearly represent revenge for her humiliation by the sadistic games he played on her in early childhood. Although she comments, 'Stop it. You're acting like a child', she also falls into childhood fears as well as having feelings of shame concerning family responsibility towards the stumbling man Johnny taunts. However, as she appears to be just about to apologise for her brother's regressive behaviour the man attacks her.[3]

At this point of the film, camera angles and movement become more destabilised with canted shots and shaky handheld movements prominent during the assault and chase scenes. The style abruptly changes from a documentary realist approach detailing the melodramatic family squabblings of two siblings (well-known from the 1960s Family series of documentaries such as *An American Family* and its British counterpart *The Family*) towards the dangerous visual instability associated with crime and horror genres. By setting the initial sequence in a graveyard Romero unconsciously evokes the spirit of the opening scene of Zola's first Rougon-Macquart novel. The early graveyard meeting associated with the young lovers in *La Fortune des Rougon* acts as a metaphorical equivalent for the whole ideological message of the Rougon-Macquart trilogy, namely the destruction of youthful aspirations and idealism by the dead hand of the past. Ironically, Johnny immediately endures assault by a representative of those very forces he sneered at only a few seconds before.

The choice of cinematic style is by no means accidental. As Paul R. Gagne (1987) points out, Romero directed *Night of the Living Dead* in a naturalist manner. His use of lighting and gritty black-and-white photography and a no-holds-barred approach to the horrific incidents gave the film a certain realistic feeling which co-scenarist John A. Russo cites as a key reason the film caught on with critics as well as audiences. Romero spoke of this as follows: 'I think that if you make something that seems real and true to people, it then becomes possible for them to have the little kinds of insights and feelings and rationales that they call "hidden meanings" and "statements" and whatever.'[4] Another corollary of Russo's statement is that the worlds of everyday reality and horror are not as far apart as most believe.

Although Johnny rescues his sister and struggles with the unknown assailant (whose physical prowess is stronger than those of his later companions), he falls to his death, his head banging on a tombstone. In one sense, this is a fittingly ironic demise for a young consumer-oriented American who is disdainful of religion ('No real sense in going to Church'). However, Johnny will soon join a new corporate community represented by those living dead members he once despised. *Night of the Living Dead*'s use of Johnny does not merely reside in his surprise appearance towards the end of the film. The very nature of his death superbly reproduces the ironic morality of EC Comics whereby characters both get their just desserts and turn into the very figures they once despised.

Barbara manages to run from the zombie and take refuge in the car. But she discovers the car keys are missing, ostensibly in the possession of her deceased brother. Releasing the handbrake, she manages to move the car automatically down a slope. But she fails in this strategy by not paying attention to the car's progress. Her neglect results in the car crashing against a tree. As Barbara flees from the zombie, Romero films her pursuit through a variety of canted angle and low-angle shots as she runs along a deserted road. As she runs away, Barbara trips and loses both her shoes before rising and fleeing again – a typical 1950s generic stereotype which Romero will eliminate from his later screenplay for the Savini version. After stopping briefly by an outside petrol pump (which will function significantly later in the film) she runs inside a farmhouse for help.

The interior proves no salvation. It is not only deserted but contains features anticipating her future fate. After finding the living room empty, she enters the kitchen and takes out a knife from a drawer. As she moves into another room, a montage of quick shots reveals animal heads on the wall with disorientating effect. Barbara has not only left a kitchen where humans once prepared meat for consumption but also enters another room where trophies ironically foreshadow the fate of the entire human species. These shots thus symbolise a reverse world where humans change from being consumers to a hunted species facing consumption; humans now face becoming sustenance for zombies. Barbara ascends the stairs to find the cannibalised head of the farmhouse's female occupant. As with earlier shots revealing her terrified perspective when she confronts the animal heads, an abrupt jump cut and zoom-in to the half-consumed head aptly conveys Barbara's terror. Although she decides to rush outside, she freezes into immobility on the porch under a car's glaring headlights before Ben appears and pushes her inside. Barbara's terrified posture represents another feature revealing human similarity to the zombie assailants since the latter often freeze before flames or car lights.

Ben immediately takes charge of the situation, 'Don't worry about them. I can handle them,' as if familiar with dealing with lynch mobs. When he later tells Barbara about witnessing zombies pursue a gas truck and fleeing from a besieged diner, his narrative evokes African-American experience of post-Reconstruction days in the American South. Also, *Night of the Living Dead*'s zombies are all white. It will not be until *Dawn of the Dead* and *Day of the Dead* that human antagonists will ironically represent the idyllic vision of a multi-cultural and multi-ethnic society that 1960s radicals promoted. Also, Ben's decision to take control (although initially from an hysterical white female), resembles the Vietnam experience of working-class, ethnic groups bearing an over proportionate share of the conflict going on at the time of the film's production and release. Ben is certainly not working class but appears to be a black man who has reached the lower middle-class ladder of economic success made possible after the gains of the 1960s Civil Rights movement.

Although ostensibly a horror film, *Night of the Living Dead* symbolically captures the mood of its era by allegorically representing an America divided against itself.

Like the films of Larry Cohen, however, Romero's cinema never engages in any sense of reductive reverse discrimination. Although Ben appears to be the nominal hero whom audiences may identify with, he is a hero who makes mistakes and also engages in a destructive masculine battle over possession of territory with his white middle-class antagonist Harry Cooper (Karl Hardman). As the film shows, the attitudes of the old society affect everyone, white and black, young and old. They also lead to chaos, disunity and destruction.

Romero's following sequences involve clever juxtapositions of image and sound, camera angle and behaviour, and rational and irrational behaviour that is indicative of a superior visual style. Before Ben and Barbara discover the presence of other humans in the cellar, he kills two male zombies outside and saves Barbara from another one entering the house. As he drags the body away, he warns Barbara who gazes at the still living corpse in fascination, 'Don't look at it.' This is the first appearance of a compelling gaze between humans and zombies, which will occur throughout the trilogy. Despite the barriers separating both species, the looks often exchanged between hunters and hunted hints at some deep, unconscious connection between the living and the dead.

Ben then tells Barbara about his experiences outside: 'I was alone with fifty or sixty of those things just staring at me.' Barbara then relates the events leading her to the farmhouse, even emphasising the supposedly irrelevant detail of Johnny's desire for candy, before she breaks down into hysteria. This foreshadows the ironic nature of the final meeting with her deceased brother. Although Barbara manages to speak intermittently during parts of the film, she relapses into a catatonic situation, a condition illustrated by Romero's revealing close-up of a music box opening to reveal panels with Barbara's fragile face fragmented through the gaps. This scene occurs after Ben orders her to search for wood. It follows a significant diagonal pan from a mountain lion's trophy head to the frail music box itself, a movement suggesting the dominance of a carnivore's world over an insignificant signifier of human culture. When Barbara switches the radio on as Ben boards up the doors and windows, the commentator speaks of an 'epidemic of mass homicide' by an army of 'unidentified assassins' composed of 'ordinary looking people in a state of trance' in areas as far removed as Pittsburgh, Philadelphia and Miami. Both Ben and the zombies are equally 'unidentified assassins'. Similarly, zombies and Barbara are 'ordinary looking people ... in a state of trance'.

The camera then performs an ominous zoom-in to the cellar door after Ben's removal of another door. This deliberately slow movement not only foreshadows the entrance of the other humans from the basement but also represents Barbara's trance-like situation of her perception. The gaze is little different from that of any zombie. The following sequence emphasises suspense and vulnerability and also questions any barriers between living and dead. When a radio commentator makes disturbing references to the assailants' cannibalist activities, two men emerge from the cellar.

The sequence appears to operate on the level of pure *frisson*. But it is much more than a formal device for generating shock. The men's entry initially suggests another form of threatening violence. But they are human not zombies. The very manner of their introduction, however, suggests little difference between either species. The film will soon depict the presence of violence among humans as the main threat to safety as Harry enters Ben's world. The two men take an instant dislike to each other especially when Ben finds flaws in Harry's story concerning his decision to remain in the cellar. Resenting Harry's aggressiveness in ordering everyone into the cellar, Ben decides that the ground floor of the house offers the best chance of safety. Although the film ironically proves Harry to be correct and Ben wrong, the conflict between them is much more than a mere question of right and wrong. The two men from different classes and races prefer to battle competitively over power and possession as they would do in a normal business situation rather than work together for the common good. While Harry appears loud-mouthed and offensive, a failed bully for whom his wife has nothing but thinly veiled contempt, Ben also goes out of his way to provoke him by calling him a 'stupid father'. He also egotistically reveals his own masculinist desires for property and control: 'Get the hell to the cellar. You be the boss down there. I'll be the boss here.' Although *Night of the Living Dead* lacks the presence of a feminist perspective which will appear in both *Dawn of the Dead* and *Day of the Dead*, it clearly recognises that the competitive arena of patriarchal aggression is no solution for the besieged humans.

Harry decides to return to the security of the cellar while Tom (Keith Wayne) calls his girlfriend, Judy (Judith Ridley), to come upstairs. The world below reveals another example of the bankruptcy of the old society represented by the nuclear family. Harry (Karl Hardman) and Helen Cooper (Marilyn Eastman) uncomfortably co-exist in a frustrating marital situation. They remain married only for the sake of their little daughter Karen (Kyra Schon) who suffers from a zombie bite. Like Ben, Harry wishes to be sole master in his domain. As he nervously mentions, 'I'm not going to take any more chances,' Helen sarcastically replies in a muted manner, 'Of course not! That's important. To be always right and others wrong!' When she learns of the presence of a radio upstairs, she insists Harry relinquish his stubborn attitude: 'We may not enjoy living together but dying together will not solve anything. These people aren't our enemies.' Tom persuades Judy to relieve Helen from attending Karen so that the Coopers can join the others. Instead of beginning to collaborate with each other, Ben and Harry combatively exist in a state of mutual antagonism, which makes any attempt at common understanding and unity impossible. Harry surveys the boards Ben has hammered against the doors and windows, sneering, 'This is ridiculous! There are a million weak spots up here.' The discovery of a television set not only supplies more information about the zombie attacks but also implicitly condemns a government that is indirectly responsible for the ensuing chaos.

Most commentators regard *Night of the Living Dead*'s rational explanation for the return of the living dead as a hangover from 1950s science fiction films. In some ways it is, since this plot device does not reappear in the rest of the trilogy. But it does have a rationale of its own; as the local television newscaster provides further reports about the 'unburied dead coming back to life and seeking new victims', he provides additional information concerning the probable cause of the outbreak. An Explorer Satellite sent to Venus encountered a mysterious level of radiation, but the authorities exploded the vessel before it returned to Earth. However, like the similar situation in *The Quatermass Xperiment* (1954), the government and scientific establishment clearly bears indirect responsibility for causing the outbreak. Officialdom left it too late to destroy the satellite; it was already within Earth's atmosphere and thus caused a disaster parallel to Three Mile Island.

Although this motif never receives further development in *Night of the Living Dead*, it does anticipate Romero's later attacks on the government/military/media and scientific establishments both in the remainder of the trilogy and Romero's other films such as *The Crazies*. The television station shows a live report from Washington D.C. as news reporter Don Quinn (played by Romero) attempts in vain to extract information from military and government figures who refuse to answer his questions. They clearly appear guiltily embarrassed over the entire incident. The newscaster then reports the latest information from the scientific establishment who now abruptly seek to overturn revered social customs due to this new life-threatening situation. Although this strategy is necessary on one level, it also ominously reveals the perspective of an inhumane scientific establishment totally oblivious to the traumatic effects this will have on surviving family members. The new measures may be essential but the method of their announcement is both callous and lacking in human sympathy: 'The bereaved will have to forego the dubious comforts that a funeral service will give ... They're just dead flesh and dangerous.' Dr Logan's world in *Day of the Dead* is not too far away.

Furthermore, after previously instructing their viewers to remain indoors, the media now suggest they attempt to reach the nearest safe station. This spurs into motion Ben's plan to fill up a truck with gasoline so they can all travel to a safe haven. However, after Tom finds the keys to the truck in the basement, Ben states that he is unfamiliar with driving the vehicle. This leads Tom to take the initiative. Later events reveal that this supposed rational strategy for survival is flawed and undermined by damaging human insecurities, especially those involving Ben as self-nominated leader. Decisions are often made hastily rather than agreed upon in a calm and rational manner.

Before Ben and Tom depart, *Night of the Living Dead* includes another redundant sequence which future generic films eliminate. This involves a romantic interlude between two young lovers who would ordinarily survive when all others are destroyed in most contemporary horror and science fiction films. But, as well as holding up the narrative, this also reveals an irony worthy of EC Comics. Original viewers identifying with Tom and Judy soon receive a nasty shock reminiscent of the best O. Henry climaxes in the original EC comic strips. Irrational behaviour and lack of foresight lead to antagonism within the farmhouse. While Harry distracts the zombies by throwing Molotov cocktails from the upper windows, Judy breaches the strategy originally agreed upon earlier by suddenly rushing out to accompany Tom in the truck. However, when Ben, Tom and Judy reach the petrol pump, Tom finds that the keys do not work. When Tom accidentally splashes petrol on the vehicle, Ben's lighted torch sets in on fire. In his anxiety to shoot away the lock, Ben threw his torch too near the truck. Tom then attempts to drive the truck away, ignoring Ben's advice to abandon it. The vehicle explodes while Tom and Judy are still inside. While their incinerated corpses provide an unexpected barbecue for the zombies, Ben makes his way back to the farmhouse and breaks down the door after Harry refuses to let him in. After both men temporarily co-operate in securing the entrance, violence breaks out. Ben assaults his cowardly partner and this leads to further tension and Harry's decision to capture Ben's shotgun despite Helen's weary admonition, 'Haven't you had enough?'

The final onslaught of the zombies on the farmhouse commences. As Harry foretold, the zombies easily break through Ben's fragile defenses. Instead of helping Ben when the zombies attempt to overpower him, Harry makes a move for the shotgun. Helen and Barbara rush to Ben's defence and free him from the zombies. However, Ben retrieves the gun and shoots Harry. Ironically, the last ditch effort of both women proves futile. Barbara snaps out of her comatose condition to save Helen from the zombies but is herself caught in the embrace of brother Johnny. The dying Harry stumbles downstairs to Karen. While Ben struggles upstairs, Helen moves to the basement to find Karen devouring her late husband. Instead of rationally re-evaluating the changed situation, she allows mother-love to dominate her feelings and falls victim to her daughter who rushes upstairs to assault Ben. Pushing her aside, he moves down to the basement and finishes off Harry and Helen before they can become a threat to him.

Night of the Living Dead returns to day with a final ironic coda worthy of the best type of EC Comics story. In an earlier scene during the television broadcast, a reporter interviewed a team of redneck hunters led by Sheriff McClelland (George Kosana) who engage in a 'search and destroy' mission against zombies. He gleefully tells an accommodating news reporter of killing three figures who attempted to crawl away to safety. We have no means of knowing whether these were humans or zombies. Since this suggests redneck lack of discrimination between the living and the dead, the comments also ironically foreshadow Ben's eventual fate in the film. Since all zombies seen in the film never appear to run away and hide during human assaults, the posse has probably killed living humans. The media representative appears complacent with the 'official verdict' and makes no attempt at any discriminating mode of investigative journalism.

The final sequence of the film begins with a high-angle helicopter shot which visually suggests that there is no real difference between posse and zombies who are seen from above like ants. Both show no humanity when pursuing their victims. As the posse shoot various zombies and move their bodies away for incineration, Sheriff McClelland spots Ben in the farmhouse also raising his shotgun at them. He urges a sharpshooter (Vince Survinski) to shoot immediately at the target without really pausing to discover whether it is living or dead. Ben's decision to aim with his shotgun at the figures outside rather than calling for help leads to the final act of violence depicted in the film. The sharpshooter kills him. *Night of the Living Dead* then moves into a series of grainy black-and-white still images reminiscent of both World War Two concentration camp footage and Vietnam War photography as the hunters enter the house, move Ben's corpse with meathooks, and place his body next to that of the first zombie seen in the film, before lighting their funeral pyre. The last image in the film is a live-action shot of the flame engulfing the corpses in very much the same manner as the napalm then used in Vietnam.

Night of the Living Dead is a significant achievement both as a horror film which would alter the genre's formal operations as well as an initial statement of Romero's thematic concerns. Like all great achievements, it has relevance far beyond its actual generic associations. In extending the boundaries of generic representation in its time, the film intuitively followed a tradition of grotesque realism, having links with both the satirical tradition of both Rabelais and Zola. As Matthew Gumpert has argued, Zola's fiction owes a debt to a transcendental metabolism in its links to Rabelais' treatment of grotesque realism as related to the treatment of the body. As he states, 'The world according to Zola functions as an immense, collective, living body, a body whose defining features and fundamental truths are the cyclical movements of metabolic creation and destruction' (1993: 93). Gumbert also relates certain significant concepts of the 'world turned into body; the universe made flesh; the life of the individual submerged in a primeval and collective *body*, the body of the people, the *folk*' to Mikhail Bakhtin's definition of the 'carnival' or 'grotesque realism' contained in his book, *Rabelais and His World* (93). However, Romero's vision represents a bleak, dark carnival depicted within the confines of the horror genre. In *Night of the Living Dead*, the word becomes flesh in many ways. The supposedly civilised aspects of rational human communication become reduced to verbal aggressiveness. Oral cannibalism soon becomes physical cannibalism as represented by the onslaught of the zombies against the humans. As the film intimates, little difference exists between both species at the climax suggesting then a naturalist determinism contained in certain works of Zola that Gumpert finds as 'levelling distinctions between sentient and insentient beings, turning the cosmos into a homogenous substance' (94) reducing everything to its basest form of animal and materialist existence. In this sense, the grainy imagery reminiscent of concentration camp footage that appears in the concluding scenes of *Night of the Living Dead* is not accidental. The camps reduced living human beings capable of culture and speech to basic material component elements of ash and dust. Similarly, the posse burn the bodies of once-living human beings at the climax of the film. The implications need little commentary here.

As Barry K. Grant notes, the film is inextricably related to its historical context. Relating *Night of the Living Dead* to the events of the 1968 Chicago Democratic Convention, the year of the film's release, Grant furnishes a much more relevant perspective for understanding the film than those who merely regard it as the first 'splatter' movie. He comments that:

> I began to understand that the *night* of the living dead is not the evening of the film's narrative, but the darkness in the human spirit brought about by the absence of compassion and understanding; and second, who the living dead *really* are – not the lurching zombies, but average folk like Harry Cooper, the sheriff and his men, and, ultimately, myself. The film didn't preach this to me, but was instrumental in providing me with an experience with which I had to admit this truth – for I remembered that, given a choice in the resolution of the tension concerning my wish to have the zombies explained, and Ben's frenzy to secure his position in the farmhouse, I would have, in effect, 'sacrificed' Ben, even as I identified with him, to satisfy that wish. Like the

repulsive Harry Cooper, I was instinctively looking out for 'number one', an attitude which the film suggests is analogous to the desensitised state of the zombies. (1986: 12)

Grant acknowledges the rich nature of *Night of the Living Dead* in terms of its challenge to audience reception. On more formal levels, the film is merely cheap exploitation or a formalist 'splatter' rollercoaster. However, by reading the film in a more serious manner, the audience member has the choice of understanding its relevance to a particular social and historical situation. Referring to D. H. Lawrence's characterisation of those who never embraced the life principle as the 'living dead', Grant sees the film as forcing us to acknowledge 'that we have the capacity to be both Ben and Harry, however repugnant this notion may be' (12).[5] In this manner, Romero also follows an important axiom of the naturalist tradition which warns its readers of the dangerous consequences of following destructive patterns of behaviour, both social and personal. The choice is up to the individual.

Although Romero never presents any false optimistic hopes in his films, intuitively following the tendency of naturalist writers such as Zola, Norris and Dreiser, *Night of the Living Dead* does thematically interrogate the dysfunctional mechanisms of a deeply disturbed society. It explicitly presented the image of an America in which the old values were now harmful and obsolete, leading to a chaos very few would survive unless some drastic personal, political and social change would follow. That was the implicit message of *Night of the Living Dead*, a message Romero would develop in his other film.

CHAPTER THREE

There's Always Vanilla

Until its recent re-release on video, *There's Always Vanilla* (aka *The Affair*) was a 'lost' film. Despite its status as the picture following *Night of the Living Dead*, it was unavailable for many years and only officially available in brief extracts on the laserdisc version of its predecessor. Romero regards the film as both an artistic and commercial failure. After gaining recognition as the innovator of a new type of generic product, Romero did not wish to be stereotyped as a horror film director and attempted to show that he could make other types of films also. Despite its independent, low-budget nature, the director also regarded it as a mistaken attempt to imitate Hollywood films such as *Goodbye Columbus* (1969) and *The Graduate* (1967).[1] The result led to the breakup of his association with many of his collaborators on *Night of the Living Dead* such as co-producers Russell Streiner, John Russo and scenarist Rudolph J. Ricci. It left a trail of painful feelings and broken friendships, the extent of which Romero is still reluctant to speak about even today. However, despite its flaws, the film is not entirely devoid of value. It anticipates themes that appear in Romero's later work and contains several relevant autobiographical elements based upon the director's experience of filming television commercials. He engages in an ironic depiction of the deceptive media practices designed to sell products no matter how irrelevant and unnecessary these items are. The television commercial Romero shows Lynn working on uses those archetypal cultural images of Western freedom and romanticism which still remain predominant in most contemporary representations. However, the film shows that they have now become hopelessly corrupt and tarnished as a result of the manipulations practiced upon viewers by the dominant media. Romero presents his two lovers as existing in a world of romantic illusions fostered by advertising and the media; he presents their relationship in a framework whereby the mechanisms whereby human beings are molded by the dominant social apparatus are revealed. Although no horror film, *There's Always Vanilla* raises questions which are inherent in Romero's better known films, especially *Dawn of the Dead*, which deal with the contamination of the human personality within a world of consumerist plenty. Both films also intuitively question whether any love relationship can really flourish and survive in such a society. Romero also questions whether it is even possible for human beings to develop on their own terms, thus opposing the dominant nature of dehumanising social structures.

Shot in 16mm and later blown up to 35mm on a budget of about $100,000, *There's Always Vanilla* derived from a 30-minute, 16mm, black-and-white film designed as an audition film for actor Ray Laine to show to Hollywood agents. Romero shot and edited the short film which Ricci wrote and directed. Judith Streiner (formerly Judith Ridley of *Night of the Living Dead*) also co-starred in a film designed merely to show-case Laine's acting talents. Both Laine and Streiner would feature in the later full-length production. This became far removed from the spirit of the original version, which Ricci describes as 'lighthearted' and 'fun': 'It was not heavy at all; just a fun romp with these two characters, namely a freewheeling creative guy and his more practical girl-friend who wanted him to think more about his career' (quoted in Gagne 1987: 43).

Angered by critical comments about *Night of the Living Dead*'s photography (due to the poor processing used at the time and corrected years later for the laserdisc version), Romero decided to make *There's Always Vanilla* resemble a Hollywood film. So he directed, shot and edited the film from an expanded script by Ricci in this manner. Unfortunately, Romero and Ricci argued over expanding the script. Ricci eventually dropped out so Romero ended up by shooting improvised dialogues for Laine to speak directly to the camera to compensate for the lack of a finished screenplay. The production took over a year to complete. Gagne traces its problems to the involvement of too many people resulting in an uncohesive film which failed both critically and commercially.[2]

There's Always Vanilla is certainly not Rudolph Ricci's definition of a type of 'elongated Pepsi commercial'.[3] The film is definitely loose, lacking the tight structure of his predecessor, and confused in its aims. However, a certain message does appear in lines spoken by the leading character's none-too-admirable father, Sam. He compares his son's lifestyle problems to visiting Howard Johnson's ice cream parlour and discovering all sorts of 'wild, exotic, flavors': 'But, somehow, you always wind up with vanilla ... There's always vanilla, Chris.' This message resembles the usual archetypal Hollywood ideology concerning the eventual conformity awaiting young Americans, even those supposedly rebellious figures embodied by Marlon Brando in *The Wild One* (1954) and James Dean in *Rebel Without a Cause* (1955) who get over their various problems and take their place within the patriarchal family. However, since one of the most discredited and morally repugnant characters in the film utters this statement this suggestively alerts viewers that it is not to be taken seriously. The film ends on an ambiguous note with neither of the two major characters ever realising their creative and personal ambitions. They instead become trapped within ideological patterns of behaviour they cannot break out of in very much the same manner as all the characters in *Night of the Living Dead*.

Chris (Ray Laine) embodies the persona of the archetypal wandering male hero familiar to readers of American literature and Hollywood cinema. He pursues a course of selfish, masculine behaviour. Chris never takes any responsibility for his actions nor does he see the need for any change. Lynn (Judith Streiner) eventually becomes trapped into following the ideologically defined role of wife and mother, which she has initially reacted against for most of the film. Although Romero regards *There's Always Vanilla* as now 'dated' as a film exercise, many features contained within its narrative have not. These involve dilemmas and problems that occur in a more developed manner in his later films.

Although the film represents a change of style from his debut, it is not too far removed from it in spirit. In *Night of the Living Dead* lack of communication condemned all the main characters to destruction. The same dilemma also occurs in *There's Always Vanilla*. But this time it appears during a love affair in a society in the process of change after the exciting 1960s decade. The society depicted in the film is actually one slowly reverting to old habits and negative patterns of behaviour which destroy any possibility for future development. It emphasises the particular forms of personal entrapment exemplified by its two leading youthful characters who should embody features of alternative patterns of behaviour inimical to the social structures surrounding them. Unfortunately, they do not.[4]

The film opens with two shots of a bizarre Heath-Robinson type machine which we later learn is constructed in front of the grounds of an advertising agency where Chris temporarily works. We then see him speaking the first of his many addresses to the camera: 'If you can dig it, the whole thing was kind of like that machine.' Two cuts showing the machine follow. The last concludes with a zoom out from the machine. Then the scene changes to Chris who adds 'everything was so confused, everything going round and round, and we didn't have to have caused that, and we couldn't understand it.' Chris's various addresses to the camera are not mere fillers to an undeveloped screenplay nor are they irrelevant to the film's structure. The affair in the film has a pertinent relationship both to the avant-garde machine set up before curious bystanders as well as the inability of the two lovers either to understand themselves or their relationship to society.

In this manner *There's Always Vanilla* begins to articulate issues which will recur in Romero's other films such as *Jack's Wife, Martin, Dawn of the Dead* and *Day of the Dead*. These involve situations where characters confront circumstances challenging their presupposed lifestyles and whether they can rationally respond to such dilemmas. Secondly, the reference to the machine unconsciously relates to the role of such imagery in naturalist novels contained within Zola's works such as *Germinal* and Norris' *The Pit*. In the first novel, the Voreux mines represent a mechanical devouring beast which both physically and mentally consumes the workers, imagery which later appears in a different context during one scene in Fritz Lang's *Metropolis* (1926). Although not as creatively written as *The Octopus*, the second novel in Norris' uncompleted trilogy depicts the Chicago stock exchange in a similar manner operating as a beast devouring its victims. Although the machine depicted in the opening scene of *There's Always Vanilla* appears as a harmless gadget, it metaphorically embodies the mechanical operation of harmful psychological factors dominating the human personality, factors which Romero's characters must always struggle against.

A placard describes the machine as 'The Ultimate Machine'. Various shots show cogs and gears in operation intercut with images of perplexed observers. Voice-over dialogue occurs when an unseen commentator asks invisible spectators about the machine's purpose: 'What do you think of that machine?' The answers are various and often reveal the ideological perspective of the addressee. One spectator describes the machine as 'marvellous' while another believes 'a genius or a student' made it. Diverse answers respond to the commentator's 'Do you think it means anything?' As the camera lens zooms out from the machine and the spectators to show the credits, two people respond. One spectator states, 'Everything that happens has to have some purpose to it.' Another angry respondent comments, 'I think they're trying to make fun of us. Some college kids made this up and they're trying to say that our society is screwed up.'

We then return to Chris's address to the audience, 'I tried to make the chick understand … I really tried to make her understand that.' Then images of the machine and audience commentary occur again. It is interesting to note that Chris refers to Lynn as 'the chick' and not by her actual name. What he tries 'to make her understand' remains to be disclosed by the film. But it will be a disclosure which reflects negatively on him. Chris may attempt to make Lynn understand about the dangers of conformity, but the methods he adopts do not really work and have the opposite effect from what he intends. He does not really try to understand what motivates Lynn as well as anticipate the problems which will affect her later, problems he bears direct responsibility for.

Audience comments on the 'ultimate machine' again reflect a diversity of opinion which never understand the real conditions of its operation. They reveal different forms of socially motivated prejudice which appear irrational and confused.[5] 'I like it … It's more or less what the country needs. I think if more time was put into things like that, things that make people happy, things that make people get out on a sunny day like this, we wouldn't be in Vietnam … our economy wouldn't be screwed up and we probably wouldn't have Spiro Agnew as our Vice-President.' Another silent majority spectator comments, 'I think if they don't like it here they should get out.' Another diverse opinion follows: 'I think basically it's camp.' One commentator compares the machine to the future zombie invasions of *Dawn of the Dead* and *Day of the Dead*: 'Pretty soon, the whole world will be covered with these things.' Another spectator gloomily prognosticates that his first impression was 'dismay': 'When I first saw that thing I knew there was no hope for us anyway.' The responses represent a mixture of absurd, irrational comment which either attempts to understand the machine or react against it. During the demonstration, an operator dressed like a nineteenth-century railway driver sits quietly by the machine watching its operation, an image evoking unconscious echoes of the train in Zola's *La Bête Humaine* hurtling on its way to destruction. The incongruity of a nineteenth-century costumed figure in a twentieth-century setting watching over an avant-garde machine ironically echoes the absurd nature of a different century unable, or unwilling, to heed the lessons of the previous one.

The image then changes to show again Chris's address to the camera as he tells the audience about the absurd nature of Army bureaucracy when a sergeant told him that a shower cabinet contained a filing cabinet without any thought of its incongruity there. The sergeant believed that the object belonged there so its presence in an inappropriate location was never questioned. Ironically, the final audience comment concerning the machine is 'It's beautiful. But what does it do?'

This introductory sequence initially appears irrelevant to the fictional concerns of the main narrative as an extra-diegetic intrusion. But it is, nonetheless, crucial to *There's Always Vanilla*'s premises. The people who comment on the machine rely on their everyday prejudices rather than rational analysis. But the key issue is 'what does it do?' The film never answers this question but leaves both audience and characters in limbo. After this scene, the film will move on to depict a relationship which just happens and goes nowhere. Both Chris and Lynn accidentally fall into an affair, but they never develop their brief personal relationship into a new, radical commitment that differs from the failed relationships embodied by both their parents. As heirs of the utopian hopes of the 1960s generation they dismally fail in realising its premises. Like Antonioni's *Zabriskie Point* (1970), *There's Always Vanilla* not only documents the failed aspirations of the 1960s generation but also implicitly argues for the rejection of deeply ingrained social modes of conditioning if any progress is ever to occur in human relationships. Ironically, when Chris later explains the reasons for quitting his job at the advertising agency to Lynn he critiques those 'gray flannelled executives ... staring at a silly old collection of gears and pulleys and trying to figure out the adjustments...'. At that point in the film, the audience then associates the dialogue with the earlier imagery contained within the prologue. However, *There's Always Vanilla* reveals that an equally unperceptive hero is the one making this remark, a hero incapable of realising the concrete nature of important personal adjustments that would make his relationship work in the first place.

Most viewers would immediately identify with the main narrator. But, like several of his literary predecessors and many key characters in naturalist fiction, Chris is an 'unreliable narrator' in more ways than one. His comments towards Lynn are extremely sexist and the developing narrative will undermine any superior claims he thinks he has. The opening sequence concludes with his final comments which compare Lynn to the spectators: 'I could never get the chick to appreciate anything like that.' However, what we later learn of his future behaviour will undermine any claims Chris has either in regard to intellectual and moral superiority or even empathy towards other people. Like Ben and Harry in *Night of the Living Dead* and Romero's future masculinist characters, Chris believes in his supposedly infallible superior judgement which leads to the breakdown of his relationship with Lynn and his continuing role as an aimless wanderer existing in his own form of personal and social limbo.

The following sequence reveals Chris's dissatisfaction with working in the music industry and his decision to return to Pittsburgh: 'I should have stayed with what I was into, playing the guitar. The money was good ... but it became a drag to listen to myself on other people's records.' Succeeding shots of the record studio reveal Chris is as frustrated as Lynn is with her work in shooting advertising commercials. Like Romero's later insert of his name on a production credit and brief appearance filming a sexually suggestive commercial, the names of *There's Always Vanilla* co-producers Russell Streiner and John Russo also appear in the recording studio. This reproduces the self-reflexive aspect of the radical European cinema of the 1960s and 1970s associated with Jean-Luc Godard which temporarily influenced the contemporary New American Cinema. It also places Romero and his co-producers in the same position as their fictional creations in terms of their complicity with an industry manufacturing illusions despite their various attempts to break free from it. Far from being a spontaneous haven of alternative music, the recording studio reveals the various constraints affecting production. A producer constantly directs the music group while an associate times their music with a stopwatch ensuring that the requisite 'three minutes and twenty-two seconds' are reached – a similar time constraint to the ninety-minute formula for most contemporary narrative feature films.

Chris expresses his discontent to a co-worker. He finds no opportunity for freedom in this environment: 'I'm leaving today. I'm tired of hearing myself on other people's records.' But his colleague cannot hear him because of the studio noise. Chris comments, 'It's this noise. It's driving me crazy ... My brain. I've lost the ability to think. I think the sound is destroying my brain.' In other words, Chris is in danger of becoming little better than a musical zombie in the industry. His remarks also uncannily foreshadow the contemporary world of action movies which aim to overwhelm viewers with spectacular, quickly-edited images and loud Dolby sound rather than evoking patterns of rational thought and reflection. Chris decides to leave the constricting world of the recording studio. Although we next see him travelling in his jeep to Pittsburgh, neither he nor Lynn will be entirely free from a system which attempts to control them and motivate their behaviour. Like Dr. Logan's trained zombie Bub in *Day of the Dead*, Chris believes he has 'lost the ability to think'. But, like Bub, he will find that socially ingrained negative patterns of behaviour still affect whatever independent aspirations he has for any type of freedom. Instead, they will result in personal frustration and creative inertia.

As he drives back home, his voice-over on the soundtrack describes his future encounter with Lynn in retrospect. However, the very nature of his comments depicts the nature of their affair as one characterised by a lack of commitment. For Chris, it is merely a new experiment like taking drugs or engaging in another aspect of a superficial 1960s lifestyle: 'It's weird but I didn't know I was coming back here ... 100 miles on the road before I knew I was coming back. I guess that was the part of me that was ready for the whole mess. I guess everybody's looking for a new thing like the chick. She was a model on local television commercials.'

The next sequence then depicts Lynn working in a similar artificially controlled environment as Chris. Like Chris, she is equally subject to a production process over which she has no control. After showing the television studio, Romero inserts various fragmented close-ups of a beer glass inserted in foam and washed to look glamorous for the purposes of a commercial. We also see the frenzied activities of the director (*There's Always Vanilla*'s actual co-producer Russell Streiner) attempting to control the events like his counterpart in the previous recording studio sequence. Before the studio take, Lynn questions her role in the proceedings. But she receives nothing but ambiguous answers from producer Michael Dorian (Richard Ricci) who is only interested in an easy pick-up. As if acting out media desires to blur boundaries between illusion and reality so that audiences accept the former in place of the latter, he places two cigarettes in his mouth and lights them both offering one to Lynn employing the Hollywood romantic gesture used by Paul Henreid in *Now Voyager* (1942). However, Lynn quickly rebuffs his overture by abruptly stating, 'I don't smoke.' She then continues questioning her role as an accessory in manufacturing false media illusions:

'Isn't that cheating? Making the beer look better than it actually looks?' Michael denies the relevance of her critique. He emphasises instead the economic and industrial dependence of all concerned in the enterprise: 'You stand there talking to me because of the beer? ... All of our salaries and our very existence depends on that beer and we're all here to make that beer look as good as it possibly can.' He critiques her glamorous posture as well as her complicity in manufacturing illusions, 'That's it. Beautiful. The *mouth* thing. Isn't that cheating?'

Another of Chris's addresses to camera interrupts this sequence. He tells viewers, 'It was just a matter of timing. I didn't have anything in mind, just my thing and the chick's.' On one level, this extra-diegetic insert may be regarded as merely another of Romero's attempts at filling out an undeveloped screenplay. But 'these raps' are much more than the 'cutesy' attempts at 'affectation' Romero later described. If viewers are expected to understand these comments retrospectively based upon Lynn's information to Chris concerning events he was never present at, then far from placing a narrator in a position of omniscient control they reveal him as lacking in a sympathetic understanding of the problems Lynn faced prior to their affair. Furthermore, even if Chris knew nothing of these events, his comments reveal him as little better than a sexist male falling into an affair with a 'chick' without making any real attempts to know her and understand her personal dilemmas. Later events in the film support both these interpretations.

The scene then returns to the television studio showing the director creating a false romantic scene for Lynn and a fellow actor to sell the beer commercial. He suggests they both kiss and make up lines. These improvisations will neither synchronise (or even be heard) in the soundtrack manufactured in the final edited illusion. The 'romantic couple' begin to insult each other: 'You are a frumpy little chick with all your brains up your ass.' Lynn replies, 'You've got a piece of spinach in your teeth.'

This scene both complements and anticipates themes in the film. Chris has referred to Lynn exclusively as a 'chick' in his addresses to the audience. He will insult her physical appearance immediately after their first encounter. The antagonistic nature of the television commercial relationship soon reoccurs in the later stages of Chris and Lynn's affair. They begin their relationship like the naive doomed young couple Tom and Judy but will end it in a manner paralleling the frustrated marital union of the Coopers in *Night of the Living Dead*.

The next scene shows Chris arriving in Pittsburgh outside a local rendezvous, Mahoney's. As he enters, a woman sings a song whose significant lines are 'The Wild and Woolly Years/Tell me where did they go?' The lyrics suggest recognition of a difference between the formerly radical era of the 1960s and the present jaded realm of the 1970s. Various influences such as the Vietnam War's lack of resolution, a screwed-up economy and the presence of Spiro Agnew as Vice-President are all possible reasons for the new decade's activist fatigue. It is an era in which *There's Always Vanilla*'s central characters all appear caught up within their solipsistic concerns. But they also bear responsibility for failing to realise those radical potentials which the previous decade offered them in terms of personal and historical challenges. Although the sexual revolution is still in force, the movement now appears compromised by the very nature of the people who attempt to follow its supposedly liberating dimensions. Chris sees his father Roger (Roger McGovern) at Mahoney's. Roger has used the sexual revolution for his own selfish ends as a means of cheating on his wife. Although he enjoys access to easy lays, he also openly sneers at other minority groups and their claims for equal recognition. Chris greets Roger with the revealing comment, 'Three years Dad and you're still here.' Roger sits at a table with a young businessman whose glass of wine Chris accidentally jostles when he approaches. After the younger man leaves for a meeting, naturally concerned about the wine stains on his business suit, Roger caustically comments, 'Business is getting full of faggots.' He then sneakily enquires into his son's sexuality, 'You're not turning into a faggot, are you?' Chris finds that his father still lives with his mother whom he describes as 'out of her mind.' When Chris's mother appears towards the end of the film, we learn that she has also adopted 1960s habits by calling police 'pigs'; yet she also relies on them to remove intruders from her property. Chris's parents are both hypocritical by appropriating selected aspects of 1960s lifestyles but never changing their patterns of behaviour inherited from the 1950s. The prodigal son is not entirely blameless as succeeding events in the film reveal.

During the scenes between Chris and Roger, Romero inserts sequences involving Lynn and Dorian who attempts a hypocritical act of seduction on her. Dorian presents himself to Lynn as a potential saviour. He talks about 'building bridges between people and skyscrapers' and represents himself as someone who will save the world from exploding. However, Dorian's method of salvation is as dubious as those paths followed by Chris and his father: 'But if [the world] is ever going to be saved, it's the communications people who are going to do it.' At this point, Lynn wishes to further her career in the advertising business and states her compliance in whatever it will take to get ahead in the profession. She states, 'I'd like to get to know everyone.' But she does not realise the full extent of the personal and professional compromises she will have to make.

The alternating nature of both sequences reveals certain parallels between hypocritical, unscrupulous males attempting to use and abuse females. But while Dorian and Roger are both clearly aware of what they are doing, Chris exists in a state of blissful ignorance blinding him to the extent of his actual contamination by patriarchal attitudes. At Mahoney's, Roger ogles a young go-go dancer and boasts about his sexual prowess: 'Your old man can still cut the mustard.' After commenting, 'You really believe that, don't you, old man', Chris takes him at his word and surprises him by fixing him up. The event results in Roger's embarrassment. Chris then inquires about his former girlfriend, Terri, whose photo they view on the wall in her former go-go dancer role as the 'Electric Madonna'. Roger significantly comments, 'She's not a real thing.' This is a pertinent statement since none of the males in *There's Always Vanilla* view women as 'real' beings but merely as disposable objects for gratification very much like artifacts in television commercials. Chris later affirms this perception in his next address to the audience when they visit Terri's apartment: 'She was just a regular screwed-up broad, but was she beautiful', a statement paralleling Roger's description of his wife as 'out of her mind'.

When we first see Terri she wears a glamorous wig similar to her objectified photo as the Electric Madonna. But she is not happy to see her former lover who has decided to return home after three years without informing her. While Roger unexpectedly finds Chris's companion eager to bed him after a night of drug taking, Terri refuses to take up their former relationship. She condemns Chris's selfish attitude: 'You spoiled my whole life, ran away from your past, from me, you prick. How the hell did you wind up back here?' After telling Chris she killed their son, Terri removes her wig and puts it on the top of a large toy signifying her refusal to play any role accommodating to male desire any longer. She tells him, 'He's across the hall with the neighbors.' The following morning, after Roger guiltily asks Chris how much money he should pay for his night's pleasure, Terri ironically introduces her son to them in words clearly denoting the shared patriarchal selfishness existing between Chris and his father: 'Chrissie. This is your Daddy. There's your Daddy's Daddy.'

Romero's intercutting of this sequence with Lynn and Dorian's encounter provides a mirror image of a world of patriarchal manipulation and female vulnerability. Lynn feels guilty about her complicity in the world of television commercials: 'I think commercials tend to break down communications rather than build them up.' But Dorian denies her critical comments about the media industry and significantly speaks of commercials in terms of being a form of artificial sexual stimulation helping viewers to deny reality: 'So much bad news comes over that tube every night that for just one brief minute, 60 bubbly seconds, I can sit back and dream of a glass of cold "Bold Gold" ... If we could live like that violently, that *passionately* [italics mine], for every 60 seconds of every 24 hours, we'd burn, we'd wear ourselves out...'

Within their respective positions in society, Chris, Roger and Dorian all yearn for a quick sexual fix rather than engage in any form of fulfilling personal and political relationships which may challenge the moribund society they inhabit. These jaded males easily appropriate any new social custom providing them with easy access to pleasure, particularly those last remnants of the 1960s sexual revolution which (feminists later correctly recognised) benefited males more than females. Lynn refuses Dorian's advances, 'Look, how do you want it?' He accuses her of 'playing games' and orders her out of his apartment. But, at least at this point in the film, Lynn opposes her male-determined role. She refuses to participate in a 'game' whereby her future media career depends upon her sexual compliance.

The next morning Chris sees Roger return home. He denies his paternity of Terri's child: 'I think she's lying. I don't think it's my kid.' Chris then accidentally encounters Lynn as she rushes to an audition for a toilet bowl commercial. After refusing Dorian's advances, Lynn has now become as disposable as the waste products ironically referred to in this type of commercial. At this point of the film, the path is open for a significant romantic encounter which could have the potentiality of benefitting and redeeming both partners according to the classical Hollywood romantic formula depicted in Stanley Cavell's *Pursuits of Happiness*. But such a strategy is both foreign to Romero and as artificial as the false romanticism seen in the depicted television commercials. Like the ironic nature of the EC comic narrative influencing Romero as a director, the events in *There's Always Vanilla* will not conclude in the normally accepted manner.

Both Chris and Lynn are affected by various aspects of their family and environment in ways similar to Zola's Rougon-Macquart offspring. Chris already has many of his father's attitudes deeply embedded within him; Lynn is vulnerable, wishes to assert some form of independence, and does not want to make the same mistakes her mother did. *There's Always Vanilla* will depict an unhappy ending for the two lovers, but it will also attempt to clarify *how* the actual family and social circumstances affecting both characters result in this conclusion. Although lacking the more mature treatment characteristic of Romero's later films, *There's Always Vanilla* suggests that the contemporary world of personal and social relationships can never bring true fulfilment.

While their attitudes differ, Chris and Lynn fall swiftly into an affair which will never benefit them either on the personal or social levels. Despite scenes showing them buying new hippie-type clothes and indulging in a lyrical outing to a zoo, their affair never exhibits any alternative and progressive signs of 1960s sexual freedom nor one leading to a rejection of the society surrounding them. Their relationship is contaminated from the very beginning. Chris makes condescending remarks about Lynn throughout the narrative as he looks back on their affair. His extra-diegetic address reveals a male reluctance to engage in a committed relationship that is fully respectful of Lynn: 'The last thing that I wanted in the world happened right then ... Then, all of a sudden, boom. There it was. I couldn't turn around and walk away from it ... I sure as hell wasn't looking for any other real involvement. I wasn't looking for another lady. I wasn't looking to get my life any more screwed-up than it was then – but...' But, despite all his reservations stated from the convenient perspective of hindsight, Chris sleeps with her, begins an affair and shows no real concern for his partner's feelings in this flawed relationship.

Despite sleeping with Chris, Lynn initially wishes to keep her independence. She provides a separate couch bed for him in her apartment, 'I've never done that before. It's the only thing I've never done.' Her statement applies both to her first sexual experience as well as accepting Chris into her personal life. Chris quickly invades her space and moves in with her. However, she soon expresses her genuine love for him. But the film makes clear that it is only Lynn who ever says, 'I love you.' Chris never utters it either in his various addresses to camera or within the narrative. He is always non-committal: 'All I could ever come up with was that she was a beautiful lady. But that wasn't enough ... There was a certain part of Lynn that got to me ... I couldn't figure it and I couldn't tell her ... I still can't figure out how the whole thing happened.' When he later presents her with a photo of them both, the image actually speaks volumes about their relationship. While Lynn faces the camera, Chris's back is to the viewer as if hesitant of revealing his true personality. Romero's consistent critique of patriarchal attitudes and his sympathy towards female characters thus already appears in this early work.

The next morning a talk-radio programme wakes Chris up. As he looks around the room, he sees a photo of her father, news commentator Lyle Harris. Lynn has left a note for him, 'I've set the programme for 11 o'clock. It's Daddy's programme.' However, Daddy's programme is nothing for her to be proud of. It is as condescending and manipulative as the talk-show programme in *Martin*. This media world is also one into which Lynn desperately wishes to gain acceptance. She does not condemn its values by developing her hesitant critiques concerning that environment's 'cheating' and manipulative nature and rejecting it entirely. Both Chris and Lynn are products of that environment and do not realise how their very personalities are formed by it.

Their inability to recognise the contaminating reality of the surrounding social world by moving towards alternative forms of personal existence results in their respective personal defeats.

From this point on, their relationship begins to deteriorate. Chris makes an attempt to become a writer. But when questioned by Lynn about what he is writing, he brusquely replies, 'Nothing.' Lynn later tells Chris about an impressionable cinematic memory from *On the Beach* (1959) which is far from romantic. She remembers the death scene between Anthony Perkins and Donna Anderson after they have taken the suicide pills: 'They had to wait. They didn't know when it would happen.' Rather than discerning that their relationship is dying, Chris denies the warning signals present in Lynn's comments concerning the eventual death of their relationship as well as denying his share of responsibility for its deterioration. He remarks in his address to the camera that 'I didn't know if the girl was stoned or not ... Who the hell knows what they want, who knows right and wrong, why they do everything they do. Sometimes we get fouled up looking for too many answers and we end up doing nothing ... Why do I have to keep spending my time trying to figure out why ... I don't know why it happened.'

This direct-to-camera sequence actually begins with a quick insert of a studio interior. Other rapid inserts reveal more shots of the studio before showing Dorian supervising a bath tub commercial with an attractive female. However, prior to these scenes, earlier images revealed Chris's hesitant look as Lynn again affirmed her need for a relationship he has no real commitment to: 'It doesn't matter why we want each other.' The studio sequences reveal the presence of an illusionary and manipulative world surrounding both protagonists. Its ideological values both intrude into and exacerbate the deterioration of personal relationships by promoting false ideals.

The next sequence shows Lynn visiting her mother in hospital before she undergoes an operation. It reveals Lynn's own particular vulnerability to a parental discourse which parallels Chris's own condition insofar as both offspring in *There's Always Vanilla* never entirely separate themselves from old values. Lynn speaks of her discontent with the phony world of television commercials: 'I just get so sick of it, sometimes. Just turning this way and that, sweating under the hot lights, trying to get excited about a lousy glass of beer. It's just frustrating. Maybe, I'm just content to be a wife and mother.' However, after asking Lynn to find her make-up, her mother launches into a tirade against marriage: 'Marriage! Look what marriage did for me? The perfect couple they called us. I was the perfect wife. I was the perfect hostess. I gave perfect dinner parties. I gave perfect small talk just to push that big baboon to the top.' After further criticising Lynn's father, she confesses her early uncertainty about which path she would follow. Her earlier problems also parallel Lynn's own present dilemma. However, she then urges her daughter to follow a path similar to Dorian's values: 'If only I had known what I know now ... I really didn't know what I wanted ... You want to get ahead and make a lot of money, your own money. That's what you want.'

Inevitably, domestic discord begins. Both Chris and Lynn succumb to deeply ingrained negative tendencies which inhibit both of them from developing a relationship uncontaminated by the negative elements contained in parental and social values.

Chris continues his freewheeling lifestyle by attempting to write the 'great American novel' and living off Lynn. Lynn yearns for a life of domesticity. She criticises Chris's inability to decide what he really wants to do. Lack of communication between them develops to the extent that neither really listens to nor understands the other. The seeds for the later-deteriorating relationship depicted between Fran and David in *Dawn of the Dead* are already present in this early couple. This lack of communication becomes explicit when Lynn reveals her pregnancy to Chris after a domestic squabble. Chris proves himself absolutely incapable of responding to her dilemma so she lies to him: 'I'm not pregnant. I'm sorry.' The next morning Chris lies on the couch after Lynn has locked him out of her bedroom. Since her mother will visit her, she expects Chris to move his things out temporarily. Although Chris regards her action as 'cheating' (the same word Lynn uses for her involvement in television commercials), he does not even attempt to understand her dilemma but whines about not having sex for three days.

Chris then decides to spend the day with Terri and his young son. But his already-disillusioned former girlfriend rejects his superficial attempt at being a 'Daddy', commenting, 'It's too late to be involved. I don't need you any more.' At the same time, Lynn attempts to speak to Dorian while he supervises a risqué television commercial using sexual innuendo to vulgarise human relationships. Romero also makes a cameo appearance as the director of the commercial here. As we learn later, she wishes to obtain information for an abortion. Chris also applies for a job with an advertising agency and infiltrates his way into the system by using language almost identical to that used earlier by Dorian in his attempted seduction of Lynn: 'A pimp makes a natural advertiser. Pimp and advertiser both deal with a public in the same way offering a release, a fulfilment of desire, a solution for frustration. One seeks a quick piece of ass, the other a new deodorant or a toilet cleaner.' Chris's 'honesty' gets him the job. But he has clearly compromised himself by selling out and soon quits when he learns that his trial assignment will involve promoting the military image during a time when the Vietnam War is still continuing.

Although this sequence contains Romero's humorous jibes at an industry whose operations he knows only too well, it conflicts with the rest of the film. It is impossible to imagine Chris even taking the job in the first place in view of his previously-voiced attitudes. However, as an indication of the personal contamination he faces and the breakdown of any true relationship he has with Lynn, it functions appropriately within the narrative. He has compromised both himself and his values by involving himself in this manipulative occupation. It is not surprising that during the next dialogue between Chris and Lynn when he upsets her by telling her about wanting to be a father to Terri's son, the sound of a machine (made either by recording studio noise or the cable car we see Dorian travelling on) both drowns the discussion and acts as a distracting background noise. This sound not only parallels the earlier noise in the recording studio (which caused Chris to quit because it drove him crazy), but also allegorically functions as an aural metaphor for dominating familial and social influences which prevent their relationship from developing positively. Ironically, Chris's camera address in this scene actually asserts, 'If Lynn and I had a kid, I would marry her.' This totally contradicts his earlier behaviour when she announced her pregnancy.

The following sequence is a crucial one. It intercuts scenes of Chris sitting alone in the apartment and condemning Lynn for not being there with her traumatic visit to an abortionist. Although Chris is not present at the visit, the editing pattern makes clear his culpability for the situation in which Lynn finds herself in. We must remember that *There's Always Vanilla* appeared two years before the Roe vs. Wade Supreme Court Decision so that Lynn now finds herself participating in both a criminal act as well as one causing her great personal trauma. The visit and Lynn's flight from the two men involved in this illegal abortion employs a sombre visual style and canted angles reminiscent of *Night of the Living Dead*. As Lynn is about to undergo a procedure supervised by a dubious doctor who utters another of the many lines spoken by hypocritical males in the film – 'I think the greatest crime in the world is for a woman to have a baby she doesn't want' – a line spoken not by a female but by a sinister male who merely views Lynn as an object, the sequence inserts shots of Chris as well as the revealing photo he earlier purchased for her showing them both within the frame. Chris shows no awareness of her predicament. His final voice-over in this sequence asserts his own selfish feelings: 'I didn't know where she was. I didn't care. I was happy she wasn't there. I was angry with her and happy to get the hell out of it.' During the preliminaries for the dangerous and illegal operation, Romero inserts three shots of the photograph showing Chris with his back to the camera and Lynn facing it. The first shot shows them both in the photo after the abortionist's sleazy-looking assistant has given Lynn a drink. When the doctor tells her to get on a table, another insert of the photo appears. This time it is a close-up only showing the back of Chris's head. After another insert of both Chris and Lynn in the photo, Lynn becomes reluctant to undergo the abortion and runs away. Her single image in the photo then appears as she flees like Barbara escaping from the zombie in *Night of the Living Dead*. After she returns to the apartment, Lynn locks the door and the photo appears for the last time in the sequence. The connection of Lynn's dilemma to her involvement with Chris is obvious. He bears responsibility for placing her in a situation of personal danger that could have resulted in her death, a result of regarding their relationship as a mere 'affair' (the significantly alternative title of *There's Always Vanilla*). The montage associations evoked by the photo in this sequence clearly equates Chris with the abortionist and blames him for causing her dilemma.

When Chris finds that Terri has vacated her apartment, he returns home to his father and mother. They find him perched on a tree like a young boy. When Chris tells his woes to Roger, he receives the dubious consolation embodied in the film's title, 'There's always vanilla, Chris,' a strategy meant to get him to accept the status quo and begin work in his baby food factory. However, vanilla is also a manufactured product like all those other exotic ice creams provided by the corporate company Howard Johnson's. Accepting the status quo will not result in any form of happiness as the next sequence shows. We see Lynn, now heavily pregnant, who has decided to pursue her option of marriage and children rather than following any other alternatives which might have developed her potentialities. She watches the finished television commercial on which she worked. It opens with her and a lover riding a horse in classic western imagery, kissing, and mouthing some sentences left silent on the soundtrack but ones we already know are false. A mailman (Vince Survinski) delivers a large package to her and her husband. When they open the light box outside sent by Chris, two blue and red balloons, symbolising the empty and fragile nature of their past relationship drift into the sky. The film concludes.

There's Always Vanilla ends on a pessimistic note with a coda depicting a failed relationship involving two characters who cannot communicate and end up compromised by their various social roles. The supposed liberatory potentials of the 1960s era have benefited nobody and its legacy is now bankrupt in a new decade where everybody becomes as compromised as their predecessors in previous generations. Earlier in the film, Lynn commented to Chris about his supposed 'honesty' after their lovemaking. During this sequence the artificially manufactured world of the television studio intruded more and more into their private world via various inserts which became more extended in length during each successive appearance. Although mistaken about Chris, Lynn expressed optimism about a relationship, an optimism which could have had positive practical consequences had things been different. After stating 'and you're honest about everything', she continues, 'People should be like that. It could be the easiest thing in the world.' Unfortunately, it is not. But the ideal remains. It is that which haunts Romero's various films, an ideal determining whether humans become free or merely another recruit to the army of the living dead.

CHAPTER FOUR

Jack's Wife

Like *There's Always Vanilla*, *Jack's Wife* became another of Romero's ill-fated ventures that sought to break away from horror films. Although it touches on supernatural elements, they are less important than its affinity with issues raised explicitly in his previous film, namely a person's unsuccessful attempt to break away from particular modes of individual and social entrapment and move towards a new form of existence. Shot in 1972 with a small crew on 16mm and later blown up into 35mm, the film suffered from budget problems affecting both production and post-production. After attempting to make a film originally budgeted at $250,000 for $100,000, *Jack's Wife* had the additional misfortune to fall into the hands of distributor Jack (*The Blob*) Harris, who drastically recut it and tried to market it as a soft-porn film under the different title, *Hungry Wives*! After releasing it in 1973 and finding it unable to attract an audience, Harris removed it from distribution and later tried to redistribute it under another title, *Season of the Witch*, as a new Romero film following the success of *Dawn of the Dead*.[1]

Even then it did not succeed theatrically and went directly into the video market. Due to its problematic history, neither the original negative nor Romero's first cut survives today. Yet, despite all the various problems affecting its production and marketing, critics such as Paul R. Gagne regard *Jack's Wife* as one of Romero's significant films, anticipating *Martin*, and described by Romero and commentators as his most accomplished film (see Gagne 1987: 46–50). Although the original version is now lost, enough remains in the re-edited work currently in circulation to trace the important message Romero has inserted into another of his early works foreshadowing themes within his later films. *Jack's Wife* is an important work whose ideas both inform and complement Romero's better-known films such as the zombie trilogy and *Martin*.

Jack's Wife certainly shares many of the problems affecting *There's Always Vanilla*, such as minimal production values, uneven acting, and a tendency to appear as merely a dated product of its time. However, it also has many positive affinities with the director's earlier work. Both films centre on confused characters who attempt to seek some form of positive direction in their lives and eventually fail miserably in the process. Gagne recognises that *Jack's Wife* deals with the nature of false perceptions. His book includes an intriguing quotation from Romero himself concerning the idea that individual perception of reality may often obscure the actual truth:

> 'The Fact is that every forward motion in the film is caused by that person ... yet she perceives the world as making everything happen to her. In fact, she can't do any of it without being able to conjure up, pun intended, a reason for it happening that is not coming from within her. She needs to be able to say, "The Devil made me do it!" Which at once is the plight of womanhood, or any minority, and the genocide – it's very hard to perceive *yourself* as the cause of something that might make it better' (49).

Romero's comments are relevant in more than one sense. They identify the director as someone who intelligently recognises the importance of contemporary modes of conduct influencing the behavioural patterns of all characters who appear in his various films. In *Night of the Living Dead*, both Ben and Harry blame each other as the enemy instead of rationally collaborating against the greater threat outside. Chris and Lynn in *There's Always Vanilla* never bother to analyse their personal flaws. They are also blind in seeing how relevant social and family patterns generating such problems affect their relationship thus making any potential alternatives for them to follow ultimately impossible. The individuals and society of *The Crazies* pursue a path leading to destruction as a result of their inability to cease looking outside and start looking within their own personalities. Those who tentatively survive in *Dawn of the Dead* and *Day of the Dead* eventually realise that the old world of capitalist acquisitiveness and possessiveness really represents a contaminating force which they must purge from their very beings. In *Knightriders*, Billy's utopian medieval society initially collapses because it lacks the power to confront and defeat such contamination while the various individuals in *Monkey Shines*, *Creepshow* and *The Dark Half* survive or die depending upon their abilities to interrogate their own selves, understand the potentials they have for engaging in alternative strategies, and cease blaming conveniently external scapegoats.

Jack's Wife anticipates all these future developments in Romero's work. Despite its production problems, *Jack's Wife* represents one of Romero's most sophisticated attempts to analyse the personal dilemmas affecting individuals in contemporary society who are often faced with different choices but who end up choosing the wrong path. Romero's various screen characters variously engage in processes of denial that harm their very personalities and prevent them realising their real potential as free individuals.

As with *Martin*, it is often difficult to distinguish the fantasy sequences in *Jack's Wife* from the world of everyday reality, although one abrupt transition from a scene showing a masked intruder attacking Joan Mitchell (Jan White) to another depicting her awakening from a nightmare does formally distinguish between the two levels. However, as in *Night of the Living Dead*, *Dawn of the Dead* and *Day of the Dead*, the fantastic levels of meaning complement, rather than contradict, the realistic aspects of the narrative. As Peter recognises in *Dawn of the Dead*, the zombies are 'us'. Despite the tendencies of most critics and audiences to emphasise Romero's films exclusively in terms of the horror genre and concentrate upon special effects, like the better examples contained within the field they speak to issues far beyond their generic boundaries. In *Jack's Wife* the fantasy eventually becomes a reality, while in *Martin* they are already indistinguishable and indulged in by the title character who cannot (or does not want to) tell the difference between them. As Romero has noted, the scene involving Nikki, Gregg, Shirley, and Joan really summarises the theme of *Jack's Wife*. After teasing Joan and Shirley over their visit to self-styled witch Marion, Gregg emphasises the power of auto-suggestion and compares it to people who worry themselves into a heart attack: 'You get a guy who believes in the power of voodoo or something and he knows the hex has been put on him, he worries himself to death.' Gregg later demonstrates his point when he makes Shirley believe she has inhaled marijuana rather than an ordinary cigarette. He succeeds not merely due to her vulnerable position following the amount of alcohol that Shirley has already consumed but also because of the fact that she already wishes to 'cut loose and do something', a tendency she condemns Joan for, despite the disastrous example she has set for her friend.

Like *Day of the Dead*, *Jack's Wife* opens with a deceptive image which seems realistic at first. But, unlike the later film, it follows it with another sequence which initially appears realistic but is nonetheless an illusion – despite its placement in the world of everyday normality. Both visions symbolically represent Joan's real life problems and challenge her to respond to them. The film opens to reveal a deserted wood. Like the opening of *Night of the Living Dead*, we then see two figures approaching the camera from a distance in long shot. Jack Mitchell (Bill Thunhurst) walks ahead of his wife. He reads a newspaper and appears oblivious to her presence. Joan submissively walks behind him. Two other shots show the couple from the camera's perspective first behind some leafless branches seen in soft focus and later with the branches in sharp focus as if contrasting two forms of vision challenging both title character and audience in terms of working towards a necessarily appropriate perspective. As this sequence proceeds, the camera reveals Joan's perspective. She watches her husband walk forward, ignore her very presence and allow branches to brush back from his body into her face. During the walk, Joan's face becomes more scratched and bloody. As they walk forward, organ music and electronic sounds appear on the soundtrack emphasising both the religious nature of Joan's self-oppression and her discordant apprehension of her current position. As Jack and Joan walk through the wood, she sees a baby seated on the ground and looks at it apprehensively as if vaguely perceiving motherhood as another link in the chain of patriarchal oppression. The next image reveals the first of the many mirror images which structure the film. Joan sees herself on a swing, its very presence suggesting a potential liberation she may eventually obtain. However, this possibility becomes brutally curtailed. Jack hits her on the nose with his newspaper and places a dog collar around her neck, seeing his wife as little better than a household pet. As church bells ring, he leads her inside a dog compound and locks her in a cage commenting, 'I'll be gone about a week.' The scene ends with Joan looking at a bulldog in the next cage before the next sequence begins suggesting a movement from nightmare into reality. But, as the film reveals, they are both the same.

This opening sequence already foreshadows the film's dilemma of a frustrated housewife experiencing both alienation and lack of self-esteem within her current social position. Like the prologue of *Night of the Living Dead*, it introduces two characters, male and female, bound in a frustrating family relationship. Jack's physical acts of violence towards Joan in this sequence parallel Johnny's verbal aggression towards Barbara in the earlier film. Furthermore, the sounds of organ music and church bells signify the role of religion as an oppressive force in Joan's life, a force which emphasises female submission as it did for Barbara in the earlier film. Jack's act of violence towards Joan in the opening fantasy sequence also foreshadows his later physical assault on her when he learns of their daughter Nikki's departure from home.

The next sequence also plays with audience expectations. A real estate agent (played by Bill Hinzman, the first zombie to appear in *Night of the Living Dead*) leads Joan on a tour. This scene initially appears realistic before the presence of discordant features lead viewers to question its veracity. Joan again exhibits silence as the agent takes her around her own home. He lists various features, both material and personal, which appear as alienating as those in the previous sequence. The agent begins by detailing the home's interior features and then opens a door to reveal Gregg (Ray Laine), smiling at her from inside. Gregg's presence initially appears unusual. It will not be until later into the narrative that audiences actually meet this character. Gregg's introductory appearance in this sequence also occurs well before Joan actually meets him in the film. This intimates that what initially appears to be a chronologically positioned opening dream sequence actually belongs to the film's actual conclusion. Romero does not only break down traditional cinematic barriers between reality and fantasy but also those dominating classical Hollywood narrative construction. According to this system, the end must answer the beginning.[2] By placing a character the audience meets later at the very beginning of the film, Romero suggests that Joan's dilemma will never reach any firm resolution but is actually circular in nature. Despite Joan's later rejection of Gregg, he still returns to haunt her in her fantasies in a similar way to the masked intruder. Thus, despite the film's conclusion in which everything appears settled for the title character who is on her way to a new life, she may actually be still wrestling with the same type of problems which initially caused her dilemma. As we shall see, she ends the film still known as 'Jack's Wife'. By employing the type of contemporary avant-garde discourses common to Hollywood cinema of the 1960s and 1970s in films such as *Mickey One* (1965), *Bonnie and Clyde* (1967), *Easy Rider* (1968) and *Alex in Wonderland* (1970), Romero suggests that his early version of the woman's nightmare will never end. It will continue well beyond the film's actual conclusion trapping her in a type of psychic-repetition compulsive situation due to the fact that she is not really as liberated as she believes.

Another door opens for Joan which also depicts a personal dead end. She sees her ladies coffee circle shot via a grotesque use of wide angle lens and roughly edited cuts whom the agent describes as 'available for luncheon, tea, bridge, etc, etc.' It is already clear from Joan's bored demeanour that the mindless chatter of her WASP female social circle provides her with no positive alternative channels for her energy. Joan is also alienated from her adolescent daughter, Nikki (Joedda McClain), as the next image reveals. Introduced to her as 'your daughter', Nikki passes her on the stairs. Nikki is oblivious to her mother's presence as if she were actually dead. In a sense, Joan is. She is already one of Romero's 'living dead' in spirit.

As she enters her daughter's room, Joan sees the first of several mirror image shots in this sequence representing her as an old woman approaching death after she has fulfilled her function within patriarchy. The images correspond to Joan's low self-esteem. She internally feels herself to be someone who is old and useless with nowhere else to go except the grave. When the agent shows Joan her own room, he points out many material artifacts such as fashionable clothes and jewellery. But these consumerist things certainly provide no satisfactory substitute for Joan's frustrated life. He also points out the supply of pills in Joan's bathroom cabinet as well as the 'phone numbers of doctor, police, priest, neighbour', all of whom play ideologically proscribed roles of trapping Joan into a life of bourgeois conformity and preventing her from reaching an awareness of fulfilling alternatives to overcome her alienated existence. The agent finally leaves after uttering an archetypal everyday American 'feel good' platitude stressing the importance of being an economically responsible housewife within capitalism: 'Don't forget to pay the bills and, have a good day.' The sequence concludes by revealing a long shot of Joan going to her dressing room mirror and again seeing the reflection of her aged self. She then sees her aged self reclining on the bed before she finally wakes up from her nightmares. Joan's schizophrenic vision reveals the true nature of her personality as a human being suffering the process of decay in a manner parallel to Romero's zombies.

Joan awakes from her dreams next to Jack in bed. Their relationship appears lifeless, mechanical and perfunctory. It appears little different from the instinctual behavioural patterns of the zombies in Romero's trilogy. Like the zombies, Joan and her husband merely perform reflex motions in their everyday life. They have no real conversation. Joan merely utters platitudes to Jack such as 'Are you up, hon?', 'Have a good day, hon,' to which he barely responds or not at all. After Jack leaves, Joan apprehensively looks at her image in her large mirror. The camera then zooms in to her diminished reflection in the small circular mirror on her left. Although Joan does not see her aged self as in the fantasy, she recognises the subordinated nature of her personality in a frustrating marital relationship.

A bell sounds before electronic buzzing occurs on the soundtrack. These two noises complement those heard in the first fantasy suggesting that a combination of religious and mechanical forces bear the responsibility both for programming Joan's behaviour and causing the unhealthy nature of the frustration with her everyday life. Already Romero suggests the presence of features he will develop explicitly in *Day of the Dead*, namely that oppressive social forces are really responsible for dysfunctional human behaviour, making their victims nothing more than living dead, whether humans or zombies.

Joan then consults her male psychiatrist. He dismisses any potentials she may have towards understanding the nature of her dilemma by describing her as 'the least qualified person to understand a dream'. It is already clear that the masculine world shows little sympathy for her plight. But the avenues Joan eventually chooses also provide very little alternative help. As her psychiatrist also states, 'The only person imprisoning Joan is Joan', a statement metaphorically envisaged by the two shots of her claustrophobically sitting inside her vehicle while it remains stationary during a car wash. The car wash is merely a temporary cosmetic process similar to Joan's psychiatric sessions. It may remove stains like the psychiatrist's attempt to explain away troubling dreams but the remedy is merely temporary. Both car stains and psychological trauma will return sooner or later.

During the party sequence, viewers gain further insights into Joan's sterile world. Various middle-aged, lavishly dressed, over-coiffered matrons engage in banal small talk ranging from menopausal problems to 'making money'. They point to another guest, Marion (Virginia Greenwald), who appears to be the outsider in their social group, as a 'good witch', and compare witchcraft to a religion. As one male guest does a 'reading of my favourite television program' intimating the cultural horizons the dominant culture allows him, Jack compares the whole party to a 'dog pound' thus equating the environment with Joan's earlier nightmare. Despite the polite levels of social intercourse, the respective positions affecting both males and females are really based upon patriarchal control whether expressed in physical violence or not.

This becomes clear in the next sequence which opens with an exterior shot of the Mitchells' house, significantly numbered '1246' which add up to the total '13'. After Joan asks Jack how long he will be away on one of his frequent business trips, the scene changes. It moves on to employ all the visual generic devices associated with horror and suspense cinema to show Joan alone, frightened by various night sounds, windows suddenly opening, and the sudden appearance of a male shadow. Joan then sees hands appearing from below her bed. But they actually belong to Jack who has been exercising before his early morning departure. Joan has thus experienced another nightmare. Like the others in the opening sequences of the film, it is one relevant to her situation as an unhappy woman. As Robin Wood has pointed out in another context, Romero's fantasy sequences often embody a particular form of a woman's nightmare within patriarchy (1987: 45–9). The hands also foreshadow the zombie hands reaching out to grab Sarah in *Day of the Dead*.

Joan is also susceptible to influences in her everyday life as well as the world of fantasy. Nikki commends her as still being attractive: 'You never think of your mother having a great body. You really look good.' After Nikki leaves, Joan decides not to swallow her tranquiliser but puts it into the toilet bowl. She then looks at herself in her dressing table mirror, decides to remove her slippers, and then her dressing gown. After narcissistically gazing at her nude body in the mirror, she lies down on her bed. This sequence may be read as one of the few instances of true mother-daughter communication within the entire film. However, the communication is merely superficial since it deals entirely with the fact of bodily attractiveness rather than personal liberation and the progressive aspects of a mother-daughter relationship. Of course, Joan is much more attractive than she believes. But Nikki's comments are really not suitable enough for a true bonding between an oppressed mother and daughter to really develop. Although Nikki resents her father's condescending attitudes such as his paternal admonition to 'Try to stay virgin' before he departs on one of his frequent business trips, her path towards liberation will be as flawed and problematic as her mother's. Nikki makes bad friendships, as we see from her liaison with Gregg, and eventually leaves home. Her action results more from pique than any carefully thought out plans concerning her future. It foreshadows Christine's attitude in *Martin* where a daughter seeks to escape from home using any means possible, no matter how much it may result in another dead end. Nikki merely influences her mother into becoming narcissistic, an attitude symbolised by Joan's self-absorbed gazing at her body. Joan may be headed towards the first stage of female pleasure, but it will not lead towards any true sense of independence and liberation. At this stage, it is merely indulgent self-exhibitionism as the following scenes suggest.

The next sequence shows Joan and Shirley (Anne Muffly) visiting Marion and pruriently investigating her involvement in witchcraft. Shirley merely indulges in gossip and voyeuristic exploration as a means of relieving her mundane life from daily boredom. She describes Joan as 'an academic' who fears taking any form of action. Joan, however, believes a witch is merely an 'exhibitionist', an ironic comment in view of her behaviour in the previous sequence. However, like the parallels between religion and witchcraft in the party sequence, these comments are revealing. They implicitly associate Joan's normal life with the supposedly alternative world of the supernatural she is tempted to enter. While Marion talks to Shirley about witchcraft, Joan superficially distances herself from the conversation. But she also skims through a primer, 'How to be a Witch', resting on Marion's bookshelf. However, as Marion continues her conversation it becomes clear that her status as a witch is merely the result of social custom rather than independent choice: 'It's a religion really. My mother was a witch. My father belonged. So it was easy for me.'

This is not only the second reference to witchcraft as 'a religion' in the film but also another indication that divisions between this supposedly alternative movement and Joan's own Catholicism are not as radical as she believes. Marion was brought up in a witchcraft family and may have unthinkingly followed the path as Joan's own family life instilled in her the virtues of Catholicism as the true religion. While Joan reads further, Marion speaks about witches in extremely vague terms: 'There's something about them that we haven't got the power to define.' This intimates a lack of rationality hindering the investigation of any supposed alternative traditions this movement may appear to have. In *Jack's Wife*, witchcraft appears to be just another ideologically-induced custom as Catholicism and family life. During Marion's monologue, Romero cuts into Joan's perspective by using a number of point-of-view shots as she observes various eighteenth- and nineteenth-century female miniatures and portraits which may depict Marion's own family members. Although these images do not represent the usual stereotypical images of witches on broomsticks, they depict fashionable, upper-class ladies who have obviously benefited from belonging to an affluent social world. Such images and dialogue actually question, rather than affirm, the path Joan is tempted towards. Witchcraft is thus viewed as another socially fashionable path rather than a radical alternative designed to question programmed behavioural patterns, both past and present.

When Joan later returns home with Shirley, she finds Nikki with college professor Gregg Williamson. As played by Ray Laine, this character again embodies all the self-assured male arrogance of his previous role as Chris in *There's Always Vanilla*. Like Bill Hinzman's earlier cameo appearance, the casting cannot be regarded as merely accidental or coincidental. While Joan wishes to do 'something meaningful', Gregg sneers at the affluent wives who engage in 'community relations' by painting the houses of the underprivileged as a 'new thing' for their group to become involved in. Although Gregg challenges Joan by using offensive language in her presence and contradicts the values she has previously lived by, his role as a *provocateur* is solely related to his male ego. He wishes to dominate her in a different, yet similar way, to Jack. Gregg demonstrates the power of suggestion to Joan by making the already-drunk Shirley believe she has smoked marijuana. However, his male victory is tarnished in several ways. Shirley is already susceptible to his influence both as a result of her heavy alcohol consumption and her personal vulnerability as a woman conscious of both ageing and being trapped in an unfulfilling marriage. As with Joan later in the film, Gregg chooses his victims carefully since he knows they lack the necessary self-awareness to recognise the nature of the manipulative patriarchal mind games he uses on them.

The already distraught Shirley compares herself with Joan and regards herself as 'past my prime': 'I'm no young chicken but Joan is a young chicken.' Shirley does not believe she is finished but wishes to 'do things'. Unfortunately, Shirley's anguish at her present position in American society as an older woman no longer attractive and chained to an unhappy marriage takes the negatively exclusive forms of self-pity, jealousy at Joan, and lack of awareness of feminist alternatives open to her as an independent woman. After Gregg has achieved his goal of manipulating Shirley, she pleads with Joan to go home with her to avoid an expected confrontation with her unpleasant husband: 'He won't be able to jump over me, if you're there.' Despite her plea for help, Shirley also criticises Joan's personal armour of opinionated superiority: 'You should really try it sometime.' 'How come you have so many opinions without having done anything?' 'One of these days you're going to find yourself with a jackass between your legs.'

Her remarks to Joan act as a catalyst in many ways. Shirley recognises her friend's tendencies to conceal her true feelings behind merely uttering opinions and not daring to experience anything. However, rather than forcing Joan to re-evaluate her personal and social position within patriarchal society and move towards a more dignified and liberating way of finding real alternatives, Shirley's criticisms have disastrous consequences. They merely lead to Joan's temptations towards dabbling in forbidden paths and not having the courage to recognise that she bears the responsibility for the decisions she makes. Ironically, Joan will soon have a 'jackass' between her legs. She remains in her car as Shirley stumbles in a drunken stupor towards her husband who waits for her behind the screen door. Although Shirley falls down, her husband makes no effort to help her up but merely stands and watches his wife pick herself up from the ground.

The next sequence shows Joan's return home. It opens with a shot of the Mitchells' house number, 1246, again affirming the 'unlucky' nature of the Mitchell family domicile. Inside, Joan finds the witchcraft primer significantly positioned next to a whiskey bottle. She then hears the sounds of Nikki having an orgasm with an unseen lover. Rather than making sounds announcing her return home, Joan goes to her bed and masturbates, thus sublimating her feelings of repressed sexuality and desire to participate in the sexuality her daughter now enjoys. During this scene, Romero constantly cuts to a bull figure in Joan's room as well as showing its shadow on her wall. Its phallic connotations are obvious. The sequence ends with a zoom-in to Nikki in the doorway condemning her mother for her voyeuristic proclivities.

After Nikki leaves home, the next sequence shows Joan with her psychiatrist. He affirms one intuitive comment she makes about her daughter's activities: 'I'm more worried about me than I am about her.' But Joan can only go so far. The next scene shows Jack's angry reaction to Joan's news about a daughter whom he earlier pompously ordered to 'Try to stay virgin'. He blames Joan and hits her twice, affirming the male's right to punitive violence: 'You kick some ass, don't you, you kick some ass.' Instead of recognising the vicious nature of a patriarchal world which has oppressed her for so long, Joan then decides 'to cut loose and do something'. But she moves in the wrong direction. Although she decides to wear different clothes as a means of asserting a different identity, she falls into another kind of personal trap by flirting with the world of sexual promiscuity represented by Gregg. However, their next meeting shows her subjected to another form of male control. Romero shoots the scene in Gregg's classroom with Joan positioned in the student area and Gregg clearly ensconced in his authoritative instructor role. Despite his taunting her as 'Mrs Robinson', Joan does not heed this early warning signal. It is not surprising that the film's second fantasy sequence follows this scene. Joan believes a masked intruder breaks into her home and rapes her. But before she can pull off the mask, the dream ends to show her waking up in bed next to Jack.

The next day, Joan drives to Pittsburgh to purchase witch culture artefacts. During a sequence in an antique shop with Donovan's 'Season of the Witch' providing musical accompaniment on the soundtrack, we see Joan purchasing various items. But Romero intercuts shots of the shop's male owner spying on Joan either through shelves or from the top of a book he reads. This suggests that Joan's alternative path is compromised by another form of patriarchal control which spies on her very moves. When Joan returns home, various shots show her practicing witchcraft rituals. One shot in particular shows her writing The Lord's Prayer backwards. Although this represents one of the well-known inverse practices of Satanism, its very duality not only relates to the frequent mirror shots employed in the film but also reveals the connection of a dominant signifier of Western patriarchal ideology to its supposedly countercultural opposite. Witchcraft is still a religion very much like Catholicism headed by a male deity. It also involves established patriarchal family control as Marion's status in the film reveals.

Before departing on one of his frequent business trips, Jack makes a belated apology to Joan. But it is clearly perfunctory. The next sequence shows Joan with her coffee circle. They all discuss the disappointing aspects of marital life. This stimulates Joan into deciding to cast her first major witchcraft spell. She clearly wishes for an extra-marital fling. But Joan can not come to terms with her conscious desires for such a drastic move away from her normal routine. Joan then 'conjures' Gregg to come to her. However, Romero provides some relevant information to viewers who may choose to benefit from a more objective perspective to analyse critically Joan's actions. Jack's wife is never capable of performing such functions throughout the entire film. As she performs the necessary rituals, bells occur on the soundtrack equating Joan's 'deviant' activities with her former Catholicism. Both systems rely upon belief and faith as well as self-deception rather than rational analysis. Romero then shows Joan switching on the television set and listening to a sports game in boredom, the type of action usually associated with tired husbands returning from work. This shot not only signifies that Joan treats the witchcraft ritual as a mere game to attract Gregg but also evokes the earlier party scene where a male guest did a performance of his 'favourite television program' as a party act. After bells occur again on the soundtrack, Joan pours herself a glass of whiskey and then decides to follow the advice of the *Letter of St. James* by relying on 'works' rather than the Pauline doctrine of faith. She phones Gregg and invites him over.

Although Joan takes the initiative, she refuses to entertain any responsibility for her action and believes Gregg's arrival results from magical spells beyond her conscious control. However, Gregg sees his opportunity for an easy conquest. He now employs some degree of strategic tact rather than the explicitly aggressive attitude he has displayed towards Joan on their previous meetings. Despite Joan's attempt to place herself into a position of control – 'This isn't going to be any kind of regular thing, you know' – Gregg suggests a truce for a guilt-free liaison. But although he appears to compromise, 'You have your reasons, I have mine', and suggests a mutual 'thank you' to begin their relationship on a note of equality, his final comments reveal the still-ingrained presence of his earlier male sarcasm towards her – 'Thank you, Mrs Robinson.' Ironically, bells again sound to signify the real nature of an exchange Joan really does not understand. Whether embodied in the figure of a religious deity or 'swinging sixties' unattached male, the Law of the Father still dominates Joan.

Joan then visits Marion and states her desire to be accepted as a witch. But, as the following dialogue reveals, Joan merely exchanges one world of conformity and self-deception for another. Marion reassures Joan that 'being afraid is necessary to believing', a comment which parallels traditional criticisms of Catholicism as a religion of fear.[3] Joan believes that she has 'caused things to actually happen'. Marion replies that witchcraft 'won't work, more often than not, if you use it lightly' which accurately describes Joan's real attitude towards it at this time. For Joan, it is merely a means of experimenting with taboo concepts as well as flirting with getting an easy lay without accepting the full responsibility for her actions. Marion also comments that 'knowing you've abused it can destroy you from within, from fear, if nothing else'. Her comments also intuitively evoke 1960s experimentation with drugs, sex and alternative lifestyles which many indulged in as a form of escapism without really understanding the full implications involved. The world of *There's Always Vanilla* sketched out the dead-end implications of the flirtation philosophy also influencing Joan Mitchell.

Marion's statement also evokes Joan's third nightmare involving the masked intruder. It abruptly ceases when her phone rings and a police lieutenant informs her than Nikki has been found. Clearly Joan's deviant yearnings conjure up the world of the supernatural in very much the same way as Thérèse and Laurent's sexual guilt in Zola's *Thérèse Raquin* evokes the ghostly presence of her deceased husband. The firm connection between the personal and supernatural realms now becomes evident in the next shot. Joan looks at her reflection in the mirror as she drinks. Her drinking now places her in the earlier position of Shirley, who wanted a new experience but wished to blame her yearnings on a suitable scapegoat, absolving her of any responsibility for her actions. When Gregg arrives, Joan announces her interest in witchcraft and begins a ritual to evoke her aptly-named familiar spirit, 'Virago'. But she now encounters her lover's explicit masculine contempt for her. Gregg describes her in terms similar to

Shirley as 'another screwed-up woman ... looking for a cop out' while really desiring 'getting balled'. Gregg then assaults her in a manner reminiscent of Joan's fantasy nightmare intruder. He later repeats this action after Joan completes her ritual to conjure up Virago; this leads to the final breach in their relationship. When Gregg drives away for the last time Joan conjures up more spells; this leads to another nightmare intrusion by the masked figure. He now wears an animal head resembling the cat which entered her house prior to Gregg's last sexual assault.

Joan fails to comprehend the nature of her personal entrapment. Her attempts to seek out false alternatives that harm her potential for true independence lead to escalating patterns of supernatural chaos and violence. The original nightmares emerged from her uneasy relationship with her boorish husband. But they also take on a sinister form of development as a result of her flirtation with a world of witchcraft which is as equally conformist as the deadly social world she seeks escape from. Joan has also hidden dysfunctional masochistic yearnings towards another male figure who is as equally contemptuous of her as her husband. In *Jack's Wife*, the supernatural imagery has close connections to Joan's middle-class world which she inhabits as a living dead victim of patriarchal capitalism. The nightmares are displaced versions of her dilemmas in everyday life. But rather than learning from them and moving towards some form of rational self-awareness, Joan exchanges one form of self-oppression for another. Her husband and lover are contemptuously violent males whose abusive actions reappear in Joan's nightmare symbolised in the figure of the dark intruder. Joan's failure to recognise the real nature of her dilemma results in cataclysmic violence and her eventual return to another form of living dead existence.

Jack's Wife ends bleakly. It appears to lead towards another nightmare which will end as inconclusively as its predecessors. Joan wakes up in bed. The ominous cat appears once more. But, outside, Jack returns home late at night. He finds the door bolted. Inside her home, Joan sees a shadowy figure of an 'intruder' before a window. She fires at the figure using the shotgun from the basement she was unable to use in her last nightmare. Romero cuts to Jack before the window and then Joan shooting him from inside. Jack collapses on the lawn outside.

The penultimate sequence intercuts Joan's initiation into a female coven with Jack's dying moments. Although these two scenes are temporally distant, they both significantly complement each other in several ways. Joan gains her freedom due to an act of mistaken violence resulting from her misinterpretation of events. Instead of gaining her freedom by asserting her independence as a woman and moving away from home she actually becomes a 'free' woman due to events over which she has no conscious control. She accidentally kills her husband. But the killing results from forces she has unleashed from her very psyche, forces she claims no responsibility for. But she has deliberately nurtured them within her own subconscious. As with Romero's other films, *Jack's Wife* suggests that there is no real necessity for the violence; other solutions are also possible. Once irrationality gains control everything is finally lost.

While Jack dies, Romero films the new rituals Joan undergoes in the initiation ceremony. Nude, silent and submissive, she passively undergoes another process over which she has no control. Joan's submission during this ritual resembles her actions in the opening fantasy sequence. Witchcraft is clearly no progressive movement which will result in her independence. It is as constrained and controlled as the patriarchal world she intuitively sought escape from. During the ritual, Marion ties a cord round Joan's neck and ties it to an altar ring, an action paralleling Jack's in the opening sequence when he put a dog collar around his wife's neck and led her to the dog pound. Also, Joan undergoes a ritual flagellation to the coven's chanting of the deterministic line, 'So, must it be.' Although Joan's chastisement is ritualistically light, it evokes those violent scenes of her beating at the hands of Jack and her rape by Gregg. When the coven chant 'Lips that shall speak the holy secret' during the ceremony, Romero cuts to a zoom-out from Jack's bleeding lips as if suggesting a dark equation between the worlds of patriarchy and the supernatural. Joan clearly exchanges one form of self-oppression for another. Finally, as Jack dies, Romero includes an offscreen comment from a policeman: 'She's lying but she'll get away with it.' This interpretation is both correct and incorrect. It is incorrect insofar as Joan has not meant to kill her husband, but it is correct since Joan has lied to herself throughout the film and allowed unhealthy fantasies to dominate her consciousness. Rather than attempting to arrive at some form of rational self-awareness and break free from an unhappy marriage and sterile social situation that will allow her to find her true identity elsewhere, Joan has taken the easy way out by resorting to violence. Jack dies as a result of repressed forces in Joan's psyche. Her act of violence represents her form of revenge for the daily humiliations she suffered at his hands. But Jack's death was unnecessary in the first place. Although the police verdict is factually incorrect it does represent the view of an angry patriarchal world which will attempt to keep women and minorities in their place. However, both Joan and law enforcement representatives are equally wrong. They refuse to investigate further and arrive at an understanding of the real complexities of the situation.

Joan now survives as a single woman, yet her victory is short-lived. She merely replaces Marion as the source for scandal in her social world. The final scene of the film reprises the party activity of the earlier sequence. Bored housewives continue to gossip about others and discuss the same petty concerns as before. These latter concerns mostly involve material affluence or 'money in your hands'. Although Joan now becomes the new centre of attention and the recipient of fawning comments, 'Everybody's talking about you, great to see you back in circulation,' she achieves no real personal victory. Although Joan describes herself as a 'witch' when another woman who obviously will be the next person to follow in her path ('I'd really like to get near to her') asks her name, Romero ironically concludes his film with two zoom-ins to Joan's face as she flinches when she overhears somebody saying, 'You remember Jack's wife.' She has really achieved nothing and has merely exchanged one form of oppression for another. As in the more supernaturally-inclined worlds of *Night of the Living Dead*, *Dawn of the Dead* and *Day of the Dead*, violence represents no satisfactory solution for real social dilemmas. Like *Martin*, *Jack's Wife* illustrates a failed route where the worlds of everyday reality and fantasy merge resulting in cataclysmic violence which solves nothing. Like Martin, Joan becomes a victim of her fantasies. Rather than moving beyond her world of self-indulgent nightmares towards a deeper form of self-realisation, she becomes trapped in her fantasies and ends up in a situation which is really circular.

CHAPTER FIVE

The Crazies

As a moderately successful Romero film, *The Crazies* remains relatively neglected in terms of critical examination despite its theatrical re-release as *Code Name: Trixie* and subsequent reissues on video. Romero described it as a rushed film lacking cohesive structure. But he also believes that 'it came close to representing for the first time, my film-making personality' (quoted in Gagne 1987: 56). Robin Wood also regards it as 'an ambitious and neglected work that demands parenthetical attention here for its confirmation of Romero's thematic concerns and the particular emphasis it gives them'.[1] *The Crazies* does contain the problematic flaws cited by Romero such as uneven acting, frenzied direction and an over-abrupt editing style. Although the last factor appeared excessive at the time it actually anticipates the mode of fast cutting typical of MTV and television commercials. However, although these factors remove *The Crazies* from any comparison to a big-budget, professional Hollywood project, they are minor in nature. Stylistically and thematically, the film is a good example of the type of contemporary independent commercial film-making that offered a more critical view of American society than contemporaneous major studio films. *The Crazies* also functions as an allegorical critique of America's denial of the Vietnam syndrome at a time when Hollywood refused to engage in any direct cinematic representations since *The Green Berets* (1968). Furthermore, the film represents Romero's development of the EC comic book style which always fascinated him. This appears in his recurrent use of movement within stationary camera angles and editing practices resembling a comic book artist's use of panels. His choice of style complements cinematic content. The predominantly 'nervous' excessive montage technique in which one scene abruptly cuts to another aptly complements the type of hysterical world depicted. Both individuals and society become equally crazy in a world heading towards destruction.

The Crazies is certainly Romero's most accomplished work prior to his association with Richard Rubinstein and the Laurel Company. It not only reveals the close association between the personal and social levels of existence characterising Romero's films but also utilises one of the key tenets of the naturalist tradition, namely the disjuncture between the biological and social circulus which often, paradoxically, results in a conjuncture between individual and historical chaos as illustrated by Emile Zola's Rougon-Macquart series of novels and his theoretical explorations in 'The Experimental Novel'.

The film also makes explicit ideas which already existed implicitly in There's Always Vanilla and Jack's Wife involving the individual's undiscerning awareness of their actual relationship to social and historical forces conditioning their very identities and behavior patterns. In Romero's earlier films, the main figures never reach any form of social awareness and pay the personal costs for their failure. The Crazies is the first film in which certain characters do obtain some degree of awareness. But it is not enough to save them from the social chaos and disintegrating fabric of their everyday world. Like There's Always Vanilla and Jack's Wife, The Crazies needs no supernatural symbols such as zombies to allegorise Romero's theme of a world which is already crazy. It is also one where boundaries between sane and insane are already becoming increasingly blurred and non-existent. The old order is not only extremely corrupt and inimical to the true development of human personality but also doomed by the very destructive forces it employs to protect its own existence.

The Crazies also emphasises a plot motif already present in Night of the Living Dead which most critics regarded as redundant to the latter film, namely government responsibility for the chaos affecting human society. In the earlier film, the Venus probe radiation appears as the science fiction generic rationalisation for the zombie outbreak. Although such an explanation typical of 1950s science fiction generic films appears marginal to the concerns of Night of the Living Dead, it does make connections between the world of individual violence and an unseen government bureaucracy actually responsible for negative consequences. By making this motif explicit, The Crazies represents the return of a political repressed already contained within the original structure of Night of the Living Dead.

In The Crazies, the government-military-scientific establishment bears the guilt for the chemical spill of a bio-toxin, code name: Trixie, into the water supply of rural Evans City in Pennsylvania. The military arrive and attempt a botched cover-up treating the citizens as little better than Vietnamese rounded up and relocated into unjustified incarceration due to the arbitrary decisions of a distant bureaucracy. The decisions resemble those made in past and present historical eras. Evans City inhabitants suddenly find themselves stripped of their supposedly secure democratic rights under the American constitution and placed in the same position as patriotic Japanese-Americans during World War Two who were rounded up and placed in relocation camps. The Crazies also parallels recent historical incidents during the Vietnam War when South Vietnamese villagers were rounded up and removed from their villages. As Mark Walker and other critics have noticed, The Crazies has distinct Vietnam allegorical associations which also emphasise many key themes implicit in Night of the Living Dead.[2] Romero's film operates as a bleakly ironic inverse allegory of

American involvement in Vietnam with Americans playing the roles of occupier and occupied, soldier and civilian, exploiter and exploited. The disintegrating chaos has relevant political associations. A priest burns himself in protest against the military like the Buddhist monk protesting against South Vietnam's Diem regime. Troops burn corpses with flame throwers. One character dies with a bullet through his head like the Viet Cong suspect in Eddie Adam's famous 1968 photo. A helicopter chases a group of fugitives through the woods only to be shot down easily by a simple weapon similar to the Viet Cong's frequent defeats of technologically-advanced enemies. During the round-up of civilians, a 'crazy' spits at a soldier's gas mask. The action also recalls the many stories of returning soldiers from Vietnam being spat upon by anti-war activists at the airport.

However, despite these interesting parallels, *The Crazies* is also a Romero film containing ideas very close to the director as well as having an indelible relationship to an influential historical period. Romero describes it not as a Vietnam film but rather 'an anti-military film' in a 'comic book context' (quoted in Yakir 1977: 64). *The Crazies* cannot be entirely divorced from this latter description. As far as its EC-influenced style goes, *The Crazies* anticipates the type of comic strip depiction used in conservative 1980s Vietnam films such as *Missing in Action* (1984) and *Rambo* (1985). But Romero's use of this style is much more mature and progressive. It belongs to the tradition of EC comic strips such as *Two Fisted Tales*, which often contained many stories avoiding the glamorisation of war typical of Cold War Hollywood films such as *The Sands of Iwo Jima* (1949), as well as containing several anti-militaristic narratives from different periods of world history. *Two Fisted Tales* also complemented the gritty realism and comic strip character depiction present in Samuel Fuller's *The Steel Helmet* (1950) and *Fixed Bayonets* (1951). Fuller's military characters were not only often reduced to basic stock generic types but also represented soldiers who reduce their personalities to the most appropriate functional mode in order to survive in a wartime situation.

As Wood notices, the opening scene operates as a reprise of those early images in *Night of the Living Dead*, moving out from its 'concentration on the family unit into a more generalised treatment of social disintegration (a progression *Dawn of the Dead* will complete)' (1986: 116). Instead of daytime, the film opens at night with a long shot of a quiet farmhouse against the sky. Rapid cuts reveal a toy, a little girl getting a cup of water from the kitchen tap (an action we later realise has ominous consequences), followed by the appropriate sound of a cuckoo clock ironically announcing the film's theme of a world gone entirely crazy or 'cuckoo'. The sound also foreshadows the pollution already in the water supply which will drive everyone insane. As in *Jack's Wife*, sounds, as well as images, occur as equal signifiers of appropriate meaning. The film is tightly directed from a meaningful screenplay in which no action or dialogue is ever superfluous.

A young boy engages in a game and terrorises his younger sister in the same manner as the more adult Johnny does to Barbara in the opening images of *Night of the Living Dead*. But this time they are not in a graveyard but inside their supposedly safe and secure home. When the little girl finds herself unable to switch on the light she finds herself the victim of her younger brother's manipulative activities. She pleads, 'Stop it,

Billy. I'm scared', as he plays the monster in their basement. However, as in *Night of the Living Dead*, such 'playful' activities herald the appearance of a much more serious threat. The real monster is not late in appearing as indicated by a shadow behind the little girl which abruptly concludes Billy's game. The next image shows their father on a rampage smashing up domestic items. As the first 'crazy' in the film, he scares his children. When the little girl rushes to her parents' bedroom she finds a sheet covering a body. A bloodstain slowly appears on the sheet, the first colour contrast in a film engaging in predominant clashes of white and red. Father suddenly appears in the doorway, but Billy flashes a torch in his face allowing his sister to escape. This feature also evokes imagery in *Night of the Living Dead* when light and fire temporarily stop any violent zombie; in the earlier film, the zombies have to smash Ben's headlights before they can continue their assault. When the little girl removes the sheet she discovers her mother dead in bed. Father then starts a fire and the film's credits roll. But they roll against the background of military drums, the first appearance of a frequent sound motif employed by Romero throughout the film.

These sounds not only anticipate the arrival of the soldiers later in the film. They also suggest that the supposedly isolated microcosmic family violence has associations with the encroaching macrocosmic threat of military violence developing throughout the film. Despite their supposedly secure constitutional rights, the American citizens in *The Crazies* find themselves treated as 'enemy aliens' by a state machinery indiscriminately regarding them as threats to the status quo. The presence of individual chaos results in the institution of brutal repression and violence approved by a government machinery intent on keeping order and showing little interest in investigating (and remedying) the actual causes. Little difference exists between military activities home and abroad.

As in *Night of the Living Dead*, a family unit violently acts out the repressed energies upon which civilisation depends for its existence. But these energies have now become uncontrollable. While a boy terrorises his younger and vulnerable sister, father has murdered mother and left her body in the family bedroom. He then goes on the rampage and destroys material items relating to the home. It is a further symbiotic enactment of repressed desires resulting from the murder of his spouse. He now removes all traces of female domestic oppression from an environment he can now claim as his own. Father then sets the dairy farm on fire after dousing the interior with kerosene. This is another intuitive recognition of the oppressive nature of an environment operating as a psychic and physical prison for all its victims. The sequence complements a later scene when a soldier ascends the stairs of a farmhouse after killing a father attempting to defend his home from military intruders. After finding the daughter playing the piano, perhaps as a means of disavowing the violence she has witnessed, the soldier finds grandmother knitting in a rocking chair. The sweet old lady then stabs him with her knitting needle in a scene whose rapidly edited montage associations evokes Karen's stabbing of Helen in *Night of the Living Dead*. As the soldier falls downstairs, the twine becomes temporarily caught in his body. It ironically renders his male presence impotent as a result of the deadly use of a supposedly harmless domestic artifact relegated to grandmother. After her most productive years as wife and mother, she is now confined to a rocking chair continuing her use-value to society by knitting. Like Karen avenging her subordinate status in the Cooper family, grandmother also appropriately reacts against a patriarchal culture which sees no use for her aged status other than being confined to a rocking chair upstairs. These two sequences also echo the return of the repressed motif occurring in many family horror films in this period whereby hidden tensions erupt against their ideological confinement.

The second sequence introduces the audience to Judy (Lane Carroll) and David (W. G. McMillan), Romero's version of the 'last romantic couple' theme, familiar from works as diverse as *They Live By Night* (1948) and *Pierrot le Fou* (1965), who would normally be expected to survive after the final reel in most Hollywood movies. However, the formative world of EC Comics and *Night of the Living Dead* already suggest that such a conclusion would be inappropriate in this context, especially when the heroine's first name evokes that of her unfortunate predecessor in the earlier film. Judy and David are unmarried, deeply in love and expecting their first child. However, although their circumstances foreshadows the later situation of Stephen and Fran in *Dawn of the Dead*, the relationship appears more intimate and closer in these brief introductory scenes. Like the mistaken proposal by Stephen in the later film, a marital union appears probable. But this fact has ominous overtones considering the depiction of dysfunctional couples such as the Coopers in *Night of the Living Dead* and the 'crazy' family seen in the pre-credit sequences. Marriage is not really a necessity for either. But Judy's comment suggests the presence of an oppressive social coercion they should both reject but which occupies a dominant ideological hold over their consciousness: 'I have a feeling that if anything happened to this baby, you won't marry me.'

As a volunteer fireman, David moves into action after hearing the fire siren. Judy also receives an emergency call informing her about a fire at the dairy farm seen in the pre-credits sequence. He leaves to join his fellow volunteers while Judy dresses to perform her function as a nurse who tends to the two badly-burned children. The scene ominously ends with Judy performing the same function as the little girl in the opening sequence by drinking water from the kitchen tap. Then the soundtrack breaks out into an ominous rendition of the old Civil War ballad, 'When Johnny Comes Marching Home', hummed ironically by a female singer. This critical militaristic musical leitmotif applies less to David but more to the future invaders and his Army buddy Clank (Harold Wayne Jones). When we first see Clank an older fireman comments on his presence at the fire station, 'Doesn't it bother you ... You must need this.' It significantly reveals the older man's recognition of Clank's aimless existence. Clank has 'no particular place to go', and depends upon the presence of action and adventure to take his mind off his present frustrations. Clank affirms this when he replies that the fire call is just 'Something to do' as he gets his fireman's uniform after hearing about the sighted presence of soldiers in the area. Clank sees Judy as she drops David off at the fire station. We also learn that she had been Clank's former girlfriend before taking up with David. Although Clank appears to have accepted the situation, Romero also shows him expressing repressed feelings of regret, feelings which will later explicitly emerge in antagonistic ways. Clank also begins the first of a series of 'one-upmanship' tactics against his romantic rival: 'You're late. I was the first one here.'

When Judy reports to Dr. Brookmyre (Will Disney) she sees a masked, white-clothed figure in the morgue performing an autopsy on one of the children. He brusquely orders her away in a domineering militaristic fashion, 'Move now.' It is not accidental that the second death we see in the film involves a female victim since Romero's films often involve an intuitive feminist awareness of who the most vulnerable victims of patriarchal society often are during times of conflict. The military doctor comments, 'The girl just died. I think I can save the boy.' But we later see that the boy survives as a 'crazy', the term the military uses to objectify their victims. This term parallels the similar objectifying term 'gook', then used in Vietnam for the Vietnamese whether they were friendly or hostile. Judy discovers Brookmyre in conference with Major Ryder (Harry Spillman) concerning toxic chemicals infiltrating the town's water supply and the necessity for martial law and quarantine: 'We never thought it would happen.' Evans City's supposedly secure civilian world, believing in democracy and freedom, soon undergoes its first shock. It discovers not only the suspension of rights supposedly guaranteed under the Constitution but also its new status as a potential enemy similar to the Vietnamese nation its government still fights in South-East Asia. Like their American predecessors such as pre-World War One Socialists, German-Americans, Nisei and Cold War-era Communists, feminists and liberals, the small community now finds itself arbitrarily designated as the enemy and stripped of their guaranteed democratic rights.

At the farm house, firemen watch the blaze. The insane father is now handcuffed to the police car, impotently asserting his last vestige of patriarchal authority as he attempts to direct the firefighters. David then learns about his situation. Father is described as a man who 'just went crazy' before a brief moment of sanity: 'When he realised what he did, he cried like a baby.' Although father obviously believed he did *not* know best, he still hysterically continues to direct the firefighting operation like the military high command seen throughout the film. As Wood pertinently notes,

> The continuity suggested by the opening between normality and craziness is sustained throughout the film; indeed, one of its most fascinating aspects is the way the boundary between the two is continually blurred ... The crazies, in other words, represent merely an extension of normality, not its opposite. The spontaneous violence of the mad appears scarcely more grotesque than the organised violence of the authorities. (1986: 116–17)

Wood also regards *The Crazies* as repeating the pattern of *Night of the Living Dead* with crazies substituting for zombies and the military for the posse. But even here divisions are not clearly drawn. Any attempted demarcation between craziness and normality becomes increasingly blurred and diffuse as the film continues. In this manner, the diffusion resembles the structure of *Jack's Wife*, where fantasy and the real world become difficult to distinguish.

As the film progresses, the borderlines become redundant, leaving both individuals and society suffering from the same type of chaos that eventually leads to total destruction. In this manner, *The Crazies* resembles the conclusions of Zola's novels such as *Nana* and *La Bête Humaine*, in which both individuals and society are caught up in a mad frenzy leading to the Franco-Prussian War depicted in *Le Débâcle*, a mood also superbly depicted by the Zola-influenced first part of *The New Babylon* (1929), co-directed by Grigori Kosintsev and Leonid Trauberg.[3]

Already personally subjected to martial law, Dr. Brookmyre wishes to save Judy, David and their unborn child from contamination. He gives her some serum, suggests she sneak away, avoid the imminent quarantine and 'Stay away from people'. Brookmyre's warning not only echoes Jean-Paul Sartre's 'Hell is other people' conclusion from *No Exit* but also contains the implicit appearance of a theme Romero develops in his zombie trilogy – the necessity for forming a new society due to the moral bankruptcy of the old order. Brookmyre already knows that the military intend to reserve the serum exclusively for themselves, a fact corroborated by a newly arrived Evans City cop: 'They're giving the soldiers some kind of injection. They say there's not enough for the town.' When Brinkmyre protests about this, Major Ryder reveals that the whole area is under a national security alert due to a plane crash. The plane secretly carried an experimental vaccine (now known to contain an infectious virus) which has now contaminated the city water supply. While news media such as the radio merely report the weather, soldiers round up civilians without any word of explanation, place them in a poorly-organised relocation camp inside a high school gymnasium, confiscate their weapons (violating the enshrined constitutional 'right to bear arms') and jam airwaves to prevent radio hams revealing information to the outside world. In *The Crazies*, Romero makes explicit an axiom relevant to both the 1960s and later decades, namely that the American military-political-scientific establishment has never believed in the best interests of its citizens at any time and regards them as expendable whenever convenient.

The following sequences emphasise this point. We next see supercilious politician Brubaker (played by W. L. Thunhurst, Joan Mitchell's disdainful husband from *Jack's Wife*) inhumanely discussing relevant options with his fellow bureaucrats about dropping a nuclear weapon on Evans City during a 'training mission'. Like those ruthless politicians in Robert Aldrich's *Twilight's Last Gleaming* (1977), they regard human life as expendable in any government cover-up operation. Brubaker intends to inform the President about his plan involving a plane containing a weapon and 'what size weapon it should carry to burn out the infected area'. This sequence also depicts supposedly rational people discussing an insanely violent scenario in much the same terms as 1950s EC Comics engaged in black satire of its culture's Cold War mentality. The scene also represents a darkly ironic American version of The Wahnsee Declaration.

At the same time, Dr. Watts (Richard France), one of the original scientists who worked on the Trixie project, faces military relocation to Evans City despite the fact that he needs essential equipment to find the antidote. We also discover that he never managed to complete his original research on Trixie because the military removed his funding. Despite his rational objections, the soldiers intend to follow 'orders' even if they are as irrational and poorly planned as the martial law operations affecting Evans City. When Watts complains, 'You'll have a hell of a job getting me on that plane, soldier', he gets the reply, 'Maybe so, sir. But we'll do it.' Although Major Ryder speaks about his superior officer Colonel Peckham's description of the occupying force as 'a highly original riot-trained army', Romero produces a quick series of ironic shots which contradict this description. They present the invaders as little better than their brutal counterparts in South Vietnam.

White-garbed, gas-masked soldiers invade motels, bedrooms and homes brusquely rounding up civilians without any word of explanation. As a middle-aged couple are led away, Romero cuts to a photo of their son in military uniform who is probably doing the same things to helpless Vietnamese in his current tour of duty. A soldier lifts up a young child performing a similar action to his counterparts in Vietnam often seen photographed in the same way as they move villagers into relocation centres, an action also reproduced at the climax of the village-burning sequence in Oliver Stone's *Platoon* (1986). Other scenes show one soldier engaged in looting as he breaks open a glass case to remove a fishing rod while others confiscate rifles from another home as they ironically walk over toy soldiers scattered on the floor, a symbolic depiction of American culture's fascination with military violence and its ideological aims to indoctrinate younger male members as early as possible.

Back at Dr. Brookmyre's office, the officer assigned to quarantine the area, Col. Chris Peckham (Lloyd Haller), arrives to take charge. Although the sheriff exclaims 'Son of a bitch!', presumably reacting to Peckham's Afro-American status, the audience has already been introduced to him as a professional soldier in an earlier scene and would naturally not share in the perception of an ignorant and prejudiced civilian. Peckham has the same racial identity as Ben in *Night of the Living Dead*. The film also represents him sympathetically as a good man performing a bad task. Nothing further is made of his racial origins. This emerges in a later scene. Peckham comments after the accidental shooting of a policeman who refuses to hand over his arms by complying to the abandonment of civil law, 'This was exactly the kind of thing we wanted to prevent.' But, like Ben, Peckham finds that he is in an uncontrollable situation as the following sequence shows. Immediately after these lines, Romero shows the military shooting a farmer who may either be crazy or justifiably defending himself from attackers. Peckham is no Hollywood-manufactured Sidney Poitier nor any black action genre hero like Jim Brown or Fred Williamson. Romero not only avoids 'identity politics' in his films, but also shows that all sectors of society can be equally trapped by the same oppressive circumstances. Although Peckham does not reproduce Ben's aggressive activities in *Night of the Living Dead*, he participates in an institutional system responsible for oppression and violence. Like Ben, he appears late in the film to take control, but Peckham is no hero. Despite his self-awareness, he does not reject an institutional structure which has provided him with a career and a social status his ethnicity would not otherwise have offered him. As Peckham remarks later to Ryder, 'I'm a combat man. I shouldn't even be here. I just happened to be available – even expendable!'

The next sequence shows David, Clank and Judy reunited before being arrested by the military and placed in the back of a van with three other prisoners, an older man suffering from the virus and father and daughter, Artie (Richard Liberty) and Kathy (Lynn Lowry). Despite Judy's pleas, the military confiscate the serum she has not been able to give to David. Although Judy received an injection at Dr. Brookmyre's office, the audience has already seen her drinking contaminated water. Clank reacts against martial law as a soldier moves him inside, deliberately concluding his comment, 'No problem', with the significantly conclusive word, '*yet*', uttered the moment he is safely inside and unheard by those outside. While David appears calm and accepts the situation, Clank regards the confinement as an affront to his masculinity and clearly relishes the moment when he can react with violence. The close-up of his angry face eloquently reveals his real feelings.

In Brookmyre's office, now the centre for military operations, Peckham informs Ryder about the real facts of the martial-law situation involving cases of Trixie ending up in the Evans City water supply. Typical of its predecessors both before and after, the American government has lied to its people. Peckham reveals that Trixie was not developed as a vaccine but as 'a biological weapon', something officially banned under the Geneva Convention but still manufactured today for possible use in any wartime situation. Although Peckham does not give further details, it is obvious that Trixie has been specially prepared for use in the Vietnam War. But now, ironically, the war has come home to America with a vengeance. Ryder replies in amazement, 'I fell for that story, hook, line and sinker.' Peckham brusquely comments, 'That was the idea.' His comment recalls the scene in *Night of the Living Dead* when news reporters attempt in vain to interview a diffident government-military establishment concerning their responsibility over the Venus space probe. The comment by the captives in the van concerning their situation, 'Maybe, we're in some kind of war' is ironic in more than one sense. Evans City civilians now find the military at war with them when they do not obey orders. This situation reveals that citizens have always been ideologically assaulted as objects of propaganda exercises which lead to bloodier reprisals if they refuse military discipline. The later image of the military shooting an escaping civilian who attempts running across a bridge in daylight illustrates this. Romero also reprises 'When Johnny Comes Marching Home' on the soundtrack as he shows soldiers gathering outside the post office and another stealing trading stamps from inside an abandoned car.

The Crazies develops Romero's consistent critique of a ruthless government establishment which is actually responsible for various types of social chaos. It is one faintly present in *Night of the Living Dead* and explicitly developed in *Dawn of the Dead* and *Day of the Dead*. When Dr. Watts appears at Peckham's headquarters, the representatives of the military and scientific establishments engage in a conflict over responsibility reminiscent of the type of debate which later appears in *Day of the Dead*. While Ryder blames Watts – 'It's you think boys who created the thing in the first place' – the scientist complains about his removal from a laboratory he needed access to in order to find an antidote. Watts also mentions that a considerable difference exists between the military's 99 per cent assurance concerning the virus's supposed inactivity and the scientific world's need of 100 per cent certainty. In any case, the difference is both minor and ludicrous in terms of the danger. Both establishments bear responsibility for the Evans City incident. Furthermore, their activity is now too little and too late: 'Trixie has been in those containers for six days. Any truck driver could have taken it out of the perimeter.' The civilian population appears. Whatever resolution the authorities adopt, questions will still remain concerning the presence of victims either dead or incurably mad: 'How can you explain away a town which has been wiped from the map or a people into mindlessness?' In either scenario, individuals do not count. Institutional calculations will lead to more chaos and destruction.

This factor emerges in the next sequence which shows an increasingly ailing Kathy and Clank following the escape from the military van taking them to quarantine. Kathy comments to Clank, 'All these people dying and my father can't feel that.' She unconsciously compares Artie to the unseen government bureaucrat Brubaker. But ironically Kathy appeals in vain to another male who shares the same attributes, 'I know you can.' Like Artie and Brubaker, Clank has his own personal agenda which does not involve any consideration for the feelings of other people. When Clank goes to the whiskey cabinet, David warns him about over-indulgence in one permitted narcotic which the status quo allows to anyone not challenging its institutions: 'Just don't get yourself tanked, Clank.' David also recognises the dangers of a world getting increasingly out of control, one in which local redneck hunters relish in following their aggressive activities. Parallels with the violent hunters of *Night of the Living Dead* and *Dawn of the Dead* appear in scenes showing rednecks engaging in shooting contests with the military in dealing with the present emergency. Kathy misinterprets Clank's character, a feature she shares in common with the heroine of *There's Always Vanilla*. Clank merely regards her as a dangerous infection. As he tells David, 'The chick's got the bug', describing her by the same demeaning term used by Chris in his debasing camera addresses to the audience in *Vanilla*. The world of masculinity will prove a woman's nightmare in more ways than one. It is a danger on the micro-level of the family as well as the macro-levels of government, military and scientific institutions. The media is also complicit in manipulating its listeners as much as the advertising world is in *Vanilla*. During this sequence, only music occurs on the airwaves, rather than news informing listeners about the present emergency. This act symbolises the type of media denial mechanism the establishment uses in concealing its oppressive activities.

As in *Night of the Living Dead*, David and Judy's relationship appears as vulnerable and doomed as the earlier one between Tom and Judy. Romero also inserts a brief lyrical interlude into the narrative that involves them both, a contrast with the violent world surrounding them. But this time the sequence appears less redundant than its earlier counterpart. While David and Judy converse in a private moment, the soundtrack plays a theme associated with their relationship, the anti-war ballad 'Tin Soldier' whose lyrics again occur in the final scenes of the film. David and Judy are no stereotyped young lovers from 1950s horror and science fiction films like their predecessors in *Night of the Living Dead*. They are mature and have more life experience. As the music plays, David tells Judy about his earlier vulnerability and macho role-playing which he now rejects: 'When I was in Nam, I thought you were Clank's girl.' He speaks of seeing her with Clank one day at a game when his friend was the 'big football hero' and reveals to her his insecure feelings at that time. David also rejects his earlier persona where he unthinkingly followed the masculine pursuits of his culture and showed no awareness of a woman's real personality: 'I didn't really know you, didn't know about you.' David's confession reveals a much more progressive perspective than one displayed by the arrogant Chris of *There's Always Vanilla*. David further reveals his pursuit of the wrong path: 'Action, adventure. Evans City's only

Green Beret. I couldn't believe this was me.' Judy consoles him, 'We're going to be all right.' Although resembling *Night*'s earlier lyrical interlude between Tom and Judy, this scene reveals the conscious development of a male hero who learns from his past mistakes, rejects the macho values of his culture, and wishes to pursue a new direction for his life. It signifies Romero's deepest concerns in articulating the necessary personal trajectory of breaking away from deeply ingrained ideologically-induced cultural habits and trying to move towards a new form of society. Romero significantly illustrates this moment in David's consciousness by framing his head in sharp focus while a rifle muzzle appears in soft focus until he pushes it away and out of the shot. No matter how fragile this movement may be, it is much better than continuing to follow the life-denying patterns of everyday social life. The scene represents an important development in his work and one highly relevant to any accurate interpretation of *The Crazies*. David also realises the whole absurdity of the situation now affecting his community: 'How can you tell who's infected and who isn't?' His sensitive character and his rejection of a weapon anticipates Peter's climactic gesture in *Dawn of the Dead*. David is also aware of the Army's dangerous involvement in this situation in a line strongly evoking the Kent State Massacre when he points out that the military 'can turn a campus protest into a shooting war'. His following sentence poignantly anticipates the tragic conclusion of his romance with Judy: 'Some of the rednecks who live in this area could be shooting at each other and not even care.'

During the next sequence, Romero reveals both the incompetence and moral bankruptcy of the old order. Peckham orders the execution of any civilian resisting the military by refusing to heed one warning shot. As in *Night of the Living Dead*, bodies are to be burned. Like Vietnam, many soldiers in *The Crazies* have no idea as to why they are engaged in this containment operation: 'Few of the men have ever been told of this ... If these men knew the whole truth they'll be breaking the perimeter themselves.' As well as commenting on the 'shoddy' nature of the operation, Dr. Brookmyre utters the premise of the entire film: 'Who can you tell who's infected or not?' Peckham describes himself as little better than an obedient soldier merely carrying out orders, a line the captured sergeant repeats later in the film. He is a 'combat officer, merely available, just expendable'. But his comment is inexcusable on more than one level. First, Peckham's argument parallels the line of Nazi war criminals which the Nuremberg trials rendered indefensible. We must also remember that during the time Romero filmed *The Crazies* analogies between American soldiers in Vietnam and Nazis were very common. The film also appeared three years after The Winter Soldier investigations when veterans openly confessed to committing atrocities and several years after the My Lai Massacre. Secondly, as succeeding scenes show, Peckham's soldiers engage in activities reminiscent of war crimes. They kill a man as well as his wife who may be merely defending home and family. After incinerating the father's body with a flame thrower, they place the mother's body on top in a manner reproducing the type of Nazi efficiency used in disposing bodies from the gas chamber. Screams erupt on the soundtrack clearly intimating that the woman is still alive. Another scene shows body bags used for dead 'crazies', another common Vietnam image. Soldiers divide among themselves the personal property they have looted from dead bodies. They also carry away little children in their arms like contemporary photographs of Americans carrying South Vietnamese infants away to 'safety'. David's comments concerning an Army who 'can turn a campus protest into a war' prove factual. Clank supports him: 'The Army's nobody's friend. We know cause we've been in.' The military's activities are little different from the redneck posse in *Night of the Living Dead*, the only distinction being that they have official approval for their actions by an establishment who find the option of dropping a nuclear bomb on the area really 'no problem'.

The following sequences depict further institutional violence and chaos as well as suggesting that old systems of personal relationships are no longer viable. As Dr. Watts works intensely to find an antidote, he removes his gas mask, an action followed by his middle-aged laboratory assistant (Edith Bell) who receives a spontaneous marriage proposal from him. Although she understands the real significance of his offer, 'I assume from that you mean our chances are good', the very nature of Watts' offer is both redundant and trivial under the present emergency. Things are never going to be the same again. Also hierarchy exists between them involving male superiority and status. When Watts later finds the antidote he never bothers to share his discovery with her. Instead he rushes away in an act of male arrogance regarding her as a lowly female technician and ignoring her pleas, 'If you can explain it to me, *sir*. I can help.'

In the next sequence, Dr. Brookmyre states that he gave Judy serum to give to Dave to ensure the safety of their marriage and future parenthood. Ironically, before he reveals this, the military doctor, first seen by Judy when she first arrived at Brookmyre's office, becomes insane. In the cases of Dr. Watts and Judy, previous forms of institutional relationships are now redundant. This is especially so when viewers reflect on these two sequences in the light of the film's tragic climax. Artie's inability to act as a real father to Kathy in the following sequences further undermines the legitimacy of the family unit. Something better is needed to replace a now outmoded system based upon patriarchal authority and male violence.

Later that night, Clank and David decide to employ their former military training by overpowering soldiers who have taken over the Country Club. Although Clank relishes the opportunity to indulge in violence by shooting them before they have a chance to surrender, David expresses unease. When they interrogate the surviving sergeant, he admits to the presence of the virus as well as absolving himself of any responsibility for his actions: 'How does the Army get involved in anything? I don't know. It's a police action. The Army only tells us what they want to. We're only following orders.' The term 'police action' ironically evokes the diplomatic language used to justify American involvement in Vietnam as well as other future conflicts. After the sergeant makes an attempt to escape, Clank shoots him in the back jeering at David's reluctance towards using violence: 'David, the Green Beret! Strong man! Hey man, you really messed up. I thought that David was Special Forces. I thought he was some kind of god. I never came close to it. Regular Army was all I made.' He takes pleasure in killing 'five of them sons of bitches' and mocks David's reluctance to resort to violence. These lines reveal Clank as an early example of those insecure males in Romero's films who take pleasure in immersing themselves in a world of masculine violence which often results in their downfall, such as David and Roger in *Dawn of the Dead* and Captain Rhodes in *Day of the Dead*. Already feeling himself affected by the virus, Clank compensates for growing feelings of vulnerability by bossing David and rushing upstairs to his former lover, Judy. After David prevails on Clank to leave, Romero depicts the second private moment between them since the crisis began, one in which Judy feels that David has a 'natural immunity' to the virus. *The Crazies* supplies no factual reason for David's immunity. Instead, it implicitly suggests that David's conscious rejection of a crazy world of patriarchal violence may be the reason for his immunity from a virus which releases repressed tensions existing within the body politic.

The next juxtaposed sequences depict the negative values contained in an old world suffering from craziness. When Clank returns downstairs, he listens to Artie revealing his feelings of patriarchal possessiveness and incestuous desires for a daughter he has never allowed to date. The moral bankruptcy of capitalist family values becomes clearly evident well before the scene where Artie rapes his own daughter. In other contexts Romero reveals the ruthless nature and corrupt values of the system Artie supports. Brubaker plans a diplomatic strategy involving the nuclear destruction of Evans City and accompanying propaganda the government will employ after the fact: 'If we have to push the button, we'll have to say that the weapon went off' (presumably by accident). Brubaker then gets the President (an unseen figure the back of whose head appears on a television monitor) to agree to his strategy. He then asks him to keep the lines of communication open for the final decision. The planned nuclear annihilation of innocent Americans is both an act of craziness and the final act of an inhumane system regarding its citizens as less than human beings and mere disposable objects.

This political resonance merges with the personal in the following scene showing Artie's incestuous assault on Kathy. Romero shows Kathy clutching a miniature portrait of a Puritan figure in a house containing portraits and pictures of family members from past historical epochs. This emphasises both the complicity of past generations as well as continuity of a family violence witnessed by the audience, a violence generated by Puritan religious repression. Clank arrives on the scene too late. Although condemning Artie for his assault, this has less to do with any sympathy he has for Kathy and more to do with another convenient situation within which he may demonstrate his male aggressiveness.

After David and Clank discover Artie's body hanging above the basement, *The Crazies* quickly moves towards its bleak conclusion. Unable to come to terms with his incestuous desires, the father has hung himself. Meanwhile, his daughter wanders outside to confront approaching soldiers. Romero significantly pans left from Kathy at the right frame of the screen to show a herd of sheep rushing away towards the military. Frightened of becoming contaminated, the men shoot her although Kathy only wishes to approach them out of friendship as she asks each one, 'What's your name?' Her association with the sheep contains ironic religious associations. It also counterpoints an earlier scene when a Catholic priest incinerated himself with a zippo lighter outside his church when soldiers refused his constant pleas to regard the building as a sanctuary. Although the priest may have been affected by the virus, his hysterical reactions may actually result from realising that socially cherished ideological beliefs supposedly guaranteed by his government are actually worthless. He becomes a martyr but his gesture is futile. A soldier shoots him and abruptly curtails his protest.

Similarly, Kathy wanders insanely like a female good shepherd anti-war protestor attempting to persuade soldiers to make love and not war.

In both cases, the actions of the priest and Kathy are futile before the violent repression of the status quo. As Wood eloquently states concerning the priest's action:

> We never know whether he is a victim of the virus (acting, in his case, on a desire for martyrdom). Once such a doubt is implanted, uncertainty arises over what provokes the uncontrolled and violent behaviour of virtually everyone in the film. The hysteria of the quarantined can be attributed equally to the spread of contagion among them or to their brutal and ignominious herding together in claustrophobically close quarters by the military; the various individual characters who overstep the bounds of recognisably normal behaviour may simply be reacting to conditions of extreme stress. The crazies, in other words, represent merely an extension of normality, not its opposite. (1986: 117)[4]

Similarly, Kathy may also be traumatically affected by the father's incestuous assault on her body as well as suffering from the virus. Both effects are not really separable. As Artie told Clank earlier, he has already previously attempted to control both his daughter's mind and body. Kathy's infected condition may really be family-related.

After dismissing David and Judy, Clank decides to make a futile 'Last Stand'. As his contemptuous comment to David reveals, 'Big Green Hat', he does this less to ensure his own safety but more to fuel his own ego and compensate for feelings of inadequacy he has towards David. After killing several soldiers, Clank's final words are 'I think I'm going to do some drinking', before a bullet passes through his head. The comment not only refers to his masculine reliance on alcohol (prior to his discovery of Artie's assault, he was seen swigging a whiskey bottle). It also metaphorically illustrates Romero's 'MacGuffin' motif in *The Crazies*, namely the contaminated water supply supposedly responsible for a virus after victims have drunk from it.[5]

After Watts' death, following his aborted attempt to reveal the discovery of an antidote to the authorities, the film moves towards its poignant conclusion. David attempts to conceal Judy from the soldiers. But he finds himself again forced to use the old methods of violence he wished to reject by killing a soldier and putting on his uniform to save Judy. Although he shoots another soldier to prevent Judy's discovery, David understands that circumstances now overcome the reluctance to use violence he has exhibited throughout the film. Finally, a group of marauding youngsters shoot at David and Judy believing them to be soldiers. One bullet hits Judy. After David kills most of their number, he lets the sole survivor live since he is merely a scared youngster who may or may not be affected by the virus. This time it really does not matter. David then throws away his rifle in a gesture anticipating Peter's surrender of his rifle in the concluding scenes of *Dawn of the Dead*. Although trapped by different sets of circumstances both men eventually realise that violence is no real solution. It is actually a virus, a form of contamination blurring boundaries between humans and zombies in *Night of the Living Dead*, *Dawn of the Dead* and *Day of the Dead*, and civilian victims and oppressive authoritarian forces in *The Crazies*. David then poignantly hears the dying Judy name their never-to-be-born child after him. This tragically acknowledges the lost potential their relationship could have had for beginning a new society especially if the son had taken after his father. The soldiers take David into custody.

The Crazies' final scenes are as bleak and ironic as any EC Comic. Peckham receives a new assignment after supposedly successfully controlling the Evans City situation. Many have died. But there are '2,100 survivors – if you can call them survivors'. He is assigned to Louisville, Kentucky, to deal with another Trixie situation. His unseen commanding officer congratulates him on the phone in absurdly inaccurate and irrational terms: 'You have one under your belt now. You have done a great job.' But the film's entire narrative already reveals this as another government lie. Nothing but chaos and oppressive violence has resulted. As Peckham moves away to his next assignment, soldiers bring David in. Both men exchange glances as they briefly encounter each other silently for the first and last time. David is about to receive a test for immunity. But a military doctor, who earlier assured Peckham that 'sooner or later' an immune human will be discovered, regards it as a waste of time. Despite his potential in providing a cure to the virus, the authorities conveniently classify David as a 'crazy'. The film concludes with an overhead helicopter shot of Peckham removing his contaminated overalls outside in the darkness, changing into fresh clothes, and moving out of the Evans City area. His solitary figure becomes more immersed by the encroaching darkness as a military helicopter circles overhead before moving him away.

Despite Romero's critical misgivings, *The Crazies* is not really a failure; it does represent a significant advance in his directorial vision. Although the structure may be bleak, *The Crazies* presents a frightening vision still relevant today about governments lying to its citizens and even planning to exterminate them should circumstances demand it. Like *Night of the Living Dead*, *There's Always Vanilla* and *Jack's Wife*, *The Crazies* also depicts a world of inhabitants dominated by past outmoded values detrimental to their full potentialities as human beings. The film presents an apocalyptic vision of a society in the process of collapse from which its more conscious survivors must remove themselves physically and mentally. Without resorting to zombies or the supernatural, Romero presents a world of living dead inhabitants. Although supposedly living human beings, many characters are dominated by the dead hand of a past controlling both their conscious minds and any possibility of moving towards positive personal and social alternatives. They operate on an instinctual basis like the zombies in *Dawn of the Dead* and *Day of the Dead*. But, as the latter reveals, these very 'instincts' are not natural and spontaneous; they result from deliberately induced dangerous mechanisms of social control. Only David escapes, but he finds his life destroyed and alternative avenues blocked. However, despite its pessimistic conclusion, *The Crazies* is an important film. It reveals Romero as beginning to articulate clearly his creative role as a knight of the living dead, whether they be fictional human characters, zombies or cinema audiences.

CHAPTER SIX

Martin

Like other films after *Night of the Living Dead*, *Martin* had its share of technical problems, such as an inappropriate budget and a few unpolished acting performances in secondary roles. Some viewers often expect cohesive narratives and, in many cases, react against those films which deliberately engage in breaking down divisions between reality and fantasy. However, as John Woo remarked on one occasion, such products characterise the type of film the industry attempts to force upon viewers rather than stimulating them towards cinematically creative and imaginative possibilities. *Martin* is not unique in questioning convenient divisions between the worlds of fantasy and reality. These issues also occur in Romero's post-*Night of the Living Dead* films. But *Martin* shows Romero extending his earlier techniques into new directions. It also reveals a more detailed interrogation of the modern world's use and abuse of traditional Gothic fantasy as well as the destructive traps awaiting not only those who choose entrapment within anachronistic beliefs but also others who submit to the debilitating world of everyday life without considering viable alternatives.

In 1985 Romero regarded *Martin* as 'still my favorite film' and his 'most realized' work (quoted in Gagne 1987: 80, 71). Paul Gagne regards it as the director's most intelligent treatment of themes appearing throughout his films. *Martin* is certainly more accomplished structurally than Romero's earlier works, but it is also indebted to its predecessors; the film develops ideas already present in *There's Always Vanilla*, *Jack's Wife* and *The Crazies*. Shot in 16mm on a budget of $100,000 and later blown up to 35mm for theatrical release, cinematographer Michael Gornick used reversal stock rather than negative to achieve a more debilitated form of colour saturation. The resulting style significantly clashes with images contained in Romero's preceding and succeeding films. Director and photographer chose the correct formal means to represent Martin's everyday world as drained of life and vitality in a manner similar to the body of a vampire's victim in traditional vampire imagery. The world of

Braddock seen in the film is an expressionistically rendered living dead environment draining its inhabitants of all vitality and rendering their lives both futile and wasted. As Gagne points out, *Martin* was originally intended to be a black-and-white film, but marketing considerations led to the eventual appearance of the colour version currently in circulation. Romero and his collaborators aimed at a saturation technique draining colours of any form of vitality, thus approximating the visual style of EC Comic books which also satirically broke down traditional barriers between fantasy and reality.[1]

Like Chris and Lynn in *There's Always Vanilla* and Joan Mitchell of *Jack's Wife*, Martin is a character who exists in a world of illusions. But his malaise is much more extreme than that of his predecessors in Romero's previous films. Martin's chosen path of personal self-expression is highly detrimental to his development and hinders any potential he has of becoming a real human being. But his dilemma is much more life-threatening by affecting both himself and others. Despite his vulnerability, he is a psychotic murderer choosing to live entirely in his self-created world of fantasy modelled according to the Gothic tradition in film and literature. Like Romero's earlier characters, Martin is victimised by self-indulgent, misleading fantasies involving his real personality. But he is surrounded by other harmful influences such as Cuda and the talk-show radio host who feed his already dangerous fantasies rather than help him towards the road of recovery. Martin is another sacrificial victim of negative tendencies existing in his own society which also seek to destroy him personally and physically in a manner akin to the victims embodied within his own destructive fantasies.

Martin's eventual fate echoes those affecting most of the characters in *The Crazies* who perish as a result of violent factors within their environment. Like Chris, Lynn and Joan Mitchell, Martin lives in his own fantasy world. His condition resembles that of Joan; as in *Jack's Wife*, he exchanges one form of oppression for another. Both Joan and Martin seek escape from a hostile family environment, but they move towards the dangerous world of harmful fantasies which they choose to nurture and end up never progressing towards a more healthy form of existence. The various roads they choose actually lead nowhere. Joan is still 'Jack's Wife' at the climax and Martin dies the death of a traditional vampire, a fate his earlier fantasies would eventually suggest. Although it is possible to differentiate formally between the worlds of reality and fantasy affecting various characters in Romero's earlier films, this strategy is more challenging to the viewer in *Martin*. Romero has created a deliberately ambiguous situation for both his title character and audience. Unlike *Jack's Wife*, no formal divisions between the worlds of fantasy and reality exist in the Gothic reproductions of Martin's life in the Old World. Viewers are now trapped within Martin's emotional world. It is impossible to discern whether his Gothic fantasies are merely imaginary or actually based upon Cuda's interpretation. The visual evidence supplied in the film is ambiguous; unlike the earlier films, viewers can no longer sit back and distance themselves from the title character's dilemma.

Despite the extreme nature of Martin's situation, Romero challenges his viewers to question whether they are also victims of oppressive social environments denied by escapist indulgence in (sometimes harmless) fantasies? Romero also stated that he went through a similar form of confusion when engaging in pre-production: 'I wound up with so many thoughts and so many directions to go that I really got confused and I sort of became Martin ... I didn't know whether I wanted my character to be a vampire or just think he was a vampire' (quoted in Gagne 1987: 71). Since Martin actually drinks blood he is a vampire in one sense but, while agreeing that the film is open to other interpretations, Romero also comments that Martin 'may not be a supernatural character. I don't believe he's eighty-four years old. I think those are things that have been drummed into him from infancy by people like his grandfather Cuda. So he's a victim and when he tries to explain his problem, the people around him don't listen or don't take him seriously' (quoted in Yakir 1977: 63).

Martin thus explores another key theme in Romero's cinema. It again examines the lack of communication between individuals who prefer to remain in their own ideologically generated fantasy worlds. They do this either by rejecting their own valid personal feelings or by denying to others the opportunity for self-development and eventual independence. The film ends tragically. Although Martin never reaches the type of self-realisation seen in David in *The Crazies* and Peter in *Dawn of the Dead*, he is on the way to moving forward before his abrupt demise. However, an institutional agent of social normality brutally curtails any possibility Martin had to develop and become a healthier person. This family agent is depicted as dangerous as the military doctor who categorises David as just another crazy in the climax of Romero's preceding film.

Martin may also be viewed as Romero's demystification of the horror genre's conventions. Although most audiences prefer gore, supernatural elements and zombies to indulge in a fantasy world, *Martin* aims to educate them into a different form of perception. Several times throughout the film Martin attempts in vain to make his cousin Cuda realise that his ideological attachment to Old World supernatural conventions is really irrational. One key scene occurs at the dinner table when Martin plays with a miniature guillotine he uses to cut celery. He attempts in vain to persuade Cuda's granddaughter Christine (Christine Forrest) to insert her finger inside. After realising that Christine will not trust him by making the attempt, Martin puts his finger inside. The blade falls into the second hole of the artifact. Martin then explains that he has held the real blade back: 'See, it has two blades, a real one and a trick one ... Things only seem to be magic. There is no real magic.' Later in the film, after escaping from Cuda's ridiculous exorcism attempt, Martin frightens his tormentor by dressing up like a traditional vampire only to spit out his fangs and reveal the real nature of his phoney masquerade. Both demonstrations have no effect upon their intended audience; Cuda (and, by implication, most horror film audiences) prefers the imaginary narcotic and spectacular aspects of magic which rely upon unquestioning emotional effect. The display is a mere box of tricks effected by real material causes. They are much more than fantastic devices aiming to condition their audiences into unquestioning submission. Everything imaginary has a particular social cause.

Martin thus attempts to stimulate its audiences into questioning the very origins of the fantastic and move them towards investigating the more relevant oppressive material causes of everyday existence which rely upon the concealing devices of superstition, fantasy and custom for their very existence. As Richard Lippe (1979) has convincingly demonstrated, *Martin* attempts to explore self-reflexively the very conventions of the horror genre itself. But it also aims to show that these conventions are actually redundant. They can never satisfactorily explain the very real social conditions generating the horror of everyday existence.

As the credits roll, Martin (John Amplas) is seen at Indianapolis boarding the Pittsburgh-New York Amtrak and selecting his next victim (Fran Middleton). Succeeding shots show him checking his equipment of hypodermic needle and razor blade before entering her compartment. Before he does so Martin experiences a fantasy depicted in black-and-white footage of the well-groomed, night-gowned female, welcoming his advances like a lover. This imagery is obviously derived from Martin's experiences of watching classic horror films, but the reality is much different. The film stock returns to colour and its supposed associations of everyday normality. After hearing the mundane sound of a flushing toilet, Martin instead encounters an unglamorous women whose face is covered in a beauty mask, making her resemble one of Romero's 'living dead' zombies. When he attacks she struggles to defend herself, using coarse language absent from most traditional horror films. Finally, the drug overcomes her, allowing Martin the freedom of performing a perverse sexual ritual upon her helpless body. He slashes her wrists in order to drink her blood. After performing his grotesque ceremony, making him appear little better than the 'rapist asshole' of his victim's description, Martin leaves the train as it arrives at Pittsburgh.

This opening sequence contains little sympathy for Martin. Although clearly insecure and vulnerable like Norman Bates of *Psycho* (1960), Martin has committed a brutal act on a defenceless female. His actions are clearly inexcusable. But the film develops a much broader picture of its title character revealing him to be both victim as well as victimiser. Martin's murderous psychotic actions are never isolated from their social surroundings, nor are they caused by any supposed individual 'bad seed' in his personal hereditary background. Like the various characters in Zola's Rougon-Macquart family tree, Martin's dilemma results from a deadly interaction of negative family and social circumstances affecting his whole being.

The first appearance of Martin's elderly cousin Cuda (Lincoln Maazel) depicts him in imagery reminiscent of a classical horror film. It is as stylistically fantastic as Martin's own imaginations prior to his deadly attack on the helpless woman in the train. Cuda suddenly appears in the frame. He is dressed entirely in white surrounded by a cloud of grey smoke. But the audience soon discovers that this supposedly living dead apparition is actually real and the suggestively magical smoke nothing more than steam from the train. Cuda's initial appearance thus foreshadows the later line in the film where Martin states that magic does not really exist. It is all superficial trickery. Cuda says little more to Martin other than ordering him to follow him to the next platform and catch the train to Braddock.

Although different in tone, the imagery introducing the film's two main characters is highly significant. It intimates that both characters choose to live a particular form of fantasy life within a declining society which they ignore in different ways. Martin is actually no traditional vampire despite the nature of his fantasies. Indeed, he denies the concept throughout the entire film. Martin's dilemma is more akin to that of a modern psychologically disturbed serial killer dependent upon sexual necrophilia like his earlier twentieth-century counterparts such as Germany's Peter Kurten.

However, Martin chooses to veil his dilemma by indulging in fantasy imagery derived from representations of traditional vampires. It is both a means of affirming his own sense of perverse individuality as well as a device chosen to distance himself from the real nature of everyday social circumstances which actually motivate his behaviour. Clearly, Martin's denial mechanisms are deliberately chosen. Any recognition of the real causes of his dilemma might result in a tentative process of self-discovery leading to a possible cure. He would be thus free of delusions and escape from his particular form of ideological entrapment. However, he does not choose this path despite the fact that he lives in the modern world and not the artificial studio-recreated European milieu of Universal horror movies. Similarly, despite Cuda's awareness of his declining New World environment, he chooses to maintain the Old World superstitions he should have discarded once he crossed the Atlantic. Both characters stubbornly affirm beliefs which are anachronistic, redundant and bear little relationship to either their real personalities or to the environment which surrounds them.

At this stage in the film, they cling to hopelessly outmoded values and blind themselves to the operation of other more relevant circumstances which condition the very forms of their existence. Cuda holds firmly to Old World values involving vampires and family superstitions. He is as much caught up in an imaginary world of fantasy as Martin. Both Cuda and Martin indulge in the same set of Gothic values and refuse to consider any other alternatives which would contradict their chosen beliefs. Cuda believes the nineteen-year-old Martin to be nothing more than an eighty-four-year-old vampire from the Old World passed on to him by family tradition. Both characters symbiotically need each other to indulge in their fantasies. At the same time, they are both victims of harmful ideologies which corrupt their different personalities. Cuda and Martin arrive in Braddock, a declining industrial suburb outside Pittsburgh. Once a key part of a strong and productive twentieth-century manufacturing industry, it is now part of America's rust-belt in terminal decline with a diminishing population. As Cuda and Martin walk to Cuda's home they pass a used car lot where once functional vehicles are now being reduced to scrap metal. Deeply immersed in reactionary patriarchal values, the ageing Cuda informs Martin that he intends to save his soul and then destroy him in terms similar to a Salem witch trial judge.

Martin is already at the stage arrived at by Joan Mitchell in the climactic moments of *Jack's Wife*. He cannot distinguish fantasy from reality. Martin is also the victim of self-induced illusions as well as his social environment. These two factors are so closely intermingled that they are impossible to separate both for Martin and the film's audience. Since Martin has a clear American accent he is by no means a new arrival from Europe, but he is arbitrarily defined as a monster by Cuda and his family values. Martin's dilemma bears a close relationship to that of those schizophrenic family victims documented by R. D. Laing in works such as *The Divided Self* as well as the Schreber case misread by Freud according to Morton Schatzman's *Soul Murder: Persecution in the Family*.[2] In two of Martin's black-and-white 'flashbacks' we see him surrounded by family members who clearly believe him to be a vampire. The imagery and costume appear to belong to the early twentieth century. Although Martin may have recently suffered from an abusive family situation, he could be repressing his traumatic pain by depicting the actual circumstances according to manifest imagery within the dream work by using his familiarity with old horror films to try to understand the origins of his persecution.[3] This is possible. But Romero leaves the interpretation open for audiences. Martin chooses to retreat into fantasy like young Amy in *Curse of the Cat People* (1944). However, as in the case of Irena in *The Cat People* (1942), no certainty is ever possible concerning the actual causes of Martin's condition. Simone Simon's character in the earlier film flees the superstitious values of an Old World designating her as a dangerous monster to seek refuge in a New World supposedly guaranteeing her respect and safety. But like Martin, she finds that the American Dream is both deadly and dangerous. As in the case of Irena, it is also impossible to tell whether Martin's fantasies represent a distorted version of the truth or whether they may be merely illusionary in nature.

Most characters in the film practice some form of self-denial. They also engage in distracting diversions as a means of denying the sterile condition of their living dead existence in a decaying environment. While Martin and Cuda bask in their own futile forms of fantasy, the latter's granddaughter Christine indulges in an apathetic existence. Like her boyfriend Arthur (Tom Savini) who wishes to make a decent living as a mechanic outside a declining industrial area, she dreams of escape and eventually uses him as her meal ticket to move elsewhere. She also spends most of her time at home, never seems to have an occupation, bickers constantly with Arthur either in her bedroom or on the phone, and denies the reality of her situation by engaging in casual sex like Martin's bored businessman's wife victim (Sarah Venable) or Mrs Santini (Elyane Nadeau). All the film's characters suffer both from frustrated personal potentials and a stagnating social system inhibiting their real needs and aspirations; they thus resemble twentieth-century versions of Zola's fictional characters. As Cuda later tells Arthur when he criticises him for wanting to move away to make a better living as a car mechanic as well as attempting to dissuade him from marrying Christine, 'This is a town for old people.' Cuda affirms a world of traditional and stagnant values in which no alternatives can ever occur. The very environment of Braddock represents as much of a deadly trap for its victims in a manner similar to the defeated realm of Plassans, under occupation by both Second Empire monarchists and Abbé Faujas in Zola's novel *La Conquête de Plassans* (1874). No equivalent to the Faujas character exists in *Martin*. However, the similar tendencies of both Cuda and Martin to engage in dangerous fantasies bearing no relationship to their real conditions of existence parallels the psychopathological patterns of behaviour Faujas evokes within the family members of the Plassans household he inhabits. The Mouret family react in different ways to the dominance of a religiously powerful force overpowering their various personalities and forcing them to submit to conditions which are really irrational in origin.

However, although Cuda disavows the obvious signs of urban stagnation affecting Braddock, he is not totally immersed in a world of supernatural prejudice. When he informs his middle-aged female customers about Martin's employment at his store he quickly rebuts insinuations concerning two young people living in the same house:

'It looks the way you want it to look, Mrs Brennan. Martin knows how to behave.' Unfortunately, Cuda's one instance of accurate insight remains an isolated one in the film. He clearly wishes to manipulate Christine and Arthur, as well as Martin, into accepting the values of the socially dead environment he has lived in for so long. But his antiquated ideological values of family prestige and supernatural possession are no longer relevant to the declining world of Braddock, as the religious service performed in the film reveals. After waking Martin up on a Sunday morning to attend church, Romero reveals the interior of the building as being in drastic need of repair. People attend the service out of a sense of bored obligation while the young neighbourhood priest Father Howard (played by Romero) clearly appears bemused by performing a ritual he obviously regards as being of little relevance to the surrounding world.

When Cuda invites Father Howard home for dinner, the young man tells him that he was transferred to Braddock after his predecessor fell ill with cancer. Worldly-wise, at home with good food and wine, Father Howard dismisses Cuda's veiled hope that he could perform an exorcism on Martin by cynically referring to *The Exorcist*'s false influence on contemporary consciousness. Father Howard also disparagingly refers to the poor state of communion wine in the parish. But Cuda does not learn from his parish priest's dismissal of Old World values. He later persuades an elderly priest, Father Zulemas (J. Clifford Forrest Jr.), to perform an exorcism on Martin. While Martin crouches before the absurd ritual performed by two elderly men, his mind appears to 'flash back' to an earlier exorcism performed on him by his European relatives. But Martin may also be recreating the experience in terms of old Hollywood movies he has viewed and used as his cultural models. Like Martin's previous memories of his past, the footage is black-and-white. In both instances, Martin runs away from an oppressive Old World ritual more concerned with affirming anachronistic values rather than attempting to understand and cure a traumatised victim.

However, Martin soon decides to take his revenge on Cuda. The following sequence shows Martin dressed like a typical vampire, stalking and terrorising Cuda in a playground. This activity lasts until he spits out his fangs in an attempt to show his elderly oppressor that it is all a silly game. It is far from coincidental that the incident occurs in a playground, aptly illustrating the nature of Cuda's childish beliefs.

Both Christine and Mrs Santini attempt to reach out to Martin in different ways but their actions eventually prove to be misguided. Although Martin does reach some form of self-realisation concerning the pathological nature of his activities, it is not enough to save him at the end. Christine attempts to give Martin the little sympathy she can afford, but she is totally caught up in her dead-end relationship with Arthur and her anger at Cuda's patriarchal attitudes. Cuda has attempted to destroy her relationship with Arthur by hinting at her supposed hereditary characteristics. He also wants to control Christine in the same way as Martin. Although Cuda's physically abusive actions finally result in her leaving home, she promises to keep in touch with Martin, yet Martin recognises correctly that she won't remember him after she leaves. Christine also suggests the importance of communication and influences Martin into getting a phone. But Martin's only telephone conversation with the outside world is with an unseen cynical talk-show host (Michael Gornick). This off-camera voice feigns sympathy and understanding to keep Martin on the line as an attraction for his voyeuristic listeners to boost audience ratings. The talk-show host feeds off Martin's dilemma like a twentieth-century vampire and tosses juicy verbal titbits to his audience like Bram Stoker's Count in the original novel, who provides his ladies of the night with a new-born baby. He condescendingly refers to Martin as 'the Count' and never attempts to talk him out of his psychological dilemma into some constructive path of healthy reality. As in *Night of the Living Dead*, *There's Always Vanilla*, *Jack's Wife* and *The Crazies*, the media is part of an institutional system designed to deceive, demean, and exploit its victims. They will never find any real form of close communication within the media as long as the present form of society remains in existence. The talk-show represents a debased form of communication which deliberately sets out to humiliate its compliant victims. Romero remarkably recognises this fact well before the emergence of the more repugnant television versions represented by Oprah Winfrey, Jenny Jones, Jerry Springer and its derivative British versions such as *Kilroy* and *Vanessa* when so-called 'quality television' proved itself as equally corrupt as its American counterpart.

Braddock's world is also one of declining cultural values as signified by the Mozart and nineteenth-century jingles heard on an ice-cream van. Again Romero anticipates the tendency of the system to appropriate and debase any creatively original achievement for the purposes of the market economy whether it be ice-cream jingle, 'easy listening' or trivial Shakespeare representations such as *Shakespeare in Love* (1998). All the characters in *Martin* attempt to reach out to others and achieve some form of communication. But like various characters in *Night of the Living Dead*, *There's Always Vanilla*, *Jack's Wife* and *The Crazies*, their efforts are often contaminated by personal prejudices, mistaken decisions and wrong actions resulting from their entrapment within negative social situations they can never really negotiate their way out of.

Bored housewife Mrs Santini becomes attracted to Martin. But her seduction is little better than an indulgent act of self-gratification. When she drives Martin home she tells him that his silence reminds her of an old cat she used to have that would just stare and listen. Frustrated by a sterile existence as a lonely housewife whose husband is often absent on business trips, she resembles Joan Mitchell of *Jack's Wife* in several ways. Like Joan, she drifts into an affair as a means to avoid confronting the drab reality of her everyday life as well as taking effective action to rise above her frustrating circumstances. After initiating Martin into his first sexual experience, she breaks out in tears. Mrs Santini possibly realises she has manipulated him for her own gratification and has cheated him out of the intimacy and communication he really needs. But this brief act of self-realisation remains undeveloped. She eventually commits suicide, an act indirectly leading to Martin's destruction at the climax.

Despite the dead-end nature of the relationship with Mrs Santini, one paralleling the type of contact between Christine and Arthur where no real communication actually takes place, Martin does undergo a tentative form of development. It could have resulted in a positive form of self-awareness leading to his eventual liberation from his unhealthy pathological practices. On his next assault on a defenseless woman, Martin again recreates the experience in Gothic horror imagery by fantasising the image of a young attractive female beckoning him and calling his name. As in his first assault, he again uses modern technology such as syringes to further his aims. Like Mrs Santini, his next victim is a bored housewife whose husband (played by Martin's producer Richard P. Rubinstein) is away on a business trip. However, after subduing the woman and her lover Lewis (Al Levitsky), Martin appears to let her live rather than slashing her wrists. His Gothic fantasy suggests this resolution since it shows his young female victim alive, rather than drained of blood, at its climax. However, Martin drags the drugged Lewis outside and this time uses his body to drink blood from rather than his usual supply of female victims. The act not only suggests deep homosexual feelings repressed in Martin's unconsciousness, which his family environment would regard as taboo as his supposed vampire origins, but also a possible deep disgust at his previous activities of preying on vulnerable females. Martin uses and abuses Lewis as a surrogate sacrificial victim in as much the same way Cuda does at the film's climax.

Like Tony Buba's perceptive documentaries *The Braddock Chronicles* (1972–85) and *Lightning Over Braddock* (1988), *Martin* depicts a world whose grim reality needs no recourse to fantastic explanations for understanding its real significance. The Braddock environment parallels those life-denying industrial worlds threatening the futures of Zola's characters in *L'Assommoir* and *Germinal* who are also affected by some form of hereditary mechanisms. Romero's Martin is a character who suffers from both these factors which will eventually cause his destruction. He is also a horror film character parallel to Jacques Lantier of *La Bête Humaine*, a character whose involvement in murderous circumstances eventually evokes the manifestation of destructive tendencies within his own personality, tendencies Zola ascribes to the character's degenerative family background.

Virtually all *Martin*'s characters parallel the attitudes of the real-life character Sal who appears in *Sweet Sal* (1979). In Buba's acclaimed first feature-length documentary, Buba plays himself as a director trying to make a film with crazy Braddock street hustler Sal, who considers himself responsible for Buba's success. As a long-time associate of George Romero, it is surely no accident that Buba has appropriated certain ideas from his mentor, particularly *Martin* which saw his first collaboration on Romero's films. Sal constantly deceives himself about his own personality and actual significance in his hometown. Sal's denials represent his way of dealing with living in a declining environment which offers no personal hope or salvation for him. In other words, he chooses to retreat into his own form of personal fantasy like Joan Mitchell and Martin rather than deal with the bleak circumstances of his everyday reality. One key scene in *Sweet Sal* shows Sal visiting his father's grave, talking to him as if alive, and kissing the small marker in a manner evocative of the opening association of *Night of the Living Dead*. Tony Buba and his brother Pasquale (another future Romero collaborator) play drug dealers in one of *Martin*'s brief, but telling scenes: Martin accidentally stumbles on them evoking the anger of the third dealer (Clayton McKinnon) before the police arrive and begin a shoot-out.

This sequence complements another when Martin attacks two winos (played by Romero's technical assistants Regis J. Survinski and Tony Panatello) and drinks the blood of one of them. Martin's action here shows him moving away from attacking defenceless women. But he is still trapped by psychopathological beliefs that he is a vampire. Furthermore, drugs and alcohol are other forms of self-indulgent escapism open to Braddock's inhabitants as is sex for bored housewives like Mrs Santini and superstition for Cuda. The film also shows adolescent punks outside a shopping mall having nothing better to do than sexually harass young housewives. Ironically, these two sequences never show the older women who appear to prefer Cuda's old-fashioned store, one of whom verbally assaults Martin. By this time, Martin has grown weary of immediate retaliation and allows his last victim to live. Prior to discovering Mrs Santini's body, he marches behind an amateur band playing a military theme. This represents another of his belated attempts at communion with others which the film will abruptly nip in the bud. It is better than indulging in deadly fantasies and experiencing exploitation at the hands of cynical talk-show hosts. Martin is at least out in the open daylight and becoming part of a living crowd.

Romero begins the film's final sequence ironically. It opens with individual shots of church spires which commenced the earlier sequence of Martin going to church. But this time, Martin will experience a deadly form of patriarchal salvation. During Martin's arrival at Cuda's house, he received the warning that any attack on a Braddock inhabitant would not be tolerated. Ironically, although not responsible for Mrs Santini's suicide, Cuda blames him and plunges a stake through his heart in typical vampire-hunter manner. Martin's death has poignant overtones since he appeared to be on the verge of breaking out of his dilemma. Like David in *The Crazies*, any future potential Martin has for development is brutally curtailed. The film concludes with images of Cuda completing his burial of Martin while the culturally debased sounds of the ice-cream jingle and talk-show host occur on the soundtrack. Although Martin can never respond to the sound of another tormentor, the host concludes by telling his audience that a listener believes he knows the Count. Martin finally comes to a physical as well as a spiritual dead end, the sacrificial victim of an intellectually bankrupt and materially debased culture which is more of a threat to its victims than Martin's pathetic recreations of Universal horror films can ever be. As Richard Lippe aptly notices, near the end of the film Martin witnesses chickens being slaughtered and prepared for human consumption, a sequence filmed in detailed close-up shots – 'a brief documentary episode in a fictional narrative film that serves to metaphorically reflect the real horror the film explores'.[4]

The episode also reveals the naturalist associations existing in Romero's work which always suggestively emphasise grim conditions within an extremely sick society. These often give rise either to violence or self-denying escapism in one form or another, whether drink, drugs, sex, talk-show humiliation or Gothic fantasies. As in all Romero's works, the divisions between humans and monsters become increasingly blurred until both conditions become identical. His next film reveals this explicitly and merges the supposedly distinct worlds of literary naturalism, EC comics and the horror genre in a highly original manner.

CHAPTER SEVEN

Dawn of the Dead

Laurel Entertainment's highly successful *Dawn of the Dead* not only saw Romero's return to the zombie motifs of his first feature film but also resulted in a synthesis of many ideas present in *There's Always Vanilla*, *Jack's Wife*, *The Crazies* and *Martin*. The primary colours and camera angles featured in scenes shot at the Monroeville mall represent a more assured and deliberate utilisation of the visual world of EC Comics both in style and content. *Dawn of the Dead* is a film which links together the special effects endemic to the horror genre as well as significant social meanings Romero always brings into his work. But the film also unconsciously refers to naturalist elements associated with Zola and other writers which have key associations with the horror genre. Since the film is popularly regarded as a 'gross-out' horror film relying on the EC Comic tradition, it is necessary at this point to note its intrinsic relationship to the naturalist tradition. Although not operating within the black-and-white 'realism' of *Night of the Living Dead* and the social worlds contained in *There's Always Vanilla*, *Jack's Wife* and *Martin*, *Dawn of the Dead* belongs to this cultural world despite its supernatural zombie context.

As Dieter Meindl points out, certain strains of American fiction illustrate significant conflicts between ideology and the real conditions of existence governing American life which may receive a metaphorical form of expression in grotesque representations.[1] One recent example of this phenomenon is Brett Easton Ellis' *American Psycho*, a work whose detailed description of the serial killer exploits of Patrick Bateman is less than celebratory. Cataloguing the material artifacts of Bateman's world in a manner akin to the factual detail of classical naturalism, along with recognising the contrasts between the increasingly divided world of rich and poor, *American Psycho* develops into an apocalyptic vision. The savage exploits of Bateman appear a natural consequence of a world in which people have been reduced to the status of dehumanised automatons functioning according to levels of basic instincts determined by their class status. Like its naturalist predecessors, *American Psycho*'s episodes of grotesque violence appear natural results of the inhumane society its inhabitants accept and profit from both emotionally and materially.[2] Bateman's violent activities are the logical culmination of those spiritual dead-ends catalogued in previous Ellis novels such as *Less Than Zero* and *The Rules of Attraction*, whose individual characters are lifeless products of consumer capitalism and little better than cannibalistic zombies with their 'use and abuse' attitudes. In *Less Than Zero*, the violence which appears in minor discordant incidents within the affluent world of its rich characters breaks out with a vengeance in full unrepressed force in *American Psycho*. It is the natural grotesque signifier of an inhumane materialist civilisation typified by its narcissistic title character. During a later scene in the novel Bateman discovers a rat which has emerged from a toilet bowl, an appropriate metaphorical signifier of his own personality and his grotesque world. This image also parallels the significance of the zombie motif in Romero's own trilogy.[3]

Such features are not new but have their origins in classical forms of representation. Meindl points out that the grotesque can express the non-rational dimensions of human life and quotes Thomas Mann's definition of grotesqueness as a 'genuine anti-bourgeois style'.[4] This is particularly so whenever authors depict the mechanical aspect of bourgeois existence as being little better than a death-in-life or 'zombie' form of existence. Meindl's description of Herman Melville's Bartleby succinctly analyses the author's manner of describing his title character in such terms: 'In preferring stasis, passivity, nonaction, Bartleby apparently prefers a deathlike state of being to the movement toward death, that is man's life' (Meindle 1996: 85).[5] Bartleby is little better than a corpse or *mort vivant*. His facial features parallel a corpse's pallor and he operates according to a passive and instinctual level of existence foreshadowing Romero's zombies throughout the trilogy. Both Bartleby and the zombies cannot exercise any form of free will. Furthermore, Meindl also sees an important relationship between grotesque imagery and violent social satire which again parallels both the EC Comic tradition and many examples of Romero's work. This also has an intrinsic association with certain literary forms such as realism which often superficially appear to have little involvement with excessive depictions. However, as Zola's explorations of naturalism show, boundaries often creatively dissolve in the practical worlds of literary and cinematic genres.[6]

During *Dawn of the Dead*'s initial release, many commentators noted the light-hearted nature of Romero's treatment, which contrasted with his earlier depiction in *Night of the Living Dead*. Although many drew comparisons to the EC Comic tradition of irony and satire, the comedic elements in the film also have significant connections to American literary naturalism. All the characters throughout the zombie trilogy face overwhelming odds which they may not personally or physically overcome. Whether threatened by the growing number of zombies outside or trapped by flaws within their own personality resulting from social conditioning, these figures confront adverse situations which are often deterministic in nature. These deterministic situations parallel those adverse social and psychological factors facing characters in American and European naturalism whether they be the unfortunate members of Zola's Rougon-Macquart family or Frank Norris' McTeague. However, as noted in the introductory chapter, determinism does not operate as a rigidly defining principle in many novels despite the assertions of hostile critics of this literary movement. As Meindl notes, 'Accepting determinism as the principle defining naturalism does not prevent one from finding in naturalist novels a determinism modified, in varying degrees, by humanistic values and concessions to individual worth' (1996: 109).

Such concessions are eventually made to characters such as Fran and Peter in *Dawn of the Dead* and Sarah and her multi-ethnic companions in *Day of the Dead*. Meindl also comments that the frequent compatibility of naturalism and the grotesque in literature relates to the presence of extraordinary and excessive features in human nature as well as the social environment influencing them. Sometimes literary treatments indulge in ironic representations as in Stephen Crane's 'The Blue Hotel' with its parallels between men and lice. For Meindl, 'Such imagery, which proceeds by grotesque diminution and distortion, contributes to establishing an ironic view of man inhabiting a disdainful universe' (110). This also foreshadows the ironic view of human nature taken in Romero's zombie trilogy where formerly live beings are now reduced to grotesque versions of their former selves. In many cases, grotesque irony becomes a central device in the narrative as Crane's *Maggie* illustrates. Frank Norris' *McTeague* and many of Jack London's writings also reveal an ironic use of animal imagery, foreshadowing the instinctual carnivore-like activities of Romero's zombies. Finally, American literature often complements the EC comic book tradition with similar representations of zombies or living dead figures. The title character of William Faulkner's 'A Rose for Miss Emily' is one such example. Her possessive attitude and special form of conspicuous consumption eventually make her resemble a bloated corpse.[7] She exists in a macabre living dead relationship which also echoes many features contained within Romero's films.

The possessive attitudes characterising characters such as *McTeague*'s Trina and Faulkner's Miss Emily anticipate Romero's zombies. *Dawn of the Dead* contains frequent parallels between the nameless army of the living dead and the quartet of human consumers inside the Monroeville mall. The mall itself represents a twentieth-century development of Zola's 'Au Bonheur des Dames' in the novel of the same name, a nineteenth-century version of The Society of the Spectacle representing the latest development of conspicuous consumption in the Paris of the Second Empire. As Rachel Bowlby notes, Octave Mouret's establishment represents the transfiguration of capitalist merchandise into spectacular effects designed to captivate the female consumer (1985: 6). Caught within the frenzy of a deliberately designed mass form of commodification and exploitation, Parisian ladies become objectified and lose their vitality, becoming little better than dead bodies within a mechanical parody of equality, a situation resembling both contemporary mall shoppers and *Dawn of the Dead*'s actual zombies (76).[8] Bowlby regards the female situation depicted in the novel as being nothing less than a form of capitalist cannibalism of individuals trapped within a Darwinist world where big beasts eat their victims. Far from being a dream palace, the 'ladies paradise' of the novel is actually a savage jungle for the unwary.[9] Zola's early vision of conspicuous consumption thus anticipates many of the features which characterises Romero's concept in the second part of his trilogy. But there is one major difference. Males, as well as females, are now trapped within the mechanical dance of death engendered by conspicuous capitalist consumption. Romero's heroine Fran soon perceives the empty nature of possessiveness when she later comments, 'What have we *done* to ourselves?' Human beings may survive, die or join a growing army of zombies depending upon the degree of self-realisation contained within their very personalities and how they mobilise to prevent their capitulation to what appears to be a life-threatening deterministic situation.

Like *Night of the Dead* and *Day of the Dead*, *Dawn of the Dead* contrasts individuals with the mindless crowd surrounding them, whether living or dead. In this sense, the film replicates Zola's perennial life/death opposition which runs throughout his Rougon-Macquart series novels from *La Fortune des Rougon* onwards. The opening chapter sees Miette and Silvère, Zola's version of Tom and Judy from *Night of the Living Dead*, meeting secretly in an abandoned cemetary. Bowlby points out that the gypsies who live near the former cemetery are 'privileged representatives of unrepressed instinctual life' which the upper classes of Plassans deny in their schemes to participate in the destruction of the Republic and the elevation of Louis Napoleon to the monarchy. Also, the burial of the dead imagery dominating the opening pages of the novel represents a harmful return of the repressed anticipating the death-in-life existence whose possessive dominance will adversely affect the younger generation.[10] It is not accidental that both Zola and Romero see the dangerous roots of possessiveness situated within the family.

When Fran reacts against the sterile existence she, David and Peter endure after gaining control over their mall kingdom and its possessions, Romero makes the following ironic comment in the script: 'It is a domestic scene. The group has become a family, with all the disadvantages of comfortable living, including the inability to communicate with one another' (quoted in Gagne 1987: 89).[11] Like Bowlby, Schor also notes the carnivore imagery which Zola often uses to describe crowds in his fiction. Romero's cannibalistic zombies have important literary precedents. They also embody a particular disease affecting the body politic in a manner similar to Zola's definition of the social circulus affecting the human constitution: 'The social *circulus* is identical with the vital *circulus*; in society, just as in the human body, there exists a form of solidarity which connects the different members, the different organs, so that if one organ decays, many others are affected, and a very complex disease develops' (quoted from 'The Experimental Novel' by Schor 1978: 127). Romero's second instalment of his zombie trilogy presents a similar situation to his audience.

As in the last of the trilogy, *Dawn of the Dead* opens with a shot of an unidentified female sleeping against a control booth wall in a Philadelphia television studio. She twitches as if experiencing a nightmare and then suddenly awakens to find herself back in the world of reality she may have sought escape from in dreams. But, as Sarah will discover in *Day of the Dead*, nightmare and reality are already intermingled. However, Romero's heroine Fran (Gaylen Ross) exists in an earlier stage of development from her successor in *Day of the Dead* but in an advanced stage of existence from her predecessor, Barbara in *Night of the Living Dead*. Unlike *Day of the Dead*, the audience does not experience the nightmare she awakes from and can easily distinguish reality from fantasy. Like Joan Mitchell, Fran becomes the key focus for audience identification. But unlike her predecessor, Fran will experience a more liberating sense of personal development and eventual freedom no matter how insecure its future may be.

Fran awakens. A supportive female colleague tells her, 'I don't know how long we can stay on the air.' Fran then sees an angry television director trying to instill order from his control desk into the increasing chaos of the studio. As in *Night*, the studio attempts to broadcast a list of rescue stations for humans to escape the zombie assault. But such sanctuaries are now becoming increasingly dangerous and ineffective. Seated next to an assistant director, the studio director (played, significantly, by Christine Forrest and George Romero, respectively) angrily attempts to create some order into an increasingly uncontrollable situation: 'Watch camera two! Who's on camera two, a blind man?' As in *Night of the Living Dead*, Romero's Hitchcock-type cameo is by no means accidental since his role represents the director as enunciator or visual signifier for the text's key meaning. Romero's director attempts in vain to articulate and put into practice principles of morality and rationality which could save his various cinematic characters facing dangerous situations. His is a lone voice amidst a growling clamour of human irrationality which will destroy any chances of survival. The situation of the besieged humans in *Night of the Living Dead* occurs once more, but the director's attempt at mobilising the dysfunctional forces in the studio is futile as he later admits to his assistant. Disturbed voices occur outside the frame. Technicians either leave or disrupt the transmission. A talk-show host performs a verbal inquisition on a guest scientist (portrayed by Richard France replaying his role as the scientist who could have saved the infected Evans City community in *The Crazies*). France's character, Dr. Milton Rausch, appears briefly in the opening sequence as another television commentator questions him. While the host later operates in the same condescending and demeaning manner as his predecessors in *There's Always Vanilla* and *Martin*, Dr. Rausch attempts in vain to explain objectively the reasons for the zombie outbreak. But, like Romero's director, he finds his attempts to bring some form of order and rationality to his disruptive community absolutely futile.

Dissension erupts over the list of rescue stations the studio manager insists on filling the screen with even though he (and everyone else in the studio) knows that half are not functioning. Despite the life-threatening situation outside, selfish desires for ratings ironically remain as the studio's only concern: 'Without those stations on the screen every minute people won't watch us. They'll tune out.' As in *Night of the Living Dead* and *There's Always Vanilla*, Romero again provides another devastating critique of the television apparatus. He depicts it as dishonest and emotionally unstable. As Fran herself mutters, 'We're blowing it ourselves.' The city of so-called 'brotherly love' is now the centre of lies and male dissension suggesting the final bankruptcy of patriarchy and the need for a different form of social organisation.

Fran's boyfriend Steve (David Emge) then arrives. He plans to steal the studio helicopter he flies for traffic reports to escape the chaos. Fran initially objects to Steve's selfish reasons – 'Somebody has to survive.' She still idealistically believes in her role of public responsibility in a broadcasting industry that was never beholden to such ideas in the past nor is capable of fulfilling them in the present. However, her objections collapse when a colleague supports Steve's scheme: 'Go ahead. We'll be off the air by midnight anyway. Emergency networks are taking over. Our responsibility is finished

I'm afraid.' He voices definitive words which both counter Fran's public sense of communal duty as well as affirming one of the key tenets of Romero's central concepts in the entire trilogy, namely the moral bankruptcy of the old order and its inability to exercise any real form of responsibility in the face of danger. This feature characterises the entire message of *The Crazies*. It now remains to be seen whether any survivors can live up to the bankrupt ideals denied by the old order and form a new society uncontaminated by past patterns of behaviour.

Before Fran and Steve leave the studio, they hear of the proclamation of a totalitarian martial law ordinance very similar to the one used in *The Crazies*. It states that 'citizens may no longer occupy private residences no matter how safely protected or well stocked. Citizens will be moved into central areas of the city.' This order not only parallels the disastrous type of relocation policies used both in South Vietnam and *The Crazies* but also reveals that citizens may no longer rely on their government to provide safety and security for them in any major emergency. When circumstances necessitate, they become as much the enemy as the zombies.

The next sequence also shows which section of the population is really affected. A SWAT team moves in to expel Puerto Ricans, Hispanics and Afro-Americans from a low-income apartment complex. Despite this action, arising from the inhabitant's reluctance to surrender dead bodies of family members for destruction, due to now redundant social values concerning people believing that 'there's still respect in dying', the real motivation is much more insidious. Romero represents it as a politically motivated act of class and racial harassment, since any enforcement against affluent whites remains questionable. Before the attack, a bigoted macho trooper named Wooley (Jim Baffico) gleefully relishes the approaching battle: 'I'll blow their asses off … their little low-life Puerto Rican and nigger asses right off. How the hell come we shift those low-lifes in those big ass fancy hotels anyway? Shit man! This's better than I got.' Wooley's attitudes represent a pathological development of Clank's aggressive masculinity of *The Crazies* and anticipates its final psychotic embodiment in the figures of Rickles and Captain Rhodes in *Day of the Dead*. Wooley then engages in a psychotic killing spree above and beyond the call of duty, venting his murderous racism on any non-white zombie or human until an appalled black trooper (later identified as Peter) kills him to end his indiscrimate slaughter. The SWAT activities in rounding up live humans resembles the actions performed by their counterparts in *The Crazies*. Roger also knows what is really going on. He advises the rebel leader Martinez not to go out before his fellow troopers fire on him.

During these events, the zombies break out of their confines to attack the living. A living wife rushes to embrace her zombie husband only to have him ravenously consume chunks of her body. The SWAT team engage in the immediate termination of all zombies who resemble once-living family members. Now, the old family ties are completely worthless and new forms of social existence need consideration. Not everyone can envisage the necessity of breaking with old patterns of behaviour. A young SWAT member, who witnessed the conspicuous consumption between living dead husband and live wife in their macabre family reunion, decides he has seen enough and commits suicide. His action anticipates one of the choices Peter (Ken Foree) faces at the film's climax. A black zombie with partially devoured limbs slowly crawls towards him and Peter appears masochistically inclined to accept his fate until Roger (Scott Reininger) saves him. As a member of the besieged community, Peter understands the reasons they left their dead in the basement instead of incinerating them according to government orders. Unlike the attitude exhibited by Johnny in *Night of the Living Dead*, respect for the dying still has a great priority in their community, but it is now redundant. Like other characters in Romero's films, Peter struggles between belief in old values and the necessity for moving forward. At this stage of the film, he becomes dangerously contaminated by a masochistic death wish which Roger rescues him from. But he will have to confront it in the film's climax when no one is around to help him. Like Joan Mitchell, David and Martin, Peter will face personal dilemmas in confronting a dangerous personal and social environment. There is no guarantee that he will survive.

However, the words of a one-legged Puerto Rican priest, who is returning from giving the zombies their last rites, move him. Although the priest represents another redundant world linked with the old society, he also suggests the necessity of change due to the different material circumstances: 'You are stronger than us ... but soon I think ... they be stronger than you. When the dead walk, señors ... we must stop killing ... or we lose the war.' The priest articulates the need for a rational strategy to deal with a situation becoming increasingly out of control. He also urges the cessation of violence, an attitude held by David in *The Crazies*, otherwise the war will be lost to the zombie forces who are already spreading like Trixie in the earlier film. It is tempting to see this figure as embodying another incarnation of the director as enunciator, especially in relation to Romero's Catholic upbringing.

Like Peter, Roger is also affected by what he has seen and retches in disgust at the carnage. After saving Peter from his masochistic desires, he establishes contact with him and reveals his escape plan to 'run' (or, really, desert) with Steve and Fran in the helicopter and invites him along. They make contact in another building, witness law enforcement officers engage in looting, and leave Philadelphia.

The disparate group of media and law enforcement employees set off on a journey both personal and physical. When they arrive at their destination, they will still have to confront the forces which they believe they have left behind in Philadelphia. As they fly across the country, they see rednecks hunting zombies. This not only reprises the concluding scenes of *Night of the Living Dead* but also articulates the Marxist axiom of history now repeating itself as farce rather than tragedy. Over satirical images of the rednecks and soldiers, Romero uses a sardonic country'n'western song, 'I'm a Man' (recorded by the British rock group *Them* and purchased as industrial library music), to reveal further both the absurdity of male indulgent violence and the reinforcement of the priest's message concerning the cessation of killing. With grotesque male figures such as those living on a diet of beer and violence, humanity will certainly 'lose the war'.

As in *There's Always Vanilla*, *Jack's Wife*, *The Crazies* and *Martin*, the quartet in the helicopter still have to make strong attempts to break away from their former personal identities or they, too, will 'lose the war'. They have to battle with issues of self-deception which hinder the necessary progress needed to cope with new challenging situations. It is Peter who first expresses his understanding of the realities of their current status when Steve suggests landing at a military airport. Despite their 'theft' of the helicopter, Steve still believes their actions fall within the law. However, as previously seen in the television studio sequences, the rule of law has broken down and the group may find themselves facing the institutional violence of a military system little better than that of *The Crazies* and *Day of the Dead*. They are now outsiders and have to develop new perspectives, as the following exchange reveals after Steve's suggestion:

Peter: Oh yeah! You got the papers for this limousine?
Steve: [Angrily] I got JON ID. So does Fran.
Peter: Right! And we're out here doing traffic reports? Wake up sucker.
          We're thieves and bad guys is what we are. And we gotta find our
          own way.

After stopping to refuel at a deserted airport, the group find themselves facing another zombie assault. Like Ben in *Night of the Living Dead*, Peter faces attack by child zombies which he barely escapes from. However, thrilled by his unexpected membership in a male-uniformed group, Steve becomes fascinated by firepower and violence to the extent of accidentally placing Peter in danger. He picks up one of their rifles and attempts to shoot zombies as Roger expresses amusement at his bad marksmanship. Peter later angrily reacts against the 'flyboy', threatening him with a gun, and warning against any further actions as if remembering the actions of Wooley the previous night.

The helicopter heads west and eventually lands on the roof of a huge shopping mall deserted except for zombies wandering aimlessly about both outside and inside. Steve intuitively understands the reason for the zombie fascination with an environment which is now really redundant in terms of their new appetites. They are there due to 'some kind of instinct. Memory ... of what they used to do. This was an important place in their lives.' Steve's response has more than one relevant association. Although the zombies cannot consume the merchandise for their basic bodily needs, they are still programmed by 'some kind of instinct' to engage in conspicuous consumption despite the fact that they do not really need to do so. Zombie attraction to the mall is redundant and unnecessary. But as their human lives were programmed by society, resulting in behavioural patterns becoming 'instinctive' or part of 'human nature', their dead counterparts continue the same form of behaviour. The living and the dead are united by desire and memory.

Despite consumerism's goal of targeting female shoppers by lavish displays of material goods, *Dawn of the Dead* ironically reveals that the mall has more fascination for the three males rather than the solitary female who accompanies them on the journey. Leaving Fran alone in an upper room after discovering food in a civil defence storage system, Steve, Roger and Peter decide to explore their new domain. Still desiring entry into an elite male military group, Steve neglects his pregnant girlfriend and joins the others to engage in a free shopping spree. He selfishly takes the weapon Peter leaves for Fran to defend herself and cynically rushes off to join the other 'boys'. Roger's comment, 'Looks like a free lunch', expresses glee at the opportunity of access to commodities they would otherwise have to pay for in their former world of capitalist exchange. Roger and Peter find the mall's control room and press devices after gaining 'the keys of the kingdom'. As the consumerist ploys of muzak, spouting fountains, and moving escalators begin, the men watch in fascination as zombies stumble around in ways little different from their former living selves. The live males are little better than small boys entranced at a new train set. However, while they play around with looting items in shopping carts and dodging zombies, Fran nearly dies at the hands of a Hare Krishna zombie. After they rescue her from a 'fate worse than death' she demands equality with the male members of the group after attempting in vain to persuade them to leave their consumerist 'au bonheur des hommes'. She also sarcastically comments that she is not willing to be regarded as 'den mother' and reacts angrily as she overhears the men discussing the possibility of an abortion when she is not present in the room. Fran regards the mall as a 'prison' symbolising everything they were trying to escape from. However, Steve cunningly overcomes her objections by appealing to her ideologically programmed female domestic instincts involving materialism and domesticity: 'Those things are out there, everywhere, and the authorities would give us just as hard a time, maybe worse. We're in great shape here, Frannie. We got everything we need right here. I'm not just being stubborn. I really think this is better. Hell, you're the one who's been wanting to set up shop.' He cunningly persuades Fran to accept the mall as their private consumerist 'haven from a heartless world'.

The group then co-operate in ethnically cleansing their haven from zombies like a successful religious group purging their sanctuary from heretics. They all engage in a killing spree, block the mall doors with huge tractor-trailer trucks and turn the upstairs storeroom they initially use as their base headquarters into an affluent-looking, penthouse-style apartment worthy of Donald Trump. Although Fran temporarily becomes one of the boys by participating in a shooting spree very similar to the redneck activities of *Night of the Living Dead* and *Dawn of the Dead*, she walks away in disgust from Steve, Peter and Roger as they view the bodies of their victims. She intuitively realises the dangerously infectious nature of violent behaviour. The Puerto Rican priest's warning that any killing must stop also operates as an evocative memory during this brief scene. By contrast, both Roger and Steve become infected in different ways. Roger endangers the group's safety when they engage in a strategy of blocking the mall doors. Revelling in macho excess and bravado, he becomes little better than the infected and irrational Clank in the later scenes of *The Crazies*. He treats the exercise as a childish game until a zombie bites his leg. Roger becomes little better than Wooley; while Wooley indulged in the earlier slaughter to vent out his rage against minority groups living in apartment blocks beyond his economic means, Roger regards the zombies as illegal squatters threatening his access to his consumerist sanctuary. His joy at 'whipping 'em' has possessive overtones as his later comment, 'We got it all', reveals. He becomes the first of the group to become a zombie while Steve will later follow him.

This change in status is neither abrupt nor arbitrary since the two men earlier exhibited signs of possessiveness and violence common to their zombie antagonists. Both Roger and Steve want to hold on to the mall as long as possible and defend it from outsiders. While the zombies remain the ultimate consumers who follow their instincts to the logical conclusion by killing and consuming humans, Fran, Peter, Steve and Roger kill the living dead so that they can gain access to a lifestyle of conspicuous consumption. However, the actions of living and dead are complementary in different ways. After indulging themselves in the material gains like victors following a colonial conquest, the humans become bored and decadent. They behave in a listless manner paralleling the zombies who once inhabited the mall. Furthermore, their rise in material status also reproduces the typical pattern of the rise and decline of most human civilisations and religions in moving from barbarism to bored decadence.

Religious analogies are not inappropriate. Romero has made this comparison himself in the shooting script by speaking of the mall as a temple of consumer greed containing within itself elements of eventual decline. He notes that 'at either end of the concourse like the main altars at each end of a cathedral, stand the mammoth two-storey department stores, great symbols of a consumer society. The images are all too familiar, but in their present state they appear as an archaeological discovery revealing the gods and customs of a civilisation now gone' (quoted in Gagne 1987: 87). Mindlessness, the suspension of any form of critically-minded independent thought and passivity, characterises any true believer whether they adhere to the realms of capitalism or religion.

Although the quartet live in relative security while the zombies wait outside, the four humans soon become reduced to conditions of mindless passivity like their living dead alter egos. Humans and zombies become equal partners in a goal of conspicuous consumption dominating personal behaviour. While the zombies graphically devour bodies of their living victims in spectacularly gory fashion, their human counterparts inside the mall mechanically indulge in their own form of consumerist consumption. They eventually become little better than mindless automatons. While the quartet initially enjoy their access to a kingdom of plenty, they all soon become bored and lethargic. Eventually, they merely indulge in the motions of consumption and show little signs of independent vitality like their zombie counterparts. The men continue their pattern of endless consuming even when their basic needs are all fulfilled. Fran either skates alone on the ice rink or tediously tries out cosmetics and wigs before a mirror until the futility of her instinctually programmed narcissistic desires become evident. As Fran over-indulges by slapping on heavy make-up, eyelashes and wigs, Romero intercuts images of mall dummies in the sequence. These parallel his other montage juxtapositions involving the same dummies during earlier scenes when the zombies instinctually shuffled along the mall. When Steve photographs Fran as she shops for clothes in the mall, she sarcastically comments, 'Great! When you finish the roll drop it off at the drug store!' The former lovers gradually lose the vitality of their emotional relationship and become little better than a stereotypical married couple passively enduring a relationship which is really dead and buried. Romero significantly illustrates this by a slow zoom-out showing Steve awake in bed while Fran stares listlessly into space. They resemble a bored and frustrated couple in an Antonioni film. Ultimately, they both engage in a stereotypical domestic argument over Steve's desire to keep the television set on despite the fact that nothing is now on.

The trio exist in a world of boredom as a result of their access to a world of conspicuous consumption. Romero significantly focuses on Fran's growing realisation of her state of ennui. In many ways, her behaviour echoes that of her naturalistic predecessor Laura Jadwin in Frank Norris' final novel *The Pit*, who 'found means to occupy her mind with all manner of small activities' until everything becomes familiar 'to the point of wearisome contempt'. Laura's access to immediate consumerist gratification leads to boredom as Norris skilfully narrates:

> Her desires were gratified with an abruptness that killed the zest of them. She felt none of the joy of possession; the little personal relation between her and her belongings vanished away ... And hardly a day passed that Laura Jadwin, in the solitude of her own boudoir, did not fling her arms wide in a gesture of lassitude and infinite weariness, crying out: 'Oh, the ennui and stupidity of all this wretched life!' (1903: 352–3)

Even before Roger's death, the quartet already began to resemble a bourgeois family out on a shopping spree with the injured Roger appearing like the baby on a mall shopping cart. After Roger's death, Peter is now the odd man out (or third party) in the stereotypical romantic pattern of 'Two's company. Three's a crowd' despite the fact there is no real necessity for this conventional exclusion to operate in a situation where civilisation has collapsed. The increasingly isolated Peter decides to remain in the background. Although he does not need to do so, he also reacts in an ideologically programmed instinctual level of behaviour. The final grotesque parodic nature of Peter's status appears when he acts as waiter at a romantic dinner for Fran and Steve before disappearing at the crucial moment when she receives a proposal and engagement ring. As if recognising the redundancy of this gesture as well as its overtones of acquisitiveness, she rejects his proposal: 'We can't, not now. It wouldn't be real.' However, their relationship temporarily resumes when Steve finally agrees to her earlier request to teach her to pilot a helicopter. Both appear equal and happy and at ease with each other for a change, yet the rapprochement is temporary since ominous forces remain outside. As an alienated Peter relieves his frustrations by playing squash on the roof, one of his balls drops down to fall at the feet of the waiting zombies excluded from their consumerist Edenic environment.

Both humans and zombies have equal desires towards control of the mall. They both act on an instinctual level of existence, involving consumption, possessiveness and violence, signifiers of an old, dead society which still exercises its hold upon both the living and the living dead. The mall's earlier zombie inhabitants represent a cross-section of the old society dominated by consumer capitalism affecting everyone – middle-aged, nuns, nurses, insurance salesman, softball players, yuppies and Hare Krishna devotees.[12] Intermittent television broadcasts describe them as functioning on a 'subconscious, instinctual level' and 'remembered behaviour from normal life'. When Peter observes the zombies waiting outside, he understands the real reason why they do not go away:

Steve: They're after us. They know we're in here.
Peter: They're after the *place*. They don't know why. They just remember
        ... remember that they wanna be in here!

Although Peter earlier repeats his grandfather's superstitious saying about the dead returning to earth when no more room exists in hell, he is the most self-aware of the whole group despite his masochistic death-wish feelings. His religious reference may also be part of family indoctrination which has become so ingrained into his subconscious that it now forms what he believes is human nature. Peter reveals that his grandfather 'used to be a priest in Trinidad'. He struggles with his religious upbringing in the same manner as Joan Mitchell in *Jack's Wife* and Martin. However, *Dawn of the Dead* distinctly reveals that these supposedly instinctual reactions really derive from programmed activities installed via the psychic operations of capitalism and the family. Dr. Logan's scientific experiments in *Day of the Dead* later make this explicit. Furthermore, as the infrequent television talk-show (now continued in a rudimentary manner) from Fran's former studio reveals, the zombies have 'little or no reasoning power' as Dr. Rausch states. He also suggests ways of controlling the zombies by feeding them dead bodies, an idea affronting the now-redundant civilised sensibilities of the remaining television studio audience. Rausch also makes an important observation relevant to the living dead practices of capitalism: 'It's the waste that kills us.' While human beings consume vast amounts of material that they do not really need, the zombies operate on a much more efficient economic level: 'They use maybe five per cent of the food available on the human body ... and then the body is usually intact enough to be mobile when it arrives.' Zombies are thus the ideal embodiment of Marx's *homo economicus*.

However, Rausch's sensibility operates merely on the level of cold rationality. He never draws obvious conclusions concerning the waste within the old society which may have caused this dilemma, yet he does suggest a strategy for future survival by suggesting the survivors consume zombie bodies, an ironic inversion of the present chaotic situation. But, like Dr. Watts in *The Crazies*, Rausch's attempts at communication fall on deaf ears. The bickering studio audience and quartet also have 'little or no reasoning power', never really communicate and fall victim to programmed methods of behaviour, finally ending in dissension. Fran later realises the implications of these findings and draws the obvious conclusion with her comment 'What are we doing to ourselves?' The surviving humans are actually responsible for their dilemmas. They may continue subconsciously to victimise themselves in various aggressive ways, both directly and indirectly, unless alternative modes of behaviour are articulated. Otherwise, the surviving humans will merely continue following programmed instinctual modes of behaviour which will result in either self-destruction or future incorporation in the increasing number of living dead outside, either literally or otherwise. Roger's insane activities in defending a useless kingdom of waste from the zombies literally kills him. The surviving trio are becoming little better than their counterparts outside by falling into alienated modes of behaviour.

Eventually, the survivors face another attack by a marauding group of bikers. Despite merely wishing to loot the place, the assailants condemn the trio for their deadly acquisitiveness – 'Hey, you in the mall. You got fouled up real bad. We don't like people who don't share' – and break into the mall allowing the waiting zombies the access to their consumerist paradise. Although Peter logically realises the necessity of avoiding a futile confrontation against overwhelming numbers, Steve immediately falls into the same selfish pattern of behaviour as Roger. He rejects Peter's advice to 'Just stay out of sight. They're after the place. They don't care about us', arguing, 'It's ours. We took it. It's ours.' But this time, Steve will have no hope of 'whipping 'em' like Roger. Before moving into action, he homo-erotically kisses his rifle, subconsciously transferring his affections from Fran to his male symbol of power. He shoots one of the bikers and begins a minor war in which the only victors are the zombies who finish off the surviving bikers.

Like Roger, Steve begins a fatal process which will make him a zombie. As with Roger, he actually becomes one after succumbing to fatal zombie bites. He emerges from an elevator to join the army of the living dead. Steve now acts in a manner equivalent to his zombie companions operating on instinct and memory. He leads his followers to break down the fake wall erected to conceal the stairwell leading to the quartet's hideout. Formerly fascinated by Peter and Roger's male group associations, Steve now ironically becomes a military commander leading his fellow zombies like a General on a campaign. However, as Gagne notes (1987: 89), Romero now depicts Steve satirically lurching along on bent ankle with an idiotic expression on his face, numbly holding a pistol he once used when he was human. It is a revealing parody of his earlier fascination with weaponry when he nearly shot Peter (accidentally) at a landing zone.

As the zombies approach, Peter orders Fran up to the helicopter while he remains behind to supposedly clear the way for their escape. However, at this moment, Peter passively submits to deadly instinctual forces ingrained in his personality from birth. After killing Steve before Fran's eyes, he clearly intends to commit suicide following the earlier example of the young SWAT team member in the assault on the apartment block. Peter retreats into Roger's room. It is the very same place where he had killed his friend after complying with his wish about not allowing him to become a new recruit in a zombie army of the dead. Peter squats in his friend's room, placing a gun to his cheek in the same manner as the young SWAT trooper. However, at the last moment, Peter suddenly decides to live, stop the killing (whether humans or zombies) and join Fran in a helicopter very low on fuel. After shooting one more zombie who blocks his path, he ascends the stepladder and joins Fran in the helicopter.

Peter's decision is highly significant on more than one level. In the original screenplay and novelisation of *Dawn of the Dead*, Peter committed suicide while Fran stepped out of the helicopter to decapitate herself with its blades. The two human survivors instinctually followed the logical conclusions of deadly masochism and submitted to Freud's negative realm of Thanatos (or Death Wish) catalogued in his 1929 work appropriately titled *Civilization and its Discontents*. During his later years, Freud became more pessimistic concerning the human condition and Romero initially reflected this feeling in earlier drafts of the screenplay. However, after shooting the first version of the conclusion, he reflected that 'I just woke up one day and decided to let them go simply because I liked them too much' (quoted in Gagne 1987: 91).[13] This evokes an unconscious reference to one of Romero's favourite directors, Howard Hawks, who finally decided on a more positive ending to *Red River* (1948) simply because he also came to like all the leading characters. But there is another, more convincing reason. Disgusted with killing and affected by the racial slur made by the leader (Tom Savini) of the bikers, who called him 'chocolate man', evoking memories of Wooley's racist attitudes, Peter falls victim to dark masochistic elements existing within his own personality, elements instinctual in nature and part of civilisation's life-denying mechanisms. However, Romero's eventual change of mind reflects a positive alternative both in terms of letting two survivors live and avoiding the reactionary elements inherent within the violent spectacular mechanisms of the horror genre itself.

Dawn of the Dead is definitely a violent film. It develops the premises of *Night of the Living Dead* by using gory, spectacular formal features which often distract audiences from recognising the important messages embedded within the film's text. Some audience members often act little differently from fictional characters (such as Romero's rednecks, Wooley, Roger and Steve) in allowing themselves to be carried away by a deadly world of masculine aggressiveness in cheering the visual spectacle of gore and slaughter. But by doing so, they lose sight of *Dawn of the Dead*'s more important concepts. The killing has to stop. Humanity has to find another path to survive. This involves rejecting obsolete patterns of behaviour which have caused the zombie phenomenon and link supposedly separate worlds of living and dead. But these deadly realms of sadistic violence and masochistic passivity are not the results of a supposedly instinctual world of 'human nature' dominating individuals. They are really programmed forms of human behaviour drilled into civilisation's victims from early childhood onwards within a family structure indelibly linked to consumer capitalism. In his 1915 essay 'Instincts and Their Vicissitudes' Freud commented upon the presence and interchangeability of two deadly forms of human behaviour – sadism and masochism. One instinct may change into its opposite; sadistic modes of behaviour may easily become masochistic under certain circumstances. Freud notes that 'The enjoyment of pain would thus be an aim which was originally masochistic, but which can only become an instinctual aim in someone who was originally sadistic.'[14] Furthermore, he recognised that the co-existence of both instincts within the same personality may embody 'the most important example of ambivalence of feeling'[15] especially in relation to the presence of male and female characteristics acting in a fluid and non-binary manner. Peter and Fran represent two characters who intuitively recognise these dangerous mechanisms of human behaviour and attempt to move in different directions.

In many ways, Peter resembles the gentle David of *The Crazies* who has rejected patriarchy and the sadistic world of male control. As a black man, he has probably joined the SWAT team to gain the status he would not otherwise achieve in society. As he tells Fran on the helicopter journey to the mall he has little option. One brother is a football player, the other is in jail. He also tells her of his regret at leaving his 'brothers' whom he regards as an important community ideal. But Peter is clearly uncomfortable with his role as officially proscribed killer. He forms a strong bond of male friendship with Roger in a manner suggesting homoerotic associations which can never be openly expressed. Affected by forces within his unconscious and lacking progressive alternatives, he exists uneasily within a world of sadistic violence. Finding no other path for him, he easily succumbs to dark, masochistic factors within his own personality at the climax. Clearly affected by Roger's death and sickened by the violence, he passively waits for death until he suddenly decides to live. Although Romero selects some mediocre library music to affirm Peter's decision, it does, at least, mark a significant movement on his part as opposed to the inappropriate goblin rock music existing in the Dario Argento version. Fran represents a more positive version of Romero's previous heroines such as Barbara of *Night of the Living Dead*, Lynn of *There's Always Vanilla*, Joan Mitchell of *Jack's Wife*, Judy of *The Crazies* and Christine of *Martin*. She also anticipates Sarah of *Day of the Dead*. Fran has the possibility of developing her intuitive potentials or regressing into some negative form of behaviour. By refusing to give in, she decides to move forward.

When Peter runs to the helicopter, he allows one of the zombies to take his rifle, following the advice he had earlier given a reluctant Roger in their assault on the mall. The same zombie who took Roger's weapon now gains another. After acquiring another material item, he drops Roger's rifle and looks in fascination at his new acquisition. Peter no longer needs any weapon to affirm his new sense of identity. Unlike Ben in *Night of the Living Dead* who aims his rifle and dies, Peter lives after relinquishing his weapon. His action parallels David's in the final scenes of *The Crazies* when he throws away his rifle.[16]

The pregnant Fran and Peter fly away as the zombies regain their consumer kingdom. No hint is given of any future typical Hollywood romantic relationship for them. Also, since the helicopter is low on fuel, Fran and Peter fly into the darkness to face no assured future. Their survival is tentative, as tentative as that facing certain characters in naturalist fiction such as Etienne Lantier of *Germinal* or Carrie Meeber of Dreiser's *Sister Carrie*. Yet the two survivors embody within themselves the potential for a new form of society by 'moving beyond apocalypse' as Robin Wood notes; *Dawn of the Dead* concludes by bringing 'its two surviving protagonists to the point where the work of creating the norms for a new social order, a new structure of relationships, can begin – a context in which the presence of a third survivor, Fran's unborn child, points the way to potential change' (1986: 121). However, as *Knightriders* will show, within a different context, any tentative possibilities for change will meet with huge obstacles, both personal and social.

CHAPTER EIGHT

Knightriders

Shot after the financial success of *Dawn of the Dead* on his biggest budget so far, *Knightriders* represents Romero's most personal film to date. It is also a creative product of an industrial system often allowing stars and directors to engage in their most cherished projects after box-office success. Seen in this light, *Knightriders* resembles Coppola's *The Conversation* (1974), Scorsese's *The Last Temptation of Christ* (1988) and *The Age of Innocence* (1993), and Jessica Lange's *Country* (1984). These all represent projects in which individual talents attempt to break away from generic and star vehicles to produce creative statements free from economic constraints. *Knightriders* belongs to this category.

But it is also a different George A. Romero film. Discarding previously familiar elements such as naturalistic concepts, zombies, EC Comic-style photography and the formal attributes of the horror genre most reviewers eagerly associate him with, Romero chose another direction to reproduce again the type of personal statement existing in his other films. However, *Knightriders* failed theatrically on its initial release. It disappointed Romero fans who wanted more gore and zombies as well as certain reviewers such as Pauline Kael and Michael Sragow who attacked the film for its simple-minded idealism.[1] Robin Wood soon saw Romero as a casualty of a 1980s decade which destroyed the radical nature of the horror genre with which Romero was associated. He defined *Knightriders* as having a certain

> symptomatic interest in relation to the persistent quandary of the American radical who wants to make some kind of positive statement yet is barred from embracing any coherent political alternative: essentially the film is another *Alice's Restaurant*, ten years too late and lacking Penn's sensitivity and complexity. It is the archetypal liberal American movie, with something nice to say about every minority group, some pious platitudes about the corrupting

power of commercialism, and a lament for the failure of a counterculture that couldn't possibly succeed. (1986: 190–1)

Although *Knightriders* contains several flaws in form and content, it does not really deserve Wood's criticism. Romero is not an explicitly political director and has always avoided overt messages. Secondly, both *Knightriders* and *Alice's Restaurant* are different films needing evaluation on their own terms. Finally, it is disputable whether *Knightriders* represents a lament for something which has failed. The film concludes with Billy's successor leading the troupe and riding away to face again the same problems that affected the group throughout the narrative. They still survive and live to fight another day. Furthermore, it is not the counterculture itself which has failed; the film focuses upon the problems facing very fallible human characters in maintaining this ideal. *Knightriders* also deals with issues raised earlier in *There's Always Vanilla* but treats them in a different manner.

The final scene of *Knightriders* not only represents the type of open-ended conclusions seen in Romero's films such as *The Crazies, Dawn of the Dead* and *Day of the Dead* but also those associated with Romero's favourite directors, Howard Hawks and Orson Welles. For example, *Rio Bravo* (1959) may conclude with John T. Chance beginning a romantic liaison with Feathers and Dude restored to his former self, but, as with Hawks' work, everything is provisional and never entirely resolved. A successful ending may have overtones of the transitory nature of life embodied in the lines of Slim's song 'How Little We Know' from *To Have and Have Not* (1944) – 'even if it's only a day'. The same is true for *Knightriders* and the tentative utopian conclusions of *Dawn of the Dead* and *Day of the Dead*. Several of Romero's films refuse the inevitability of predetermined closure. It is a feature that Michael Anderegg finds characteristic of Welles' late Shakespearian films as well as Theodor Adorno's understanding of an art work as opposed to a manufactured artifact.[2]

Romero's fictional characters face different problems involving survival and over-coming external and internal problems. They also attempt moving towards a better world where the odds for finally succeeding may be a little better. Although utopian strains are present, his films realistically never give any easy answers. They also seriously depict the huge obstacles his various characters struggle against whenever they attempt to realise their own destinies. Although Billy (Ed Harris) may exhibit signs of wistful idealism similar to Falstaff and Shallow reminiscing about their youthful activities in Welles' *Chimes at Midnight* (1967), the represented worlds in both films are far from Edenic.[3] Ironically, if Welles' Falstaff 'longs for an Edenic world only because he has long since forfeited it' (Anderegg 1999: 129), Romero's Billy has long since lost the knightly prowess that justifies his leadership of the troupe and his current position as king. He has suffered from injuries long before the first combat with Morgan seen in the film. These necessitate Billy's knights riding to his rescue so he can retain his pre-eminent position.

As with *Dawn of the Dead* and *Day of the Dead*, Romero also decided to make *Knightriders* to show people 'they still had a chance'[4] as well as revealing the odds they face in taking up challenges involved with such a chance. In this respect, *Knightriders* also parallels the utopianism of Zola's final novels, *Fécondité* (1899), *Travail* (1901) and

Vérité (1903). But the film avoids the naïve progressiveness contained within those texts. In Zola's final trilogy, the three Froment brothers eventually succeed and overcome all obstacles in unrealistic 'happy ever after' conclusions which never appeared in the earlier Rougon-Macquart series.

Despite its medieval trappings, *Knightriders* is also a self-reflexive work about film-making. It resembles Howard Hawks' *Hatari!* (1962) which is not solely about an African safari. It is also a work indirectly dealing with the process of making a film on location and having 'fun' at the same time.[5] *Knightriders* was an obvious labour of love for all concerned as the acting of all participants testifies. But *Knightriders* also deals with key Romero concepts such as the problems of leadership, self-control and various attempts towards following an alternative life-style in an increasingly commercialised and commodified era.

One major contradiction in *Knightriders*' vision is the adoption of a feudal life-style based upon hierarchical concepts, a factor certain reviewers recognised. In an otherwise sympathetic review Ed Sikov comments upon the fact that 'the *Knightriders* cult is governed strictly by the right of kings, and is an autocracy based on wish-fulfilment and the ridiculous subjugation of an entire group to a battle's victor'.[6] But this begs several questions. Undoubtedly, the group engage in a wish-fulfilment fantasy which appears strangely at odds with the surrounding world. But it is a fantasy which is neither as self-deceptive and self-serving as that generated by Joan Mitchell in *Jack's Wife* nor as morbid and violent as *Martin*'s nocturnal activities. The knightriders group have clearly decided to participate in the creation of an Arthurian myth which has more to do with a Hawksian ethos than the dark feudal connotations of the actual era. It is a hierarchical group. But the participants have clearly chosen their roles within this new society and are respected as individuals. The knightriders society is as inclusive as Hawks' idyllic groups which include not only heroic figures such as John Wayne's John T. Chance, but females such as Feathers, aged disabled characters such as Stumpy and ethnic non-macho figures such as Carlos who is master in his own hotel and who knows more about women than Chance. Significantly, Chance's final victory against Nathan Burdette owes more to Stumpy and Carlos than it does to his own individual prowess and strategy. Similarly, the knightriders society is comprehensive rather than rigidly hierarchical.

When Billy angrily disrupts the impromptu meeting arranged by Morgan with impresario Bontempi, he asserts that it is not a real council meeting because not everyone is present. That includes non-knights as well as knights. Furthermore, the troupe follow Billy's leadership in terms of his prowess in being King but they also recognise his vulnerability in the same way in which the non-heroic members of John T. Chance's group in *Rio Bravo* look out for his own interests. Despite being leaders, both Chance and Billy actually depend on others. Also, the knightly contests represent Romero's version of Hawksian professionalism in being 'good' at combat as Rocky (Cynthia Adler) states, or following 'the basics', as she tells a defeated biker opponent: 'It looked great for a while, but you don't have the guts to do what we do. That's basic number one.'

Rocky represents Romero's development of the Hawks woman. Rather than being marginalised when the male group engage in their professional goals, she represents the logical culmination of Hildy Johnson from *His Girl Friday* (1940), the newspaperwoman who is as professional as her male counterparts and obviously wasted in any normal marital relationship. Rocky functions as an accepted member of Romero's professional male group rather than operating from the sidelines like Angie Dickinson's Feathers in *Rio Bravo* where her only active contribution to the group lies in causing a diversion so Chance and Colorado can defeat their enemies. Significantly, her lesbian identity may not be accidental but rather the logical response to those feminist critics who regard the Hawks woman as a male in female costume as well as others such as Robin Wood who note a 'gay subtext' in the director's work.

Billy eventually decides to relinquish his leadership to Morgan at the end of the film in a manner resembling Hawksian precedents. Although the knightriders no longer face life-threatening situations like their predecessors in *The Dawn Patrol* (1930) and *Only Angels Have Wings* (1939), Morgan now has to take on the burdens of leadership as Douglas Scott does after the heroic death of Captain Courtney in *The Dawn Patrol*. Like Dude in *Rio Bravo*, Morgan was formerly a 'stray sheep'. But he returns to the fold purged of his aggressive narcissistic attitude and fully aware of the dangers lurking within the world outside. He once again becomes a team player and realises the value of community like Winocki (John Garfield) in *Air Force* (1943). Morgan (Tom Savini) is similarly tempted by a woman who arrived in town (and not on a stagecoach like her predecessor in *Rio Bravo*), who seduces and abandons him after he performs his pleasurable use-value role. In *Knightriders*, Billy is a much more flawed leader than Chance. He has to cope with the same type of personal demons affecting characters such as Peter in *Dawn of the Dead* before he can move on to any form of self-realisation. Although not ageing like the Wayne characters in *El Dorado* (1966) and *Rio Lobo* (1970), Billy is fighting a 'dragon' which could eventually destroy him and the troupe who have made, as Linet points out, an 'adult' decision to follow his ideals. Like Cole Thornton in *El Dorado* he has to deal with an injury which affects his physical prowess. But, as *Knightriders* affirms, this ailment is also metaphysical.

Billy also resembles Romero's Martin in so far as he is torn between visions of the past and his present role in contemporary society. But, unlike John Amplas' tragic figure, Billy reveres a more healthy past world of glory and honour which he attempts to apply to the present rather than Martin's pathologically regressive behaviour. While Martin's behaviour has obvious family origins, Billy's world has divorced itself from the contemporary malaise affecting human beings as seen in its worst examples of Julie Dean's abusive alcoholic father and Stephen King's slobbish hoagie man.

Whatever the contradictions affecting Billy's choice of a medieval alternative it is far more preferable to the values followed by the world outside. Billy, Merlin (Brother Blue) and the troupe all seek a certain form of 'magic', or spiritual idealism, in a world in which it is noticeably lacking – if their audiences, the media, and corrupt Deputy Sheriffs are anything to go by. But the magic in *Knightriders* represents a much more positive path than the sterile dead ends followed by both Martin and Cuda in Romero's earlier film. It does, at least, recognise the presence of the world outside and the necessity for withdrawal to maintain both the group's pragmatic idealism and the necessary self-respect for continuing existence.

Knightriders is also a romantic vision drawn from previous Hollywood models. Originally, influenced by genre films of his youth such as *Ivanhoe* (1952), *Knights of the Round Table* (1954) and *The Adventures of Quentin Durward* (1955), Romero wished to make a film that realistically shows the knights as they actually were. But fascinated by his discovery of travelling Renaissance fairs and The Society for Creative Anachronisms in particular (the inspiration for Billy's troupe), he developed the screenplay which later became *Knightriders*. As Sam Arkoff recognised, a grimly realistic knight movie would have failed at the box office for the same reasons that pessimistic images of other genres like the western depicted in films such as Frank Perry's *Doc* (1971) and Michael Cimino's *Heaven's Gate* (1981) have done.[7] However, although classical Hollywood directors such as John Ford and Howard Hawks depicted a West which often bore little relationship to its historical dimensions, this did not prevent them from directing significant works which often indirectly comment upon the problematic historical circumstances influencing their formations.

Generic precedents also exist for Romero's creative venture. During the 1950s American stars such as Robert Taylor and Tony Curtis often appeared in historical epics. The latter graced films such as *The Prince Who Was a Thief* (1951), *Son of Ali Baba* (1952), *The Black Shield of Falworth* (1954), *The Purple Mask* (1955) and *The Vikings* (1958) with a barely disguised, incongruous Bronx accent derived from his former existence as young Bernard Schwartz. Neither did Robert Taylor engage in a medieval Anglo-Saxon accent for his roles as Ivanhoe and Sir Lancelot. Since a generic knight movie was impossible, Romero developed the anachronistic aspects of the original genre into a creative dimension in line with the ideas appearing in his previous films. Ed Harris' Billy is no Taylor or Curtis but another of Romero's tortured male figures struggling with masculine ideas of leadership and the path he has chosen to follow. Finally, although *Knightriders* lacks the EC style of *The Crazies*, *Dawn of the Dead*, *Creepshow* and *Day of the Dead*, it does have a different type of comic strip precedent, namely *Prince Valiant* (1954), a film based on Hal Foster's well-known newspaper comic strip, and featuring Robert Wagner, Sterling Hayden, Janet Leigh and Victor McLaglen all articulating medieval roles in contemporary movie accents.

Similarly, *Knightriders* contains a mixture of different accents, ethnic groups, and characters from other medieval legends such as *Robin Hood*. Similarly, Sir Walter Scott's knightly romance *Ivanhoe* also incorporated Robin Hood and his Merry Men into his fictional narrative. Like other Arthurian adaptations, such as Mark Twain's *A Connecticut Yankee in King Arthur's Court*, it mixes various elements both medieval and modern in its own special way. While classical Hollywood cinema mixed American, English and Irish-American actors (such as William Bendix in the 1949 film version), Romero introduces Afro-American actors such as Ken Foree and Robert Williams into his version of King Arthur's court as well as Boston-accented Sir Ban (Marty Schiff) and Newark native Sir Hector (Ronald Carrier) into the team. He also changes gender, making Morgan male rather than female, includes a lesbian knightrider and incorporates figures such as Alan, Friar Tuck and Little John (now black, rather than white) from other heroic legends. Romero also borrows

Warner Shook's Pippin from the legend of Charlemagne (see Harty 1991: 15). These appropriations also evoke the many historically inaccurate borrowings Hollywood genre cinema often uses for specific works in the name of creative license.

Knightriders begins with lyrical shots of a forest located in a non-discernible time-period. A black bird arises in the distance during the second long shot of the forest landscape. A montage juxtaposition of images characteristic of Romero's editorial techniques in films such as *The Crazies* then follows. Swiftly edited cuts change from exterior images of the bird in flight to its own point-of-view perspectives of the landscape as it moves in rapid flight. Romero then concludes this introductory sequence with the bird's call appearing predominantly on the soundtrack. The next shot shows Billy waking up in response to its summons. As in *Jack's Wife* and Romero's other films, sound montage plays a significant role in this opening sequence. On the most basic level, the bird's cry wakes Billy up, but as in *Martin's* opening scene, levels of fantasy and reality intermingle. *Knightriders* seductively invites the audience to take an objective perspective by viewing the landscape and flight in realistic terms. However, the sound montage suggests that we, like Billy, have merely witnessed a dream. Whereas Martin attempts to persuade Cuda that there is really no magic anymore, the opening images of *Knightriders* reveal that fantasy and reality are both intertwined. But *Knightriders* reveals that a crucial difference exists between the tricks Martin employs to awaken Cuda away from his superstition and the fantasies they both adhere to in the earlier film. Like Martin, Billy is caught up in his own personal fantasy but in a less pathological manner than his cinematic predecessors. He is also a Don Quixote figure, yet unlike the original literary character, Billy has attracted an entire group to his vision, not just a solitary Sancho Panza figure, who readily acknowledge the differences between fantasy and everyday reality their leader wishes to avoid. Billy does recognise the differences. But he initially does not want to deal with them and stubbornly adheres to the values he personally holds until denial becomes impossible. Also, these differences are negotiated in several ways by various members of the Knightriders and not just one individual. Like all Romero's main characters, Billy has to recognise and come to terms with negative features within his own personality before advancing further into self-realisation.

After revealing Linet (Amy Ingersoll) at his side, the next shot shows Billy in a lake flagellating himself with a tree branch in a ritualistic manner. He appears like a medieval knight of old engaging in a purification ritual ceremony watched by his lady fair. The still naked Billy performs a ritual vow in the forest as he holds out his version of Excalibur. Billy then puts on his crown and armour and appears to ascend a steed. However, the camera reveals the steed to be a motorcycle and thus abruptly changes the audience's temporal perspective into modern rather than medieval times. In one sense, the magical illusion is broken. It is not real. However, Billy and Linet create their own form of magic in the twentieth-century world. Unlike Cuda and Martin who are dominated by adherence to old visions no longer relevant to their everyday world, Billy and Linet live their ideals but in a manner fully aware of the different world in which they exist.

After the credit sequence showing Billy and Linet riding on their motorcycle, the next scene shows the medieval fair where Billy's troupe actively prepare for the afternoon's jousting tournament. While Whiteface (John Amplas) entertains the crowds, other members of the group either sell wares or prepare for the forthcoming combat. Several scenes show troupe members such as Little John (Ken Foree) either working at an old blacksmith's forge or using modern Black and Decker tools. The individual group members combine medieval and modern practices in their work. Billy's group is a multi-ethnic community comprising different races and genders working together in a common cause often performing roles different from everyday social expectations. They represent the utopian ideals of the 1960s existing in a hostile universe threatening to disrupt their chosen life styles. Master of ceremonies Pippin (Warner Shook) is gay and initially uncertain of his sexual identity. Knightrider champion Rocky (Cynthia Adler) is a self-assured lesbian while the group's spiritual advisor Merlin (Brother Blue) is a middle-aged black man who is also a qualified doctor. Most group members embody opposites within their personalities, but they eventually come to terms with contradictions which might destroy them in everyday life. Others, such as Morgan (Tom Savini), Marhalt (Scott Reiniger) and the rest of his rebellious group will eventually face their personal dragons and overcome them without any outside interference from a leader figure. Like John T. Chance in *Rio Bravo*, Billy understands that salvation can only come from within after the experience of strong temptation. No friend can help another from dealing with their own personal dragons individually.

In contrast to most generic representatives, Little John is black (played by an actor familiar to audiences in his role of Peter from *Dawn of the Dead*). He is engaged in an interracial relationship that represents the logical consequences of Fran and Peter's 'last romantic-couple' symbolism which concludes Romero's previous film. After working on manufacturing jousting lances and other artifacts – 'Go in a little deeper. It's got to snap easy. We don't want anyone being killed out there ... This damn thing's solid ... The head's made out of rubber. This thing's got its own inertia' – he expresses concern over Morgan's heavy mace. Alan (Gary Lahti), the Sir Lancelot figure in the group, also feels uneasy about the damage it may inflict: 'We don't have to make it rougher than it already is.' Despite the arrogant and narcissistic attitudes expressed by Morgan, Billy later allows him to use the weapon in the belief that every member of his group must follow their own conscience.

In *Knightriders*, Romero paints a highly unflattering picture of certain audiences passively viewing the tournaments. Cynical, disdainful, often lusting for blood and belittling the efforts of performers, they appear as the director's depiction of those elements who view his films merely for visceral excitement and nothing else. Julie Dean's (Patricia Tallman) father, Lester (Jim Baffico) is little better than the 'fat slob' she describes him. His paternal role typifies the worst aspects of Romero's woman's nightmare which depict the patriarch as wife-batterer or economic cheat. Like Jack Mitchell in *Jack's Wife*, he beats up his wife and attempts to do the same to his daughter. Lester also tries to cheat one of the troupe by not paying for an item. Later, a slobbish 'hoagie man' and his wife (Stephen and Tabitha King) look on as the knights engage in dangerous combat. Like the popcorn guzzling, coke-swilling member of an average cinema audience, he disdainfully sneers at the knights, 'Acrobats. That's all that they are!' and later dismisses the injuries they suffer. He brags, 'It's a fake. It's all a fake. They have to make it look tough, look dangerous', after Billy suffers a dangerous neck injury in his conflict with Morgan. Immediately, after this comment Romero cuts to Julie gasping in shock at the real wound on one of the knights. This montage juxtaposition concisely expresses Romero's knowledge of the injuries stuntmen actually suffer during location shooting.

Billy's world uneasily attempts to juxtapose an idealistic visionary past world with the vulgar realm of the present. Yet it is not one involving the choice of a hopelessly anachronistic utopian retreat to the past by rejecting everything associated with the present. Prior to Pippin's introduction, heralds with medieval trumpets announce the day's events. As they blow their horns, Romero cuts to inside the tent, revealing tape players with the appropriate music. This particular act of demystification not only continues *Martin*'s project of showing that not everything is magic but also self-reflexively reveals elements associated with the cinematic apparatus to the informed viewer. As if imitating an everyday occurrence on location when a knob falls off the sound system rendering the equipment useless, the heralds resort to improvising the sound of trumpets. Billy's magic is actually physically created, but the real point involves how that technology is used. Similarly, Billy's knightriders are not merely engaged in a spectacular performance for viewer pleasure but are professionally involved in something they regard as a vocation rather than a day's entertainment. The knightriders all participate in a philosophy they sincerely believe in. It is designed to promote an idealistic world of a medieval honour missing from contemporary life, but they also utilise modern aspects of technology to further their vision. In many ways, it is akin to Romero's own ideals; his films add up to much more than zombies, gore and special effects. Romero's aims may not be those of Billy's but they contain an affinity of spirit.

Referring to T. H. White's *The Once and Future King*, Pippin announces the heroic ideals of the day's events: 'I, through magic, says who may honour the king ... a knight's fighting skills are the symbol of that hero ... to the future may nobility also reign.' However, few of the audience feel such noble ideas. Prior to the performance, Deputy Sheriff Cook (Michael Moran) hustles for a bribe and threatens to close the show down in a manner possibly reflecting Romero's own experience during film locations. While Morgan sees the need to compromise, Billy vehemently refuses and articulates the group's ideals: 'We're not paying. It's wrong to pay this scum off, Morgan. He's not going to shut us down. He's not going to do shit.' Despite Alan's reservations concerning Billy's fitness to engage in combat, he accepts Morgan's challenge and falls in battle (as he has on previous occasions). This necessitates the knightriders coming to his rescue before the opponent makes him yield. While the combat becomes more dangerous and Billy's wounds more life-threatening, the hoagie man merely sneers 'It's a fake. It's all a fake...' after Morgan's blows just miss piercing Billy's artery.

After the contest, a close-up of an owl introduces the sequence of Billy's debate with Merlin while his injuries are attended to. It complements the images of the black bird associated with Billy in the film's opening scenes. Both men appear as complementary soul brothers. In White's novel, Merlin's constant companion is an owl named Archimedes. Although both believe in the values of the troupe and their recreated world of Arthurian magic, Merlin is more aligned with the spiritual values of wisdom rather than Billy's fascination with the dark side of a destiny he appears pathologically driven towards. While Billy is obsessive in his goals, Merlin is more balanced and omniscient. The two men represent competing tensions within the mind of anyone assuming a leadership position. Balance and objectivity are important concepts in Romero's films, yet not everyone is capable of reaching this combination and Billy is as mentally divided as other central characters in Romero's films. He tells Merlin of his dream involving the Black Bird. Merlin attempts to draw Billy away from pessimistic forebodings by suggesting the dreams result from his various wounds. Billy then counters his friend's balanced counselling by suggesting that he should follow the very solipsistic ideals which contaminate both Martin and Cuda, 'You're supposed to believe in those things.' However, Merlin replies both by affirming his belief in magic and by suggesting that material and mental causes often govern the operation of magical principles rather than arbitrary forces of destiny:

> If I didn't believe in magic, I'd still be treating gall bladders, prosthetics, and stuff like that. See magic ain't got nothing to do with organs and glands and broken necks. Maybe it's got to do with soul, man. Only the soul's got destiny, it got wings, it can fly. That's magic.

Although Billy gravitates towards the arbitrary nature of events and relies too much on supernatural mysticism, Merlin gently attempts to make him see that he is also responsible for his own beliefs, present circumstances and future destiny. This is a lesson various characters in *There's Always Vanilla* and *Jack's Wife* never learn. Despite Billy and Merlin's belief in the magical nature of the world they inhabit, it is Merlin who articulates Romero's key belief in human responsibility and the capacity for making changes rather than submitting to supposedly arbitrary forces of destiny. When Billy comments, 'You see things before they happen', Merlin rejects any mystical abilities: 'That's probability. Some things are just sure to happen, seeing them coming is nothing.' Billy still clings to the arbitrary nature of predestination: 'You taught me too good, magician. You taught me to believe that black bird is going to get me.' Merlin replies, 'You'll make it happen yourself.' He emphasises factors of 'probability' and Billy's tendencies towards dropping his guard and allowing destiny to get him, something which does happen in the concluding segment of the film. When Billy submissively comments, 'Maybe, that's my destiny', Merlin dismisses it and refers to Malory's tale of Arthur's attempt to avoid his destiny. He thus counters Billy's pessimism and affirms the possibility for individual change. But one arbitrary circumstance does hinder such a possibility. Merlin suggests that there are certain things beyond human control. But he also denies the dubious comforts arising from masochistic submission to these factors. For Merlin, 'destiny' is really a 'big deal!' 'Probability' is the more important factor in both his and Romero's universe. It is thus highly 'probable' that Billy's self-destructive behaviour will lead to his future 'destiny' in much the same way as the actions of characters in the divided environments of *Night of the Living Dead* and *Dawn of the Dead* lead to eventual doom. Similarly,

Roger's refusal to listen to Peter's admonitions and David's egotistic desires in the latter film also lead to their downfall.

Once Billy recovers, he walks outside Merlin's tent to the relief of all concerned. But he refuses to autograph a photo of himself on a motorcycle for a little boy significantly named Billy (Chris Jessel) on the grounds of contributing to the media hype he wishes to avoid: 'I'm sorry. I don't like this kind of stuff. I can't. This is Evel Knievel. It's got nothing to do with what we're doing.' Young Billy, sadly but intuitively, understands the reasons. However, as well as neglecting to see the sincerity behind his request, Billy loses sight of the fact that the young boy genuinely needs a seriously heroic role model in a world where such types are now lacking. It would not have cost him anything to compromise his beliefs in view of the nature of the request. However, at this point of time, Billy is both inflexible and rigid. Ironically, Morgan gratuitously seizes the opportunity to donate an autograph 'from the next king', an honour he would have gained had Billy's knights not ridden to their leader's rescue.

Billy's personal problems also resemble those of Tom Dunson in Howard Hawks' *Red River* (1948). Suffering from the decline of his former youthful prowess and affected by physical infirmities, Billy stubbornly adheres to his own rigid principles and ignores the concerns of those around him. When he returns outside, Alan criticises Billy's unconscious masochistic desires, 'What were you doing over there, man. It looked like you wanted him to smash you. I mean ... you didn't have to do it.' Linet similarly condemns his behaviour in the following sequence. She notes that Billy is no solitary individual and his actions have consequences for those who decide to follow him. She points out, 'Everyone has made a conscious adult decision to be here. When you're crazy, you make them think about that decision. You have to...' Billy fills in her concluding word, '... compromise'.

Like Wayne in *Red River*, Billy similarly refuses to listen to Linet's version of 'You was wrong, Mr Dunson.' He adheres to his way of doing things while she attempts to make him see reason in the best manner of Romero's affirmative female characters such as Fran and Sarah: 'Change doesn't have to mean compromise. You're bigger now. Things are different. Publicity helps the overhead by bringing in more crowds.' However, like a horror film director assailed by producers and audiences for not delivering enough gore, Billy criticises the crowds who attend his spectacles: 'More suckerheaded American driftwood who can't tell the difference between me and James Jones ... or Charles Manson or the Great Wallenda. Even that kid thinks I'm Evel Knievel!' Although Julie's father, the hoagie man and the later crowd lusting for blood in Kansas support Billy's critique, this is not true for everyone as Linet correctly asserts: 'That kid thinks you're Billy Davis. Sir William the knight. You're his hero.' However, Billy is too caught up in his own personal dilemmas at this point in the film and cannot really discriminate between those who deserve his condemnation and others who really appreciate his ideals. He sticks to a rigid form of leadership and loyally accompanies Bagman (Don Berry) to jail after Deputy Cook plants an incriminating bag of marijuana in his trailer rather than accepting Morgan's pragmatic advice to pay off the corrupt official. Although Billy's stand is admirable in one sense, it is also futile. During the jail scene, he has to watch impotently while Cook batters his friend to a bloody pulp.

All Billy's troupe have made a conscious decision to join him in a low income existence. His world offers them the possibility to be themselves whether gay (Pippin), lesbian (Rocky), or harmoniously living in an interracial relationship (Little John) the very nature of which receives no comment whatsoever. Julie Dean decides to join this community with Alan and leave her battered mother (Iva Jean Saraceni) who is last seen poignantly framed and trapped in the domestic prison of her kitchen like the archetypal victim of a classical Hollywood melodrama. However, Billy's community is not totally inclusive. It really involves a rigorous form of apprenticeship in which any outsider has to earn the privilege of acceptance as Julie will later discover.

After Billy and Bagman's release from prison, they both debate the nature of compromise with the world outside. Their agent Steve (Ken Hixon), who negotiates their bookings, tells them that their low-budget independent status prevents him from negotiating higher fees. Speaking like a conscientious guerrilla film-maker, Billy is reluctant to contaminate his art by demeaning it to the status of a mere 'act' and 'setting up with fancy new costumes and cycle manufacturers'. His dialogue foreshadows what would happen to most films in the 1980s which became mere conglomerate 'movies' linked with concession stands and specially-scripted scenes to feature corporate-sponsored products. However, the dragon Billy fights involves not just his personal demons but also the hard realities facing any independent venture no matter how idealistic its origins. Steve cogently comments about Billy's business practices which parallel Romero's organisation before Richard Rubinstein's involvement:[8] 'You take on any long hair who knows how to make sandals. Do you know the price of hamburgers? Two by fours? So you want to pick up the Blue Cross tabs?' Although Billy fears the dangers of commercialism, Steve attempts to move Billy away from his idealistic superstructure towards the hard economic realities of the actual base factor determining everyday existence: 'It's money, Billy. It's all got to do with money. Money makes the world go round, even your world.'

However, Billy rejects Steve's picture of a *homo economicus* model which would increasingly dominate the world of the 1980s and 1990s and beyond. He affirms an ideal whose spirit dominates most of Romero's work:

> No. It's just getting too tough. It's tough to live by the code. It's real hard to live for something you believe in. People try and they get tired of their diets, their exercises, their marriage or their kids or their jobs or themselves. Or they get tired of their God. You can keep all the money you make off this sick world. I don't want any part of it. Anybody who wants to live for themselves don't belong with us. Let them go out and buy some pimp psychiatric paperback which says it's O.K. Don't ask me to say O.K. It's not O.K. by me.

Bagman makes a counter-argument from his own experience. He tells Billy of his earlier existence as a Civil Rights agitator in the South. After suffering from a brutal beating in jail and experiencing bad depression associated with that incident, he nearly committed suicide 'because of what was all around me'. However, he was able to laugh off Moran's brutal beating because 'I'm now in Camelot'. Like Steve, he attempts to show Billy an alternative direction pointing out the two paths they all face:

Truth and justice and the American way of life. That's got to take a back seat to staying alive. Man, you can have the most beautiful ideals in the world. [Cut to Billy thinking.] But when you die, your ideals are going to die with you. The important thing is staying together and we've got to keep the troupe together and if keeping the troupe together means that we have to take this practical way then I suggest let's take it and get some sleep.

Romero gives equal screen time to Steve and Bagman's arguments. They appear rational in recognising a world of everyday reality which sometimes involves compromise. However, despite the excessive idealism dominating Billy's character, later events do prove Billy correct. The machinations of sleazy promoter Bontempi (Martin Ferrero) and his contemporary Morgan Le Fay associate Sheila (Amanda Davies) corrupt and nearly destroy the troupe. Finally, Billy's ideals do live on after his death as the concluding scenes of *Knightriders* reveal.

After contemplating Bagman's arguments, Billy looks at Bontempi's Silver Bullet business card, crumples it, and tosses it into the fire. He wakes up Bagman and denies there are two different paths, affirms the fact that ideals do not die with the person who holds them, and rides out to counter the commercial dragon in the person of Bontempi threatening his troupe: 'The troupe is the code. I can't let people walk on that idea, I can't.'

Despite his wounds, Billy rides at night and finally arrives at his troupe's Kansas location, angrily criticising an undemocratic meeting like a demented and tired Tom Dunson in *Red River*. He finds Tuck, wearing a revealing horned-devil's cap, enjoying the pleasures of Sheila's corpulent photographer Judy (Maureen Sadusk). Billy finally storms away after throwing a take-away pizza (another symbol of a commercial world) at Bontempi's trendy clothes. Upset at the troupe's disobeying his order to remain at their previous Pennsylvania location, Billy becomes more moody and angry. He now begins to doubt his cherished ideals. His leadership ability becomes more questionable. Although Linet criticises his attitude and their developing alienation, she does recognise the change he has brought to her life. Once, giving up on fantasy, she became attracted to Billy not his 'dream'. However, despite speaking affirmatively of their two years together as King and Queen, Linet now sees the importance of his vision: 'I don't know if its because of you Billy. But I'm here.' An ideal certainly lives on after the death of a relationship in her case as the climax of *Knightriders* will show.

The Kansas tournament represents the beginning of the end for Billy's leadership. It also reveals the initial appearance of a corruption which seriously threatens the entire troupe. Despite the absence of Julie's father and the hoagie man, the Kansas audience appear more grotesque and bloodthirsty than their Pennsylvanian counterparts. Lacking any awareness of the knightriders' dedication to their art and the nobility of their ideals, they gaze atavistically at the combat, roar for blood, or bop like mindless zombies when the PA system accidentally plays a crude rock number, 'Let's get it up'. Although one member of the troupe speaks positively about 'that spiritual feeling' motivating the majority, others are ready to sell out. The narcissistic Morgan decides to form his breakaway group, sign a contract with Bontempi and become king in his own way: 'I don't want his crown. It's a crown of thorns.' But Billy will soon face another avatar of his destiny.

When Morgan rode through a small Kansas town, one shot showed him filling the frame after Sheila tempted him with commercial stardom. When Morgan rides out of the frame, the camera reveals a silent Indian (Albert Amerson) watching the procession. Both figures are instrumental in fulfilling Billy's destiny. While Morgan is the future king, the Indian represents the death-wish destiny Billy has so eagerly pursued. The Indian appears melodramatically in a dust storm caused by the motor-cycle. He wears an emblem depicting a black bird. Despite Alan's reservations and attempts to prevent him fighting, the still-wounded Billy rides out to meet his opponent: 'If I refuse to fight. I have to yield.' Despite further injuries, Billy defeats his opponent and forces him to yield. A beautifully composed shot reveals blood dripping from Billy's body along his blade which falls on the Indian's bird emblem. It will be Billy's last heroic moment of glory. But, like his predecessors, Billy is the injured sacred king who will soon lose his authority according to the Arthurian legend and Golden Bough philosophy he espouses.

Billy later watches in sadness as Morgan's associates, Alan, Julie and Bors (Harold Wayne Jones) ride away from the troupe. But he believes they will be back. Although arrogant and one-dimensional in his ideals, Billy also recognises his flaws. In one scene, he attempts to apologise for his neglect of the loyal members of his team due to his focus upon the 'lost sheep'. However, like Linet's recognition of Billy's lasting influence, his musician friend shrugs off the apology and replies, 'Man, you gave us everything. You gave us a chance.'

The world outside offers no sanctuary for either Morgan's knightriders or Alan's group. Despite sampling the affluent life of Washington D.C., Morgan finds himself the degrading object of a sleazy photo shoot with his surplus associates such as Tuck and Judy liable to Bontempi's ruthless business 'termination' policies. Initially attracted by Bontempi's comparison of his breakaway knightriders to a pop group – 'The smaller the group, the greater the profits' – he finds this vision realised in a manner he never envisaged when he returns one night to find his associates fighting and trashing a hotel room in a manner similar to the exploits of The Who's drummer Keith Moon. Alan decides to visit some married friends who have chosen to live out in the country. But he finds their domestic bliss empty in relation to what he has experienced as a member of Billy's group. As with Julie's parents, the marital ideal appears deficient in comparison to the democratic life of Billy's troupe where marriage and domesticity appear conspicuous by their very absence (or, at least, non-mention). Alan appears bored as they sit at a table dominated by a huge fast-food corporate carton. Bors begins an artificial impersonation of Marlon Brando's acting, the imitative nature of which contrasts sharply with his active prowess as a knightrider. Julie sits lethargically by a pool, her attention focused on earphones, and calling to Alan like a bored housewife, 'Let's party!' The following scene abruptly shows Alan delivering an incomprehensible Julie back to her parents at night. It initially appears callous on Alan's part.

But the action is much more complex and does not deserve Pauline's Kael's condescending and inaccurate comments concerning Julie having a 'legitimate gripe' since Alan 'seems to remember that it's Lancelot's destiny to love the queen'.[9] This remark typifies Kael's usual inability to read a scene in its appropriate cinematic context; Alan's action has nothing to do with his supposed destiny as Lancelot. Unlike Linet, Julie has not developed into understanding the significant nature of Billy's ideals which motivate Alan and others. She, instead, remains on the level of indulging in a relationship which is little better than a 'fling'. Julie shows no sign of any deeper awareness of the type of society which has allowed her access. She does not understand what the knightriders really represent in terms of their appropriation of Howard Hawks' professional code. As a result, she is 'no good'. Ironically, Julie finally realises this as Alan and Bors ride away and the light in her parents home switches on. She mouths 'oh fuck', realising that she has blown it. Her position resembles that of Gent in *Only Angels Have Wings* (1939) whose reluctance to undertake a mission leads to his expulsion from the professional group. The Hawksian associations also apply to Billy's rival; Morgan's character parallels that of fallen heroes such as Bat in *Only Angels Have Wings*, Dude in *Rio Bravo* and J. P. Harrah in *El Dorado*. Like the latter two characters, Morgan has temporarily fallen due to the machinations of Sheila's 'no good' woman. Although she never arrives on a stagecoach and promptly leaves like her unseen predecessors in *Rio Bravo* and *El Dorado*, she uses and abuses Morgan for commercial purposes. Once Morgan discovers that his bodily presence merely represents a temporary holiday away from her permanent boyfriend, his eyes become open. Like his fallen Hawksian predecessors, Morgan redeems himself by returning to the fold and eventually inheriting his leader's mantle.

Alan reunites with Morgan and the lost sheep all return home. The knightriders then decide to engage in their chosen activities for their eyes only without any intrusive and uncomprehending audience present to demean the nature of their personal ritual battles. Billy enjoys the dedication they all show in their skills and then decides to resign his crown to Morgan. He significantly experiences a final pleasure in seeing his group return without any prompting on his behalf. As with his earlier decision over Morgan's mace, Billy has left decisions to their own collective conscience. Aware of his morality, Linet's feelings for Alan, and the fact that his ideals will outlive him, he leaves after saying poignant farewells, especially to his spiritual mentor Merlin, 'I love you'. Billy then rides away followed by the Indian he has knighted.

Before Billy can die, he has to perform two more heroic deeds. He returns to Pennsylvania, finds Moran gorging himself on junk food in a fast-food establishment and punishes his adversary, gaining the applause of everyone inside. As with the earlier junk food reference in *Knightriders*, this act seems a self-conscious ironic deed from a director who has commented elsewhere on the 'McDonaldization of America'.[10] Billy defeats another dragon and the applause of the audience suggests some hope for the future. He then makes amends with young Billy, entering his schoolroom, and presenting him with a symbol of a heroic ideal – his own Excalibur. His body increasingly bloodstained, Billy rides away followed by his Indian companion. Both pass a sign marking Gettysburg Park. Like the previous sequence showing Billy riding past the model of a crow's head as the camera pans left to show a truck with a grille resembling a winged bird passing the camera, this emblem is symbolic in more than one sense. Gettysburg was one of the bloodiest battles in the Civil War in which the South, with its emblems of chivalry and nobility, suffered a crushing defeat. But it was also the site of Lincoln's Gettysburg address which looked forward to the end of the Civil War and the eventual reunification of North and South. The dying Billy rides to his destiny and finally achieves his cherished ideal of seeing himself in a vision as a medieval knight riding a real horse before a heavy truck kills him. Although Billy's fate may appear pessimistic, his death finally reunites the Knightriders in a poignant climactic scene in a cemetery. As a gentle rain falls, the lyrics of a song, 'I'd Rather Be a Wanderer', pronounce the knightrider ideal of community, professionalism and chosen exile in an increasingly contaminated and commercial world.

The knightriders have experienced their own version of a Civil War. But they become reunited and much stronger in their ideals thanks to Billy's vision and his symbolic sacrifice on their behalf. Morgan wears the crown. But he will also bear the burden of Billy's crown of thorns as well as the poignant responsibility of leadership characterising Hawksian heroes in *The Dawn Patrol* and *Only Angels Have Wings*. As a black bird symbolising Billy's spirit watches from a tree, the knightriders led by Morgan now ride away to face new challenges and the world outside which will continually threaten their existence but one which they will attempt to overcome in each new contest.

Knightriders is a highly personal and sincere film revealing Romero's utopian ideals in a cinematically allegorical manner. Although flawed by its long running time and some over-emphatic dialogue scenes, it is nonetheless one of the director's major achievements which deserves better recognition. The film is somewhat idealistic and sentimental and represents a complete contrast to its more commercially successful predecessor. However, despite its formal problems, *Knightriders* is as close as any Romero film may be to the articulation of the goals which inspired the director throughout his career. The fictional knightriders represent a type of community composed of individuals who succeed in continuing their different forms of 1960s idealism as opposed to those lost souls in *There's Always Vanilla* who have spiritually failed. They also embody the type of attitude seen in Romero's own ideas of a film-making community who form an alliance, break apart and then recombine to continue practicing the very ideals which brought them together in the first place. *Knightriders* may not have the visceral appeal of the zombie trilogy, but it is a crucial film in understanding the necessary type of alternative the human survivors actually need.

CHAPTER NINE

Creepshow

Scripted by Stephen King, *Creepshow* deliberately attempted to appropriate cinematically the visual style of EC Comics. The film promised to be the beginning of a collaboration between the two authors which would eventually lead to a film version of *The Stand*.[1] Romero and King both knew that the EC comic tradition had been a significant influence on American popular culture both in terms of alternative images of the Cold War era and its satirical and subversive views of a conformist world.[2] As Ron Hansen noted, Romero shared EC's ironic treatment of fantastic situations ever since *Night of the Living Dead.* Hansen also quoted director of photography Michael Gornick's observations concerning the similarities: 'Aside, from the physical differences here, the lighting affectations and so forth, I think much of the way I normally shoot and George's style of shot selection and cutting pretty much lend themselves to the comic-book format. The overall feel has always been with us.'[3]

However, although condemned by critics such as Robin Wood (who had no knowledge of the EC Comic tradition) as representing the worst of both King and Romero in 'a series of nasty anecdotes in which nasty people do nasty things to other nasty people, the nastiness being the entire point and purpose' (1986: 191), and Michael Sragow as a film indulging in 'gross-out',[4] *Creepshow* is much more complicated than its detractors assume.

At the same time, it is by no means successful. Ironically, like *Knightriders*, the emphatic depiction of ideas cherished by the author by no means guarantees the commercial success of the finished product. Explicitness does not necessary guarantee the creative expression of authorial ideals. Both *The Crazies* and *Dawn of the Dead* combine selected elements of EC style with allegorical messages. But if style dominates substance, the message may get lost amidst visual excessiveness. Such a danger affects *Dawn of the Dead* whose significant levels of meaning may be deliberately ignored by an audience wishing to dwell consciously on the gross-out factor and become little better than Stephen King's slobbish hoagie man from *Knightriders*. But a key analysis of the text may reveal other elements in operation which counter certain indulgent aspects of audience reception.

However, *Creepshow* problematically relies too much on knowledge of the important cultural EC traditions which few outside America may be aware of. Like *Night of the Living Dead* and *Dawn of the Dead*, 'common sense' associations concerning the supposedly trivial nature of comic strip representations may hinder appropriate understanding of relevant structural operations and drown out other significant levels of meaning. At the same time, it is not an entirely 'gross-out' production or a 'feeble echo of the Amicus omnibus series'.[5] On the one hand, *Creepshow* may represent a cultural indicator of a work appealing to the slob factor where 'the lowest common denominator isn't a term of derision but an admirable goal' (Sragow 1982: 48). If the film is seen entirely in terms of terrifying the viewer by the 'gross-out' factor then this interpretation is relevant. However, other meanings are also present within its cinematic structure.

The 'gross-out' factor also affected EC Comics. These culturally marginalised productions also contained important allegorical messages within their versions of 'gross-out'. Both EC Comics and Stephen King's writings put their respective audiences in touch with the 'nightmare anxieties' of youth, which are often socially based. The youthful readers of EC comics certainly noticed the differences between perception of real-life injustices and the hypocritical activities of the adult world. Vulnerable before the dominant hold of adults and parents, 1950s children often retreated into a fantasy realm where social justice would prevail in forms different from the realistic level of everyday existence. However adults, as well as children, formed a key component of EC comic readership, a fact the film's epilogue significantly notes. The work of artists on war comics such as *Two Fisted Tales* as well as those other comic strips featuring narratives dealing with American outbreaks of lynching and anti-semitism in the pre-Civil Rights era would certainly have offended Cold War censorship forces. Ron Hansen noticed *Creepshow*'s embodiment of that recovered sense of childhood's certainties, of what is good and what is evil and of just desserts, and quotes producer Richard Rubinstein:

> I think George has always regarded fantasy and horror as basically allegorical, and that's something he has in common even with Grimm's fairy tales. He says it's a way of doing morality plays and still remaining commercial. You look at these stories in *Creepshow*, and it's sin and retribution in almost every case. (1982: 76)

Romero and King's publicised desires to 'just go for scares' may have hindered audiences recognising other significant ways in which *Creepshow* operates.[6] A close analysis of the film reveals EC's morality-play discourse as well as other associations appearing in Romero's films. Although admittedly a minor part of Romero's work and revealing his lack of fear of competing with the mainstream, *Creepshow* contains qualities which necessitate a second viewing. Yet they are not enough to furnish claims for regarding it as an unjustly neglected work; *Creepshow* is certainly far below the level of Romero's better work. It represents an attempt to play explicitly with a formative cultural tradition revered by the author, but Romero had also achieved significant results elsewhere and really did not need the collaboration of Stephen King. Despite King's screenplay employing elements common to his horror fiction and film adaptations (see Williams 1996: 238–49), Romero had achieved better results elsewhere.

Like the opening scene of *The Crazies*, the film begins with a long shot of a family home at night. Off-screen sounds of domestic dissension occur on the soundtrack. An angry father (Tom Atkins) screams at his young child: 'I never saw such rotten crap in my life ... I told you before I didn't want you to read this stuff anymore.' After a mid-shot of the house brings the viewer further into this harmonious world of family values, Romero abruptly changes to an interior shot framed by a low-angle close-up from young Billy's (Joe King) perspective as his father brutally hits him for reading 'Creepshow', a comic book in the EC tradition. As in *Night of the Living Dead*, Romero intercuts images of animal heads on the walls to emphasise the fearful nature of this family home during certain moments. Mother (Iva Jean Saraceni) attempts to intervene criticising her husband for hiding 'girlie' books. Played by the same actress who portrayed the battered wife and mother in *Knightriders*, this mother's intervention is also ineffective as her husband continues to chastise Billy: 'Not only do I find he's reading this crap but he's a damn little sneak as well.' Romero then associates rapid montage cuts of animal heads in his familiar manner of equating the so-called civilised domestic world to the savage natural world human beings have supposedly evolved from. The animal imagery is also an oblique reference to the naturalist tradition appearing throughout Romero's work. Despite Billy's denials, the father asserts his patriarchal authority by threatening further violence and throwing his son's comic into the garbage bin. After he sends Billy up to his room, father brushes off his wife's concerns: 'Don't you think you are a little hard on him?' He counters by critiquing his son's fascination with the grotesque imagery of contemporary comic books, 'Do you want your son to read that?'

However, by depicting the father slouching on a couch and grasping a full whisky glass as he pompously asserts his parental rights, 'That's why God made fathers', Romero brings to viewer attention the contrast between appearance and reality which structures *Creepshow*'s entire narrative. As well as hypocritically denying his own retreat into fantasy, the father asserts dominance of a patriarchal world of normality within everyday life wherein 'father knows best'. He also asserts religious authority for his activities which rely both on violence and female domestic subordination for their operation. However, although his pronouncements concerning family life seem to represent the way things appear to be, they are also based in reality upon the savage exercise of patriarchal violence which the father and mother would deny as being an operational control mechanism of everyday life. Furthermore, although his punitive activities now appear to us as untenable, they are a fundamental part of everyday existence, one both based upon denial and the repression of any imaginative alternatives to everyday life. Deprived of any positive outlet for his imagination, Billy curses his father for throwing away his comic book: 'I hope you rot in hell.' Billy is alone in his bedroom which is dominated by horror film artefacts such as a poster of

Bela Lugosi as Dracula and various monster toys. Living in his world of EC comics, Billy imaginatively evokes a decaying figure who actually typifies the reality of the grotesque world he inhabits as a little boy existing in a family world of supposed normality. The figure also represents his revenge on a hypocritical adult world.

Billy conjures up the Creepshow host outside his window whom he welcomes with great pleasure. When the screen images change from real to comic strip representations, 'the Creep' retrieves Billy's comic book from the trashcan by a camera movement impossible in real life but possible within the imaginative realms of animation and comic strip fantasy. The credits roll before the pages magically turn to the first story which, more than coincidentally, is titled 'Father's Day'. Like the old EC comics, *Creepshow* will present the viewer with five separate stories interspersed with adverts and other matters. They are both stories remembered by Billy and displayed to the audience as well as narratives influenced by the EC 'moral tales' tradition concerning the punishment inflicted on representatives of an errant everyday world of normality by avatars of the fantastic. Both *Creepshow* and the EC comic tradition utilise the horror tradition of the 'return of the repressed' whereby signifiers of the injustices perpetuated by the world of normality return in a distorted, corrupted and decaying form to avenge themselves upon the representatives of a normal, but corrupt, world. These horrific signifiers are by no means 'real' but they represent the wish-fulfilment victory of a fantastic world whose appearance contradicts a world of everyday appearance whose supposed normality may be more corrupt than anything represented in a horror comic. In *Creepshow*, the worlds of appearance and reality conflate in the same manner as the introductions and conclusions of each individual tale – by moving from a comic strip style to reality and back again. Veteran EC Comic artist Jack Kamen provided the opening 'splash page' for each of the five stories as well as the concluding graphic image when the story dissolves away from live action.

'Father's Day' begins with a clock chiming inside the Grantham mansion with family members gathered reluctantly for their celebration of the day their greataunt Bedelia (Viveca Lindfors) murdered her senile father seven years before. Like Barbara and Johnny's visit to the graveyard in *Night of the Living Dead*, it is a ritual they have no real feeling for. But, as Aunt Sylvia (Carrie Nye) explains, it is a ritual dominated by hopes of inheritance, a motivation binding the disparate family members of Richard Grantham (Warner Shook), his sister Cass (Elizabeth Regan) and her husband Hank Blaine (Ed Harris) together despite the evident fact that they hate the sight of each other. The Grantham's annual Father's Day family dinner never intends to honour a beloved father figure. It is rather to celebrate the fact that the 'old bastard' is dead. Every year since his death, Aunt Bedelia makes an annual pilgrimage to his grave to wallow in guilt. As Silvia comments, 'You can set your watch by her', a comment which relates both to the clock introducing the interior sequence as well as the lifeless, mechanical, ritualistic living dead patterns of behaviour they all follow. When introducing Bedelia, Romero employs a visual tradition associated with EC Comics by using two adjacent framed strips lying on top of a rectangular one showing her in freeze frame. Then the image tilts to fill the screen with the rectangular shot which then reveals its occupant in motion smoking an exaggerated, but highly ironic large phallic cigar. It is almost as if Bedelia is little better than a frozen corpse who becomes reanimated to participate in a meaningless ritual pattern of behaviour. The snobbishly British-accented Silvia begins her off-screen voiceover narrative telling both family members and audience about past history. As Silvia relates the family tale, the film moves into flashback visually reproducing the stylistic techniques of EC comics by framing the past events in stylistically askew angles and presenting its characters imitating the grotesque Delsarte-type expressions typical of 1950s comic reproductions and 'non-realistic' acting traditions.[7] The characters are exaggerated for a particular purpose since the grotesque world presents a dark Gothic reflection of the supposedly clean world of everyday normality. During the quick flashback neither Jon Lormer's Nathan Grantham nor Viveca Lindfors' Aunt Bedelia are meant to represent real people, as the distancing nature of the antique gold frame bearing the caption 'Seven years earlier...' signifies.

As the dislocatingly framed images of the past unfold, Silvia describes Bedelia's father as being 'possessively jealous' of his daughter 'all her life, a complete Freudian relationship'. This latter remark certainly contradicts Romero's often-repeated disavowals concerning the psychoanalytic significance of his work. 'Father's Day' is not only a Freudian horror tale but a reworking of ideas previously seen in *Night of the Living Dead*. Although scripted by King, the film is Romero's and may bear traces of his involvement in the screenplay. This is particularly so in terms of the symbiotic relationship between the warring family within the house and the external threat existing outside. Although the Granthams do not resort to physical violence like Harry Cooper in *Night of the Living Dead*, their aggression takes the form of verbal sniping and humiliating remarks against each other, a behaviour pattern metaphorically paralleling cannibalism.

The flashback continues to show the death of Bedelia's 75-year-old suitor Yarbro (Peter Messer) in a hunting accident arranged by Nathan and the incessant verbal aggression practiced by the father against his beleaguered daughter: 'Where's my cake, Bedelia? I want my cake you fucking bitch.' As he angrily repeats his demand for his 'Father's Day' cake, Nathan's desires parallel Freudian repetition compulsion mechanism symptomatic of unhealthy neurotic patterns of behaviour. After preventing the departure of his daughter by ensuring his continued possession of her in the family's Gothic mansion, he articulates his incestuous feelings by repeatedly emphasising the need for oral satisfaction that is little better than cannibalism. As in Romero's zombie trilogy, cannibalism, possession and pathological behaviour of the bourgeois family are all intertwined. Nathan's further comments also articulate the avaricious nature of a deeply dysfunctional family relationship based upon verbal aggression: 'Bedelia, you bitch. You're just like the others, you're really like that band of vultures.' Despite the grotesque nature of the visual and acting devices employed in this sequence, 'Father's Day' is much more a Romero morality play than the redundant copying of the EC style Stephen King believes it to be. With no avenue of escape, Bedelia reacts against the possessive hold of her father – 'Where's my cake? I'm your father. You're supposed to take care of me' – by murdering him.

She stabs her father repeatedly like Norman Bates in the *Psycho* shower scene, venting her repressed sexual frustrations against the oppressor whose equally thwarted desires take the form of verbal abuse. As family maid Mrs Danvers (Nan Mogg) overhears the deadly event, Romero intercuts the murder scene with his characteristic use of animal head jump cuts.[8] They symbolise those dark, primeval features still dormant within the human psyche no matter how 'civilised' certain environments may appear. They may include the Norman Rockwell farmhouse interior of *Night of the Living Dead*, the consumerist mall paradise of *Dawn of the Dead*, Billy's 1950s family home in the prologue or Nathan's rich Gothic mansion. Bedelia's comments made during her repeated stabbing of her father are revealing. They link together various associated themes of incestuous desires, possessiveness and the traditional family's role of transmitting the psychopathological nature of so-called 'instinctual' behaviour which civilisation transmits from one generation to the next: 'You screwed it all up. You screwed-up my mother. You screwed up me. You called me a bitch ... You taught Silvia. You taught us all.'

The narrative returns to the present showing Bedelia by her father's grave. Her life is now reduced to bearing the burden of oppressive family guilt and dependence upon civilisation's narcotic remedies for unhappiness such as smoking and hard liquor. Bedelia now faces the return of her father from the grave. Emerging as a disintegrating corpse in classic EC tradition, Nathan (John Amplas) also follows the pathological nature of repetition-compulsive patterns of behaviour he exhibited in life by once again expressing patriarchal acquisitiveness: 'Where's my cake, Bedelia? I want my cake. It's Father's Day, Bedelia. I want my cake.' He then strangles her.

The next image shows the clock chiming inside the Grantham mansion. Cass and Hank dance to rock music while Richard and Silvia look on in disdain. Noting Bedelia's absence, the quartet bicker before Hank decides to go and look for her. Striking his match on a cherub headstone, an action paralleling Johnny's irreverence in the opening sequence of *Night of the Living Dead*), Hank discovers Bedelia's discarded whiskey bottle, and drinks from it before Nathan's appearance causes him to fall into the grave. In an act of poetic justice, Nathan's headstone falls on Hank and crushes him.

Inside the house, the remaining family members remark on Hank and Bedelia's absence and wish to begin their Father's Day meal of ham. Cass, significantly, wishes to fulfil two appetites. She has married Hank for his stud qualities and wishes to engage in her own form of consumerist pleasure: 'I want him and I want my dinner. I'm hungry.' The possessive cannibalism linking the Granthams again returns with a vengeance. Silvia decides to look for Hank. Her dialogue also suggests her wish to fill another type of appetite: 'I'll go and get him. He's such a sweet guy.' However, when she reaches the kitchen she discovers Mrs Danvers' dead body, the head of which is framed in a circular window, intimating Silvia's own fate as the nominal head of the Grantham family. She is also a person whose avaricious nature benefited from Nathan's earlier education. Bedelia once commented to her father, 'You taught Silvia.' Ironically, father now returns from the grave to possess the daughter figure whose avariciousness matches his own. Repeating once more the phrase, 'I want my cake', he twists Silvia's head off.

'Father's Day' concludes in an appropriately grotesque manner. Cass and Richard go in search of Silvia and discover traces of Nate's gory activities in the kitchen. Nate then triumphantly appears carrying Silvia's head in the middle of a tray. His final lines are now different: 'Father's Day. I got my cake. Happy Father's Day.' Romero frames the three characters in a triangular position reminiscent of significant groupings in Hitchcock films such as *Rope* (1948). Nate is at the apex in the background. Cass and Richard appear left and right of the frame in the foreground. Silvia's head occupies the centre of the frame. It is gruesomely decorated with frosting and candles, making it resemble the head of the Statue of Liberty. This macabre conclusion associates the typical ironic ending of an EC comic with one of Romero's cherished themes. Like the American flag seen in the opening of *Night of the Living Dead* flying over the graveyard, Silvia's final appearance in 'Father's Day' links a pathological living dead family unit to one of the key signifiers of the American ideal, an ideal now redundant and bankrupt in the twentieth century. 'Father's Day' concludes with the victory of Freud's 'Death Instinct' firmly entrenched inside the American family and literally continuing beyond death as embodied in Nate's decaying corpse. As played by John Amplas, Nate resembles the later stages of Romero's zombies in *Day of the Dead*. All these figures are shuffling bodies in advanced stages of decay but still animated by pathologically possessive desires which motivated them in life. Despite the jocular EC-influenced style employed in this sequence, Romero's intentions echo those operating in his more serious films.

EC humour and exaggerated performance style also dominate 'The Lonesome Death of Jordy Verrill'. Despite some amateurish mugging by Stephen King in the title role, the story offers much more than Tom Milne's dismissive description of its premises as 'the most drearily predictable of the five tales' (1982: 216). A deterministic premise worthy of literary naturalism's bleak premises operates within this narrative. But the deterministic nature of Jordy's fate is not entirely due to the arbitrary arrival of the meteorite on his farm. Although Jordy's contact with the object seals his fate, other factors are also involved. Jordy lives alone in a ramshackle farm somewhere in Maine. When the meteorite lands on his property, he talks to it as if it were a living person and regards it solely as an opportunity for making money. Although Jordy sees it as chance to pay off a $200 bank loan, his motivations are really more avaricious. He sees it in terms of making a fast buck. Jordy first comments, 'I wonder how much they'd pay for it at the college'. As with the flashback in 'Father's Day', Romero uses canted angle shots and frame-within-frame images. But this time his images depict Jordy's fantasy desires. As he enters the local college's Department of Meteors, the soundtrack ironically plays a version of a traditional English academic song which sounds as inappropriate as Aunt Silvia's cultural pretensions in the previous story. As 'The Crate' will show, academia is little better than those other corrupt institutional mechanisms of civilisation Romero sees as prejudicial to human development. A grotesque series of images show Jordy and a professor bargaining over the economic aspects of possession. When the scene changes to the present, Jody then announces his desire to 'Pay off the bank loan. That's the ticket. Got to cool that son of a bitch off.'

He pours a bucket of water over the hot meteorite to see it crack open and release a gooey liquid which Jordy describes as 'meteorshit'. Imagining his dreams of economic gain dissipating as the professor comments, 'You must be joking. I wouldn't give you two cents', he walks away hoping, 'Maybe, I can glue it together in the morning.' Jordy's 'meteorshit' comment is by no means accidental. It evokes the Freudian motif of wealth as 'filthy lucre' in terms of its anal associations developed by Norman O. Brown in *Life Against Death*. Furthermore, the colour of the vegetation is green which is also the colour of the American dollar. In view of Romero's final identification of Aunt Silvia with the Statue of Liberty in the concluding scene of 'Father's Day', such an association is certainly not accidental.

Jody then goes to sulk in front of his television set. The 1950s programmes he views contain significant insights into his own personal dilemma. He first watches a wrestling match, a contest not only symbolising his own lack of masculine aggressiveness but an entertainment commonly known for its fabricated manufacture of violent spectacle before a bloodthirsty audience. As Jordy opens his bottle, the frame successively dissolves to the meteorite, Jordy's head, the bucket he has discarded outside, and again to the television set. These images are arbitrary in nature. But they all equally depict a collective contamination affecting the main character. They range from physical contact with the meteorite to the more subtle civilised elements of passive television consumption and alcoholic oblivion. As the exotic green weeds spread outside, Jordy discovers them sprouting from his blistered fingers. He also undergoes a castration fantasy as he imagines himself visiting a doctor and awaiting the removal of his offending members with a meat cleaver.

As Jordy and his environment gradually change to green, the television plays an old black-and-white Hollywood film where a grandmother and granddaughter talk about the old pioneer ideals. Certain lines are significant: 'There's a difference between dreaming and doing and more'; 'We've got to make a new country and to see our dreams come true.' These lines from *A Star is Born* (1937) function ironically in terms of their juxtaposition with Jordy's passive figure and the Popov bottle of Vodka he consumes. As the descendant of the old pioneers, Jordy's figure provides a telling contrast both to the ideologies of the old Jefferson farmer yeoman ideal as well as to Hollywood fantasies. Finally, a religious broadcaster appears to urge his congregation of viewers to 'begin a good thing'. His message finishes with an off-screen announcer mentioning that the image was pre-recorded and not real. Jordy's dilemma is not just related to the random appearance of a meteor in his back garden but also to other pertinent social factors conditioning his everyday existence.

Jordy Verrill is a solitary figure. We learn nothing about his life other than the information contained in the segment. He dreams rather than acts, lives in a ramshackle farm and passively indulges in the mass-produced narcotic fantasies provided by his culture; Jordy is little better than the vegetation he is on his way to becoming part of. As he attempts to take a bath to curtail the growth affecting him, his father's image appears in a mirror warning him about the consequences. Like Nathan Grantham, the father's role is punitive and threatening, embodying patriarchal damage affecting his son's personal development. His warning also attempts to stop Jordy reversing the contamination. Father (Bingo O'Malley) comments, 'You get into that water, Jordy. You might as well make up your death warrant.' He appears to be another agent in the contamination process physically represented by the inhuman vegetation slowly making his son less than human. However, Jordy vainly attempts his final cleansing. As he wakes in the morning, the radio broadcasts a positive forecast of rising grain prices and new high profits. The commentator also ironically remarks that the favourable weather will result in the landscape becoming 'green in the next few months' which will be 'about miraculous'. His remarks also parody the agrarian ideal featured in the old movie Jordy briefly listened to as well as the pre-recorded message of the religious commentator. However, the Jeffersonian yeoman farmer ideal and religious motivations of early American history now become perverted into promoting a contaminating capitalism which will eventually infect everyone in the same way as the meteor vegetation consumes Jordy.

Jordy can no longer share in this new American Dream. The 'meteorshit' rapidly turns him into a living embodiment of vegetation making him little better than a zombie functioning on basic instinctual patterns of behaviour. Left with the remaining vestiges of the little conscious thought he has, Jordy finally attempts a successful suicide by blowing his head off with his shotgun. Like certain human victims of Romero's zombies, he makes a last-ditch effort to avoid the final stages of contamination which will take away the remaining features of his humanity. Jordy's act also parallels Peter's abandoned plan in the final scenes of *Dawn of the Dead*. But, unlike Peter, Jordy has no real hope or chance of survival. The sequence concludes with the real-life image of the vegetation slowly creeping towards inhabited town areas in a manner similar to Hitchcock's final image in *The Birds* where the winged threats to human survival ominously dominate the landscape. Although Jordy's death appears both arbitrary and deterministic, enough evidence appears in this episode to suggest the indirect involvement of other culturally relevant factors contributing towards his personal downfall. Both the legacy of America's historical past and human agency face contamination by a malevolent plague. Despite its jokey imagery, this *Creepshow* segment contains a message as serious as those in Romero's other significant films.

'Something to Tide You Over' links together the domestic possessive motif of 'Father's Day' as well as Romero's ironic criticisms of the television apparatus appearing in *Night of the Living Dead*, *There's Always Vanilla* and *Dawn of the Dead*. Possessive husband and technological fetishist Richard Vickers (Leslie Nielsen) plans a vindictive revenge against his wife Rebecca (Gaylen Ross) and her lover Harry Wentworth (Ted Danson) for violating his patriarchal rights. As with the rest of the *Creepshow* tales, the key theme involves destructive possessiveness. But while Harry and Rebecca wish to live their lives freely – 'She just wants out. No alimony. No community property rules' – Richard, like Nathan Grantham of 'Father's Day', regards family as his own personal property: 'I keep what is mine. No exceptions to that rule, Harry. No exceptions, whatever.' Threatening Harry with his hold over Rebecca, Richard forces his victim to accompany him to the beach and buries him up to his neck in the sand. As the water approaches, Richard provides his own perverse form of live entertainment for Harry. He places before his victim a television monitor showing Rebecca drowning in another part of the beach. Richard also has video cameras recording the deaths of his wife and lover as she drowns before his helpless eyes.

Richard's deadly technological game has definite Hitchcock associations. Like 'the master of suspense', Richard is fascinated by technology in pursuing his own form of murderous gaze. While she drowns, Rebecca becomes Romero's version of Laura Mulvey's cinematic female dominated by the male gaze. However, Rebecca's position is not one which the males gain sexual pleasure from. Buried in the sand up to her neck, Rebecca is reduced to the helpless position of a passive fetish object. But her visual image results from an explicit patriarchal revenge fantasy in which the husband disposes of his property in the manner he thinks most fitting. Richard takes a sadistic voyeuristic pleasure in the proceedings, but Harry gazes in sympathy and masochistic helplessness while his lover drowns. The deaths of Harry and Rebecca occur in the ironically named 'Comfort Rest', an environment which is 'very private'. As Richard comments in his usual proprietorial manner, 'I own it all.'

When Richard returns home, Romero reveals television monitors showing his car arriving. As a Buddha image appears on the screen symbolising the compassionate and non-avaricious qualities absent from its owner, Richard switches on two television monitors to watch the last moments of Harry and Rebecca. While Richard gazes at this live television entertainment, Harry voices his revenge. When Richard later returns to the scene of his crime, he finds the television monitor and VCR still there but Harry absent. Believing the current has dragged his victim out to sea, he returns home.

However, Richard will not live long enough to enjoy any further employment of his murderous gaze. After a monitor showing an old black-and-white movie blacks out, Richard hears the voices of his drowned victims who confront him in his bathroom and reduce him to helpless insanity. 'Something to Tide Over Me' concludes in typical EC Comic poetic morality mode. A video camera appears on the beach at night. Two pairs of feet imprinted in the sand lead towards the ocean. The final image shows Richard buried up to his neck while the tide rushes in. He insanely laughs and challenges his executioners to do something he urged them to do before: 'I can hold my breath ... a loooonnnggg ... time.' As this possessive husband meets his fate on his private beach still affirming anally retentive qualities in his final moments, the image changes to comic strip form.

'The Crate' begins with an overhead shot showing janitor Mike (Don Keefer) toss a quarter into the air in a college basement zoology lab to decide which area he will clean. When it falls behind the grille in the stairway, he discovers a crate from an 1834 Arctic Expedition delivered to Horlicks University. Although the fictional name for the location appears trivial in nature, it does relate to the very premises of the plot which involves both the awakening of a creature from slumber as well as the similar awakening of Professor Henry Northrup (Hal Holbrook) to perform in reality one of his most desired wish fulfillment fantasies.

The next sequence shows a stuffy faculty party where Henry's vulgar, lower-class wife Wilma (Adrienne Barbeau) embarrasses her husband and eminent guests by her brash behavior. Attaching herself to a new faculty couple, the Raymonds (the demure faculty wife superbly portrayed by Christine Forrest), Wilma (or 'Call Me Billie') vocally disrupts the genteel nature of the proceedings. Although one guest asks, 'Why do they keep inviting her?', everyone suffers in polite silence according to unspoken taboos of the academic world whereby hypocritical convention and sterile rituals dominate more rational forms of behaviour. 'The Crate' is a story which brings together two opposing realms of academic self-deception and direct activity into conflict via the MacGuffin device of the creature released from its long captivity. It also satirises the world of higher learning which is equally as hypocritical and deceptive as the other institutional realms of government, media, and the military Romero condemns elsewhere. Adrienne Barbeau's Wilma certainly appears as a human monster throughout the film or a human equivalent of the creature in the crate, as Gagne notes (1987: 130). But beneath the superficial level of laughing at Wilma's fall and Henry's revenge, other salient factors operate. Who is the real monster in the film? Wilma? Henry? Or even the average member of the audience who laughs at the episode without considering its wider implications?

During the party, Wilma spies Henry's friend Dexter Stanley (Fritz Weaver) chatting with a young female graduate student. Dexter then receives a message from Mike asking him to investigate the crate. Although regretting his lost opportunity as an authority figure to further 'converse' with his willing audience, Dexter is relieved to be away from Wilma's presence. At the same time, Henry dreams of shooting her in the head with a Magnum to the polite applause of his fellow faculty members. He later fantasises about strangling her with his tie. These two fantasy sequences are important since they numerically correspond to the deaths of Mike and graduate student Charlie (Robert Harper) later in the film. They also contribute to the 'dreaming and doing' motif which also occurs in 'The Lonesome Death of Jordy Verrill' as well as the fluid lines dividing reality and fantasy in Romero's work.

The most basic level of audience reaction to the plot would appear to be pleasure at Henry's eventual disposal of Wilma. However, although she is definitely annoying and irritating, she is also a human being. Furthermore, one may ask why Henry married her in the first place since they are obviously mismatched as a couple. Certain answers are possible. Firstly, although we never learn whether Wilma has an actual job we do know that she is supposedly attending classes later that evening. Despite the fact that she returns drunk after a night on the town, the possibility remains that she was once Henry's student whom he married under duress. Two instances in the film support this. First, Wilma takes great pleasure in looking at Dexter talking to his female student. Secondly, when Henry later tells her that Dexter has got into trouble with a graduate student who has 'crawled into a dark corner and won't come out', this acts as a sufficient bait to entice her to the basement. Perhaps Henry did get himself into trouble once and extricated himself by a hasty marriage to Wilma? Anyway, certainty on this matter is impossible since everyone exists in an academic environment based on duplicity, hypocrisy and evasion of the realities of everyday life. It is an environment Wilma knows all too well. As she loudly tells the Raymonds, 'Some of these so-called academics make the shark in *Jaws* look like fucking Flipper!'

When Dexter arrives at the laboratory, he and Mike open the crate and find an ape-like creature inside who devours the janitor. After the distraught Dexter enlists Charlie to his aid, another victim falls prey to its appetite. Dexter hysterically rushes to Henry's house and tells him about the incidents on the evening they usually play chess together. When Dexter relates the details, Romero films a chess set in the foreground while Henry tells his colleague, 'I can't do anything unless you stop being so damned hysterical!' The contrast between the rational world of chess and the irrational behaviour of Dexter is visually evident. Two people have already died. However, Henry now sees an ideal opportunity to remove Wilma from his life for good. He feeds his friend a drink mixed with a sleeping potion and phones his wife from the zoology basement to entice her to Amberson Hall.[9]

Once inside, he pushes her next to the crate, vainly attempting to rouse the creature from its slumber. After looking at her husband in amazement, Wilma then begins attacking his impotence on every conceivable level. Henry is 'no good at departmental politics, making money ... anything. When was the last time you made it in bed?' This last comment finally evokes Henry's return of the repressed as the creature emerges from its crate to claw her and take her body inside. Henry then tells his wife, 'Just tell it to call you "Billie".' He soon chains up the crate as the creature's claws extend from the inside before dumping the crate and its contents into a deserted lake.

Henry then tells Dexter the events of the previous evening. The two honourable academic gentlemen subsequently decide to remain silent over the whole affair as they sit down to a game of chess. Despite the fact that the activities of both men have resulted in deaths (one accidental, the other intentional), they agree to maintain an institutional silence over a disturbing affair, one based upon academia's perennial 'use and abuse' syndrome. They deny anything has happened. Dexter comments, 'I hate doing anything to anybody.' Henry replies, 'Neither have I' before realising the possible consequences: 'What if it gets out, gets out of the crate?' The final images reveal the creature active within the depths struggling to break out of its confines before a shot ends in a close-up of its eyes. There is no need to show the eventual outcome. The suggestion remains that Henry will be forever haunted by the fear of a future revenge as much as he was haunted by the figure of his deceased wife. As the final image changes to its graphic counterpart, the close-up of the eyes intimate that Henry's moral punishment is not too far away.

'They're Creeping Up on You' is *Creepshow*'s final episode. It appropriately unites the EC graphic style with underlying social comment in a manner which remains both true to its original source as well as Romero's own concerns as director. Like 'The Crate', this episode opens with a foreboding overhead shot which changes from comic to 'real' style as the narrative begins. It introduces us to financier Upson Pratt (E. G. Marshall), a reclusive Howard Hughes figure who lives in a white antiseptic apartment complex at the top of a Gothic brownstone mansion in New York.[10] As he meticulously sprays a roach which has invaded his environment and disposes of the remains down a waste chute, his 1950s Wurlitzer jukebox plays jazz music reminiscent of the Roaring Twenties.[11] This incongruity is by no means accidental. Both sound and image link two separate, incongruous, but revealing periods. Despite the glamour of the Roaring Twenties, the era was one of political oppression and racism, a decade which would end in the Wall Street Crash. Pratt is going to face his particular version of a 'Crash' in more ways than one. His 1950s jukebox would normally play 1950s rock music rather than the sounds from Pratt's youthful days. He, quite obviously, chooses what he wants to remember. But the presence of a 1950s artefact in his modern sterile complex evokes the decade of EC comics which contained graphic morality revenge plots against vindictive characters.

As Pratt removes the offending roach from his sight, he comments 'I'm going to get bugs.' But his later remarks reveal that he regards human beings as little better than insects. Irritated at the fact that his modern white, climate-controlled environment does not protect him from his insect phobia he immediately plans vindictive reprisals against his employees: 'Heads are going to roll. I promise you that.' Pratt then harasses executive employee George Gledhill on the intercom, abusively insults black handyman Mr. White (David Early) and threatens building superintendent Reynolds with dismissal unless he return immediately from his family vacation in Orlando, Florida, to deal with the situation.

As Pratt examines his latest stock values on a machine, Gledhill informs him that business competitor Katzenmeyer committed suicide after failing to stop Pratt's corporate takeover. The ruthless tycoon selfishly comments, 'Wonderful. Now we don't have to offer that old fart a seat on the board of directors.' Like the Grantham family and Richard Vickers, Pratt is another of *Creepshow*'s greedy capitalist figures who will soon face his destiny. Like the others, his downfall will result from a factor symbolising the pathological nature of his possessive qualities. But, in his case, roaches, rather than cake or a television monitor, will cause his downfall. As Pratt reacts against a brown-coloured roach invading his person, he remarks 'Once they get a foothold in the building, you never get rid of them.' This also applies to human beings. He separates himself both from the outside world and any form of human contact. He prefers to live in an antiseptic world built upon his ruthless methods of personal acquisition. Pratt demeaningly regards his victims and employees as 'stupid' and little better than disposable roaches as the following remarks show: 'Katzenmeyer! Reynolds! Bugs! That's all they are!' However, the roaches represent Pratt's particular form of the 'return of the repressed' as the cake and television apparatus do in 'Father's Day' and 'Something to Tide You Over'.

Pratt receives a phone call from Katzenmeyer's widow who condemns his vicious selfishness. She ends her message with the curse, 'I hope you get cancer in the right place'. The bugs not only perform the role of her avenging agents but also represent Pratt's personal fears equating them with a deadly disease. Pratt comments, 'I grew up in Hell's Kitchen. I know what to do with a bug when I see it.' Like the title character in Budd Schulberg's novel *What Makes Sammy Run?* (1941), Pratt is running away from memories of his early deprived environment. He has become an oppressor the more he attempts to distance himself from it. But the bugs will eventually avenge both themselves and the countless human victims who have perished in Pratt's ruthless rise to the top of the economic ladder. Ironically, his very position at the summit of an apartment complex will not save him. Although the inside environment is antiseptically white, the building's exterior is brown. The colour significantly parallels Pratt's New York brownstone mansion and the roaches who will eventually invade his territory as well as his body. It also symbolically evokes the economic anality which has motivated his entire existence.

A blackout disrupts the power mechanisms inside Pratt's apartment. Although he attempts to enlist White's aid, the black handyman expresses relish at being unable to answer Pratt's call. White looks at Pratt through the glass porthole of his apartment door. The reclusive magnate resembles a human looking at an animal or a pre-Civil War Southern gentleman viewing a caged slave with bemusement. Since Pratt earlier made racially disdainful comments about White's race and occupation, this latter interpretation is more appropriate under the circumstances. Pratt then retreats to his sealed bedroom vowing revenge on both humans and insects: 'You'll never get in here and when the blackout is over people are going to pay. I've been beating bugs all my life and I'll beat you too.' However, after hearing Mrs Katzenmeyer's last judgement, 'I hope you die', Pratt looks in horror as his bedspread vibrates and bugs emerge from it. He collapses in terror.

The following morning when the power returns, Romero films the apartment as if nothing has happened apart from an overturned cereal bowl. White calls to Pratt from outside: 'What's the matter, Mr Pratt. Bugs got your tongue?' We then see Pratt's dead body on his bed. His chest vibrates like John Hurt's stomach in *Alien* (1979) prior to the chestburster's appearance. Swarms of roaches them emerge from Pratt's mouth. They have feasted on him internally in an inverse manner to Romero's zombies and cover his bedroom in a brown tide. It is a fitting revenge both in terms of Pratt's aversion to dirt and the excremental associations of the 'filthy lucre' he has devoted his entire life to acquiring.

Pratt becomes consumed by the objects he fears most. These objects represent the return of a pathologically repressive possessiveness. It is often denied by the main characters but acts as a motivating characteristic affecting virtually all the *Creepshow* stories. The film then moves towards its epilogue with young Billy achieving a poetic justice in regard to his abusive father by sticking a voodoo doll he acquired from a Creepshow advert full of pins. Two garbage men find the comic but decide not to throw it away; one (Marty Schiff) comments, 'My kids love those things' and his companion (Tom Savini) adds, 'I love 'em too.' His remark underscores the fascination an adult world has for the subversive nature of the EC comic strip both in the 1950s as well as the early Reaganite era. This latter era saw the 1950s values of rapacious conspicuous consumption capitalism return to America with a vengeance. It was now time to bring the zombies back to centre stage.

CHAPTER TEN

Day of the Dead

To date, *Day of the Dead* remains the last episode in the original, allegorically-inclined, unpublished story George A. Romero wrote many decades ago under the title of 'Anubis'. It was initially composed in three movements which roughly corresponded with the themes contained within his cinematic zombie trilogy. The first movement involved a group of people taking refuge in an isolated farmhouse as the zombie plague begins. They all end up eaten. The second movement begins some six months later with a civilian and military posse moving through the area exterminating zombies. However, the surviving zombies find some weapons accidentally left behind and remember how they used these implements in their former life as human beings. This movement concludes with an army of zombies chasing a solitary wounded human being across the country. The human reaches the farmhouse and dies when the zombies drill him full of holes. 'Anubis' then leads towards its conclusion which involves the theme of an army of zombies controlled by human masters. Romero looked upon 'Anubis' as an allegory dealing with the consequences of an incoming revolutionary society represented by zombies who replace an existing social order of humans. Ironically, the moral is that nothing really changes at all (Gagne 1987: 24–5).[1] It is not hard to see in this treatment certain parallels with the issues raised in his second film, which involved the failure of 1960s ideals and the movement towards conformity on the part of the younger generation. *There's Always Vanilla* is a title applicable both to the earlier film as well as several issues raised throughout Romero's work.

In 1978 Romero expanded his vision of 'Anubis's' final movement by writing a forty-page treatment which elaborated on the images of a zombie army chasing a living human being contained in his original treatment. This eventually became the basis of the first and second screenplay drafts which Romero finally altered into the present film version due to a production deal necessitating its theatrical appearance by 1985 (see Gagne 1987: 147–50).[2] An outline of the earlier version reveals not only the exciting allegorical nature of Romero's approach but also the manner in which the film version differs from the director's earlier ideas. Although Romero regretted his inability to film his original vision, *Day of the Dead* is, nevertheless, one of his major achievements as critics such as Robin Wood have recognised (see Wood 1986b: 45–9). It is an extremely remarkable work, one whose premises make it a fascinating production appearing in a Reagan era characterised by a reactionary cinematic focus on conservative 'mindless entertainment'.[3] Despite its emergence in the reactionary 1980s, *Day of the Dead* is one of the few horror films of that decade which keeps faith with the radical generic traditions of previous decades. The majority of contemporary horror films such as the *Friday the 13th* and *Nightmare on Elm Street* series did not live up to the pioneering trends set by their predecessors in the 1970s.

The initial screenplay drafts begin with images of a Florida city some five years after the zombie plague. As in the film version, shots of an alligator crawling out of an abandoned bank, useless dollar bills littering the floor and a decaying zombie, lacking a lower jaw bone, appear symbolising the detritus and decay of a vanished civilisation. However, the earlier versions of the screenplay introduce a boatload of disparate human refugees searching for sanctuary as well as showing other humans arriving at the city marina. Sarah, Miguel, Tony, Chico and Maria immediately find themselves fighting other humans as well as zombies before three survivors escape to a tropical island. Like his counterpart in the film, Miguel suffers a zombie bite and Sarah quickly slices off his arm to prevent infection. She also cauterises it with a flaming torch. Tony dies from gunshot wounds but Maria prevents Miguel shooting him in the head to prevent him returning as a zombie. However, like the unfortunate housewife in *Dawn of the Dead*'s early housing project sequence, she suffers from her returned lover's zombie bite. Sarah and Chico finish off Tony while Maria slips over the side of the boat and commits suicide. This character follows the pessimistic path chosen by her two predecessors in the original climax of *Dawn of the Dead*.

On the island, the survivors discover a huge elevator of an underground military installation. A group of soldiers led by Captain Rhodes emerge. They are followed by a band of uniformed zombies wearing red vests. Rhodes supervises their 'boot camp' training. His surprising success in controlling a zombie horde which overran human survivors in the early films results in living soldiers feeding their zombie counterparts with human meat from refrigerated cartons. Human trooper Toby and his companion Tricks react in disgust at Rhodes's enjoyment of this perverse operation. Both Toby and Tricks represent Romero's development of David's character in *The Crazies*. A battle begins leading to the death of the already infected Miguel. The wounded Chico is captured, but Toby later performs a mercy killing to prevent him becoming a zombie.

Sarah escapes but is rescued by Caribbean islander, John, and his alcoholic mechanic friend Bill McDermott. They are inhabitants of the island's lower echelon, the Stalag, and tell her about the nightmare society she has discovered. The island represents a gross parody of capitalism and is divided into three class sectors. Its lower level comprises the island's 'lumpenproletariat'. This includes not only humans relishing violence, depraved sex, drugs and disease but also others regarded as disposable units of society such as blacks (John), Irish (McDermott), dissidents (Dr. Logan) and disabled (female deaf-mute Spider). Stalag 17 is made up of what appears to be a cesspool of human dregs whose condition results from the labels applied to them by the upper echelons of the island society. While some individuals – such as Spider – are allowed to perform menial tasks on other levels, the vast majority are regarded as little better than human fodder for the zombies. Rhodes relishes any opportunity given him to exercise military discipline and increase the zombie food supply. John conceals Sarah in the Stalag away from Rhodes and his men.

The next level of the island society comprises an underground scientific establishment headed by Mary Henreid and assistants Julie Grant and Fisher. They attempt to find ways to study zombie behaviour. The unit's star zombie pupils are Bluto, former American Indian Tonto and Bub. Like his later counterpart, Bub is the most advanced of them all. He not only takes on Rhodes in a Clint Eastwood gunfighter manner described later in the screenplay but also has deep feelings for Mary like a son towards a mother. However, like the Los Alamos scientists working on the Atomic Bomb, the island doctors exhibit a warped attitude toward survival since the military establishment headed by Rhodes intend to use the zombies as an army of the living dead. Romero leaves the most grotesque parody of Reagan-era lifestyles for the screenplay's mid-section. Former Florida Governor Henry Dickerson controls the island society. He lives in affluent luxury parodying the escapist world of popular Reaganite television series such as *Dallas*, *Dynasty*, *The Colbys* and *Falcon Crest*. Dickerson inhabits a gymnasium which Romero describes as a mixture of Elaine Powers and a harem chamber which also comprises 'good ol' boy' country club cronies and political yes men. Nicknamed 'Gasparilla' after a notorious Caribbean pirate, Dickerson lounges in a 'coffin-shaped' tanning device in his second appearance within the screenplay surrounded by some conservatively dressed females who are obviously wives left over from the good old days of official monogamy and scantily clad women who represent the mistresses of the old political establishment.

Like Rhodes in the film version, Dickerson expresses a sexual interest towards Mary. Furthermore, in the second draft screenplay, Dickerson also expresses relish that the retirement state of Florida (where senior citizens previously migrated to die) is now the stronghold of the living dead. He not only sees his island as a secessionist state in any future union but also envisages extending his domain over America and the rest of the world by recruiting millions of zombies into his army. Dickerson's fantasies represent a bizarre version of Reaganite militarism and his Star Wars philosophy.

Eventually, Sarah joins forces with Mary, Toby, Logan, Spider and others to start a rebellion. While the demented Logan wishes to destroy the entire island like a biblical Jehovah, Toby argues that other innocent people exist in the camp and elsewhere who do not deserve this fate. The zombies also participate in the ensuing chaos in an eager attempt to find their own food. They consume Logan, Julie and Dickerson's affluent community in the process. Eventually, the island community explodes while the survivors (including a group of children) escape to another island. The screenplay ends with John and Sarah standing vigil over Tricks's body hoping that, like Miguel's (which they discover in their flight), it will not reanimate. Since it does not, Romero suggests that the zombie plague is now over and humanity can reconstitute itself along new lines.

Romero's original vision necessitated a budget of $6.5 million dollars for many of the astounding sequences contained in his first and second draft screenplays. According to Tony Buba, the first draft screenplay contained scenes involving helicopters flying into battle against zombies and playing 'Amazing Grace' on the PA system.[4] Unfortunately Laurel's desire to refuse to compromise by agreeing to industry demands for an 'R' rating led to the constraints of reduced budget and further screenplay revision (see Gagne 1987: 147–50). Although Romero regretted the loss of his original idea, *Day of the Dead* certainly stands on its own merits whether one knows about the original concept or not. Many characters are dropped or conflated from the original screenplay drafts resulting in a much more concentrated and dynamic film. The screen version retains much of the original opening scenes but makes Sarah part of the scientific team. It drops the Stalag and Florida condominium characters and lower-class levels of island society but retains the middle-class ones of military and scientific establishments. Sarah is now a composite of her original fugitive character from the first two drafts and the earlier figure of Mary Henreid. Miguel survives into the final scenes but his eventual fate resembles Julie Grant's in the original. Although Romero suggests a romantic relationship between Sarah and Miguel in the original versions, the Toby and Mary Henreid characters with their love for one another now become conflated into their screen successors. Miguel dies in the same way as Julie Grant while Fisher remains. Captain Rhodes is as odious as his screenplay draft counterparts while Bub remains as the only star zombie pupil on the block. Since Stalag 17 disappears, Dr. Logan now becomes head of the scientific establishment. But he still remains as demented as his original counterpart.

Despite Romero's feelings concerning his revisions, the final product does make the film more concentrated in focus with less characters appearing to confuse the viewer from appreciating the implications of the narrative. Although the final film does lack the explicit tension between the different social classes that were represented in the first two drafts, it does reinforce a key element in the trilogy existing as far back as *Night of the Living Dead*, namely the real threat to survival being the class-based verbal savagery different characters exhibit towards each other rather than the zombies outside. These outside forces really externally embody internal tensions within the human beings raging within their fragile fortresses. Furthermore, like Fran in *Dawn of the Dead*, Sarah is the film's main point of character identification. Penetrating the futile and superficial face of social masculinity, she vainly urges the importance of co-operation during two sequences in the film. Finally, although the explicit political allegory remains absent, it is certainly present in the film on a much more subtle level and available to anyone 'who has eyes to see and ears to hear' – to quote the biblical references occurring in the screenplay drafts and John's dialogue in the film. Dickerson and his Reaganite associations may not be as explicitly present as they were in the original screenplay versions but they still spiritually remain in the final film as implicit signifiers.[5] *Day of the Dead* opens in a similar manner to *Dawn of the Dead*. A woman appears asleep in the opening scene. Shot against the white background of a brick cubicle, Sarah (Lori Cardille) appears in long shot leaning against the wall with her head resting on her knees. As she slowly raises her head, the mid-close-up image cuts to another one revealing her point of view. It shows a calendar hanging on the opposite wall. Sarah walks towards the calendar on which all the October dates are scratched out. She gazes at the autumnal picture of a pumpkin patch with a little girl in the background. As if wishing herself into this wonderland imagery, this somnambulistic Alice in Wonderland figure begins slowly moving her hand down the calendar dates. Suddenly, scores of zombie arms emerge through the wall and claw at her. The next shot shows Sarah abruptly emerging from what appears to have been a dream in the back seat of a private helicopter.

The opening image appears redundant to the rest of the film, laying itself open to the 'It's only a dream' type of dismissal for an audience impatient to move on to the world of action, zombies and gore. But this sequence is not so peripheral as it initially appears to be. Unlike *Dawn of the Dead*, where we do not experience what the sleeping Fran dreams about before she awakes, *Day of the Dead*'s viewers participate in Sarah's nightmare. On one level, the sequence appears to resemble the well-known Val Lewton 'bus' shock effect where a frightening succession of incidents eventually turns out to be based on nothing at all. However, the protruding zombie arms also resemble that key moment in Val Lewton's *Bedlam* (1945) when the arms of mental patients reach out to the hero in an asylum corridor, an image also used by Roman Polanski in *Repulsion* (1965). Admittedly, this sequence lends itself to this type of formal 'shock horror' interpretation. However, other levels of meaning exist in this brief, but pertinent, introduction making it much more than the type of cute cinematic citation overused by lesser talents in 1980s cinema and beyond.

First, Sarah looks at a calendar where all the October dates are crossed out. In America, October is the key month leading up to the Presidential and State elections before voting occurs in the first week of November. Secondly, the image above the calendar shows a field full of pumpkins which resemble the pods in the various screen versions of *Invasion of the Body Snatchers*. In the latter film, pods threaten human society with a brave new world removing pain, pleasure and freedom of choice. Romero's zombies certainly exhibit no freedom of choice and his trilogy depicts a world both as insane as Master Simms' asylum in Val Lewton's *Bedlam* (1946) as well as one whose insanity mirrors the supposed sanity of the civilised world. When she moves, Sarah appears about to exercise some form of freedom of choice. But decaying zombie arms reach out to overpower her before she can do anything else. It is not too coincidental to see this scene as Romero's bemused anticipation of the probable results of the 1985 Presidential election which would give Ronald Reagan his second term in office. The Reagan era certainly represented the return to life of supposedly dead values and policies with a vengeance. Furthermore, the military build up and escalation of the Cold War threatened to plunge the world into a situation little better than that revealed in *Day of the Dead*.

After Sarah awakes, the next shot shows her emotionally distraught lover Miguel (Antone DiLeo) sitting next to her in a helicopter. He wears a scruffy military uniform and gazes out of the window in terror. The next images show Bill McDermott (Jarlath Conroy), an alcoholic Irish electronics technician, and John (Terry Alexander), the Jamaican helicopter pilot flying over a Florida coastal city in search of human survivors. This group represents the potential nucleus of Romero's new society. Rather than the one white female and four Hispanics of earlier screenplay drafts, this group is a much more diverse unit that resembles the utopian community earlier envisaged by *Knightriders*. They also embody minority groups often denigrated by a racist and patriarchal society, especially in jokes such as 'Did you hear the one about the woman, the spic, the Jamaican, and the drunken Irishman?' However, as in all his films, Romero respectfully invests these outsider characters with indisputable qualities of human dignity.

Despite John's reluctance in landing when he says, 'It's not in our contract,' Sarah compassionately insists on reassuring herself that no human survivors exist. As the credits roll, Romero reveals images of a decaying city which was even more derelict in the original script. *Day of the Dead*'s audience would naturally see the city's condition as due to human abandonment, but Romero's original intention was much more subversive in terms of commenting upon the 1980s era. He envisaged the city in the original screenplay as embodying the type of disintegrating urban structure seen in older American cities. The environment not only parallels Braddock of *Martin* but also those poorly built newer urban environments which collapse in ten years rather than two hundred. Romero also commented that this social critique existed in the film despite the fact that most critics and the audiences merely looking for exploitation and thrills tended to ignore this feature (see Gagne 1987: 159). Although this meaning is not explicitly present in the actual film, the opening sequences do implicitly exhibit several instances of Romero's black humour, especially when we think of Florida's conservative retirement community ethos as the most appropriate American state for the living dead to conquer in the final part of his zombie trilogy.

When a bullhorn attempts to summon any human survivors, the credits roll as Romero reveals the city's condition and its actual inhabitants. An alligator crawls out of a bank while now-useless currency blows in the wind. Consumer debris and garbage juxtapose with money now littering the streets. Insects crawl over a decomposing skeleton while the dead gradually awake to the sound of their expected feast. Romero's screenplay and director credits appear appropriately over the image of a deserted cinema, peculiarly named 'The Edison'. The name itself evokes one of the founding fathers of a cinematic mechanism often used by the system to promote conservative ideological illusions and images of conspicuous consumption rather than other more socially relevant concerns such as awakening audience consciousness. Like other capitalist artefacts, cinema has now become redundant. Possibly, Romero's selection of this telling image parallels Jean-Luc Godard's final credit at the climax of *Weekend* (1968), another film about the breakdown of civilisation with its survivors reverting to cannibalism – 'Fin du Cinéma'.

A low-angle shot of a zombie lacking its lower jawbone appears against the sun. Another zombie emerges from behind the kiosk of The Edison grasping a now useless set of ticket stubs. Other soldiers in the army of the dead slowly move towards human sounds. They moan in unison like damned souls. The humans then decide to return to their island sanctuary, an underground military installation resembling the claustrophobic confines of *Night of the Living Dead*'s farmhouse. It is an environment to which the Washington government has despatched a discordant military and scientific team in the final days of civilisation hoping for a cure to the zombie plague.

When they return, Johnson (Gregory Nicotero), a soldier tending a makeshift garden, enquires 'Did you find anything?' John sarcastically replies, 'Real estate at close out prices.' They see a new graveyard and learn about the death of the installation's commanding officer, Major Cage. John ironically remarks, 'And then there were twelve!' His comment not only echoes the biblical language he will later use to explain the chaos in imagery, evoking Peter's in *Dawn of the Dead,* but also exemplifies Romero's satiric humour within this latest, bleakest, chapter in his trilogy. The twelve survivors echo the twelve disciples of the old Christian era. But rather than being united under the leadership of a saviour figure they all exist in a condition of savage tension stimulated and dominated by the macho megalomaniac figure of Captain Rhodes.

Both John and Bill exist separately from the rest of the community and live in underground trailers reminiscent of those reserved for stars on a film location. Although Sarah wishes to gain their active involvement in the precarious situation, John continually attempts to persuade her to move to their own private island, 'to spend what time we have soaking up some sunshine'. However, like Fran in the opening chaotic scenes of *Dawn of the Dead,* Sarah remains committed to salvaging what is left of the old society until it is clearly impossible to do so.

Deep in the cavern, two aggressive soldiers, Rickles (Ralph Marrero) and Steele (Gary Klar), enlist the already mentally disturbed Miguel into joining them for their continually dangerous assignments – providing zombies as specimens for the scientific establishment. Although *Day of the Dead*'s zombies are in a more advanced process of decay than their predecessors, they exhibit more basic patterns of thought, memory and intuition. This development is due to the fact that five years have already passed since the first outbreak. Zombies, like humans, have the ability to learn from their experiences! When Sarah protests in vain against Miguel's unfitness for duty, she is overruled by Rickles and Steele despite the fact that they all recognise that their opponents are really much more than 'dumbfucks'. As Steele calls the zombie specimens towards the bull pen area, Rickles and Sarah note a new hesitation in the movements of the living dead. Rickles remarks, 'They're scared. They know what'll happen when Dr. Frankenstein gets them.' Sarah answers, 'You're right Rickles. They're learning. They're actually learning.' This is one of the few remaining references to the zombies advanced abilities occurring in the original screenplay drafts. They are becoming even more dangerous than their deadly predecessors in *Night of the Living Dead* and *Dawn of the Dead.*

While the zombies above and below the installation experience frustration in being unable to reach their prey, their human counterparts exhibit no hesitation in displaying verbal aggression towards one another. The military and scientific establishments are constantly at each other's throats. Although removing themselves from active involvement in institutional activities, both John and Terry exhibit a sullen demeanour and conceal their contempt for all parties except Sarah. The new military leader Captain Rhodes (Joseph Pilato) exhibits verbal aggression towards everyone. His savage warrior nature is illustrated by the excessive two holsters and bandolero he wears under his combat jacket. Like Governor Dickerson in the original screenplay, he threatens Sarah sexually and also nearly shoots her when she disobeys orders.

By contrast, Sarah makes at least two unheeded requests for cooperation during the film: 'We need each other. Can't we just get along?' Like Fran in *Dawn of the Dead*, she also recognises that their involvement in the now-bankrupt remains of the old civilisation inhibits any forward movement: 'Maybe, if we tried working together we could achieve something. We're pulling in different directions.' Her last remark also applies to the equally brutal and inhuman world of the scientific establishment.

Although part of this team, Sarah hopes that science will eventually provide a cure. But she finds that old institutional interests still rule the supposedly disinterested and objective world of scientific discovery. Although Fisher (John Amplas) expresses sympathy towards Sarah and warns her against antagonising Rhodes, he is a weak male unable to prevent his superior Dr. Logan (Richard Liberty) from continuing inhumane experiments. Derived from a minor character in the original screenplay whose insane reactions to his scientific work exiled him to Stalag 17, Dr. Logan is appropriately nicknamed 'Frankenstein' by his military antagonists. Rather than wishing to find a cure, Logan really wants to understand how the zombies function so he can control them like an authoritarian parent. He works on specimen after specimen like a vivisectionist gone mad and shares the same pleasure in tearing apart helpless victims like his zombie counterparts. He represents the insanity of a scientific establishment which also mirrors Rhodes' embodiment of the violently mad military mind. Sarah criticises Logan for his fascination with 'what's happening rather than what's making it happen'. His fascination seems to involve no search for a cure to end the zombie plague and rebuild civilisation once more. Instead Logan exhibits a morbid fascination with the plague's symptoms. Like a military scientist engaged in investigating deadly germs for use in biological warfare, he really wishes to develop his own form of social control over the zombies, a control having many features with a now defunct old society.

While Sarah views his zombie specimens in disgust, Logan gleefully informs her about his findings. As in *Dawn of the Dead*, the humans recognise that the zombies operate via some form of remembered instinct. Logan shows Sarah a gutted zombie attempting to bite his fingers despite lacking a stomach. Another specimen has its exposed brain wired with electrodes attached to a spinal column. Logan is less interested in any cure or medical reversal; he aims at a more developed totalitarian form of control where zombies may be more compliant and obey orders better than subjugated humans. Despite the danger and uncertainty, Logan believes zombies can be conditioned to behave. His ideal colonised zombie will thus eventually become 'civilised' and 'domesticated the way we want it to be'. As he later tells a disbelieving Rhodes, Logan believes in 'domestication as control' and verbally demonstrates his adherence to the values of the old society. While Rhodes believes in the military values of obedience and control, Logan articulates its civilian parallels. Although he never achieves the goals of Dickerson in the original and fails to persuade Rhodes, Logan is a potentially dangerous figure fascinated with the very authoritarian ideology characteristic of the old society. As he tells Rhodes, 'You've lost control unless you make them behave … keep them in check and keep them from eating us.' Logan's attitudes thus parallel those of other scientific establishments who ignored their responsibilities to society and eagerly worked with totalitarian regimes.

As Sarah observes later, Logan's prize pupil Bub represents his most successful experiment. Bub has a dim memory of his past life. He becomes fascinated by the objects Logan places before him such as a toothbrush, razor and paperback copy of Stephen King's *Salem's Lot*. Bub later appreciates classical music on a Walkman such as Beethoven's Ninth Symphony with its conclusion praising universal, brotherly love. This Symphony (with its male chorus acclaiming 'all men' becoming 'brothers') functions not only as an ironic cultural signifier of an old patriarchal society (excluding women) but also foreshadows the encroaching zombie world where everyone becomes one and the same in a consumerist and violent manner no matter what their original human forms were originally. The advanced process of decay exhibited by the zombies in this film blurs every distinguishing boundary between male and female, black and white, adult and child. Everyone becomes instinctually consumerist and conformist representing an advertising executive's desired world. But they, ironically, achieve this goal in death rather than life. Unlike other humans, Bub does not view Logan as a meal. But the audience later learns the reason for this when they discover the master feeding his prize pupil with human flesh. As Logan states, 'Civility must be rewarded. If it isn't rewarded ... why ... there's no use for it. There's no use for it at all.' It is doubtful whether Bub had any filial feelings towards Logan before this indoctrination process began. Also, despite Bub's touching puppy love for his teacher, his advanced pupil status may owe more to his former military training where obedience was the norm rather than the exception as we see when he salutes Captain Rhodes. Although Bub later exhibits pain when he discovers Logan's body in a scene paralleling the creature's discovery of Ygor's corpse in *The Son of Frankenstein* (1939), he is really the successful product of a military-style type of education. Bub's progress involves the basic stimulus-response training shown in the case of Pavlov's dog and animals trained to perform tricks. But although Bub represents no zombie future alternative, he appropriately brings down Rhodes later in the film in a manner resembling EC's poetic justice tradition.

When Logan shows Sarah the latest successful results of Bub's training, he also articulates *Dawn of the Dead*'s message of the zombie relationship to human society: 'They are us. They are the extensions of us', having 'the same animal functions'. Logan also stresses the need for a reward system identical to civilised educational techniques so as to trick zombies 'into being good little girls and boys as we were tricked by the promise of a reward to come. They have to be rewarded.' These lines also refer to religious doctrines used to control human beings in society in both past and present. However, another one of Christianity's premises is now coming true. The dead are returning to life. Logan hopes to control them by using the same educational and social techniques applied to human beings in the old order. He sees Bub as exhibiting 'the bare legacy of social behaviour, civilised behaviour'.

Day of the Dead also continues the radical tradition of the American family horror film in revealing psychic darkness existing within the midst of an institution traditionally revered in society and hysterically promoted from the 1980s onwards. Ironically, Logan's discovery of 'what's happening' to the zombies involves his recognition and utilisation of disciplinary measures used in the traditional family system. When Sarah, John and Bill infiltrate Logan's laboratory at night they discover the dead body of an infant zombie and the decapitated head of a soldier ominously illustrating the type of experiments Logan conducts. These involve an educational system of rewards and punishments involving the civilised realms of private property and parental obedience. Logan's tape recorder reveals the real nature of his experiments. Bill switches the tape on accidentally. They all listen to a grotesque version of family education with Logan playing the parts of both punitive parent and chastised child. The tape begins with the 'child' claiming a parent's possession: 'It's not father's stocking. It's my stocking!' The 'child' then obeys 'mother's' voice by putting it away. Logan's actual voice then occurs on the tape as he disciplines a zombie to act like an obedient child: 'Bastard! Be civilised! Take that!' The 'child' then articulates its obedience: 'Five minutes mother. Just five minutes. Father's stocking has a stripe. I wouldn't wear one of father's stockings.' 'Mother's' voice then concludes, 'Mother is very proud of you, very, very proud. You did quite nicely today.'

The information on the tape supports the thesis of Ethel Spector Person concerning family mechanisms which involve the conditioning of infantile dependence by a fixed system of rewards and punishments.[6] It also reveals the patriarchal nature of Logan's methods. They involve the operation of disciplinary violence in the furtherance of unquestioning obedience towards the status quo. By this point, Sarah and her companions have reached the level of Fran's perceptions in *Dawn of the Dead*, namely that the old society is irretrievably doomed and the former patterns of human relationships are now bankrupt.

Long before this revelation, which only occupies a brief segment of *Day of the Dead*, Sarah slowly began to see the end of her delusions. She can no longer attempt to recuperate things which are now lost. Although Sarah offers sympathy towards Miguel, he masochistically chooses to relish in self-pity and refuses any offer of help she gives him. This occurs in the first sequence involving zombie specimen capture. Taunted by Rickles and Steele, Miguel still wants to act like a man although it is clearly evident to himself and others that he can no longer perform a former military role which defined his masculinity. Despite Miguel's lack of the macho qualities displayed by Rhodes and the other soldiers, he expresses resentment at Sarah's strong personality especially when it evokes his symbolic fears of male castration. He soon becomes as verbally antagonistic towards his former lover as the other soldiers are. Sarah intuitively recognises this in the second nightmare she experiences in the film. She dreams that Miguel awakes and his guts pour out on the floor like the zombie of the previous sequence in Dr. Logan's laboratory. After deciding not to tolerate his insults any longer, she throws him out of her room. When Miguel later experiences zombie bites, Sarah immediately attempts to stop the infection by cutting off his arm.

But by this time it is too late on all levels. Miguel's masculine resentment of Sarah already brings him back to the military mentality despite his obvious weakness. He is infected on more than one level and eventually becomes a zombie in all but name. His final act in letting the zombies into the compound and transporting them underground is not beyond criticism; although he may believe he is performing the heroic role of the sacrificial soldier in helping to wipe out Rhodes and his remaining men, his act is also vengeful and selfish. He may believe he is taking revenge on Rhodes and the other soldiers who humiliated him, but he is also placing his former lover and the two men who offered him sanctuary in personal danger. Miguel's motivations remain ambiguous; he may be in the last stages of an infection which render him as inhumane as the attacking host feeding on his body, but whether his actions are the result of conscious or irrational desires, his climactic sacrificial 'gung ho' performance remains questionable.

The zombies invade the compound and conquer the last remnants of the old society in very much the same way as the Franco-Prussian War destroys the Second Empire and ushers in a period of violent revolutionary chaos as in Zola's penultimate contribution to the Rougon-Macquart cycle, Le Débâcle. The older order has perished, yet, unlike the surviving figure of Jean Macquart in the final paragraph of Zola's novel, the survivors of Day of the Dead have no desire to rebuild anything pertaining to an old order. They will, instead, attempt to start anew.

As in his other films, Romero depicts the bankruptcy of the old society, but he does not outline in detail any utopian alternatives. The only conclusion possible is that anything else has to be better than the old order. When Bill rescues Sarah from the fighting soldiers after her breach with Miguel, he takes her to the trailer he shares with John. When John sees her, he greets her warmly as an old friend now that she is on his own personal territory and he is no longer in a subordinate capacity to her. They are now equal individuals inhabiting a common space outside the boundaries of an inhumane institutional status quo. Sarah observes that John has converted his backyard into a fantasy environment; he lounges against a painted backdrop of a tropical beach very much like a film director relaxing on his own personal film set. Both John and Bill welcome Sarah into their fantasy world, but it is a world very different from those morbid dark environments created by Martin and Cuda and very akin in spirit to Billy's recreation of his own personal dream in Knightriders. Bill and John both know the difference between their own form of magic and the world of outside reality. But, rather than symbolically drowning themselves in irrational fantasies which leave them vulnerable to the onslaughts of a world of powerful reality, they nourish their ideals as utopian values while being fully aware of the dangerous world outside.

Fantasy occupies an important role in the work of Romero. But his idea of fantasy never involves pure escapism. As There's Always Vanilla, Jack's Wife and Martin all show, some forms of escape can involve negative self-destructive avenues. But, others, as in Knightriders, offer people 'a chance' and a dream to make life better despite the many obstacles hindering this achievement. The title character in Martin may lament that magic does not exist any more, but his chosen magic is harmful to himself and others. The climactic tragedy of Martin is that the title character was slowly coming to realise this, yet he never had the opportunity to follow his intuitions to their logical conclusions and break away from his negative illusions to construct other more positive alternatives. Neither the Braddock of Martin nor the Bakersfield of Knightriders offer their inhabitants any form of salvation. But the important goal is to break away, find some positive solution or utopian dream befitting each individual, and not lose this important opportunity as Julie Dean does in Knightriders.

Although alienated from their institutional surroundings, neither John nor Bill become as masochistic as Peter in Dawn of the Dead. John dreams of his desert island

and Bill enjoys his flask of whiskey. Ironically, when they later escape up the silo ladder, both men finally throw away their various props which they recognise as now being useless. When Bill rescues John, he throws away his empty whiskey flask while John does likewise with his empty gun. When we last see them in the film, they are both engaged in the productive act of fishing by the beach. John frequently attempts to persuade Sarah to 'drop out' and find their island in the sun rather than propping up a corrupt system. As he earlier tells Sarah in the first trailer sequence, 'What you're doin' is a waste of time.' This time Sarah is more open to the idea as John further defines his feelings for a higher plane of existence, feelings which may not be intended to be taken literally: 'S'long as there's you and me and maybe some other people, we could start over, start fresh. Get some babies.'

John's feelings are vague and utopian. He may not be suggesting a literal plan but suggesting that whatever they do in the future has to be much better than the bureaucratic, institutional, statistical past world whose records and products of dangerous ideological illusions are all stored away safely in the underground bunker. As John looks at a record inventory before him, he lists the various items stored for safety by the government – defence budgets, immigration documents, records of five hundred companies, 'negatives of your favourite movies', tax forms, all left in what John describes as a 'fourteen mile tombstone'. He envisages this new generation as having a different type of education than the one Logan delivers to his obedient zombies. John hopes the new society will teach its children 'never to go here and dig these records out'. Like *Dawn of the Dead*'s Peter, he uses religious imagery to explain their predicament. But he expresses his ideas in a metaphorical and non-doctrinaire way despite comparing the zombie plague to a divinely punitive version of the fall of the Tower of Babel. However, both the biblical story and the now-defunct old civilisation involved the dangerous features of institutional arrogance which led to cataclysmic disaster. When the survivors ascend the ladder and climb up their own utopian tower, John speaks optimistically about 'flying away to the Promised Land'.

They reach the top of the compound and find that the zombies now roaming above ground have somehow not reached the helicopter. As they run towards it, hoping that the soldiers have filled the gas tank during the previous night (another parallel to the tentative conclusion of *Dawn of the Dead*), Sarah manages to pull open the helicopter's back door only to encounter a zombie hand reaching out towards her. The image then abruptly changes to reveal Sarah recovering from another nightmare. She awakes near the helicopter and sees John and Bill fishing in a tropical paradise with seagulls flying above them. We also see the calendar which appeared in the very first sequence. But this time, the month is November with the initial three days crossed out. Seen in association with the previous images, the calendar suggests a new beginning on more than one level.

Unlike the previous screenplay drafts, *Day of the Dead* ends on a note of ambiguity. The zombies still remain in control but the three survivors *appear* to be in a more fortunate position than Fran and Peter in *Dawn of the Dead*. At least, they have had sufficient fuel in their helicopter enabling them to fly 'away to the Promised Land'. But have they? Since the audience never saw the soldier filling the tank at night as earlier requested, no guarantee exists that sufficient fuel is there. Furthermore, the final zombie assault on Sarah appears real. A possibility exists that the epilogue may represent the dying visions of all three survivors before their eventual annihilation. However, throughout the entire film the worlds of illusion and reality clash frequently whether in terms of personal ideologies (Rhodes, Logan, John, Sarah) or the conflicting worlds of hope and despair. *Day of the Dead* is a film structured upon duality: Sarah experiences two nightmares; Miguel undergoes two tours of duty in the bull pen; the audience sees Logan training Bub on two occasions; Logan verbally debates with Rhodes twice; Bub demonstrates his knowledge of firepower twice throughout the film. Duality is often a key mainstay of the horror genre with its contrasts between the worlds of normality and abnormality. However, if Sarah has lived and experienced three nightmares then this tentatively breaks the dualistic pattern structuring the entire narrative of *Day of the Dead*.

As in *Dawn*'s climax, Romero allows his human survivors to live on and struggle for another day. They have that chance which the musician thanks Billy for in *Knightriders*: 'Man, you gave us everything. You gave us a chance.' As Dave Kehr noted, their escape is little short of miraculous, an event revealing 'an inexplicable touch of grace' (quoted in Gagne 1987: 155), in terms reminiscent of John's religious use of imagery. As with Peter in *Dawn of the Dead*, religion contains metaphorical associations involving both hope and warning as long as they remain on the spiritual plane and not the institutional levels of the old society. Somehow, as if by magic, Sarah and her fellow survivors have escaped death and miraculously arrived on a peaceful island. Like the opening nightmare sequence of the film, Sarah appears to have abruptly awoken from a dream. But, whereas the initial sequence moved from a horrific fantasy to a deadly world of everyday reality, the climactic sequences of *Day of the Dead* move from another life-threatening situation affecting the heroine through her awakening to a tranquil world in which everyone lives in harmony with their environment.

According to the usual operations of the classical Hollywood editing system, the abrupt cut from the zombie hand threatening Sarah to her awakening on the island appears both arbitrary and disruptive. Something is missing in-between both sequences. However, this violation of the norms of the classical Hollywood editing system, norms which became more predominant during the 1980s and beyond, also represents Romero's homage to a radical montage system which Hollywood employed during the 1960s and early 1970s under the influence of the European art movie. Originally, within the modernist realms employed by 1920s Soviet cinema, this type of editing practice involved an attack upon the conventional mode of audience spectatorship and an attempt to move towards different forms of intellectually alternative practices. Although *Day of the Dead* operates in different ways, its use of this abrupt editing device not only represents a brief return to the practices Romero employed in *The Crazies* but also involves a challenge to the audience. How may characters suddenly move from a situation of extreme danger towards a utopian realm of harmony and peace?

CHAPTER ELEVEN

Monkey Shines

Partly due to financial and industrial problems that resulted in compromises affecting the final version of *Day of the Dead*, Romero officially ended his involvement with Laurel Entertainment (see Gagne 1987: 147–70). He now wanted freedom to pursue other projects. Although Romero maintained his base in Pittsburgh, he still hoped for that optimistic union between his mode of independent film-making and Hollywood industrial support. *Monkey Shines* is the product of this ideal. Financed by a major studio (Orion) but shot in Pittsburgh with the involvement of as many of his creative team as possible, the film also represents his first major literary adaptation. Michael Stewart's original novel was set in Oxford, England, but Romero transfers the setting to Pittsburgh. The film appears to represent a radical change for the director both stylistically and thematically. On a first viewing, it initially appears to be the unfortunate product of compromise and seems to lack the type of visual style and thematic concerns present in Romero's other films. During pre- and post-production phases, Romero experienced several examples of creative frustration. Despite Christine Forrest's abilities as an actress, the studio insisted that she test for the role of Nurse Maryanne Hodges before they would accept her. Also, after previews, Orion added a last-minute gratuitous shock ending combining the already shopworn audience scare tactics seen in *Carrie* (1976) and *Alien* (1979) which jarred with the director's type of more subtle climax. The studio also insisted on a traditional happy ending to replace Romero's more ambiguous and ironic conclusion. Naturally, *Monkey Shines* did not attract the same degree of critical and popular acclaim surrounding other Romero films.

With these factors in mind, it would be natural to dismiss *Monkey Shines* as one of Romero's failed works deserving little attention. However, although it fails to reach the creative levels of *Night of the Living Dead*, *The Crazies*, *Dawn of the Dead* and *Day of the Dead*, it is by no means a total failure. Despite the compromises affecting its production, the film has several points of interest both in terms of the cultural concepts influencing Romero as well as parallels to his authorship concerns elsewhere. In many ways, *Monkey Shines* resembles *There's Always Vanilla* as a compromised work. While the latter film represented Latent Image's attempt to 'go Hollywood', it also exhibited many traces of the director's future concerns. Stylistically, *Monkey Shines* lacks the exciting rawness and dynamism of Romero's brand of low-budget film-making and superficially appears to resemble an average Hollywood production. Yet it contains many key Romero themes and its more intuitive employment of acting and direction deserves further investigation.

Like many other Romero films, the important elements appear indirectly within the text awaiting excavation by discerning viewers who move beyond the superficial mechanisms of gore and thrills to penetrate the real causes motivating such excessive displays. In an era dominated by the *Friday the 13th* and *Nightmare on Elm Street* series, *Monkey Shines* was doomed to failure if Orion regarded it as a rival to such gratuitously popular competitors. But, based on an understated, underrated novel,[1] *Monkey Shines* actually operates on much more subtle levels which would appeal to a director hailed for introducing new, explicit forms into the horror genre but also interested in other more mature and subtle avenues of exploration. Careful attention to the film reveals an extremely ambiguous and complex work, both in terms of the creative screenwriting Romero employs as well as his masterful direction of acting performances. *Monkey Shines* is a film containing much more than meets the eye; it is a work in which the plot operates as a mere device for the director to engage in further explorations of the human condition. As with gore and zombies in Romero's other films, the device of a murderous monkey is really equivalent to Hitchcock's 'MacGuffin'. Other important things are going on in *Monkey Shines*.

Although lacking naturalism's stylistic features, *Monkey Shines* does have several parallels to one of the genre's major premises, namely the thin division between savagery and civilisation characteristic of late nineteenth- and early twentieth-century literature. Like Jacques Lantier in Zola's *La Bête Humaine* and Frank Norris' McTeague, Allan Mann (Jason Beghe) has to struggle with atavistic feelings. His subconscious feelings of resentment emerge in anger against his betrayers and a mother who wishes to keep him in a state of infantile dependence. Although many of Zola's unfortunate Lantier family often succumb to the curse of hereditary degeneracy exacerbated by malign environmental influences, Allan Mann's dilemma is more the result of those conditioned civilised instinctual patterns of behaviour motivating Romero's zombies and human characters.

For most of *Monkey Shines*, the audience believes the collision with a truck 'explains' Allan's quadriplegic condition. However, halfway through the film, Dr. Williams (William Newman) suggests that a 'congenital problem' may really have caused his condition: 'The accident could have been just a tragic coincidence.' This scene follows two significant associated movements in the screenplay. When Allan's mother Dorothy (Joyce Van Pattern) announces her intention of giving up her independent existence to move in and 'mother' him as before, her son's hand briefly moves. When Allan excitedly points out to her this sign of his possible improvement, Dorothy denies it and complains instead about his behaviour towards her. She refuses to recognise that her son's irritation results from his resentment at her wish to dominate and make him dependent upon her as in infancy. In the next scene, Allan expresses his fear of capuchin monkey Ella whom he will later blame for subsequent murderous events. Like his mother, he denies several unpleasant facts in his life and conveniently places the blame elsewhere upon a scapegoat in a manner paralleling the denial mechanisms employed by the main characters of *There's Always Vanilla* and *Jack's Wife*.

As with other figures in Romero's films, Allan of *Monkey Shines* is not totally admirable. He is a complex individual with several negative features buried within his own personality which he refuses to come to terms with. As a result, *Monkey Shines* is a much more ambiguous film beneath the surface. Romero directs Jason Beghe's Allan so that he depicts several complex layers of human behaviour ranging from a character attracting audience sympathy due to his condition to an angry profane white male who manipulates others emotionally. Despite the studio's attempt to find an easy explanation by blaming Ella, Romero's screenplay and direction suggests other more ambiguous levels of meaning. Although the visual style of *Monkey Shines* appears to differ from Romero's more independently conceived works, its characters and content are not entirely divorced from previous concerns. Like many characters in Romero's other films, the leading players in *Monkey Shines* are complex figures exhibiting contradictory tendencies who often engage in aspects of duplicity and self-deception threatening their entire personalities.

After a studio disclaimer concerning the treatment of capuchin monkeys used in Boston University's programme to help the disabled, *Monkey Shines* opens with a tranquil image of Allan's house. As the credits roll, the camera slowly moves right to zoom towards the upper window in a manner resembling the opening sequence of *Psycho*. Like Hitchcock's film, this opening shot suggests that the future horrific events of Romero's film are somehow connected with a character we will soon see. The scene changes to an interior view as Allan moves into the frame from below appearing in a mid close-up as he awakens. Next, the camera moves slowly right to show his sleeping girlfriend Linda Aikman (Janine Turner) at his side before zooming out to frame them both in mid-shot. As he demurely covers her nude body with the sheet, he whispers his intention of going for a morning run. The next show shows him exercising nude in another room before he raises the outside blinds and looks outside. Before the beginning of David Shire's lyrical music, Romero shows Allan's hands putting bricks into his backpack prior to his morning run.

These opening shots are not superfluous to the following narrative. They suggest several things about Allan and his relationship to Billy of *Knightriders*. Like Billy, Allan is a perfectionist and takes pleasure in his physical prowess. However, Romero subtly suggests that his hero has certain unwholesome features in his personality that he is unaware of. Although Allan is not living in a medieval fantasy outside society like Billy, he is wholeheartedly committed to a pursuit of perfection into which he channels his whole energies. He follows two demanding paths of being a law student as well as a college athlete, either of which would ordinarily tax the energies of any individual. Rather than remaining in bed with Linda, he decides to go out for an early morning run. His desires have masochistic undertones; while Billy exhibits these features by flagellating himself ritually every morning, Allan puts heavy bricks into his backpack thus making a run which ought to be a pleasurable exercise more of a punishing ritual. Although the audience gains little explicit information about Allan's real motivations in these opening scenes, it does receive certain suggestive information warning them not to identify with *Monkey Shines'* nominal hero but rather to engage in objective observation and analyse particular features motivating his character.

As Allan runs through the peaceful streets, a series of shots alternate between objective views of him running before the camera and his subjective perceptions of the people he sees. Romero also films his running feet making him appear like a Pegasus figure following the novel's description of its nominal hero. However, as Allan runs further, a sudden subjective shot shows the presence of a large dog looming before a gate, its restraining leash hidden by the bushes. It lunges forward, causing Allan to collide with a truck. A slow-motion low-angle shot shows Allan flying through the air, ironically attaining his Pegasus ideal, before the succeeding image reveals bricks from his backpack disintegrating on the ground – an apt metaphor for his disabling injuries. Again, these images foreshadow others which will occur later in the film involving alternation between objective and subjective perception as well as the atavistic motifs contained in the screenplay. Significantly, the dog appears to be running wild. However, both the audience and Allan see that it is restrained by a leash similar to the leash binding Ella's body in certain scenes of the film.

The next sequence shows the hospital operating room. Individual shots reveal a monitor and respirator before showing Allan on the operating table. Then, the camera pans left to show the operating theatre staff. Allan's body is now regarded as little more than a piece of human machinery which Dr. John Wiseman (Stanley Tucci) crudely rejoices over as something he can exhibit his egotistic sense of authority. His repugnant manner reveals itself in the opening lines following a nurse's affirmative comment concerning Allan's unconscious position on the operating table once the anaesthetic takes effect: 'Good. Then we can talk about him. Martha. His ass is even hairier than yours.' After ending the sequence with the surgeon's knife beginning the operation, the next scene silently and poignantly reveals the tragic circumstances surrounding Allan's new position in life. Like the silent but meaningful introductory sequence in Hawks' *Rio Bravo*, Romero opens with a close-up of a black-and-white photo of Allan in his athletic prime winning a race. The camera then pans slowly right to reveal a Roadrunner cartoon 'get well' card, a colour photo of Allan, Geoff, Linda and Coach Charlie Cunningham, a single photo of Linda and other 'get well' cards. Then the camera passes a table containing Allan's medication, and finally halts at a close-up of a now bearded Allan immobile in bed fully conscious of his new situation. Romero visually conveys Allan's feelings in a camera movement also reminiscent of Jean-Luc Godard's cinematic examples of montage in *mise-en-scène*.[2] He then lap-dissolves from Allan's face to show Wiseman's car arriving outside Allan's house. Although this appears to be a natural cinematic transition from one scene to another, Romero's rare use of this technique in *Monkey Shines* (as well as most of his other films) suggests some implicit connection between Allan's condition and the responsibility of the surgeon, a connection which later events will affirm. A lap-dissolve also significantly occurs later in the film after Allan has phoned Linda's house and discovered Wiseman's presence there. The lap-dissolve changes from the embrace of Linda and Wiseman to a close-up of Allan's angry face.

Dorothy sees Wiseman arrive and rushes to greet him at the door. She appears overjoyed at his arrival as if expressing pleasure at the presence of a man who has put her son in a dependent condition. She eagerly introduces him to everyone at the welcome party as 'Dr. John Wiseman, the genius who saved my Allan's life.' However, Allan's law professor, Dr. Esther Fry (Tudi Wiggins), rejects Dorothy's fascination with institutional titles and insists on being addressed by her first name only. Unlike Dorothy, she is also concerned about Allan's progress towards some form of independence and asks Wiseman whether he will be able to continue his studies. Wiseman replies, 'Physically yes. The question is *will* he want to.' His answer also emphasises the main concentration of *Monkey Shines*, namely its focus on human consciousness and related responsibility.

After meeting Charley Cunningham (Tom Quinn) whose hesitation ('I'm ... I was Allan's coach') he does nothing to contradict, Wiseman asks Linda 'How're you holding up?' Her guilt-ridden reticence together with the penetrating nature of his question leads her to go to Allan's bathroom and clear away her personal things. Tensions are clearly in the air prior to Allan's arrival. They are evident in the meaningful, but understated, performances directed by Romero and professionally delivered by his actors.

When Allan arrives, Dorothy overenthusiastically utters the toast, 'To Allan, to the start of his new life.' Linda belatedly arrives and places her night bag containing personal possessions unobtrusively in the corner before guiltily rushing up and kissing him: 'I should have come to visit you more often at the hospital. I'm sorry.' Recognising the strain on Linda, Wiseman complicity removes her from the scene by asking her to get him a large whiskey for Allan which he has medically 'prescribed'. Wiseman manipulates this tense situation in several ways. He wishes to deflect Allan's attention from losing his girlfriend by getting him intoxicated. Wiseman also dominates Linda in the same supercilious manner he used towards a conscientious nurse in the earlier operating room sequence. When Linda goes to the kitchen, she drinks some of Allan's whiskey before hired nurse Maryanne Hodges (Christine Forrest) appears on the scene to take control of the situation. She removes the glass from Linda's hand, pours the contents into a plastic container, refuses the use of ice cubes and dilutes the whiskey with tap water. Wishing to remove herself from an embarrassing situation, the distraught Linda tries to phone Allan's friend, Geoffrey Fisher (John Pankow), a researcher in craniology, who is absent from his office.

These masterfully underplayed performances in the film's third sequence aptly suggest tensions which will explicitly emerge into violent manifestations later. They also reveal Romero's competent and intuitive control of acting performances which are often neglected by audiences who prefer more 'gory' effects rather than complex acting. Without explicitly spelling out meanings, the various characters in this welcome-home sequence reveal many hidden sides of their motivations. Dorothy seems to relish the celebration much more than any grieving mother should. Wiseman appears uneasy at his requested presence; so does Linda in her role as obligatory grieving girlfriend. When Allan arrives, he puts on a brave face for his new role as quadriplegic but it is unnatural, suggesting deep frustration and unhappiness. Wiseman 'prescribes' a large whiskey for Allan which Maryanne immediately modifies ('and if we use alcohol we water it down'). Maryanne's character immediately exercises the type of control that Allan soon negatively reacts against. Most of the characters take advantage of his vulnerable position to dominate him in one way or another. Despite the superficial veneer of a homecoming party, Romero suggests that the actual event is not really positive and that dark repressed tensions exist below the surface.

The next sequence shows Geoff arriving at his laboratory with a container holding a human brain from a Jane Doe donator who died on the operating table. As he enters his laboratory containing capuchin monkeys, he switches from the red light to normal fluorescent illumination as he shows his prize to his favourite female monkey, 'Number Six'. After injecting himself with a drug to ward off sleep, he slices off portions of the brain before boiling it in a solution and eventually injecting a dose into 'Number Six'. Geoff aims to increase her intelligence in his experiments. The sequence appears straightforward in nature, but, like the previous party scenes, many disturbing factors appear here.

Despite his seemingly harmless appearance, Geoff has much in common with Dr. Logan of *Day of the Dead*. Both men are exclusively devoted to their work and show no real understanding of the broader consequences of their experiments in terms of the effect on others. Secondly, while Rhodes nicknamed Logan 'Frankenstein', Geoff is also a similar figure. Rather than the Gothic laboratory of the Universal films, Geoff inhabits an antiseptic laboratory flooded by white fluorescent light. However, his clinical environment is by no means devoid of the satanic associations connected with scientific experiments in earlier films such as *Metropolis* (1926) and *The Bride of Frankenstein* (1935). Before Geoff switches the fluorescent lights on, his laboratory is immersed in sombre red safety lighting making it more reminiscent of a hellish environment than a modern clinical area. Also, when Geoff mixes the brain in his chemical solution, he utters the witch chorus from *Macbeth* – 'Double, double, toil and trouble. Fire burn and cauldron bubble.' Unlike the witches who stimulate Macbeth's ambitious desires by acting as outside agents who, nevertheless, know their victim better than he knows himself in the earlier part of the play, Geoff knowingly nurtures his own ambitions for scientific achievement. But his objective scientific activities are as deadly as the witches' brew in *Macbeth*. He is also a Dr. Frankenstein who will create a bride of Frankenstein for a friend who will use the 'bride' as an agent to activate his own unrepressed desires in the same way as Colin Clive uses Boris Karloff in James Whale's film. Also, another reference to *The Bride of Frankenstein* appears in Romero's reference to the human brain. Like the brain in the original film, Geoff's specimen has 'no apparent abnormality'. However, unlike the hunchback (Dwight Frye) in *The Bride of Frankenstein*, Geoff does not damage it. Romero thus avoids the flawed rational scientific explanation which mars Whale's film. He intends to show that Ella's activities really emerge from Allan's 'dark half'. Unlike Karloff's creature, Ella is the result of a successful, not an accidental, experiment.

When Geoff plays his answer machine he belatedly receives Linda's message and arrives later in the evening when Allan is in bed. Announcing his presence by tapping on the window and using the key he had when he lodged with Allan, Geoff walks through the house which contains poignant reminders of his friend's past and present condition. On the wall are travel posters of places Allan will never visit again such as Jamaica and Barbados. A point of view shot reveals Geoff's perspective of the winch in his friend's bathroom. During the following dialogue, Allan reveals two items which suggest his deep resentment. He feels economically dependent on Dorothy who has provided money for the home facilities. Despite knowing the real facts concerning his friend's inability to ever pay off the debts, Geoff remarks, 'Don't worry. You'll pay her back. Lawyers get rich', without dwelling on the fact that there are very few rich successful quadriplegic lawyers. Allan also reveals his knowledge of Linda's alienation from him despite the fact that 'She didn't say anything.' When Geoff responds, 'If she walks out on you now, fuck her', Allan replies poignantly, 'I can't.' His feelings of impotence, sexual jealousy and revenge will later emerge when he has both the relevant *will* and means at his disposal to achieve his goals.

Allan also harbours deep feelings of resentment against his mother since early childhood. During the next scene, Dorothy runs a home movie despite Allan's lack of interest. It shows him playing in a back yard with other children. However, an ominous note sounds when Dorothy reminds Allan that the Patterson family who rented their Chicago Lake Side adjoining property moved away and that Allan blamed her for their departure. Allan obviously missed the only companions he had in his youth. When Dorothy mentions Allan blaming her for the Patterson family's departure, Maryanne's budgie, Bogie, suddenly flies into the room and flaps over him in a manner reminiscent of the winged representatives of repressed violent desires in Hitchcock's *The Birds* (1963). Although Bogie does not have the same associations that Ella will later have for him, the bird's appearance at that particular moment suggestively represent Allan's repressed embodiment of aggressive feelings towards Dorothy in the same way as Hitchcock's winged avatars represent Lydia Brenner's resentment towards Melanie Daniels. This will not be the first time in *Monkey Shines* that a human being will use an animal to express feelings of resentment and deny that very form of manipulation.

The next scene in the home movie shows young Allan refusing to wear the Halloween costume Dorothy has purchased for him. He looks resentfully towards the camera expressing his irritation. Allan comments, 'I always wanted to be Robbie the Robot. Guess, I finally got my wish.' Romero's reference to *Forbidden Planet* (1956) and its 'monster from the id' theme is not accidental as succeeding events reveal.

Geoff also faces his own form of pressure. After chasing away animal rights activists spray-painting the outside walls, he faces his departmental head, Dean Burbage (Stephen Root), a threatening administrator who relishes appearing on talk-shows (Romero's favourite media bogey) to promote vivisection. Burbage also regards medical science in the university as another institutional arm of capitalism. Burbage wishes his subordinate to provide 'results'. When Geoff attempts to argue with Burbage on his own ideological terms, 'It's not costing anything', his tormenter beats him at a game he knows only too well. Burbage replies, 'It's costing time, Geoffrey. I don't want to fire you. I just want you to *produce*.' Burbage also snoops into Geoff's lab, wishing to discover his results and claim it as his own work similar to the activities of certain senior academics who exploit their graduate students. As in 'The Crate' episode of *Creepshow*, the world of higher education is a negative institutional environment. Later, Burbage describes himself as a 'realist', rather than Geoff's more accurate description of 'sadist'. As Geoff views in horror Burbage's malignant experiment with a drowning rat, the latter comments, 'By the carrot or by the stick. I prefer the stick. It's close to what we experience in real life.' Little difference exists between Burbage and Logan of *Day of the Dead*. Although the latter believes in rewarding his zombies who show 'civility', his tape recording reveals that punitive methods are also involved in his methods.

These encounters set in force a chain of circumstances which will eventually lead to disaster. Geoff feels pressured to increase Number Six's dosage: 'You should be playing chess with the dosage you get. My ass is on the line. So is yours. It has to work. You're half human. Why don't you show something for Christ's sake?' Allan's later attempt at suicide leads him to remove the monkey from its other less-developed companions and give it the human stimulus it needs, one which is beneficial neither to animal or human. Despite his supposedly offering Number Six the 'carrot' of Allan's human contact, Burbage's 'stick' philosophy also motivates his actions.

Geoff injects the monkey with serum attempting to make it more human. Ironically, he believes that it will benefit all concerned. Unfortunately, like the scientists in *The Crazies* and *Day of the Dead*, he is so closely bound up in his work that he does not realise that human civilisation is really a mixed blessing and not something to be emulated in its present form. Even the unscrupulous Wiseman (who has by now appropriated Linda) recognises that civilised human family life has its dangers when he argues against Dorothy's postponing her return to Illinois. He sees it as harmful for both herself and her son: 'I think you might be aggravating the situation. Go back home. Go back to your business.' But he also dismisses Geoff's concern over Allan by brusquely commenting that 'six out of ten quadriplegics attempt suicide at one point or another', before walking away with Linda and leaving Allan to his fate. Geoff then decides to enlist the aid of animal trainer, Melanie Parker (Kate McNeil) ostensibly to help his friend as a household friend for the disabled but also to continue his experiments unethically from afar. Like many characters in *Monkey Shines*, Geoff's motivations appear ambivalent. It is extremely difficult to decide which one really dominates his mind. Does he really want to help his friend? Or use him for a scientific experiment? Both factors may compete with one another so that any certainty is difficult. Dorothy definitely wants to look after her son, but she also desires to dominate him. Allan later becomes a human battleground torn by conscious attempts to control dark desires. However, he also unconsciously enjoys the release of unrepressed violent energies channelled against whom those he hates.

Monkey Shines is thus really a complex film dealing with the ambiguous nature of human motivations. Such motivations exist within the personalities of people unable to deal directly with the consequences and responsibilities of human desires and energies. It is a feature common to *There's Always Vanilla*, *The Crazies*, *Jack's Wife*, *Martin* and the zombie trilogy.

Despite Maryanne's irritation, Geoff and Melanie introduce Number Six (now named Ella) to Allan's home. Ella and her human master eventually form a close bond, so much so that Allan comments, 'She does so much for me. She seems to want to do things for me.' However, this is Allan's perception. Although the audience may fall into the trap of reading the Frankenstein 'damaged brain' explanation into *Monkey Shines* like the scientific explanation in *Night of the Living Dead*, other explanations are equally possible. Despite her booster shots, Ella may not be acting independently but really serving Allan's desires to the same extent as the zombies in Romero's trilogy enact basic human instincts their supposedly deceased status appears to deny. Later, Allan significantly recognises that Ella is also 'part' of him.

During the opening scenes of *Monkey Shines*, Allan engaged in a masochistically punitive system of training. Now no longer able to channel his negative energies into athletic pursuits, he transmits them against his nurse Maryanne. Although Maryanne resembles Wilma of *Creepshow* with her non-appealing personality, the audience has no evidence to believe that she is as culpable as Allan believes her to be. With the exception of figures such as Captain Rhodes of *Day of the Dead*, Romero's fictional characters are very rarely one-dimensional. Naturally, Maryanne does not like her job. She sits around most of the time due to Ella now taking over most of her duties and becomes irritated at her client's negative behaviour resulting from his resented immobility: 'I'm sick and tired of your insults.'

But these factors do not really justify the way Allan treats her. He blames Maryanne for the lack of hygiene and dismisses her complaint that Ella is really responsible for the state of his house. However, when Allan shouts '*We* get pissed off', Maryanne immediately suspects some negative intonations concerning his use of the plural tense. She intuitively responds, 'It's unnatural! You and that monkey.' After Bogie flaps over Allan's face and appears to nearly peck out his eye (an action foreshadowing Ella's later use of the syringe over Melanie's immobile body), Ella later disposes of the offending object at night. Undoubtedly, she performs Allan's desired wish as Maryanne recognises when she blames him in front of Dorothy for Bogie's demise: 'You killed my Bogie. Not with his hands. He had his little demon do it. You did it. The two of you together.' Maryanne significantly terms Ella a 'demon'. It is almost as if she intuitively understands that the monkey resembles a familiar spirit of one of the witches in *Macbeth*. When Allan sarcastically rages against Maryanne concerning the reasons for her beloved pet's death – 'Who gives a shit? It deserved to die' – his unrepressed anger both certainly affirms Maryanne's suspicions as well as suggesting to the audience that Ella may not have acted on her own.

At the same time, Dorothy returns after deciding to sell her home and business to move in with Allan. Already feeling embarrassed at Dorothy taking over Maryanne's task by bathing him as if he were still a little child, Allan learns about a female conspiracy. This revelation further fuels his angry feelings concerning his resented dependence upon others. Dorothy informs him that Maryanne gave notice of quitting a week before; Mother immediately decided to devote herself exclusively to Allan without informing him of this change and allowing him the possibility of making other plans. When Dorothy puts Allan to bed she exhibits pleasure at dominating her son once again by commenting, 'I'll be here when you need me.' However, his hand suddenly moves in reaction to his feelings of angry dependency. Although she never sees the movement, Dorothy perversely refuses to acknowledge any sign of her son's recovery and encourage him to leave his dependent condition: 'Your hand did not move. It cannot move.' She then provokes Allan's angry outburst and refuses to acknowledge its real causes by retreating into her closed world of genteel civility: 'I don't like how you're behaving. I don't like it at all.' Significantly, Allan experiences his first vision of moving outside the house in Ella's body that very same night. Romero conveys this to the audience by using a low-angle, Steadicam subjective shot from the perspective of a monkey. This shot complements the earlier credit Steadicam objective shot of Allan's feet running before the camera. It suggests a deep symbiotic relationship between master and animal servant parallel to that existing in *The Bride of Frankenstein* (1935).

Like many Romero characters, Allan is torn by conflicting desires which he can never really overcome. When Geoff examines the attic and finds evidence of Ella's nightly excursions, he denies this in his desire to continue using his friend for his own ends. Allan now becomes afraid of Ella and wishes her removal. However, he conveniently projects his fears on to a surrogate object and blames Ella. This resembles the very same manner that Colin Clive's Dr. Frankenstein abandons and blames a creature whose creation he was directly responsible for in *The Bride of Frankenstein*. Allan expresses his fears to Geoff and Melanie: 'It's like I was in Ella's body, running with her strength, seeing through her eyes. I'm part of her and she's part of me.'

The following sequence strengthens the screenplay's suggestion of a deep symbiotic relationship existing between Allan and Ella in which the human factor is really the dominant factor motivating the animal's actions. After consulting Dr. Williams for a second opinion, Allan and Melanie learn that his quadriplegic condition is much more complex. Indirectly criticising 'the brilliant Dr. Wiseman', Dr. Williams informs Allan that his condition may be actually 'part of a congenital problem, an abnormality that doesn't look like it was caused by a truck. The accident could have been part of a tragic coincidence.' Allan's condition is thus psychosomatic rather than material. The film does not choose to explore what exactly this 'congenital problem' actually is. However, Romero's screenplay and the excellent acting performances by Jason Beghe and Joyce Van Patten suggest that Allan's condition really results from a dysfunctional family situation affecting them both. Dorothy has always attempted to dominate her son since he was little as the revealing home movie showed. Allan thus resented her controlling manner from an early age. His masochistic training techniques appear more related to his psychological condition rather than being a part of a normal training exercise. Allan appears to have channelled his violently sadistic feelings against his family upbringing into masochistic channels. He desired to achieve in the solitary goal of winning, both as an athlete and as a law student, as a means to exert independence from a constraining situation. Ironically, he had ended up in the situation of family dependency he attempted to escape from. As Dr. Williams suggests, Allan's 'accident' has deeper causes than the 'tragic coincidence' of his random collision with a truck. The symbolic appearance of the savage dog attempting to escape from its leash in the credit sequence has already intimated such a possibility.

Dr. Williams maintains an institutional dimension of professional silence when Allan asks him about Wiseman's operation: 'So if he had looked harder and found what caused it, he could have fixed it?' Allan then forms the logical conclusion. Ella immediately jumps on Allan's shoulder as Romero uses a voice-over to articulate the injured party's angry thoughts: 'Wiseman! That motherfucker. That smarmy self-satisfied son of a bitch.' This technique only appears once in this sequence. Its very arbitrary appearance suggests that the director intends that his audience arrive at a significant meaning. The next shot shows Melanie's eyes through the front window of her van as she listens to Allan's anger: 'He put me through this whole fucking thing due to his own incompetence.' The thought mediated in a previous scene through a voice-over making the audience knowledgeable about Allan's feelings now becomes explicit for another character in this scene. As Allan rages, Romero cuts from a close-up of Ella to her angry master, suggesting a deep bond between them. Melanie also discerns certain unhealthy feelings: 'I don't like this change in you, Allan.' As the next sequence reveals, thought becomes translated into action. This intimates that, like Karloff's Frankenstein's monster, a creature is not entirely guilty since it merely performs its master's desires.

When Allan gets Ella to contact the phone numbers of Wiseman and Linda, he finally learns the double nature of his betrayal. Romero pertinently concludes the scene of Wiseman and Linda embracing with a lap-dissolve to Allan's hurt expression. Juxtaposed matching close-ups of the eyes and teeth of Allan and Ella then follow. When Allan bites his lip in emotional pain, blood trickles down his cheek. Ella immediately leaps to comfort her master by licking the blood away. The next sequence reveals Ella as a 'blood sister' in both thought and action. Point of view shots then follow in rapid succession revealing Ella's progress to Linda's house, Wiseman and Linda coupling in the bedroom and a shot of fire filling the screen.

The next morning Allan exhibits his knowledge of the deaths of Linda and Wiseman before Dorothy actually tells him. He informs Geoff about his desire for Ella's removal and blames her for the deaths. However, as the dialogue reveals, the issue is really ambiguous. While Geoff asserts, 'Ella would never have done it', Allan replies, 'I wanted it done ... I thought about ways of doing it. I knew that old cabin. I knew it would burn fast.' However, when Melanie confronts Allan with the revealing question, 'Did you do it, or did she?' he chooses to absolve himself of any responsibility for his actions in a manner resembling Joan Mitchell in *Jack's Wife* – 'She did it. She acted on her own.' Allan's explanations are also contradictory as the following lines reveal: 'Geoff, I've been so full of anger. I've had the most horrible thoughts lately, vomiting up every resentful thought I've had, everything ugly, vicious, and sinful. That's what it is – it's sin. It's the desire to sin, Geoff. Ella's played into that.' Allan's refusal to take the full consequences for his actions by deciding to blame supposedly supernatural forces places him in the same culpable category as Joan Mitchell.

Significantly, after appearing to take responsibility for his actions, Allan retreats into an anachronistic and implausible explanation which bares no relationship to any of the film's events. He is eager to blame his servant for executing the master's desires. When Ella instinctively retreats before a match, thus disproving Allan's contention that she set Linda's home on fire, Allan remarks, 'Is that an instinctive reaction? Or does she know what fire can do?' He is clearly putting his legal training into action to absolve himself of any responsibility for his role in the murder of Wiseman and Linda. Geoff decides to take Ella back to the laboratory to perform tests even though he sees through Allan's religious excuses: 'But I don't expect to find sin in a urine sample.' Ella also reacts to her removal and poignantly appeals to her master when Geoff drags her away. However, Allan ignores her pleas and tells Geoff, 'Don't bring her back', rejecting her in the same way Colin Clive's Frankenstein ignored responsibility for his creation in Whale's film.

Melanie then decides to take Allan away to a different environment which turns out to be her country home. Despite his angry reaction against Dorothy's manipulated attempts to return him to a state of infantile dependence, Allan weeps in Melanie's arms like a little boy expressing his desire to 'try to' get better. This action certainly reveals both Allan's own form of manipulative tendencies and the type of cunning tactic he will later use against Ella at the climax of the film when he deceives her about his real intentions. Although Allan expresses his indebtedness concerning the supposed benefits of tranquil surroundings – 'I can feel myself coming back to normal' – Melanie humorously, but significantly, questions his motives, 'Every minute you're away from me, or Ella?' Allan replies, 'Both.' He then nuzzles up to Melanie in the same manner Ella did to him and initiates love-making. Allan's movements again appear manipulative rather than spontaneous, suggesting that he is the real puppet-master and not Ella. When Allan apologises to Melanie, he has a knowing expression on his face like an actor delivering a prepared performance rather than a spontaneous response.

In the meantime, Geoff attends to Ella in his laboratory noticing the difference she has from the rest of the capuchin monkeys. His remarks are extremely significant in suggesting not only Allan's undeniable role in Ella's activities but also the fact that he may be manipulating her: 'They're all getting the same dosage. The missing ingredient must be Allan.' After noting Ella's lack of pain during her next injection, Geoff remarks to her, 'You didn't do all that stuff Allan's been blaming you for ... you couldn't have committed murder.' If Allan is the 'missing ingredient' in Ella's case, the same is also true of the brain serum Geoff injects her with. When he notes Ella's lack of pain afterwards he comments, 'I've turned you into a fucking junkie.' Geoff, of course, has performed similar actions to Dr. Logan in *Day of the Dead* by making his subject all too human and deadlier than a mere animal. Furthermore, the animals respond to human anger and do not act on their own initiative as two later scenes reveal. When Geoff returns to find Burbage has stolen his experiments, the caged monkeys reproduce his anger by jumping around in their cages. They enact Geoff's frustration in the same way as Ella responds to Allan's dark desires. Secondly, after Geoff injects himself with the serum and experiences Ella's perception, the monkeys escape from their cages and destroy his laboratory as a way of responding to his murderous intention of killing Ella. They certainly wish to protect one of their own species who has undergone a devious form of human experimentation. Geoff also switches off the florescent lighting and undergoes the experiment while infernoesque red light bathes his laboratory. Although he begins the experiment by saying to Ella, 'If this shot can plug you into Allan's head then maybe it can plug me into yours', like Allan he denies the fact that he may also be using Ella in the same way that Allan does.

While Geoff performs the experiment, Allan and Dorothy engage in another domestic conflict. Already angry at his weekend tryst with Melanie, Dorothy bathes Allan. Unlike the costumes she wore earlier in the film, she is now dressed as a traditional mother with pinafore and unattractive gown. Romero intercuts the scenes showing the development of the explosive resentment between mother and son with subjective shots of Ella's journey to the house and Geoff immobile in the laboratory. Humans and animal are equally involved in experiencing dangerous conflicts and tensions. Boundaries between the supposedly rational world of humans and the more violent animal world dissolve. Romero's screenplay deserves careful attention since it develops important levels of meaning during this sequence. Although Allan attempts to 'bury the hatchet' twice, Dorothy's resentment against Melanie and the refusal of her son to return to a desired state of infantile dependency finally leads to verbal and physical violence.

In many ways, the scene is highly reminiscent of *Night of the Living Dead*'s interior farmhouse conflict where humans war against each other while dangerous inhuman enemies wait outside to overpower them. Despite Allan's realisation of the dangerous effects of his emotional behaviour, he immediately regresses to abusing Dorothy verbally and blaming Ella for actions he has initiated himself. After 'sensing' Ella's presence in the house, he pleads with Dorothy: 'These rages. Ella pulls them out of me. Ella pulls them to the surface.' Despite attempting to warn his mother, Allan also denies his real responsibility. She also engages in denial and expresses her resentment for domestic slavery against her son, blaming Allan for a decision she made in the first place: 'I've given up everything for you.' Allan angrily responds, 'Who asked you to give up anything?' He also vehemently unleashes all his repressed anger against her: 'You're nothing but an empty, greedy black hole. You've been trying to suck me into it for as long as I can remember. I cannot stand it anymore. I cannot stand your bullshit. You conniving, clinging, bloodthirsty, bitch!' Allan's verbal assault leads to Dorothy's physical attack on him before she leaves the room.

Allan's anger against Dorothy appears initially justifiable under the circumstances. However, he is not entirely innocent. Some of the things he accuses Dorothy of also apply to himself. In his later strategy against Ella, Allan reveals himself as equally 'conniving' and 'bloodthirsty'. His tendency to blame Ella for carrying out his own repressed desires is also 'bullshit'. Like many Romero characters, Allan struggles between rational control and succumbing to dark, self-destructive tendencies buried deeply within the human personality. Realising the presence of his 'familiar spirit' in the house, he attempts in vain to warn Dorothy before Ella electrocutes her. Also, when Geoff arrives at the house, he asks Allan, 'Ella's not in here with you?' When Allan replies, 'No, I don't think so', Romero zooms out from Allan on the bed. He finishes the movement at an angle equivalent to Ella's perspective seen in a previous shot which revealed her perched on top of his bedroom cabinet in the very same position.

Allan still vacillates between admitting his responsibility for Ella's action and denying it. When Allan finally admits, 'It's me. I've killed them, all of them', Geoff replies, 'You couldn't kill anything, Allan.' However, at this moment, Allan knows himself much better than his friend: 'I've had five thousand years of civilisation in me. But what if I wasn't civilised anymore? What if I was an animal? Then, I follow my instincts. That's what this all is, instinct. Animal instinct. It lives in us all, lives by it's own set of laws, laws of the jungle.' However, when Geoff admits his own responsibility, Allan sees an escape route so he can now avoid blaming himself and engage in denial. Geoff gives the 'scientific' explanation which most audiences would readily accept. Unlike Allan, he also blames himself and sees his culpability in the affair. Geoff thus arrives at a state of understanding far exceeding Dr. Logan in *Day of the Dead*: 'You didn't do it, Allan. I did. Ella has been genetically altered. I've had her on a new drug all this time. I lost track, Allan. I lost track of everything but my work.' However, the human factor is still important since the 'new drug' enabled Ella to reach a higher stage of development not entirely advanced or ethical. Both scientist and patient bear equal responsibility for programming an animal to enact violent desires which are really part of an instinctually violent human condition.

Allan immediately seizes on Geoff's admission and angrily reacts against him in a manner recalling his earlier attitude against Wiseman: 'I was just part of an experiment? A guinea pig? What did you do to Ella? What did you do to me?' Interestingly enough, these last two sentences reveal again that he intuitively still regards Ella as inseparable from himself. Ella then attacks Geoff and proves herself more intelligent than her human adversary by using his deadly syringe on him. Although Geoff still has some final moments of consciousness, he refuses Allan's request to use the phone to enlist help choosing instead to go for medical treatment and save his already discredited scientific reputation. His final stubborn desire to keep Ella's activities secret lead to his demise. Allan then realises that his Frankenstein monster now wishes to control him as she begins to feed him like a child. However, Allan also realises their deep bond: 'You can't hurt me. I'm part of you.'

When Melanie later arrives inside the house and sees Geoff's body, her lines reveal a much more accurate understanding of the real situation. She asks, 'Did you do that or did she?' Allan again engages in denial, 'She did it.' But, before Ella attacks her, Melanie knowingly responds, 'That's right, Allan. *You* had nothing to do with it.' At this point in the film, Ella is really kin to Bub of *Day of the Dead* rather than being an external threat. Allan now faces a threat to himself as well as Melanie. He turns against his creation, verbally abusing her in a more aggressive manner than his now deceased mother. The very nature of his language suggestively denotes his repressed anger not only at his infantile condition but also one paralleling the traditional role of the female confined to the home. Fearing and resenting the female side of his own nature, he aggressively channels his anger against Ella who then exercises her own form of poetic justice and urinates on him. Seeing Ella attempting to kill Melanie with Geoff's deadly syringe, Allan manages to turn on his cassette to attract Ella by the romantic music which then plays. On one level, Allan rises to the situation by seeing Melanie's danger. But, alternatively, he may be motivated by aggressive desires towards a former pet who now treats him like an infant in the very same way his mother did. Both motivations may be present in Allan's mind and it is impossible to suggest which one is really dominant. However, Allan then uses the very 'conniving' qualities he earlier condemned in Dorothy by coaxing Ella to approach him for an act of loving intimacy so he can bury his teeth in her neck and kill her. Allan's act is one of bloodthirsty savagery illustrating his kinship with 'animal instincts' lying dormant beneath his 'five thousand years of civilisation'. On one hand, his action is the result of a human being defending himself against a murderous primate, but it also denotes the final deadly bond he has with Ella when he now kills without using a convenient surrogate sacrificial victim.

The sequence ends on a note of deep ambiguity. Allan has overcome his monster. But he will have to live with the consequences. Unfortunately, studio politics dictated that Romero shoot two different endings rather than the ambiguous and ironic conclusion he originally intended. One ending reveals Dr. Williams about to operate on Allan and Ella emerging from his back like the 'chestbuster' in *Alien*. The other shows Allan leaving hospital, getting out of his wheelchair and using crutches to join Melanie in her van to depart for a romantic weekend. Neither ending does justice to the complexity of *Monkey Shines*; Romero originally wanted the film's climax to follow Michael Stewart's original novel where Allan never recovers from his accident. The final sequence of the film depicted Dean Burbage breaking into Geoff's laboratory to steal his research findings. However, before he can do this, the final shot showed a monkey suddenly appearing in the frame to condemn another human manipulation of the animal world. But, despite studio interference, *Monkey Shines* is another significant chapter in Romero's examination of a human condition necessitating neither zombies nor deadly monkeys for relevant levels of meaning.

CHAPTER TWELVE

One Evil Eye and The Dark Half

After the release of *Monkey Shines*, Romero virtually lapsed into silence with the exception of his contribution to the Dario Argento-produced two-part film, *Two Evil Eyes* and *The Dark Half*. The creative era of the American horror film to which he contributed much had now declined into insubstantial slasher films such as the *Friday the 13th* series and the trivial *Nightmare on Elm Street* saga. Like Romero's zombie trilogy these films promised and delivered gore in abundance. But, unlike the director's more challenging films, they contained little narrative meanings other than sheer exploitation. Supposedly, Romero's association with a stimulating era in American history was exclusively responsible for his best works. However, like Larry Cohen, Romero is not really a director of horror films. Although he is popularly associated with the genre, his significance lies in other areas contained within his films, but the dominant conservatism of the Reagan-Bush and Clinton eras and industrial problems concerning distribution did affect his work. Rather than capitulating to the system Romero retreated and remained in Pittsburgh instead of following the disastrous trail to Hollywood chosen by directors such as Wes Craven and Brian De Palma. Although Romero's next two films lacked the excitement and innovation of his previous work, they were not entirely devoid of merit.

Both 'The Facts in the Case of Mr Valdemar' and *The Dark Half* share a Gothic heritage, a feature also common to the novels of Stephen King. During this period, Romero unsuccessfully attempted to direct film versions of King novels such as *Salem's Lot*, *Pet Sematary* and *The Stand*, which fell by the wayside for one reason or another. However, although the Gothic aura of the supernatural appears ideal territory for Romero, the director's concerns lie elsewhere as Kim Newman has shrewdly noticed. Expressing disappointment in his review of *The Dark Half*, Newman commented that although Romero works in the horror genre his 'films prefer science fiction to the supernatural'.[1] As already noted, the supposedly redundant radiation explanation in *Night of the Living Dead* is far more pertinent to the film than any supernatural associations. Furthermore, although supernatural and scientific explanations clash in most of Romero's films, their intuitive intelligence and emotional weight firmly supports the latter's rational dimensions. However, the Gothic associations surrounding 'Facts' and *The Dark Half* tend to suffocate, rather than develop, the ideas Romero attempts. The first film attempts to avoid the Gothic style entirely and aims (apart from the unfortunate presence of the ghostly 'They' towards the climax) at naturalistic levels of meaning while the second cannot discard the trappings entirely.

As Andrew Britton significantly pointed out, the Gothic is more of a hindrance than a help in developing radical implications inherent within the horror genre, implications which Romero had previously successfully transmitted in his other films. Speaking of contemporary horror films, Britton noted the problem with this formula:

> The Gothic no longer registers a hesitation at the surface of the text, but produces an esoteric sub-text which is directly at odds with the offered significance. Metaphor, in this instance, engenders and is engendered by misrecognition: the return of the repressed isn't cleanly distinguished by the return of repression, the very image which dramatizes the one enforcing the other.[2]

Romero's earlier films oppose the redundancy of this imagery. The acting performances and screenplay of *Monkey Shines* stimulate any alert viewer to pause before ascribing blame to Ella rather than its manipulative hero Allan. However, 'Facts' concludes by featuring certain supernatural tendencies which gradually creep into the Romero text until it finally contaminates the structure of *The Dark Half*.

Romero's version of Poe's story deliberately avoids the Gothic trappings adopted by Roger Corman in his *Tales of Terror* (1962) anthology. While Corman's version of 'Facts' stresses the Gothic style of colour expressionism and a gory climax emphasising Valdemar's disintegrated body (a scene censored from the British version), Romero stylistically adopts a different approach and emphasises a message not entirely dependent upon the literary source. Despite the fact that Romero delivers his message too blatantly (perhaps in frustration at society and Hollywood distribution patterns), his version of 'Facts' is not entirely devoid of interest. Despite its mood of despair and exhaustion, Romero's version of Poe's tale has many connections to his vision as a director.

In the first place, Romero's deliberately chosen muted style for 'Facts' reflects another of his cinematic adoptions of literary naturalism. In many ways, his direction in this film often resembles the type of naturalistic techniques common to many uninspired examples from American and British television drama. However, Romero here chooses to emphasise the domestic chamber-drama aspects contained in the narrative of 'Facts' rather than its Gothic horror trappings. Valdemar's resuscitation and the climactic supernatural appearance of the borderland spirits are actually more irrelevant than necessary in this production. Although Poe's influence demands some Gothic appropriations, Romero makes this aspect a subordinate part of the production.

Romero also employs several naturalist associations derived from Zola's *Thérèse Raquin* in an adaptation which emphasises the guilty feelings and personal dissensions between his loving couple who undergo similar torments to their literary predecessors. Like Thérèse and Laurent, Jessica Valdemar and Dr. Hoffman conspire against her husband aiming at a future life based upon economic security. However, Jessica and Hoffman are not Zola's petit-bourgeois couple but people living on a higher socio-economic scale. Furthermore, they do not collaborate in murdering the husband but conspire in robbing his assets, leaving death to perform the final act. Also, like *Thérèse Raquin*'s Camille, Ernest Valdemar returns from the dead to haunt them. But his manifestation is physical rather than having the symbolic return of the repressed associations in Zola's original text. Also, unlike Corman's earlier adaptation, Valdemar's return is not the actual climax of Romero's version.

Zola and Poe appear worlds apart in literature. But Romero cinematically unites them by making the latter's Gothic associations subordinate to his naturalist concerns. Also, as noted in the introduction, certain examples of literary naturalism often contain elements of horror and grotesque. Zola's naturalistic plot of *Thérèse Raquin* underwent many borrowings and stylistic changes over the past hundred years ranging from French poetic realism, Italian neo-realism, American film noir, French film noir, and American neo-noir in diverse works such as Pierre Chenal's *Le Dernier Tournant* (1939), Luchino Visconti's *Ossessione* (1942), Billy Wilder's *Double Indemnity* (1944), Tay Garnett's *The Postman Always Rings Twice* (1945), Marcel Carne's *Thérèse Raquin* (1953) and Bob Rafelson's David Mamet-scripted *The Postman Always Rings Twice* (1981).[3] Since film noir borrowed from both French poetic realism and German expressionism (which also contributed to the classical American sound horror film), there is no compelling reason why Romero should not return to the original style of a text which influenced all these diverse adaptations.

Romero's contribution to *Two Evil Eyes* begins with an opening shot showing a taxi driving past a graveyard, an introduction deliberately echoing the opening scenes of *Night of the Living Dead*. As the viewer will soon realise, associations between bodily decay and social contamination also appear in Romero's particular version of 'Facts'. The next shot shows Jessica Valdemar (Adrienne Barbeau) rehearsing her lines for the forthcoming meeting with her husband's lawyer Pike (E. G. Marshall). This brief introduction has more than one significant association. First, a greedy wife rehearses her imminent performance. Secondly, the scene self-reflexively evokes the performative strategies employed by the actress Adrienne Barbeau rehearsing her lines for the film in which she will appear. Actress and character both perform a role. Romero's fictional characters also perform roles based upon their social conditioning. Very few of them ever escape from this particular form of personal entrapment. Thirdly, her thrice delivered lines – 'Is that an *accusation*, Mr Pike? Is that *some* sort of accusation? Is that some sort of accusation, *Mr Pike?*' – contain the aura of a ritual performance that both she and her audience understand as being necessitated by their imminent meeting. Both Jessica and Pike intuitively understand the real reasons involved in terms of their social confrontation. But like other Romero characters they deny the actual realities governing their respective performances. Here, denial is by deliberate design rather than governed by the operation of irrational or unconscious forces. This type of procedure parallels Renoir's recognition of 'The Rules of the Game' governing any upper-class social situation or the academic role-playing of 'The Crate' where denial, rather than honesty, echoes the title of George Stevens' final film, *The Only Game in Town* (1970).

When Romero cuts to Pike's office, the opening shot reveals that both players are united in a game they know all too well. The director begins with a mid-close-up of Pike as he sceptically examines Valdemar's written instructions concerning the liquidation of assets. Then the camera dollies round to include Jessica in the frame. As Jessica and Pike parry their words like actors in a play trying to grandstand each other, Romero then adopts the classical Hollywood editing pattern of shot/reverse-shot. This feature emphasises both their performances and the dialogue. Despite their personal antagonism, Jessica and Pike operate as experienced role players fully cognisant of their expected patterns of behaviour in a socially sanctioned economic game.

The following dialogue emphasises the contaminating nature of survival within a capitalist system leading people to perform social patterns of behaviour clearly detrimental to their humanity. Both Jessica and Pike are complicit victims of a familiar system seen in Romero's films which dominates individuals. Pike comments that Valdemar's desire for liquidation represents 'bad timing' in terms of the stock market. He asks why her husband did not give her 'assets' on paper. Jessica coolly replies, 'I don't need assets, Mr Pike. I need *dollars* to live on.' She also emphasises her need for economic security during the two-year period when her dying husband's will becomes free of all legal technicalities: 'What do I live on while I'm waiting? Take a job as a waitress? I'm not society, Mr Pike. I have nothing of my own. I was a flight attendant when Ernie brought me home from the "red eye" to the shock and horror of you and everyone else in this town. I married a rich, *old* man. I let him use me for pleasure and for show. Now, I'm going to let him pay me for my services.'

Jessica's speech not only echoes radical feminist criticisms of marriage as a form of legal prostitution but also emphasises the socially denied (but actual) fact of everyone's recognition of her role as a performer in a masquerade which is both private and public. Jessica has performed sexually for her husband in private and displayed herself as a commodity in public. She now naturally demands payment for her services.

Pike then compares Valdemar's signature on the liquidation document with an earlier one. When he finds a difference between them, Jessica then launches into her curtain-closing line, 'Is that some sort of accusation, Mr Pike?' She begins to phone her husband. Pike hears both the dying Valdemar (Bingo O'Malley) and his physician Dr. Robert Hoffman[4] (Ramy Zada) who reassure him concerning the request. She wins the game and announces her intention of returning the next day to pick up the 'necessary forms'. When she returns home, she finds Hoffman hypnotising her dying husband and reading him a script which he will perform for any future calls to his lawyer: 'I want to do it. I owe it to Jessica.' These lines are similar to the ones Pike heard on the phone. Furthermore, Valdemar's rehearsal ironically parallels Jessica testing her lines in the opening scene.

When Jessica enters the house, she is about to pour herself a drink. But the camera tilts up to reveal Hoffman watching her from above holding two drinks. The shot itself appears merely perfunctory by introducing to the viewer Jessica's partner-in-crime.

However, Valdemar later appears in this very same area after he revives to kill his deceitful wife. By this use of *mise-en-scène* in two separate scenes in the film, Romero suggests the manipulative role of patriarchy as bearing full responsible for Jessica's social contamination. She is viewed from an area from which two manipulative males look down on her. Although Jessica is far from being an ideal Romero heroine like Fran in *Dawn of the Dead* and Sarah in *Day of the Dead*, the director suggests that her negative qualities may arise from her complicit involvement in a corrupt social structure which demeans both her individuality and alternative potential as a human being. In this light, her nearest counterparts are Dorothy and Linda in *Monkey Shines*.

Despite the audience learning that Jessica and Hoffman were previously lovers before Valdemar's appearance on the scene, Romero has little sympathy for them. Although Hoffman's lines concerning the dying man appear to represent his real feelings, he also plays a role as a jealous lover from the wrong side of the tracks: 'He's a ruthless old man who takes pleasure in treating people as if they were possessions. He's spent his whole life taking what he wanted without a care for anyone else. He took you away from me.' However, Jessica's earlier lines before Pike made it clear that she was also complicit in Valdemar's appropriation of her sexual assets. She also tells Hoffman, 'He didn't take me. I went.' Both lovers are contaminated by economic greed, a fact Romero emphasises when Hoffman attempts to resume his sexual relationship with Jessica with the following ploy – 'Time to liquidate a few assets of our own.' Despite Jessica's hesitation over this impropriety happening near her dying husband, she is deeply complicit in Hoffman's scheme to rob her husband and cannot break away even if she wanted to. Romero's depiction of the dissension and greedy nature of his lovers in high society forms an admirable complement to Zola's own interrogation in *Thérèse Raquin*.

Virtually all the characters in 'Facts' have few redeeming values and certainly not Hoffman and Jessica as major players in the economic game. While audiences might have conceivably sympathised with an old man dying in agony, his painful outbursts against Jessica also reveal evidence of his attitude towards her in life which resembles that of the patriarch in the 'Father's Day' segment of *Creepshow*: 'Where is that bitch of a wife of mine? Out spending my money?' Eventually, after collecting further economic assets from Pike who knowingly threatens her – 'If anything should happen to Ernie, you'll have a hard time collecting. So, do your best to keep him alive' – she finally decides to agree to her lover's proposal and 'liquidate a few assets of our own'. However, Valdemar's death interrupts both their sexual foreplay and dreams of imminent economic wealth. Hoffman decides to conceal the body in Jessica's basement freezer to allow for the necessary three weeks to liquidate the assets she has acquired from Pike.

Although Romero shoots this episode in a style differing from Poe's Gothic sensibility, he does introduce several strands of his own black humour. Hoffman puts Valdemar's body in a food freezer which he and Jessica empty of its contents. Valdemar now becomes little better than 'dead meat' or a commodity the guilty lovers will use to feed their economic desires. They act in a manner little different from Romero's army of the living dead in the zombie trilogy who continue their consumerist habits well after death. Although deceased, Valdemar is still under Hoffman's hypnotic spell.

So he, too, is another unit of Romero's living dead community. Jessica and Hoffman intend to feed off Valdemar's wealth in the same way as Romero's zombies desire human flesh. Like the zombies, both lovers reveal their participation in a form of mental telepathy; Hoffman finishes Jessica's sentence for her showing he knows what is in her mind – 'In three weeks, he'll be...' 'Yes. He'll be melted.' In order to prevent Valdemar's liquefying, Hoffman hits on the idea of preserving it in Jessica's freezer so they can use the dead man's body to liquefy his assets and live off the proceeds.

Everyone is implicated in this economic chain. Hoffman alleviates Jessica's fears over Pike: 'He gives you a hard time. But underneath it all, he doesn't give a shit as long as he gets his fees. That's all he cares about. That's all anybody ever cares about in the end.' Jessica gets the message: 'Money.' Hoffman points out the moral to her: 'Yes, it has a way, doesn't it?' His axiom also extends to the nurse (Christine Forrest) who has attempted to persuade Jessica to place her husband in a hospital. When she suddenly appears at the door during Hoffman's removal of Valdemar to the freezer, she appears relieved to hear that Jessica has finally agreed to her suggestions. But she also states that she will still charge her for the visit. Although the nurse is completely within her rights on legal grounds, she exhibits no real sympathy for the wife of a dying patient and only cares about her fees in very much the same manner as Pike.

When the guilty lovers later find Valdemar dead, but still conscious from Hoffman's hypnotic techniques, they decide to continue with their scheme. Despite Hoffman's recognition of their joint guilt in committing 'grand larceny and fraud', he emphasises the importance of conducting business as usual, a message which Jessica finishes telepathically in a manner complementing Hoffman's earlier trait. When Hoffman begins his sentence, 'We are felons. We have committed grand larceny and fraud. We have to maintain...', Jessica completes it for him, '...an air of normality'. These two transitions have supernatural associations. They represent for Romero the real nature of the film's particular magic which involves a deadly material desire for the destructive values of society. This desire will eventually lead to the respective deaths of the couple.

Romero's message in *Martin* emphasised that magic no longer existed in its original sense. Instead, adherence of various characters to a 'living dead' form of existence and their inability to break free from its various manifestations embodied a lifestyle little better than that of a medieval villager dominated by the power of the church or vampire. Most characters in *Martin* displayed a lack of true independence and an inability to move towards healthier, alternative modes of existence. Martin, Cuda, Mrs Santini, Christine and Arthur were all involved in their own versions of spiritual dead ends. Unable to break free from deadly patterns of behaviour, they had accepted the status quo and became little better than dehumanised slaves or human zombies. As the zombie trilogy revealed, humans and zombies are identical in nature operating according to similar 'instinctual' desires resulting from social construction and manipulation. The naturalist elements Romero employs in 'Facts' emphasises this meaning. It also dialectically operates oppositionally against the supernatural features inherent within the horror genre. The supernatural really represents a metaphor for those controlling devices individuals submit to in various ways whether they are conscious of these operations or not.

Also, in many instances, the supernatural elements often act as allegories for the human condition. In one scene, Jessica sits in a park; behind her is a stone gargoyle. Romero begins the shot by showing the gargoyle and then tracking away so that Jessica's body appears in front of the image. She is the real monster, an interpretation supported by a little child's voice uttering the word 'monster'. Her attachment to economic gain appears 'instinctual'. But it is really the result of her own conscious and unconscious desires. When we first see Hoffman's apartment, Romero reveals a pentagram ceiling window before tilting down to reveal the interior. However, although the supernatural Gothic associations of 'Facts' appears to emphasise the role of the unknown, the really powerful elements in operation belong to the everyday world of the known and 'normality'. These latter features are actually the dominant ones operating to control its victims. Romero uses the supernatural as an allegorical device to suggest that our everyday world now occupies an oppressive hold on human consciousness in much the same manner as the old powers of religion and superstition.

Another key scene makes this evident. Upset at Valdemar's continuing existence, Jessica spends the night sleeping on Hoffman's sofa, not his bed. She wakes the following morning when a radiogram mechanically emerges from its closet to report the business news. The movement of this device resembles a coffin in a funeral parlour prior to its final journey, but it moves up rather than down to invade the human world as if symbolically representing the deadly nature of an economic system turning all its victims into living dead automatons. Although Hoffman's apartment sequence begins with a shot of a pentagram ceiling, the camera movement concludes in showing objects from everyday life. The radiogram reports important economic news relevant both to Jessica as future heiress and the living subjects of a capitalist economy dominated by the currency of a dead object.

However, even Jessica cannot stomach the pleas of her deceased husband for release, particularly when he refers to the presence of certain mysterious figures in the afterlife who wish to use his body to 'pass through'. She finally shoots Valdemar leaving Hoffman with the problem of disposing of his remains. Although Jessica has ruined the first scheme, Hoffman has another one ready. He intends circulating news of Valdemar's burial in Harrisburg after they inter him in his garden. Hoffman cynically comments, 'People won't ask any questions. They'll co-operate – as long as there's enough money.'

However, like Romero's zombies, the forces from the afterlife cannot be easily bought off. They return to wreak vengeance on the two deadly lovers in a similar manner to the director's other monsters, namely, in employing the repressed violence operating in the everyday world of normality. Jessica confronts her husband in their home. He informs her that he now functions in an instinctual manner due to forces beyond his control. The living dead Valdemar announces her fate: 'They're coming for you, Jessica ... It isn't me Jessica. It's the others, Jessica, using my body.' Valdemar echoes Johnny's similar threat in *Night of the Living Dead*, 'They're coming to get you Barbara.' After witnessing his lover's body fall down at his feet, Hoffman looks up at the banisters to see Valdemar standing in the same position he occupied in his opening appearance. Although Hoffman finally wakes up his patient, he learns from him that it is now too late. Despite this, Hoffman takes monetary assets from Valdemar's safe significantly concealed behind a mounted stuffed bear, and leaves for his apartment.

The next sequence shows the police at the Valdemar home. One cop surmises that Jessica shot her husband and then committed suicide. They learn about the presence of blood in the freezer. The investigating detective (Tom Atkins) utters a line which is both unnecessary and over-emphatic: 'Rich people! Sick stuff always turns out to be rich people.' Since he also utters a variant of this line in the climactic scenes, the reference is too didactic for Romero's cinema and more fitting for the world of Oliver Stone. They then find the decayed body of Valdemar. Although Roger Corman's *Tales of Terror* builds up to this final revelation, Romero makes it redundant to the concerns of his narrative since the final act of his drama has yet to unfold.

In the following sequence, the camera movement again begins with an establishing shot of Hoffman's pentagram window ceiling before tracking down to reveal money from Valdemar's attaché case and Hoffman asleep on his bed. As in an earlier scene, Hoffman uses his triangular metronome to hypnotise him to sleep. But shadowy forces from the underworld arrive. They pierce Hoffman's body with the metronome which still continues its mechanical motion.

The next scene significantly opens with a triangular skyscraper dominating the city. The two cops, previously seen at the Valdemar residence, arrive to investigate reports of screaming from one apartment. Apparently, the sounds have occurred for nearly two weeks. As if echoing an appropriate form of EC comic book poetic justice, the time coincides with that agreed upon between Jessica and Hoffman to conceal news of Valdemar's death. The apartment supervisor reveals to the cops that the affluent apartment dwellers share many characteristics with Jessica, Hoffman and Valdemar in terms of their lack of humanity. He tells them that he 'couldn't get anyone to do anything about it. You know how people are.' The cops break into the apartment and find money scattered around. One makes another redundant observation: 'What'd I tell you? Another rich guy.'

After the cop (Atkins) leaves Hoffman's blood spattered bedroom, he closes a mirror door. As the door moves back it reflects Hoffman's now decaying body with the metronome still intact ticking away mechanically. Hoffman appeals to him, 'There's no one to wake me. No one to wake me.' 'Facts' ends with bullets firing from the cop's gun. The final shots reveal blood spots falling on dollar bills. Romero then cuts to the final image prominently displaying the triangular image with the overseeing eye which appears on 'The Great Seal' of the American dollar bill on the reverse side of George Washington's image. Two Latin inscriptions appear above and below this triangular object, 'Annuit Coeptis' and 'Novus Ordo Seclorum'. The overseeing eye on the bill's triangular object matches the red eye still functioning on the metronome embedded in Hoffman's body now making him another of Romero's 'living dead'. Hoffman now becomes a *homo economicus* in death as he did so in life. He is little better than a programmed machine moving instinctually according to the rhythm of a triangular metronome which ticks like a human heart. In life Hoffman desired an affluent existence based upon the dollar bill, a dead fetishistic object with excremental associations. His rapidly decaying body not only resembles a zombie but also embodies the decomposing aura of a previous human existence devoted towards anally-acquisitive ends. Romero reveals that the American dollar bill conflates two different realms: the magical world of the supernatural and the supposedly secular realm of everyday life. This is significant visual message concludes his contribution to 'Two Evil Eyes'. Romero makes the dollar economy the 'one evil eye' in his version of 'Facts'.

This episode thus represents an interesting aspect of his work. It is Romero's attempt at making a naturalist horror film in which supernatural elements deliberately play a supporting role, not a dominating one. The film works best at the level of suggestive dialogue and *mise-en-scène*. It does not really need the Gothic associations of either Valdemar's survival beyond death or the ghostly 'They' to operate effectively. However, despite its interesting associations, 'Facts' appears tiring in execution and over-emphatic in delivery. No need exists either for Tom Atkins' lines about rich people or its repetition. Romero could really have let the 'Facts' speak for themselves rather being over-emphatic here. Such meanings also appear implicitly in his other films without any need for over-emphasis. However, although 'Facts' is a lesser work, its flaws may be attributable to a period in which Romero expressed despair at a film industry in the grip of over-commercial, banal and reactionary concerns, the type Andrew Britton significantly described as 'Reaganite Entertainment'. The director's pessimism may have led him to become too over-didactic in spelling out the message and his despair at audiences wanting gore and zombies may have led him towards this direction.

However, in 'Facts', Romero expresses Andrew Britton's definition of artistic hesitation by employing Gothic associations which hinder, rather than help, his creative development. He is a director whose work always promises a movement away from stifling generic confines into some significant direction. His next association with Stephen King reveals the same problems which have affected his work in the horror genre, namely the limiting nature of supernatural meanings.

King's work is often more significant for its insights into the material dark half of the American Dream rather than thrills and scary monsters. But, like his surrogate character, Thad Beaumont in *The Dark Half*, King's devoted audience reads his fiction for chills rather than comments on the American condition. As with the films of George A. Romero, Stephen King's fiction is mostly dependent upon the formulaic demands most audiences expect. This factor limits its potential significance and hinders development of the possibility the author has of making pertinent critical comments on the American way of life within his fiction. King's often cumbersome writing style and over-productive output embodies further problems. The author merely becomes a mechanical entity churning out product rather than engaging in an interrogative examination of his society; book after book appears to just emphasise the horror in a formulaic manner rather than investigate the real material causes underlying it. *The Dark Half* as fiction and film pertinently reveals this dilemma. It is a work which really does not need a supernatural 'dark half'. As Kim Newman insightfully notes in a review written from the twin perspectives of horror film critic and novelist, a problematic confusion exists in the film concerning the villain, 'who never decides whether he is a pseudonym come to life, the ghost of a dead twin, or another incarnation of that malignant Elvis currently stalking American popular culture' (1993: 40). One of the innovations Romero's screenplay brings to King's novel is the motif of Presley's twin brother who died at birth which appears both in the 1950s rocker persona of George Stark as well as the use of the Elvis ballad 'Are You Lonesome Tonight?' Romero obviously borrowed this idea from John Carpenter's 1979 television movie *Elvis* where the King's morbid communion with the shadowy persona of his deceased brother forms an important Gothic motif within the text. However, although Romero appears to have directed a seemingly faithful adaptation for mainstream audiences, other familiar concerns also appear throughout the film.

Like the film, King's *The Dark Half* begins with young Thad Beaumont's 1968 brain tumour and the discovery of the remains of a twin brother inside his brain during an operation. It then moves directly to Thad's 'burial' of his fictional alter ego, George Stark on the cover of *People* magazine in 1988 and deals with the reasons for this in retrospect before proceeding in a linear narrative direction. By contrast, Romero's version never engages in flashbacks and moves in a concise linear manner throughout its duration. It depicts creative writing professor Thad Beaumont's encounter with blackmailing student, Fred Clawson, after his class with the events leading to the decision to bury his violent pulp writer surrogate for good. Unlike the novel, Romero provides different reasons for Thad's decision which primarily involve the encouragement of his wife, Liz (Amy Madigan).

Although the female perspective of *Dawn of the Living Dead* and *Day of the Dead* occupies a subordinate position in this film, it is nevertheless significantly present during key moments within the narrative. *The Dark Half* certainly emphasises the critique of violent masculinity present in Romero's other films such as *Night of the Living Dead, The Crazies, Dawn of the Dead, Day of the Dead* and *Monkey Shines* as well as paralleling King's own real life decision to expose himself to the general public as the author of the Richard Bachman books. But it also reproduces the theme of masculinity as the woman's nightmare (see Wood 1986b). Although the female roles in *The Dark Half* appear thankless, during several key moments Romero emphasises both the supportive, knowledgeable qualities of characters such as Liz Beaumont and Reggie Delesseps (Julie Harris) as well as concerns of minor players in the drama such as Annie Pangborn (Chelsea Field). This last character apprehensively notices the effect of the pattern of violence on her husband, Sheriff Alan Pangborn (Michael Rooker), who later becomes emotionally affected by the negative incidents he has to deal with. Pangborn nearly shoots her when he returns home one night fearing that George Stark has invaded his home. Also, when Pangborn angrily bullies Thad into revealing the truth, Romero inserts a brief shot of his wife's knowledgeable, but fearful, reaction concerning a pattern of male violence also affecting her husband. Her worried expression complements Liz's when she hears her husband on the phone threatening Stark like a character from the latter's novels: 'I'll hear the birds and I'll come and tear you apart.' It is almost as if Mrs. Pangborn realises that her husband needs a scapegoat to distract his increasingly negative energies away from the realisation that perhaps George Stark is as much his dark half as Thad's. Liz comes to the same realisation in both novel and film.

Unfortunately, the film's 'happy ending' omits the intuitive understanding between Liz and Pangborn that George Stark will continue to haunt the Beaumont marriage long after his departure to the underworld.[5] Also, Romero changes Thad's consoling male faculty colleague in the novel to the female character played by Julie Harris. Like Liz, she also intuitively understands that George Stark is much more than a supernatural threat to Thad Beaumont.

The pre-credits sequence begins with a flock of sparrows who embody the supernatural forces of the Greek psychopomps who fly skywards conducting human souls back and forth between the realms of the living and the dead. When the date '1968' appears, Romero uses the significant lines, 'Are you sorry we drifted apart' from Presley's 'Are You Lonesome Tonight' to suggest Thad's ambivalent feelings concerning the loss of his twin brother. After revealing young Thad's operation, the discovery of the remnants of a twin not fully 'absorbed into the system', and depicting a huge flock of sparrows flying outside the hospital, the film moves to the present. The first scene shows Thad (Timothy Hutton) gazing at his image in the mirror. His hair is slicked back almost like that of his future *alter ego*, George Stark. While the novel barely mentions the physical resemblances between Thad and George, the film's use of the same actor playing both roles emphasises the Jekyll and Hyde personality of its hero who really does not need an externalised supernatural twin brother.

Romero introduces the Beaumonts to the audience via a scene that does not exist in King's novel. While Thad looks at himself in a mirror as if expressing reluctance to part entirely with a George Stark persona (who has provided money as well as an avenue to divert away his frustrations with domestic life), Romero reveals Liz reading a page of his new manuscript. Their twin children William and Wendy play near her. Thad then finds William playing with a page of his manuscript, which he retrieves before any harm occurs, and humorously remarks, 'A born editor'. This incident appears a more positive image of the life of writer and family than the one contained in King's novel *The Shining*, where alcoholic frustrated writer Jack Torrance violently reacted when he found his son, Danny, playing with his manuscript. However, as Thad's fascination with his mirror image shows, dark currents exist beneath this harmonious domestic surface. Unlike her fictional counterpart in *The Shining*, Liz affirmatively supports her doubting husband who expresses little confidence in his talents and clumsily drops toys. When Thad asks, 'Not that bad, is it?', Liz replies, 'Not much. It's wonderful. It's great. It's a great book. You've actually really done it.' Thad also mentions, 'It's not coming out of me easy', a statement expressing both his creative efforts as well as contrasting with his George Stark books where the dark side of masculine violence easily expresses itself and no doubts occur whatsoever. Liz's influence in supporting her husband as writer as well as gently urging him to perform domestic duties unthinkable for George Stark reveal her as positively influencing Thad's gentle role as a father no matter how much he may unconsciously react against it.

Romero's direction of Timothy Hutton as Thad reveals a personality at war with himself. Thad appears intuitively wishing for his worst side to emerge to escape from his mundane domestic world. This feature occurs in the next sequence which shows him teaching his creative writing students and urging the values of freedom from repression: 'The writer has to get that inner being out of the locker, otherwise the work will be inhibited, timid. Without passion it will be a pack of lies.' But the presence of blackmailer Fred Clawson (Robert Joy) forces him to confront his darkest desires.

Reacting against Clawson's economic threats of losing an audience who pay hardback novel prices and believe the author resembles his characters, Thad refuses to submit to blackmail. He, instead, threatens him in a violent manner more appropriate to his fictional surrogate than his everyday persona.

Although Thad later expresses irritation concerning Clawson's invasion into his life, Romero has Liz suggest that her husband go public with the information and bury George Stark forever. This differs from the novel where Thad appears to have made the decision himself. Amy Madigan's Liz appears in the film as Thad's 'better half' as opposed to George Stark's macho 'dark half'. Although Thad agrees with her suggestion, his playfully violent comments to his baby after diaper duty suggests that he does not entirely regret the decision to regard George Stark as dead and buried. While Thad gleefully comments, 'I'd like to knock him through the loop, let Alexis Machine get him, cut off his pecker, shove it in his little rat mouth, so they'll know he's a squealer', Romero cuts to Liz's worried expression. She knows that George is a significant part of her supposedly gentle husband's personality and may not easily go away.

The key role of gender difference operating as a key structural element in *The Dark Half* also exists in the characters of Thad's literary agents. Although divorced, Miriam (Rutanya Alda) and Rick Cowley (Tom Mardirosian) continue their business relationship. But former husband and wife have different attitudes concerning Thad's announcement of a decision which will affect their profits. While Miriam utters her full support, Rick expresses concern on both the financial and consumption levels: 'I read George Stark because it's fun. I read Thad Beaumont because it's my job.' Miriam then significantly comments, 'That's why we live across town from each other.' Unfortunately, despite their different attitudes, they will both face the revenge of an author who does not wish to die.

The scene then dissolves from the New York skyline to show Thad and Liz sharing the same concerns. Thad expresses regret for killing off a profitable source of income. But Liz both reassures her husband about the decision he has agreed to follow as well as expressing relief at the demise of a vicious fictional character. However, she does recognise a disturbing affinity between writer and creation noting some regret in her husband: 'You don't want to give up George. You've become attracted to him … He can do anything you want, be anything you want. He's your drinking buddy … You really don't realise what you're like when you write the books, do you. It's like witnessing Jekyll turning into Hyde.' Despite Thad's denial of such a relationship as well as his concealed alcoholic tendencies (which are exposed when George later finds Thad's hidden whiskey bottle in his study drawer), Romero subtly shifts the weight of the argument on Liz's side rather than Thad's. In this scene, Liz appears much more straightforward than her evasive husband who does not appear to relish the prospect of entirely jettisoning a significant part of his personality.

By playing the dual roles of Thad Beaumont and George Stark, Hutton's performances form a perfect psychological match. While Stark takes pleasure in the joyful release of his violent libido, Thad generally engages in subdued threats as if secretly hoping his dark half will perform the vicious actions he cannot bring himself to do. As well as enjoying his earlier threat against Clawson of disposing of him like Stark's fictional character, Alexis Machine, Thad also takes sadistic pleasure in scaring New

York writer Mike Donaldson (Kent Broadhurst). When Donaldson remarks that the links between author and creation suggest 'classic symptoms of schizophrenia', Thad relishes Stark's reaction towards such civilised definitions. Thad's attitude resembles Allan Mann in *Monkey Shines* who secretly wishes that a convenient monster fulfil his darkest desires. He is also irritated by the garrulous presence of elderly photographer Homer Gamache (Glen Colerider) who rambles on about death in philosophical ways while having no clear ideas about its brutal alternative versions. Although Thad consciously expresses relief at the death of his literary twin, he subconsciously resents his new commitment to the full-time role of devoted father without having recourse to the psychological release provided by George Stark's aggressive fictional world. This results in the remains of Thad's unborn twin brother emerging from the family graveyard to evolve into Stark who embarks on a bloody trail of vengeance against all those responsible for his 'death'.

After the brutal killings of Homer and Clawson, the police suspect Thad since his fingerprints appear on the scene of both crimes. However, at this point of the film, Romero's subtle constructions begin to collapse into formulaic representations. The audience has already seen George Stark's shadowy presence twice in the film before his full appearance at Miriam's New York apartment. He now becomes an external embodiment of Thad's dark desires. However, although Romero's films contain precedents for Stark's monstrous appearance in terms of zombies and deadly monkeys, George Stark becomes little better than a figure from the average horror film whose rampages have little relationship to the human dilemma which have caused his appearance. Earlier Romero screenplays often balance competing claims of the horror genre's excessive violence and their strong connection to relevant social problems in a concise allegorical manner. Unfortunately, in this adaptation of a King novel where the Gothic element clearly overwhelms significant aspects of human psychology, the result becomes an incoherent film which lacks the development of key potentials in the material.

Although King's work contains both social and supernatural features, his readers often prefer the latter to the detriment of understanding the former elements which are really responsible for key developments within the narrative. It is a similar dilemma shared between Thad Beaumont and George Stark as well as a director such as George Romero in relation to an audience who constantly request more bloodshed for sensual gratification. Stark sells more copies than Beaumont. Zombies appeal more to the average fan than *Knightriders*. Problems exist whenever any talent employs a genre noted for its excessive qualities and usually regarded as devoid of any relevant social meaning. Romero often works himself out of this dilemma by finely crafted screenplays which explicitly attempt to raise audience awareness of the tensions existing between the special effects and the social conditions which really generate such manifestations which often remain submerged amidst excessive fetishistic signifiers. Unfortunately, *The Dark Half* (like its original source) raises the question of personal control and responsibility (always a key issue for Romero). But it finally ends up by drowning it in a deluge of scary incidents.

Although Stark's explicit presence in the film later takes attention away from the real reasons concerning his appearance as Kim Newman pertinently notes,[6] individual fragments still remain scattered throughout *The Dark Half* suggesting one direction the film could have taken. It would have involved dispensing with Stark entirely or clarifying Thad's guilty responsibility for creating and nourishing his dark half. However, despite Liz's urging Thad to tell Pangborn the truth – 'you're keeping secrets, Thad. That's no good, never was ... This is not a good time to hold things back' – the film's version of the 'truth' is a convenient monster on a slaying spree and not individual responsibility. Stark's bogeyman figure is clearly a surrogate scapegoat device.

Romero inserts into the film an important confrontation between Reggie and Thad which never appears in King's novel. It is one urging Romero's axiom of confronting hard questions directly and taking human responsibility for trying to control events whether they be supernatural or otherwise. Like Romero's other positive female characters, Reggie knows more about her faculty colleague's problem than he does himself. Her dialogue forms a rare moment of reflection which *The Dark Half* loses in its climactic special effects ending. She comments that Stark is really a creation of Thad's will: 'We all have something of the beast inside us. We can either suppress it or encourage it. In your case, you encouraged it too much. In your subconscious you wanted it to live. You wanted it so badly it actually came to life. Your characters have always been vividly written, Thad.'

Reggie's lines concerning human responsibility and an author's fascination with the dark side of his personality gain support from earlier scenes in the film such as Thad's threat to Clawson, his 'playful' discussion of its implications with young William witnessed by Liz, and Thad's unconcealed enjoyment of the way Stark would deal with a cynical, New York intellectual reporter such as Donaldson. Even Thad admits his guilt at this point when he confesses to Reggie his realisation of George Stark embodying his 'dark half': 'I wanted him to live. God forgive me. It's true. Part of me has always admired George Stark, admired his simple violent nature, a man who doesn't stumble over things, who never looks weak or silly, a man with a straight answer for everything.'

Reggie also embodies Tania Modleski's definition of 'a woman who knows too much'.[7] But unlike her cinematic predecessors she belongs within Romero's particular cinematic world. This allows her the capacity to interrogate patriarchy and confront self-deceptive males such as Thad with the responsibility for their guilt. Although Thad denies Reggie's assertion that he still 'admires' Stark, she emphasises that his desires represent the key issue: 'If you don't want him here, he can't remain.' However, Stark is the one who is trying to take 'real life' away from Thad feeding on his creator's dark desires in very much the same way as Romero's zombies feed on human flesh and instinctually follow the worst patterns of civilised behaviour. She counsels Thad that both he and Stark are symbiotic blood brothers who know each other intimately. She warns Thad, 'Don't let him seduce you, don't.' But, finally, as Reggie affirms, 'In the end, it's what you believe.' Thad leaves and expresses his gratitude to her for giving him 'the weapon I need'.

The film moves towards its final confrontation between Thad and his twin brother. Stark has kidnapped Liz and the twins and holds them captive in Thad's country retreat. Realising that Thad's psychological struggles are beginning to cost him his life, the now decomposing Stark wishes his twin to begin a new Alexis

Machine novel that will reverse the decaying process. Thad's struggle is really internal. But, despite Timothy Hutton's performance as Thad, Stark's physical presence in the film unfortunately reinforces the horror genre's frequent recourse to convenient externalisation and distracts the viewer away from the battle going on inside its main character. As the psychopomps fly against the windows to carry away the loser, a deadly psychological chess game continues between Thad and his dark half. Both begin to take on each other's attributes. When Stark overcomes his hesitation of a fictional character becoming his own creator, his body begins to heal while Thad's begins to deteriorate. However, Thad rallies by initially overpowering his antagonist and stopping his bodily deterioration, but Stark soon revives. Both men are now physically healed and balance each other's personality more than ever. Stark knocks over a book in Thad's manner, a fact the author recognises by his comment, 'Clumsiness, George.' Thad then begins to speak like his dark half relishing the threat to his twin's existence in a similar manner to his earlier encounter with Clawson: 'I'm not doing anything, Hoss. I'm just waiting around to see how things turn out.' When Stark then attempts to shoot Thad's children, Thad then moves against him using a typewriter to knock the gun away; he had earlier used a Black Beauty pencil (Stark's favourite writing implement) against him, but he now uses Thad's preferred instrument to win the battle finally. The birds then break into Thad's study and dismember Stark's body before carrying the remains away to the underworld. Alan Pangborn eventually arrives to witness the final act and the film ends.

Thad has clearly overcome his dark half. But his initial use of Stark's preferred writing instrument against his adversary and his final threat resembling Stark's own speech appear to question any positive outcome the film may attempt to move towards. Thad may have reverted back to his own persona by using the typewriter against Stark, but Stark's clumsiness also shows that he has also become like his weaker twin. However, the intriguing ambiguity of this final act remains in doubt since the film moves to a perfunctory, rushed ending, indebted to a spectacular display of special effects that Romero very rarely indulges in. Possibly, studio demands may have resulted in this hasty ending since it leaves many questions unresolved. Will Thad be totally cured after realising the violent tendencies in his own nature? Romero's better films end on a note of provocative ambiguity. Unfortunately, *The Dark Half* does not provide this. It is a film which does contain some intriguing insights. But it is also the product of a studio system now almost exclusively devoted to 'mindless entertainment', disavowing important classical and 1970s traditions which made films much more than that. Romero's retreat from direction since 1992 may represent his recognition of this very factor.

CONCLUSION

In his posthumously collected series of essays, Theodor Adorno regarded the real function of art as not involving a denial of the real world. He believed that:

> Art undergoes qualitative change when it attacks its traditional foundations ... and becomes a qualitatively different entity by virtue of its opposition, at the level of artistic form, to the existing world and also by its readiness to aid and shape that world. Neither the concept of solace nor its opposite, refusal, captures the meaning of art.[1]

Although a vast difference exists between Adorno's aesthetic theory and the films of George A. Romero, these comments by the Frankfurt School's major spokesman contain relevance for this under-appreciated independent Pittsburgh director. Romero exists outside the Hollywood system, operating in an era when the critical community needs to reject the fallacious arguments of certain realms of cultural studies and say, 'Come back Frankfurt School. All is forgiven!' The films of George A. Romero oppose the currently monolithic Hollywood system both formally and thematically. They express oppositional utopian yearning for a better world but realise that such a world is impossible unless audiences actively seek to change the present system. Otherwise, they are little better than the 'living dead' of Romero's films, a collective including both humans and zombies alike.

Neither naively affirmative nor cynically pessimistic, the films depict fictional situations in which characters may try to change their lives or submit to the system at great personal and emotional cost. Although films such as *Dawn of the Dead* and *Day of the Dead* suggest potential re-awakenings for their surviving characters, the possibility for change still remains tentative and under threat from internal and external forces. However, Romero functions as a knight of the living dead for those aware of the values of his films and open to a liberation only they can achieve for themselves. Romero is the knight who loosens the chains. The realisation of liberation is a factor that can only be achieved by those who read the films and act on their warnings. This aspect runs through his entire work as a link. Hence, this concluding chapter will compare his most recent work to a short he directed more than thirty years ago. Both express a common message.

It is a message naturally antithetical to the corporate world of contemporary Hollywood. Thus, Romero's absence over the last decade is not surprising in which both he and actresses such as Meryl Streep have been compared to 'yesterday's pizza – cold!' Although different in nature from his previous works, his latest film, *Bruiser*, again raises familiar issues concerning individual dehumanisation in late-capitalist society. Stylistically, *Bruiser* differs from Romero's other films: it is shot in an antiseptic, almost clinical, manner, which resembles both dehumanising professional Hollywood and television techniques of representation as well as the empty, spiritually unfulfilling, affluent environments dominating its protagonists. Dedicated conformist Henry Creedlow (Jason Flemying) works for a slick magazine 'Bruiser' aimed at the 'me' generation. But he wakes up and discovers himself faceless one morning. He uses his newfound anonymity to avenge himself on those who have wronged him such as a thieving Hispanic domestic, cheating wife Janine, bullying boss Milo and treacherous friend Jim, who have all participated in different ways of robbing him of his identity. Henry becomes infamous, featured in the tabloids, and a celebrity for the first time in his life. Because the police cannot catch him, Henry revels in his anonymity and uses it for revenge.

The heroine, Rosemary (Leslie Hope), is in the process of divorcing Milo Styles (Peter Stormare), the wealthy owner of 'Bruiser' magazine, a former Communist and refugee, who has now sold out to Western material values. But Rosemary cannot make the final break until she discovers the identity of the faceless killer and sees what actually motivates his avenging acts. When the police discover the body of Henry's murdered wife, with whom Styles is having an affair, they try to set her up as the murderer. Tom Atkins's Detective McCleary exhibits similar patriarchal tendencies as his counterpart in *Jack's Wife* when he brusquely remarks, 'The dame did it.'

Although lacking zombies, the film contains much of the social criticism which has been a key factor in the other films of George A. Romero.[2] *Bruiser* opens with Henry waking up in the morning and listening to a talk-show. Its host abuses his listeners evoking the previous situation in *Martin* as well as paralleling the verbal tactics employed by Milo. As Henry listens, a distraught male commits suicide on the air after bemoaning the loss of his house due to taxes. Since the 'house poor' Henry lives in a sterile, affluent neighbourhood inside an unfinished house, the event affects him emotionally despite the fact that his face registers nothing. The caller states his entrapment within materialistic values: 'You shovel shit all your life and you don't leave a mark at all. It's as if you've never been here at all.' Henry then appears to commit suicide but the following shots reveal its fantasy nature. Later, at the station, Henry supposedly decapitates a woman and injures an affluent male. He becomes enraged when the woman jumps the queue waiting to board the train and takes out his frustrations on her. Yet the sequence ends by revealing that it is another of Henry's fantasies. He will wake up one morning to find that his features are covered by a blank, white mask, a situation which appears to be real and not fantasy. As a result, his masochistic tendencies illustrated by the suicide he listens to on the talk-show and his imaginary suicide before his bathroom mirror turn into their sadistic opposites as he plans revenge on all who have betrayed him. These include his cheating wife, false friend and bullying boss, Milo, who have humiliated him in one way or another. The two opening 'fantasy' sequences, which compare masochistic and sadistic solutions to psychological dilemmas in the realms of fantasy, again creatively evoke Sigmund Freud's essay 'Instincts and Their Vicissitudes'. They also reveal that *Bruiser*'s screenplay represents one of Romero's significant achievements in terms of how the film is constructed.

Like *Martin*, *Bruiser* plays with boundaries dividing fantasy and reality so that both realms appear to merge. But unlike *Martin*, there are no Gothic sequences in which we can be certain that the events are really fantasy. Society has now reached such a state that what once passed for normality no longer exists. The pursuit of false goals of affluence and materialism have resulted in personal existence being little better than a living nightmare. When Henry awakes one morning to find his features have altered into the mask which Rosemary modelled from his face during Milo's barbecue, the supposedly deceased victim of the talk-show host also appears on the radio. He announces that he has 'risen from the dead' that he is not going to take 'any shit from rotten bastards like you anymore'. This Lazarus figure also announces, 'You can't turn a man into nothing', a statement that has parallels with Henry's past and present situation. When Rosemary modelled the mask, Henry commented, 'It didn't look like anything.' She replied, 'It's an exact replica', and advises him to 'see if you can work on your image'. Later that evening, Janine criticises Henry, 'You swallow your emotions. You take any shit ... You're nothing, nobody.' After discovering that a colleague has witnessed his murder of Janine, Henry warns him, 'I used to take every kind of shit handed to me. Don't develop a taste for it.' When his face finally returns after his murder of Milo, Henry tells another office colleague that he finally 'stood up' for himself.

Although Henry's character respectively evokes both the title characters in The Beatles 'Nowhere Man' and Jim Thompson's *The Nothing Man* (1954), *Bruiser* also contains Romero's critique of violence as a solution. Although she sees the justification behind Henry's actions, Rosemary reacts against him in ways reminiscent of Romero's previous heroines. Despite her reservations, she helps Henry to escape by donning his mask and costume during Milo's masquerade ball. She exits from the film by walking into the background after giving Henry's mask to McCleary; Rosemary wears Henry's costume but without the mask. An earlier scene showed her wearing a similar mask while bathing in a jacuzzi, revealing her own form of entrapment. After enduring an unsatisfactory marriage with Milo and existing in a rich and sterile environment representing the final version of Henry's unfinished house, Rosemary is free to pursue her own goals. However, in an ironic epilogue, Romero shows Henry now working as an office boy and reacting against a bullying boss by changing once more into his masked avenging persona. The cycle of violence will continue anew with the implication that only radical changes in society and personal behaviour will finally end it.

For Romero, who described this film as a 'parable about disenfranchisement' during his presentation at the Film Center of Chicago in September 2000, modern society has now become a dark nightmare, a situation envisaged in the climactic 'masquerade' where Henry takes his final revenge on Milo. The masked ball is a late-capitalist version of Edgar Allan Poe's *The Masque of the Red Death* where Milo's Prospero ironically perishes by a red laser beam, becoming an egotistic spectacle in death as well as life. It is also a descendent of those excessive grotesque visual displays found in Zola's Rougon-Macquart novels such as *La Curée, Son Excellence Eugène Rougon* and *Au Bonheur des Dames* which revealed the decadence of the upper levels of society. Deliberately depicted in demonic terms, Milo's masked ball represents another celebration of crowds who are little better than living dead. Here again, Romero intuitively merges the naturalist aspects of Zola's crowds with the supernatural associations of his earlier films. As McCleary ironically remarks, 'Everybody here is faceless.' His line also evokes those faceless zombie legions in Romero's trilogy. Although the director needs no actual zombies in this film, he significantly cuts to certain scenes showing dismembered body parts as candy on trays devoured by the partygoers. The masquerade thus represents the logical culmination of Zola's earlier vision concerning commodification, spectacular displays and consumerism. Organised by the twentieth-century version of Octave Mouret from *Au Bonheur des Dames* who also uses and abuses his female employees as bodily commodities, the masked ball also metaphorically represents key themes present within Romero's films. If not actual zombies, the participants are all living dead versions of late twentieth-century capitalism, the descendants of those affluent consumers seen in the 1920s films of Cecil B. DeMille.[3]

Henry also appears as a masked figure, his costume reminiscent of the title character in Louis Feuillade's *Judex* (1916). Although Romero has frequently referred to Georges Franju's *Eyes Without a Face* (1960) as one of the sources for *Bruiser*, the French director had also remade *Judex* in 1964 and finished his career with *L'Homme sans Visage* (1974) whose title bears a more than coincidental analogy with the dilemma of Henry Creedlow. Like *Monkey Shines*, *Bruiser* is a film where the director has deliberately chosen to change his style towards a more minimalist form of representation. But his different stylistic choice should not deceive viewers. Many of the director's familiar themes still operate. Like other directors reaching the summit of their powers, he has realised that less can actually represent more in terms of significant meaning.

Unfortunately, *Bruiser* never gained a theatrical release in America but went straight to DVD and VHS. Presently, Romero is working on several projects. The final chapter in his cinematic odyssey as a director has yet to be written, but as we move towards the conclusion for this book, some comments are necessary concerning a remarkable 25-minute advertising documentary which was never released: *The Amusement Park*. Despite its current unavailability, this short film significantly illustrates the real concerns motivating Romero's role as a director throughout his entire career.

In the early 1970s, a religious group commissioned Latent Image to make an advertising documentary expressing concern for the plight of American senior citizens. It suggested positive ways to avoid the problems of ageing, but when completed, its clients expressed concern at what Romero directed. A prologue and epilogue was later added with actor Lincoln Maazel (who would later appear as Cuda in *Martin*) appearing alone in a deserted amusement park like an American salesman. He voiced concern over the events depicted in the documentary and warned his audience to take appropriate measures to avoid the incidents depicted in the film. However, *The Amusement Park* was never shown. The backers claimed that the film was too difficult and would confuse its audience. Since they still own the rights, the film still remains unseen today.

Despite its length, *The Amusement Park* is one of the most radical indictments of American callousness towards the most vulnerable members of its society. It implicitly articulates the need for a social and humanistic revolution, a goal which today appears far more distant than it did nearly three decades ago. What gives *The Amusement Park* its edge is its keen combination of fantasy and realism within an allegorical condemnation of selfish materialism. In an era which now rigidly categorises individuals on purely economic grounds, Romero's documentary takes on an added perspective. Where fantasy has its greatest power is in its relevance to social conditions and the presence of a more realistic utopian dimension totally lacking in the infantile authoritarian wish-fulfilment spectaculars represented by *Star Wars* and *Close Encounters of the Third Kind* (both 1977). By combining fantasy with realism, *The Amusement Park* represents another example of that powerful use of cinematic naturalism intuitively influencing George A. Romero. The film begins by showing an optimistic looking old gentleman in a white suit (played by Lincoln Maazel). He encounters his mirror image in a white room. His counterpart is in a bruised, bleeding and despondent condition. A door leads to the outside. The dishevelled figure warns his spruce counterpart not to venture outside: 'You won't like it out there.' However, the other man ignores his advice and ventures out into the amusement park.

This park is nothing less than America, an America of commercialism and entertainment, a place where the individual is valued only for his purchasing power, and an environment which represents the decadent entertainment world of Zola's Second Empire where theatrical spectacles foreshadowing the debased values of the Lucas-Spielberg version of Hollywood now take centre stage. The old gentleman purchases tickets for the various events and begins a journey into humiliation and despair. As he attends the various sideshows, he is economically exploited or patronised and treated like an imbecile because of his age. He attempts to help an elderly couple whose dodgem car is attacked by an aggressive driver played by Romero himself (perhaps this is the director's recognition of the contemporary Western phenomenon of 'road rage'?). The old man is ignored because he has forgotten his spectacles as well as being robbed and assaulted by Hells Angels. When he attempts a kindly conversation with a little girl, a young man violently assaults him as a child molester.

This last incident occurs during a particular section of the film. A young couple go to a fortune teller to see what their life will be like in an America fifty years into the future. They see themselves aged, living in slum conditions and regarded as useless members of society. The man suffers a heart attack; his wife attempts to phone a doctor. After problems involving the right coins for the phone box and unsympathetic telephone operators, she finally reaches the doctor, but he is too busy pandering to his rich, pampered clients to come to their aid. The young man leaves the tent horrified at his fate in a future America. He then sees the old man and vents his fear on him by a violent attack; a convenient scapegoat who represents his fear of what he will become in a future America. This is not the first or last time that a character in a Romero film will find a convenient scapegoat upon whom to vent out internal fears and frustrations.

In another section of the film, the old gentleman enters an exhibit where he is assured he will be looked after, but he finds himself in an old people's home which is little better than a funny farm. The inmates are patronised and humiliated. Finally, the man escapes and becomes despondent. He attempts one last act of kindness by trying to read a story to a little girl, but her parents treat him in an aggressive manner and believe him to be a child molester. His final attempt to realise a kind world of utopian fantasy collapses. The old man becomes a broken wreck, a despised product of an uncaring society. The wheel finally comes full circle when the old man encounters another spruce, dignified alter ego about to venture outside. He warns him, 'You won't like it out there...' as the camera dwells on his despondent face.

In the added epilogue, Maazel attempts to reassure the audience like an encouraging salesman attempting to promote a product. But it fails entirely. Any attempt at recuperation has been disrupted by the previous events of the main narrative. They resemble a living hell as grim and uncaring as those earthly fates awaiting the old and sick in Zola novels such as *L'Assommoir* and *La Terre*. The film is far too powerful for American society then and now. It must remain under lock and key never seeing the light of day.

The above was first written from memory some twenty years ago.[4] But, despite its date, it stands as a fitting epitaph to the cinema of Romero. *The Amusement Park* is one among a number of his most accomplished films which uses the cinematic machine to jerk his audience into some form of awareness concerning the problems affecting their society. They reveal what that society has become and act as a potential spur to action. In this manner, George A. Romero may be appropriately described as a 'knight of the living dead'. Although his films are misunderstood by most audiences who go for the gore, they have other important social dimensions; they call upon both his fictional characters and audiences to leave the realm of the living dead and change themselves and the society they belong to. Romero and his films continue an important nineteenth-century legacy into the twentieth century and beyond. The title of Ibsen's naturalist play 'When We Dead Awaken' is one significantly relevant to Romero's particular cinematic legacy.

It is a legacy deeply indebted to the radical aspects of cinematic and literary naturalism that have unconsciously influenced Romero throughout his career. Although Romero has never read Zola, his films indirectly reflect concerns appearing in many of the writer's novels which take issue with the human oppression and rampant materialism characteristic of the Second Empire of Louis Napoleon and beyond. The entire body of Romero's work is an important twentieth-century cinematic equivalent to Zola's pioneering social justice pamphlet *J'Accuse*, yet Romero's approach is much more subtle. Zola's and the naturalist tradition are key cultural components within the textual formation of Romero's films. As Ken Mogg has argued concerning the influence of Schopenhauer on Alfred Hitchcock in his scholarly MacGuffin website, although the director may not have read the works of this important philosopher the ideas formed part of a contemporary cultural climate infiltrating the films themselves. The same is true of Zola's influence on Romero. Zola pioneered a naturalist tradition which moved to America and influenced many writers such as Dreiser, Norris and London. However, it was more than coincidental that this movement became marginalised in periods of conservative reaction such as the Roaring Twenties and the Cold War era. Even in later times, the academy is often hostile to works articulating issues of social injustice which contrast with fashionable discourses such as postmodernism. Romero's work cannot be safely recuperated into any bland apolitical domain. Hence, its current marginalisation.

Robin Wood described *Day of the Dead* as 'the last great American horror film'.[5] Reynold Humphries acclaimed Romero's zombie trilogy for its attack on the values of American consumerism.[6] Both writers mourn the passing of the radical American horror film and express reservation about the genre's future. However, Romero has left an important legacy that both he and others may develop in the future. This involves the recognition of the realist horror film and its social implications which have not been given proper attention until fairly recently.

During the last few years, several scholars have moved away from concentrating on the excessive aspect of the horror genre towards reconsidering its realist dimensions. Due to the decline of *Screen Theory* and recognition of its limited and now obsolescent theories, a much broader perspective has emerged involving a much broader understanding of realism far beyond Colin MacCabe's definitions made three decades ago. As Julia Hallam and Margaret Marshment have recently argued, 'Realism is not a single homogenous mode that always works in the same way; on the contrary, it is important to identify the particular strategies at work in any particular text.'[7] This is much more of a critical approach rather than the monolithically dogmatic definition which once held dominance in critical discourse. Romero's work really belongs in this area. It also has associations with the naturalist tradition.

Romero's cinema is a critical cinema far removed from the infantile representations of George Lucas and Steven Spielberg as well as the escapist concerns of recent horror films. The director's work has also suffered from the trendy appropriation of solipsistic postmodernist concepts, a discourse now becoming appropriately moribund.[8] Now that attention is moving towards the social dimensions of the horror film, Romero's work may gain better appreciation for its contribution towards a more oppositional form of cinema employing the radical dimensions of the genre than has been the case over the past twenty years. Recent work on realist horror and naturalism traditions are moving in this direction,[9] an area to which George A. Romero firmly belongs. Hopefully, the director will be further involved in this significant movement now developing in both critical study and cinematic representations. He has already contributed several landmarks to its growth and will, undoubtedly, continue to furnish more important examples to a movement in which he has been a creative founding father.

APPENDIX ONE

The Romero Screenplays and Teleplays

Romero's screenplays for the films he did not direct deserve some notice. The same is true for certain of his teleplays. Although they rarely reach the heights of films he had creative control over, they do reflect several ideas occurring in the other films as well as negative industrial constraints affecting his talent. These latter components vary from being highly disappointing to suggestive developments of themes appearing in his other films as director. The projects Romero worked on in a screenplay or producer capacity also appear to be designed to give his collaborators such as Michael Gornick, John Harrison and Tom Savini director credit.

Both *Creepshow 2* (1987) and *Tales from the Darkside: The Movie* (1991) contain little, if any, redeeming value. They appear contractual products which Romero felt obligated to undertake for the Laurel organisation he left in 1985. Directed by Romero's cinematographer, Michael Gornick, *Creepshow 2* reflects the type of empty Hollywood 'sequelitis' product Romero would have found himself forced to direct had he ever made the mistake of relocating from Pittsburgh. Shot for $4 million in association with New World Pictures, this Laurel production appears a tired version of the earlier *Creepshow* in which none of the original participants appeared to have any interest whatsoever. Richard Rubinstein functioned as executive producer while Romero's screenplay was based on story ideas provided by Stephen King. Despite acknowledging EC Comic veteran Jack Kamen in the final credits, *Creepshow 2* is less satisfactory than its predecessor. Although the three stories 'Old Chief Wood'nhead', 'The Raft' and 'The Hitchhiker' formally reflect EC moral codes, their individual renditions are often glib and perfunctory. Unfortunately, with the exception of Lois Chiles' erring wife in 'The Hitchhiker', the acting performances are uninspiring. Certain Romero's themes occasionally appear, but they are never developed to any satisfactory degree so that they creatively complement those ideas found in films the director had complete control over.

In 'Old Chief Wood'nhead', Ray Spruce (George Kennedy) speaks about wishing to contribute to a declining town he had benefited from while the economy was healthy. But, as Nigel Floyd notes, the episode incongruously introduces a banal 'Spielberg world of cutesy old-timers' before changing its tone abruptly to end in three climactic gory scenes.[1] The grotesque college students in 'The Raft' represent the worst type of cartoon characterisation imaginable so that their demise appears as a welcome relief. Although one of them wears a 'Horlicks University' T-shirt from the original *Creepshow*'s hypocritical academic establishment, nothing further is made of this reference. Finally, although the class and racial components of 'The Hitchhiker' episode dealing with a rich, adulteress killing a poor black hitchhiker in a hit and run accident initially appear as the most promising of all three tales, significant implications within the plot remain unrealised. During one point of the story Annie Lansing (Lois Chiles) attempts to engage in a characteristic Romero act of denial after she has killed the hitchhiker by telling herself, 'There was really nothing at all. There was no hitchhiker.' But this promising theme is thrown away in a plot which is formulaic and mundane. Virtually all three stories operate on the banal levels of grotesqueness and shock far removed from the original intentions of the EC tradition. *Creepshow 2*'s screenplay resembles the product of a tired talent forced to contribute to a production that appears totally uninspired.

During 1983 Romero wrote the pilot episode, 'Trick or Treat', directed by Bob Balaban, which was included in the 1984–85 season of *Tales of the Darkside*. Overall, Romero's contributions to this series fell far below his usual standards. The most promising of his teleplays, 'The Devil's Advocate', dealt with bitter talk-show host Mandrake (Jerry Stiller) who appropriately ends up in hell to fulfil the role he has bitterly fulfilled during his lifetime. The story begins with Mandrake entering the television studio and complaining about a dead wino being found in his car. He then begins his sneering performance on his unfortunate listeners who are masochistically drawn to his show. After sarcastic comments made against the wife of a recently unemployed man suffering from the contemporary manufacturing recession and a low-income Afro-American night watchman, Mandrake finds himself promoted. As self-styled 'devil's advocate', Satan has decided to reward a person who has made his job easier by making him listen to anguished calls from all historical eras. Mandrake appropriately finds himself locked into a studio existing in a hell of his own creation.

'The Devil's Advocate' is another of Romero's social criticisms of an institution designed to use and abuse its listeners. Its attack has much in common with the images of the talk-show apparatus seen in *There's Always Vanilla* and *Martin*. However, the brevity of the running time allows little opportunity to develop its attack further despite the powerful performance by Jerry Stiller of a man who has turned against the whole human race due to misfortunes he has suffered in his own personal life. Romero's other two teleplays, 'Baker's Dozen' and 'Circus', also appear insufficiently developed.

Romero's 'The Cat From Hell' screenplay for *Tales from the Darkside: The Movie* (1991) represents another lost possibility. Directed by John Harrison and based on Laurel Entertainment's problematic and insipid television series, this three-part anthology again resembled the *Creepshow* format which by now had served its purpose. Romero is a director who never wishes to repeat himself and his screenplay contribution appears to again be another example of something he had to do, rather than wanted to.

The episode begins with a taxi pulling up at an old mansion at night. As its occupant gets out, an old man in a wheelchair welcomes him. They walk into a deserted hallway seen from an overhead perspective shot which resembles a cat's point-of-view. The wheelchair-bound figure, Drogan, is the head of a pharmaceutical company, who offers his visitor, hitman Halstead, money for the execution of a cat. Despite his supposed wealth and comments such as, 'Over the years I've filled this place with everything you could want, everything you could ever want', both the present narrative and past flashbacks reveal the mansion as being little better than a frugal version of *Citizen Kane*'s Xanadu. During the numerous flashbacks, Harrison's introductory and concluding visual techniques seem reminiscent of the ones used in Welles' 1941 film in which characters often appear in lap-dissolves while the past events they narrate either begin or end. As Drogan's first references to the previous occupants killed by the cat states, 'We were a dull collection of rich and unhappy people.'

Both Drogan and Halstead are mirror images of a deadly capitalist economy. While the former has gained legitimate wealth by manufacturing a 'remarkably habit forming' drug combining 'painkiller, tranquilliser, and mild hallucinogen' which is 'one step up from street junk', the latter has also performed services for businesses. Drogan comments, 'And you've done well yourself' in terms of the 'last two jobs you've done for members of the professional community'. A mysterious black cat has murdered Drogan's sister, companion, and butler at various times on the stroke of midnight. The executive believes 'It's been sent to punish me' as he reveals that his fortune is built upon a four-year series of tests upon the nervous systems of five thousand cats. Drogan then leaves the hitman to perform his service during the night with 'everything you could want, everything you could ever want'. As the hitman cynically observes, 'Everything you could ever want! Why is it the rich guys always buy the cheap stuff?' However, despite his efforts, the feline adversary proves stronger – it kills the hitman. The next morning, when Drogan arrives home, the cat emerges from its opponent's body to scare its last adversary to death. Ironically, the clock chimes midnight after a night accident has rendered it dysfunctional.

Romero's screenplay has several ingenious touches. It is a horror version of *The Magnificent Ambersons* meets *The Chimes at Midnight*. But the direction and performances lack Romero's magic touch. 'The Cat From Hell' obviously represents a screenplay Romero devised for an anthology film from a television series he had little feeling towards (see Gagne 1987: 201–6).

Naturally, Tom Savini's 1990 version of *Night of the Living Dead* never surpasses the heights of the original version. Like Romero's screenplay contributions to *Creepshow 2* and *Tales from the Darkside: The Movie*, his involvement again appears to be on the level of helping a collaborator gain a director credit as well as ensuring the sequel rights remained in the hands of the original Pittsburgh associates. However, Romero's screenplay for Savini's film is one of his major achievements in relation to a film he did not direct. Like 'The Cat From Hell', production circumstances necessitated his involvement. As Kim Newman stated, although a remake appeared ludicrous 'this enterprise was embarked on partly because a rights quirk meant that if the original production team did not undertake a remake, anyone else could do so'.[2] Romero had also agreed to colourisation of the original version as a way of financially reimbursing those who had worked on it.[3]

However, although Savini's version naturally suffers in comparison to the original, it is also a significant example of Romero's authorship as screenwriter rather than director. While Romero did not direct this version, it gave him the opportunity of further reflecting on the original and revising and rewriting several scenes. As Barry Grant (1992) notes, the Savini-Romero text changes Barbara's character from catatonic victim to feminist heroine making the original's critique of patriarchy even more explicit. He traces Barbara's new status to the influence of Fran in *Dawn* and Sarah in *Day* and also relates her character to other figures such as Joan Mitchell of *Jack's Wife* and the Hawksian professionalist ethos seen in *Knightriders*. But while Grant astutely notes the new Barbara 'as a *corrective* to the narrowness of masculine professionalism, rather than, as in Hawks, having to be measured *by* it (in that key Hawksian phrase, to be as "good" as men)', he also loses sight of the exact manner *Jack's Wife* relates to the new version.

In the earlier film, Joan Mitchell attempts to find a new direction but becomes hopelessly lost in the end. Although Barbara's situation is different, she, too, finds herself in a blind alley at the climax. Although the ending involving Barbara's execution of Harry may be read as a 'woman's response to patriarchy' (Grant 1992: 210), it may also have ironic associations by criticising the heroine in the same way as her gaze criticises the hysterical masculinity she sees before her. Romero's films often operate in an ambivalent manner. Savini's *Night of the Living Dead* concludes by interrogating the motivations of its female character in the same way Romero examined those of various male characters throughout his films. It is a measure of his penetrating vision as a director that he recognises problems within feminism as conceived in the 1990s. Barbara puts on military attire like Sigourney Weaver's Ripley in *Aliens* (1986) yet thinks she stands apart from the violence and believes that she is not a guerilla fighter in the *Rambo* mode. However, she has also become contaminated by that very violence, a characteristic Romero criticises in his various male characters such as Clank in *The Crazies* and Roger and Stephen in *Dawn of the Dead*. As Newman recognises, 'It is ironic that the 1990 Barbara's anti-zombie violence is seen to be as insane as her 1968 predecessor's retreat into a psychological shell' (1993: 52). Romero usually approves of the actions of characters who finally throw their weapons away such as David in *The Crazies*, Peter in *Dawn of the Dead*, and John in *Day of the Dead*. Romero's revised Barbara is in a much more ambiguous and precarious situation. Like Hitchcock in his various reworkings of earlier films such as *The Man Who Knew Too Much* (1934) and *The 39 Steps* (1935), Romero engages in a characteristic screenplay revision of his most well-known film to good effect by developing new implications in the light of changing historical and social conditions.

The new version begins with Johnny's famous line, 'They're coming to get you, Barbara', spoken against a black screen. Most audiences who saw Savini's version knew Romero's original thoroughly. The reference to Johnny's scary comment evokes both audience familiarity with the original as well as suggesting how Romero's screenplay will differ by emphasising and reworking well-known aspects of the narrative by citing an already well-known line in the opening shot. Savini begins the film with long shots of a car driving along a deserted rural Pennsylvania road. As the credits roll, Romero's screenplay emphasises the family tensions between both siblings implicit in the original version. Various lines place the opening scene firmly within the tradition of the American family horror film. Barbara (Patricia Tallman) asks Johnny (Bill Mosley), 'Why do you have to be so mean?' He replies, 'I'm your older brother. Being mean and heartless is part of my job', articulating the vicious sibling rivalry endemic within the patriarchal family. However, unlike the original, it is now the mother's grave they visit rather than the father's. Clearly, the visit is an act of posthumous revenge from beyond the grave by a mother both siblings had no real feeling for when she was alive. As Johnny remarks, 'This is the fourth time I've been up here in the three months since she died. I'm spending more time with her now than when she was alive.' He correctly sees this empty 'charade' as another means of maternal control since she knew Johnny would have to accompany his sister on a trip to a deserted area 'two hundred miles away from the next glass of beer'. Johnny also attacks Barbara's denying the real 'truth' affecting their family life. 'She drove our father crazy ... and she damn near drove you into a convent. When was the last time you had a date? ... The one thing she never did was to drive two hundred miles to visit anybody.'

When the vehicle finally stops, the audience sees Barbara and Johnny for the first time. Like the original character, Tallman's Barbara is also afraid of the cemetery and Johnny plays on these fears. But unlike Judith O'Dea's earlier version, Tallman's character appears more repressed as seen by her spectacles, neckerchief, tightly buttoned high-neck blouse, brooch and demure skirt. By contrast, Johnny is more 'scary' than the original character played by Russell Streiner. Portrayed by Bill Moseley, well-known for his Chop Top character in Tobe Hooper's *The Texas Chainsaw Massacre Part 2* (1986), this new Johnny is already a monster created by the patriarchal family. He also already resembles a zombie by his exaggerated gestures and semi-grotesque make-up.

Romero then displays the conventions of the family horror film to good effect. After showing mother's tombstone, Johnny plays around crying, 'There's no escape. *No mother!*', as he drops behind the tombstone. Ironically, the first zombie will emerge from this very same area to frighten Barbara. However, unlike her predecessor, she immediately fights back using mother's bouquet wreath to impale an opponent who has now killed her brother. Although indebted to the original version, the sequence differs from it in several ways rebutting those inaccurate critical perceptions describing the entire film as one which 'copied the original version practically scene-by-scene'.[4] Unlike her earlier counterpart, Tallman's Barbara at least has the option of knowledge about a feminist movement which has been active for at least three decades.

As in the original, Barbara escapes to the farmhouse and encounters its living dead owner, Uncle Rege (Pat Logan) with the severed hand of his son, Satchell, who has committed suicide. Ben (Tony Todd) then arrives. Unlike the original, both Ben *and* Barbara battle with the zombies as complementary equals in the combat. Romero intercuts Ben's fight with Barbara's. Although they utter the same word, 'Die', as they kill their opponents, it is Barbara who is fighting the largest zombie, Rege, with a poker. Although upset by what she has seen, Tallman's Barbara does not collapse into a state of useless catatonia. Also, although Todd's Ben does take over, he also attempts to communicate with her and urges that she rally round: 'I don't need you falling apart on me. Fight what you're feeling. Fight what you're thinking about. Keep strong.' Like Peter in *Dawn of the Dead*, he realises she needs survival skills. However, unlike Peter, Todd's Ben is already compromised by negative masculine traits like Roger and Stephen in the earlier film.

When Ben describes his experiences to Barbara, he refers to two Romero critiques concerning talk shows and redneck violence. He tells her, 'All I heard was trash talking. Same as always, people making out they knew what it was all about.' As in *Night of the Living Dead* and *Dawn of the Dead*, survivors have much more to fear from rednecks than zombies. Ben tells Barbara about witnessing 'assholes trying to round them up and put them in the back of trucks as if they knew what they were going to do with them'. He also mentions being in a diner when a 'good ol' boy' began chasing after zombies and firing at random making no discrimination between the living dead and any unfortunate minorities. Ben also caustically dismisses media explanations: 'It wasn't no prison break. It wasn't no chemicals. This is hell on earth.' When he finds the farmhouse telephone dead, he remarks to Barbara, 'It doesn't take long for the world to fall apart, does it?' But Ben's comment will also apply to the small remnants of human society hiding within.

After discovering others in the cellar, Ben enquires as to why they remained below. This time Tom (William Butler) offers the real reason which Harry (Tom Towles) is reluctant to admit when he mentions that they were 'scared to hell when they heard banging'. As in the 1968 version, Ben and Harry take an instant dislike to each other. But while they argue, Savini shows Barbara acting fully aware of the dangerous situation affecting them. She also goes immediately to the toolbox looking for items to board up the windows. But she suggests an alternative strategy which both Ben and Harry reject: 'We could walk right past them. We wouldn't even need to run. If we're careful, we could get away. This place is not safe, upstairs or down. You told me to fight [to Ben]. Well, I'm fighting. I'm not panicking. We should get out before it's too late.' This version affirms her strategy as being the correct one. Barbara's development and intelligent awareness of the dangerous situation threatening everyone makes her, as Grant recognises, 'the film's one true Hawksian professional' (1992: 206).

However, Ben's decision to board up the farmhouse proves disastrous. Savini shoots two scenes showing zombies attracted towards the humans by the sound of hammering rather than an instinctive awareness of live human flesh. The tensions between all human characters become more explicit in this version. Harry both verbally and physically abuses his wife, Helen (McKee Anderson). Judy (Kate Finneran) is less sympathetic than her 1968 counterpart. Since Tom's uncle owned the farmhouse, she immediately asserts family and property rights at one point when Ben and Harry argue: 'Where'd you be if we kicked you the hell out?' Tom then intervenes telling his girlfriend, 'We're not going to kick anybody out, Judy Rose.' Although Judy is not yet married, she behaves in a manner reminiscent of Zola's property-conscious grasping bourgeois heroines such as Félicité Rougon of *La Fortune des Rougon* and Lisa Queneu of *Le Ventre du Paris*. She later indirectly causes the petrol-pump explosion by driving in a reckless manner resulting in Ben falling off the truck. Lacking Ben's guidance and finding they took the wrong key, Tom shoots the lock off and causes disaster. However, unlike the original version, Savini does not dwell on the gory banquet the barbecued lovers supply for the zombies. Indeed, the film is curiously muted in terms of spectacular gory effects. The real violence goes on inside a house divided by patriarchal violence and the adherence to now redundant ideological behavioural patterns.

Family values are now bankrupt in more than one sense. New patterns of behaviour have become necessary, patterns Barbara seems to embody as a heroine different in certain ways from her 1968 counterpart. Tom admits that he could never have killed Uncle Rege even though he changed into a cannibalistic zombie. When the Cooper daughter, Sarah (Heather Mazur), turns into a zombie, Harry cannot bring himself to kill her. Barbara immediately does so. Judy freaks out when Barbara kills the now living dead next-door neighbour, Mr Magruder. Since Barbara has no real love for a family system which made her life miserable, she appears to move towards a new set of values. She becomes more rational and self-controlled demonstrating to the hysterical Judy that the attackers are really dead by shooting one several times. When Ben accuses her of 'losing it', she responds, 'Whatever I lost, I lost a long time ago and I won't lose anything again. You can stop talking to me about losing it when you stop screaming at each other like a bunch of three-year-olds.' Her comments also relate to Harry as well as Ben. They later fight over a television set and destroy an important means of communication with the outside world. Barbara makes her second attempt to persuade Ben to walk away but to no avail.

After the death of Tom and Judy, Barbara witnesses Ben and Harry more interested in fighting each other than repelling the zombie invasion. The wounded Ben tells her to go while he escapes to the basement and Harry hides in the attic. The last image viewers see of the still-living Ben reveals him laughing when he hears the media finally giving up its lying explanations. A radio commentator admits that the previously broadcast rescue stations are 'no longer in operation' and affirms the existence of the living dead.

At this point in the film, male values have proved absolutely irredeemable. The resilient Barbara thus appears as the film's feminist heroine who 'takes back the night of the living dead'. But Romero's perspectives towards his heroine are often more ambiguous and complex in the film. Barbara's attitudes are certainly more positive than the rest of the humans in the farmhouse. The film also reveals her strategy as being the correct one under the circumstances. But Harry Cooper in Romero's original version also had the right idea despite the repugnant nature of his personality. Characters and ideas do not necessarily cohere in Romero's cinema.

Barbara survives. But the nature of her survival also involves some degree of personal cost. Her rationality has its limits. She exhibits Hawksian professionalism at its best by adjusting to changing situations and being aware of other alternatives. In this manner, she resembles Matthew Garth in *Red River*. However, she also becomes as contaminated by violence as Tom Dunson in the same film. Barbara does recognise how she can get past the zombies waiting outside; she uses violence to defend herself and others in life-threatening situations, but two significant scenes in the film reveal her submitting to irrational violence. After witnessing the futile struggle over the television set, she goes outside with the others. Recognising the zombie who killed her brother, she immediately shoots it. By this action, she acts in a contradictory manner and resembles an avenging heroine in a family melodrama rather than recognising that the zombie operated according to instinctual rather than rational motives.

The opening scenes revealed Barbara's personal entrapment in a family situation when her brother tormented her. Johnny's demise was no real loss to her. Also, the zombie is too far away from the house to do any real harm. Barbara's gesture is both unnecessary and contradictory in nature. Secondly, when she returns to the farmhouse, she finds Harry still alive and shoots him through the head. She believes correctly that her redneck companions will assume Harry to be just another zombie like Ben. Again, Barbara's action appears justified under the circumstance; is she not taking vengeance upon a horrible patriarch? However, the gesture is also unnecessary and animated by arbitrary personal desires for revenge. Harry is also in a state of shock as his traumatic response, 'You came back. You came back', reveals. Barbara afterwards, ironically, utters the line spoken by the redneck sheriff in the original version when her companions appear: 'There's another one for the fire.' Although Grant believes the line endorses Harry's fate as 'a woman's response to patriarchy as defiant as the killing of the salesman in Marlene Gorris' militantly feminist *A Question of Silence* (1982)' (1992: 210) the real implications are far more questionable.

Although female, Barbara has once again operated according to the behavioural modes of male violence Romero criticises within his films. The director takes a much less violent view of his zombies than many of his screen characters: 'You have to be sympathetic with the creatures because they ain't doin' nothin'. They're like sharks: they can't help behaving the way they do' (quoted in Yakir 1977: 62). The zombie who killed Johnny certainly could not help his behaviour. No love was ever lost between brother and sister. Also, on her flight from the farmhouse, Barbara became upset at seeing a zombie mother carrying a baby doll. But rather than walk away, she shot a figure who really was not 'doin' nothin''. The repugnant Harry also cannot help the way he behaves but does this excuse shooting every abusive husband on this planet rather than trying to find alternative ways of healing? Romero once asked, 'Have we conjured up creatures and given them mystical properties so as not to admit that they are actually of our own race?'[5] Unlike Fran in *Dawn of the Dead*, who sympathetically allows a trapped zombie nun to escape and frequently silently recognises the relationship she has to the living dead outside the mall's glass door, Barbara can not admit this.

Barbara's climactic lines, 'They're us. We're them and they're us', apply as much to her as the rednecks she sees taunting captured zombies and consuming the hot sausages and spit-roasted pork supplied by a truck. Although Barbara is no frightened and helpless woman like the independent female of most horror films,[6] she still reacts like her generic prototypes in her encounter with the mother zombie. She denies the relationship she has to a once-living being in very much the same manner Joan Mitchell denies her involvement in sexual promiscuity and witchcraft in *Jack's Wife*. The concluding images of Savini's version are thus more ambiguous. They do not merely represent Barbara's perspective concerning a repugnant and monstrous patriarchy (see Grant 1992: 209) since they are also critical of her very motivations. The camera zooms in to her face, intercutting it with still shots of rednecks, zombies and funeral pyres. Then the final image zooms in to a huge close-up of her eye. It interrogates her as much as it does the spectacle she witnesses.

Romero's screenplay for the new *Night of the Living Dead* thus contains several significant ideas. Yet it also interrogates the female character in a similar manner to the director's earlier investigations of male behaviour. This change is not accidental. In an era which has successfully co-opted feminism, allowed women into the military to kill and press buttons of technological destruction as easily as any man Romero now challenges his female characters, as well as their male counterparts, to recognise the dangerous nature of ideological entrapment. They, too, may easily join that growing army of the 'living dead' present on cinema screens as well as in everyday life. Males such as David, Peter and John previously relinquished their weapons in Romero's films. In an increasingly dangerous world where certain women avidly wish to prove they are 'deadlier than the male', Romero now challenges Barbara to arrive at the same awareness characterising her female, as well as her male, predecessors.

APPENDIX TWO

Chronology

1940   Born in the Bronx, New York City, on 4 February.

1954   Began filming on 8mm in the Scarsdale area of New York. Arrested for throwing a burning dummy from a roof while shooting 8mm short *Man from the Meteor*. Education at Suffield Academy, Connecticut.

1956   8mm short productions, *Gorilla* and *Earthbottom*. Wins Future Scientists of America award for *Earthbottom*, a geology documentary made at Suffield.

1958   Begins studying art, design and drama at Carnegie-Mellon Institute, Pittsburgh, Pennsylvania. Shoots 8mm short *Curly* and 16mm short *Slant*. Both are co-scripted with Rudolph J. Ricci who described the latter black-and-white film as 'a Bergmanesque study of a lonely girl's fantasies during a Pittsburgh winter'.

1960   Begins work as an actor, director and set painter in Pittsburgh.

1962   Completes work on first envisaged ambitious feature *Expostulations*, co-scripted with Rudolph J. Ricci. This was an anthology comprising several unrelated vignettes and satirical shorts such as 'The Froomistan' about a mad scientist building a contraption in his backyard; 'The Rocket Ship' dealing with a spaceship landing in an ice-cream cone; 'The Trilogy' viewing the experiences of a black in the ghetto; and 'Door Against the Rain' about a boy finding his fantasy world outside his back door. Although Romero shot some two to three hours of silent 16mm colour footage, it was never edited into a finished film. Established TV production company 'Latent Image' for industrial and commercial films. Shot Latent Image Promotional Reel. This was a 16mm compilation short running six to eight minutes promoting the company and featuring fast-motion scenes of the crew at work. (During 1962–73 the Latent Image shot 30-second and 60-second commercials for companies such as US

Steel, Calgon, Westinghouse, Koppers Inc. and H. J. Heinz. It also worked on political campaigns film such as *Lenore Romm*.)

1967   Co-directed and scripted *Screen Test* with Rudolph J. Ricci. This was a 16 mm black-and-white short which anticipated the theme of *There's Always Vanilla* and was designed to demonstrate the talents of Ray Laine who would later play the lead in the future film.

1968   Directed, photographed and edited *Night of the Living Dead*, co-scripted with John A. Russo, based on a story by Romero. Alternative titles *Night of the Flesh Eaters/Night of Anubis*. Image Ten Company formed for feature production.

1970   Begins extensive work as TV director.

1972   Directed, photographed and edited *There's Always Vanilla* (aka *The Affair* for Southern drive-in circuits), scripted by Rudolph J. Ricci. The film was shot on 16mm colour and blown up to 35 mm. Working title, *At Play with the Angels*.

1973   Directed, photographed, edited and scripted *Jack's Wife*. This 16mm colour film was blown up to 35 mm but reduced from its original running length of 130 minutes to 89 minutes by Jack Harris Enterprises for general distribution under the title of *Hungry Wives*. It also circulated as *Season of the Witch*. Directed, edited and scripted *The Crazies* (aka *Code Name Trixie*) from an original script by Paul McCollough titled *The Mad People*. Enters into partnership with Richard P. Rubinstein to form the Laurel Group.

1974   Directed *O.J. Simpson/Juice on the Loose* for *The Winners* series with Richard P. Rubinstein as producer and executive producer. Aired on ABC TV during December.

1975   Directed the following titles for *The Winners* 'sports profile films' with Richard P. Rubinstein as producer and executive producer: *Reggie Jackson/One Man Bunch*; *Franco Harris/Good Luck on Sunday*; *NFL Films/The 27th Team*; *Bruno Sammartino/Strongman*; directed and produced *Tom Weiskopf/On Tour*; *Willie Stargell/If I Didn't Play Baseball*; *Johnny Rutherford/ Eleven Year Odyssey*. Co-executive producer with Richard P. Rubinstein of *Magic at the Roxy* directed by Michael Gargulio on videotape. Producer/executive producer/co-producer and co-executive producer of the following 'sports profile films' for the ABC TV syndicated series *The Winners* during Autumn 1975 following *Monday Night Football*: *Kareem Abdul Jabbar/Nobody Roots for Goliath* directed by Richard P. Rubinstein; *Driver: Mario Andretti* directed by Richard P. Rubinstein; *Lou Brock/ The Thief* directed by Michael Gornick and co-produced with Richard P. Rubinstein; *Pittsburgh's Front Four/ The Steel Curtain* directed by Michael Gornick and co-produced with Richard P. Rubinstein; *Rocky Blier/I'm Back* directed by Michael Gornick with Richard P. Rubinstein as co-executive producer; *Terry Bradshaw/Thank God I'm a Country Boy* directed by Michael Gornick with Richard P. Rubinstein as co-executive producer.

1977   Directed, scripted and edited *Martin*. Photographed by Michael Gornick in 16mm colour with sepia inserts and blown up to 35mm. This film marked Romero's first collaboration with make-up and special effects artist Tom Savini.

1978   Directed, scripted and co-edited *Dawn of the Dead* (UK title, *Zombies – Dawn of the Dead)*. Produced by Richard P. Rubinstein, a different version lacking four minutes with slight re-editing agreed upon by Romero was accomplished by Dario Argento.

1981   Directed, scripted and co-edited *Knightriders*. Produced by Richard P. Rubinstein.

1982   Directed *Creepshow*. Produced by Richard P. Rubinstein with screenplay by Stephen King.

1983   Original teleplay 'Trick or Treat' for pilot episode of *Tales from the Darkside* included in 1984–85 season, directed by Bob Balaban. Romero was executive producer for this series.

1985   Directed and scripted *Day of the Dead*. Produced by Richard P. Rubinstein. Original teleplay 'The Devil's Advocate' for 1985–86 season of *Tales from the Darkside* directed by Michael Gornick. Laurel Group partnership dissolves.

1986   Teleplay 'Baker's Dozen' adapted from 'The Gingerbread Witch' by Scott Edelman for *Tales from the Darkside* directed by John Sutherland. Teleplay 'Circus' adapted from a story by Sidney J. Bounds for *Tales from the Darkside* directed by Michael Gornick.

1987   Produced and scripted *Creepshow 2* directed by Michael Gornick. Stories by Stephen King.

1988   Directed and scripted *Monkey Shines*. Produced by Charles Evans.

1990   Directed and scripted 'The Facts in the Case of Mr. Valdemar', episode in *Two Evil Eyes*, a two-part anthology with Dario Argento. Produced by Achille Manzotti for ADC Gruppo Bema Production. Executive producer and scenarist on *Night of the Living Dead* directed by Tom Savini. Produced by John A. Russo and Russ Streiner. Released by Twentieth Century Fox as a Menahem Golan production. Scenarist for 'The Cat from Hell' episode of *Tales From The Darkside: The Movie*. Directed by John Harrison. Producer: Richard P. Rubinstein.

1993   Directed, scripted and executive produced *The Dark Half* based on the novel by Stephen King. Produced by Declan Baldwin for Orion Pictures.

2000   Directed and scripted *Bruiser*.

NOTES

CHAPTER ONE

1   See Jim Hillier (1992) *The New Hollywood*. New York: Continuum; Jon Lewis (ed.) (1998) *New American Cinema*. Durham: University of North Carolina Press. For an interesting perspective on Hollywood corporate development see also Dennis McDougal (1998) *The Last Mogul: Lew Wasserman, MCA, and The Hidden History of Hollywood*. New York: Crown Publishers.

2   Andrew Britton (1986) 'Blissing Out: The Politics of Reaganite Entertainment', *Movie* 31/32, 1–42; Robin Wood (1985) '80s Hollywood: Dominant Tendencies', *cineACTION!* 1, 2–5; Wood (1986) *Hollywood: From Vietnam to Reagan*; Tony Williams (1996) 'Trying to Survive on the Darker Side: 1980s Family Horror', in Barry K. Grant (ed.) *The Dread of Difference*. Austin: University of Texas Press, 164–80.

3   For the history of this specific form of cinematic mechanism see Tom Gunning (1990) 'The Cinema of Attractions: Early Film, Its Spectator and the Avant-Garde', in Thomas Elsaesser (ed.) *Early Cinema: Space, Frame, Narrative*. London: BFI, 56–60

4   Robert Singer, personal correspondence. See Zola (1964) 'The Experimental Novel', in *The Experimental Novel and Other Essays*. Trans. Belle Sherman. New York: Haskell House, 28.

5   The studies he refers to are June Howard (1985) *Form and History in American Literary Naturalism*. Chapel Hill: University of North Carolina Press; Walter Benn Michaels (1987) *The Gold Standard and the Logic of Naturalism*. Berkeley: University of California Press; and Lee Clark Mitchell (1989) *Determined Fictions: American Literary Naturalism*. New York: Columbia University Press.

6   Howard 1985: 36–8.

7   See Louis J. Budd, 'The American Background', and Jacqueline Tavernier-Courbin, '*The Call of the Wild* and *The Jungle*: Jack London's and Upton Sinclair's Animal and Human Jungles', *The Cambridge Companion to American Realism and Naturalism*, 21, 47–71, 238.

8   See *The American Film Institute Catalog, Feature Films 1911–1920*. Berkeley: University of California Press, 1988. Surviving footage from Hobart Bosworth's Jack London adaptations such as *Martin Eden* (1913) and *An Odyssey of the North* (1914) reveal the presence of a distinctively cinematic naturalist style particularly in the former's use of location in the industrial districts of Oakland. Photographic evidence from non-extant Jack London films such as *The Sea Wolf* (1913), *John Barleycorn*, and *The Valley of the Moon* (both 1914) testify to the naturalist influence. *Destruction* (1915), *The Marble Heart* (1916), and *A Man and the Woman* (1917) were respectively based on Zola's *Labor*, *Thérèse Raquin*, and *Nana*. D. W. Griffith's Biograph films such as *A Corner in Wheat* (1908),

The Musketeers of Pig Alley (1912) and 'The Mother and the Law' episode from *Intolerance* (1916) reveal that such imagery was inescapable during an era which also witnessed the filming of works by American naturalist novelists such as Frank Norris and Upton Sinclair. Examples include *The Pit* (1914), *The Jungle* (1914), *Life's Whirlpool* (1916), *The Adventurer* (1917) and *The Money Changers* (1920). Griffith's last film, *The Struggle* (1931), appeared during the last years of Prohibition. Despite its historically inappropriate box-office appeal, the film has connections with both literary naturalism (especially *L'Assommoir*) and late nineteenth-century critiques of the menace of alcohol on everyday life. Furthermore, naturalist depictions of consumerism, the commodification of female bodies, and spectacular displays in works such as Zola's *Au Bonheur des Dames*, occupied a prominent role in American cinema of the 1920s. See Sumiko Higashi (1994) *Cecil B. DeMille and American Culture: The Silent Era*. Berkeley: University of California Press, 89–92, 104.

9   For an example of 1960s reactions against the reductive nature of naturalistic reproductions in television still dominant in PBS *Masterpiece Theatre* and *Mystery* productions today see Don Taylor (1990) *Days of Vision: Working with David Mercer: Television Drama Then and Now*. London: Methuen. As the novels of Brett Easton Ellis depict, not everyone is capable of either escaping damaging psychological mechanisms of materialism let alone understanding the real implications of *Dawn of the Dead*. Trapped within mindless consumer-culture gratification victims become little better than Romero's zombies. They may also develop into future versions of Patrick Bateman, the 'hero' of *American Psycho*. See Ellis (1987) *The Rules of Attraction*. London: Penguin, 40, 58; Ellis (1991) *American Psycho*. New York. Vintage.

10 Lehan (1995), 'The European Background', *The Cambridge History of Realism and Naturalism*, sees the crowd theme as characteristic of naturalism. He describes *Germinal* in terms of Zola's ideas of biological determinism, ideas we may also read in a different manner as noted above: 'The murderous nature of Etienne in *Germinal* takes us close to Zola's belief in the atavistic, and grounds the industrial conflict between mine owners and workers in a kind of animalistic struggle, a theme that is clearly established when the brutal crowd is described as an uncontrollable animal' (58). See also Naomi Schor (1978) *Zola's Crowds*. Baltimore: Johns Hopkins University Press, whose mythical reading of Zola's fiction sees the operation of both repression and the return of the repressed involving the buried dead in *The Fortune of the Rougons*. She also comments that 'The invisible dead, Homer's "silent majority", are familiar characters in Zola's works. Not only his cemeteries, but his gardens, his rooms, his very cities (see *Rome*), are strangely animated by the palpable presence of the dead. The invisible crowd of the dead is one of the most active in Zola' (120). Rachel Bowlby notes that *Au Bonheur des Dames* contains the theme of the reduction of women to dead bodies as well as their repression. See *Just Looking: Consumer Culture in Dreisser, Gissing and Zola*. New York: Methuen, 1985, 76. Fran escapes from both in *Dawn of the Dead*.

11 See Richard Wight Fox and T. Jackson Lears (eds) (1983) *The Culture of Consumption: Critical Essays in American History 1880–1980*. New York: Pantheon – an important collection of essays dealing with the consumerist mentality within American society. Romero's films employ the concept both literally and metaphorically.

12 See Wade Davis (1988) *Passage of Darkness: The Ethnobiology of the Haitian Zombie*. Chapel Hill: University of North Carolina Press; Davis (1985) *The Serpent and the Rainbow*. New York. Simon and Schuster. Davis also cites Zora Neale Hurston's belief that zombies were not created by magic and mentions the use of drugs which parallel the methods used in both *White Zombie* and *Revolt of the Zombies*. See Davis 1988: 66–7.

13 See Tony Williams (1981) '*White Zombie* – Haitian Horror', *Jump Cut*, 28, 18–20; Gary D. Rhodes (2001) *White Zombie: Anatomy of a Horror Film*. Jefferson: McFarland.

14 Howard (1985: 53) notes an interesting opposition between nature and culture in the early chapters of Jack London's *White Fang*, where humans lose their traditional privileges by dominating animals and now become the hunted species rather than the hunter. She views this reversal as one of the particular forms of antinomy characterising American literary naturalism. See also Diane M. Smith (1989) 'Confronting Socialism: The Naturalist Novel and its Reception in Europe', *Works and Days* 7.2, 86. She notes Zola's description of the rioting Montsou miners in *Germinal* as having 'jaws of wild animals' and Gissing's rebellious crowd in *Demos* bellowing with a 'wild beast roar'. As Walter Benn Michaels astutely demonstrates in *The Gold Standard and the Logic of Naturalism*,

the naturalist novel has an intrinsic connection to capitalism whatever the mode of expression. The beast imagery within many naturalist novels is a key example. During his early life Jack London feared becoming little better than a 'work beast' and adopted the symbol of the wolf as his emblem. In Theodore Dreiser's *Sister Carrie*, the downwardly mobile Hurstwood finally merges into the mass of pitiful drifters who have 'ox-like stares' and wait patiently 'like cattle'. See also Howard 1985: 101–2.

15   Robin Wood (1989) *Hitchcock's Films Revisited*. New York: Columbia University Press, 288–302. Similarly Howard (1985: 71) notes that naturalist novels contain many ideological discourses. She further states that naturalist fiction generally incorporates conventional elements from popular literary genres like the adventure story and the domestic novel in terms of their complex relation to mass culture. She also notes that naturalism exists in constant dialogue with realism (142). If Walcutt (1956: 22) recognised American naturalism as involving a 'continual *search* for form' there is no reason why it may not find expression in the cinematically different form of Romero's specific appropriation of the horror genre. Howard (167) also sees affinities between naturalism and mass cultural popular social melodramas such as Harriet Beecher Stowe's *Uncle Tom's Cabin*, Frank Norris' *The Pit*, Sinclair Lewis' *Main Street*, and even Margaret Mitchell's *Gone With the Wind*. For the horror film's relationship to the Hollywood melodrama see Tony Williams (1996), *Hearths of Darkness*. New Jersey: Fairleigh Dickinson University Press, 24–6.

16   Donald Pizer (1966) *Realism and Naturalism in Nineteenth-Century American Literature*. Carbondale: Southern Illinois University Press, 63. See also Pizer (1982) *Twentieth-Century American Literary Naturalism*. Carbondale: Southern Illinois University Press, and James R. Giles (1989) *Confronting the Horror: The Novels of Nelson Algren*. Kent State University Press, who relates Algren's work to the grotesque excessiveness in the novels of Louis-Ferdinand Céline and other French existential writers. See also Giles (1995) *The Naturalistic Inner-City Novel in America*. Columbia: University of South Carolina Press; Herbert Selby (1997) 'John Rechy, and Latter-Day Naturalism', *Excavation*, 9, 167–71; Robert Singer, 'Only the Dead: Urban Milieu in the Contemporary Naturalist Film', op. cit. 194–203; 'The Impulses of Humanity: Naturalism and the Contemporary American Film', *Excavatio*, 11, 143–8; and Carl Rollyson, 'Susan Sontag: A Postmodern Naturalist', op. cit. 119–23.

17   Howard 1985: 63–4. Eric J. Sundquist notes that in certain naturalist texts 'the abnormal becomes the barely submerged norm' resulting in a 'Gothic *intensification of detail* that approaches the allegorical'. See 'Introduction: The Country of the Blue', in Sundquist (ed.) (1982) *American Realism: New Essays*. Baltimore: Johns Hopkins University Press, 13. This interesting association of Gothic excess and allegorical readings also parallels features in Romero's films. Commenting on some elements also relevant to the temptation of rigid definitions concerning literary and cinematic texts, Mitchell notes, 'We need, if only for the moment, to relax the stranglehold of literary "standards" in order to fully appreciate how fully any enacted philosophy depends on its style – or rather, to recall that the two are one and the same, and that an extreme philosophy can only be realised in correspondingly extreme styles. Inquiring this into the sometimes awkward, invariably disruptive styles of determinism may well compel us into a larger reconsideration of narrative standards themselves. In any event, we will discover how much a larger pattern to grammatical improprieties can alter some of the deepest assumptions we bring to bear on the world around us' (1989: x).

18   See Howard 1985: 104–41 for her interesting discussion on naturalism and the spectator in *Sister Carrie*, Stephen Crane's *Maggie*, Jack London's *The Sea Wolf* and Frank Norris's *The Octopus*.

19   Witek's first chapter contains a useful comparison of the conformist imagery of comics produced by the Gilbertson Company, which marketed the *Classics Illustrated* series, with the more dynamic style of EC comics.

20   See the biographies provided in both the EC Comics reprints by Gemstone Publishing and the Internet site www.gemstonepub.com/ec/bios.

21   Les Daniels has significantly noted the debt these comics owed to an American cultural tradition represented by both Edgar Allen Poe and Ambrose Bierce. He sees *Tales from the Crypt*, *The Vault of Horror* and *The Haunt of Fear* as possibly owing their success 'to the theories and practice of Poe, who had called for short stories planned to achieve a single effect and ceasing when the effect had

been achieved.' Daniels also notes that the hosts introducing each story and commenting upon conclusions 'had a significant function in providing a sense of aesthetic distance between the shocks they presented and the readers to whom they presented them' in a manner 'reminiscent of the works of that master of sarcasm and satire, Ambrose Bierce, contained in the articulations of radio announcers on programmes such as *Inner Sanctum* and *The Hermit's Cave*' (1971: 63–4). Jack Davis' 'A Stitch in Time' certainly resembles an EC Comics version of themes common to both literary naturalism and Zola's fiction. Unlike most EC stories, the setting is a late nineteenth-century sweatshop where female employees exact a militant feminist revenge (in the best traditions of Zola's *Germinal*) on their bullying slave-driver boss, appropriately named Mr Lasch, for causing the death of an elderly worker. Lasch repeatedly utters the word 'production' and the story contains Marxist overtones usually absent and unthinkable in that era of American Cold War hysteria. This may explain its 'unusual' setting in the safe confines of a historically distant past. See *The Vault of Horror* 12 (1995) reprint of the 1952 issue. Other EC retribution themes occurred in the present and used supernatural elements for their realisation. According to Steve Bissette in a 9 March 1999 telephone conversation, two non-fantasy EC stories criticised prevalent Southern 1950s tendencies of lynching Negroes while another condemned a mob who lynched a soldier who did not salute the American flag by revealing that the victim was blind! For cultural parallels see M. Thomas Inge (1990) *Comics as Culture*. Jackson: University of Mississippi Press, 117–27; Robert M. Stewart (1980) 'George Romero: Spawn of EC', *Monthly Film Bulletin*, 47, 40. Several critics have noted that some of the better crime and horror comics 'took a stand on social issues of the day. By condemning all references to race as being racist, for example, reviewers effectively closed off any discussion of racism.' See here Amy Kiste Nyberg (1998) *Seal of Approval: The History of the Comics Code*. Jackson: University of Mississippi Press, 30, 63–5, 73. EC comics also adapted ideas from Gothic films such as *Gaslight* (1944) and *The Beast with Five Fingers* (1946). See, respectively, Johnny Craig's 'Madness at Manderville', *Tales from the Crypt 2* (1992) reprint of *Crypt of Terror* 1950 issue and Al Feldstein's 'The Maestro's Hand', op. cit. Furthermore, Johnny Craig's 'Mute Witness Murder!', op. cit., forms an interesting link between Cornell Woolrich's 1942 short story 'It Had to be Murder' (better known as 'Rear Window') and Hitchcock's 1954 film. Johnny Craig also used the basic plot of *The Cabinet of Dr. Caligari* (1919) to feature a female protagonist which anticipated the disastrous 1962 American version starring Glynis Johns. See 'Whirlpool', *The Vault of Horror* 6 (1991) reprint of the 1953 issue. For the proletarian grotesque concept see Michael Denning (1995), *The Cultural Front: The Laboring of American Culture in the Twentieth Century*. New York: Verso, 118–23.

22 *Tales from the Crypt* 5 (1993) reprint of December 1950/January 1951 issues. See also Graham Ingles (1996) 'We Ain't Got No Body!', *The Vault of Horror* 17, reprint of January 1953 issue; and Ingels' (1995) 'Horror! Head It Off', *Tales from the Crypt* 11, reprint of 1951/52 issue. Unless otherwise indicated, all references are to the Gemstone Publishing reissues.

23 *Tales from the Crypt* 3 (1993) reprint of 1950 issue; *The Vault of Horror* 17 (1996) reprint of December 1952 issue. Witek also notes that 'the critiques of American society in the EC's were oblique and implicit' (1989: 70).

24 See *The Vault of Horror* 13 (1995) reprint of 1952 issue; *Tales From the Crypt* 11 (1995) reprint of 1951/52 issue. 'Madame Bluebeard' also anticipates family horror films of later decades since the title character does not just murder her husbands to gain a rich lifestyle but also abandons them as sacrificial victims for the death of her mother whose husband adored her. Like Mrs Edgar in Hitchcock's *Marnie* (1964) she teaches her daughter that men are nothing more than 'beasts' and only good for money. Decaying corpses also return from the grave to take revenge on two unscrupulous car dealers in Jack Davis' 'The Death Wagon!', *The Vault of Horror* 13 (1995) reprint of 1952 issue. Another returns from the dead in Graham Ingels' 'Funeral Disease', *The Vault of Horror* 6 (1991) reprint of 1953 issue, and a deceased husband and wife similarly return to take vengeance on his second gold-digging wife in Ingels' 'Staired in Horror', *The Vault of Horror* 12 (1995) reprint of 1952 issue.

25 The cover illustration illustrated Jack Davis' 'Out of His Head', *The Vault of Horror* 6 (1991) reprint of 1953 issue.

26 See Kurt Anderson, 'A perfect mad man', *Time* (15 June 1972), 139, 24, 63. 'Gaines' magazine was the only place for children to have an uncensored glimpse behind the perky façade of 1950s bourgeois life.

It was where they could get clued in to the fatuousness of civics-books sanctimony, to the permutations of suburban phoniness, to grown-up dissembling and insincere hucksterism of all kinds. *Mad* infected children with a healthy degree of antiestablishment scepticism, a Dada-dissectionist attitude toward all media.' This last sentence ironically echoes the opening scenes of *Dawn of the Dead*, set in a television studio. Even 1990s conservatives expressed their debt to Gaines. See 'Editorial', *National Review* (6 July 1992), 44, 13, 18: 'Many upstanding conservatives including some on *NR*'s editorial board will confess under mild torture that *Mad* was an early influence and source of malicious pleasure at the expense of parents, mass culture, and other institutions of our society.'

27 For King's relationship to the American cultural tradition see Douglas Winter (1986) *Stephen King: The Art of Darkness*. New York: Signet, 23–4; Gary Hoppenstand and Ray B. Browne (eds) (1987) *The Gothic World of Stephen King: Landscapes of Nightmares*. Bowling Green, Ohio: Popular Press; Anthony Magistrale (1988) *Landscape of Fear: Stephen King's American Gothic*. Bowling Green, Ohio: Popular Press; Jeanne Campbell Reesman (1991) 'Stephen King and the Tradition of American Naturalism in *The Shining*', in Anthony Magistrale (ed.) *The Shining Reader*. Washington: Starmont House, 121–38; and Jonathan P. Davis (1994) *Stephen King's America*. Bowling Green, Ohio: Popular Press.

28 For King's connections to European naturalism in *The Shining* see Tony Williams (1997) 'Stephen King, Naturalism, and *The Shining*', *Excavatio* 9, 156–65.

CHAPTER TWO

1 See Maria Reidelbach (1991) *Completely Mad: A History of the Comic Book and Magazine*. Boston: Little, Brown, 187–8. Although concentrating on *Mad*, Reidelbach's book is fully aware of the links it had with EC Comics. The various biographies of the illustrators as well as her second chapter provides a wealth of relevant information. Reidelbach notes the insidious role of the Comics Code Authority after the demise of EC comics which 'had virtually eliminated representations of ethnic groups in comics'. She quotes historian Pamela B. Nelson who comments that Code restrictions had 'intimidated many cartoonists into avoiding ethnic images altogether'. Reidelbach also quotes Joe Orlando's recognition of the Code's more insidious consequences which echo the 1980s and 1990s: 'It reflected the society. Look at the advertising, the magazines like *Saturday Evening Post*, the kind of people they represented were certainly not a melting pot, they all looked like WASPs, and they were hairless, and they didn't sweat, and the women all wore white gloves. Feldstein and Gaines had been severely burnt enough by the code to avoid the kind of pointed racial and religious morality tales that had been the suspense comic's redeeming feature, but in *Mad* they reveled in contrariness, exalted in pointing out skeletons in closets and dirt swept under the rugs.'

2 For a colour reproduction of this illustration see Reidelbach 1991: 7.

3 Barbara mentions this in her account to the occupants of the farmhouse. It may have been on her mind but the actual event shows her embarrassed and wishing to avoid the zombie.

4 Paul R. Gagne (1987) *The Zombies That Ate Pittsburgh: The Films of George A. Romero*. New York: Dodd, Mead & Co., 38. This is an invaluable resource book for Romero's films to date.

5 The film has also stimulated several other intelligent readings. See Jane Caputi (1988) 'Films of the Nuclear Age', *Journal of Popular Film and Television*, 16, 3, 100–10; Richard Dyer (1988) 'White', *Screen*, 29, 4, 59–63. While the first essay relates *Night of the Living Dead* to the apocalyptic climate of the nuclear age, the second significantly stresses its racial and political context. Dyer concludes his treatment of the film's relationship to both *Dawn of the Dead* and *Day of the Dead* by noting certain particular connotations: 'The hysterical boundedness of the white body is grotesquely transgressed as whites/zombies gouge out living white arms, pull out organs, munch at orifices. The spectre of white loss of control is evoked by the way the zombies stumble and dribble in their inexorable quest for blood, often with intestines spilling out or severed limbs dangling. White over-investment in the brain is mercilessly undermined as brains spatter against the wall and zombies flop to the ground' (1988: 63). Dyer concludes his examination by noting that the fear of control of one's body 'and the fear of not being able to control other bodies, those bodies whose exploitation is so fundamental to capitalist economy, are both at the heart of whiteness. Never has this horror been more deliriously evoked than in these films of the *Dead*.

1   See Dan Yakir (1979) 'Morning Becomes Romero', *Film Comment*, 15, 3, 60, 64–5; Paul R. Gagne (1987) *The Zombies That Ate Pittsburgh: The Films of George A. Romero*. New York: Dodd, Mead & Co., 41–6.

2   See Gagne 1987: 44–6 for a description of the creative and production problems which affected the original Latent Image production group over the making of this film.

3   See Gagne 1987: 41, 43.

4   When interviewed in 1973, Romero stated that the premise of *There's Always Vanilla* 'was going to be what happens to the youth culture in five or ten years' when it experienced 'a full cycle back-around' to parental values. Despite his reluctance to discuss this film further it is remarkable how much it still contains this very relevant idea. See Fran Lebowitz *et al.* (1973) 'George Romero: From *Night of the Living Dead* to *The Crazies*', *Andy Warhol's Interview*, 3, 31. According to an earlier interview Romero stated that the film had the working title of *At Play with the Angels* and was to be a work 'looking at "the American hippie" four or five years from now and where he is going to be and where the people are going to be around him and what happens to their whole communication'. See William Terry Ork and George Abagnalo (1969) '*Night of the Living Dead* – Interview with George A. Romero', *Andy Warhol's Interview*, 1, 4, 22.

5   Ironically, these comments are juxtaposed editorially with Chris's remarks to the camera in a similar manner to the later studio production inserts. When Lynn later decides to seek help for an abortion from Michael Dorian after learning about Chris's selfish desire to want to be a father to his abandoned son, Chrissie, an insert showing a studio dial, 'Turn to Clear Vision', follows a shot of her upset on the sofa. This is the first example of Romero's fascination with montage which will reach its stylistic culmination in *The Crazies*.

CHAPTER FOUR

1   For relevant information concerning Harris' similar marketing strategy for Larry Cohen's first film *Bone* (1972) see Tony Williams (1997) *Larry Cohen: Radical Allegories of an American Filmmaker*. Jefferson, NC: McFarland, 302–3.

2   See Thierry Kuntzel (1978) 'The Film Work', *Enclitic*, 2, 1, 38–61; Kuntzel (1980) 'The Film Work 2', *Camera Obscura*, 5, 7–69.

3   Over thirty years ago, I attended a lunch organised by Manchester University's Department of Biblical Studies. When Professor John Allegro remarked to a female student that Catholicism was generally understood as a religion of fear, the woman replied that the fear generally resulted from knowing what would happen if one did not believe!

CHAPTER FIVE

1   Robin Wood (1986) *Hollywood: From Vietnam to Reagan*. New York: Columbia University Press, 116; Robin Wood and Richard Lippe (eds) (1979) *The American Nightmare: Essays on the Horror Film*. Toronto: Festival of Festivals, 93. The first work duplicates the second and will be referred to in terms of its easier accessibility from this point onwards.

2   Mark Walker (1991) *Vietnam Veteran Films*. Metuchen, NJ: Scarecrow Press, 90–3; Tony Williams (1996) *Hearths of Darkness: The Family in the American Horror Film*. Madison, NJ: Fairleigh Dickinson University Press, 143. For the relationship of the Vietnam War to Romero's *Dawn of the Dead* and *Day of the Dead* see Robert C. Cumbow (1994) '*Dawn of the Dead, Day of the Dead*', in Jean Jacques Malo and Tony Williams (eds) *Vietnam War Films*. Jefferson, NC: McFarland, 105–6.

3   For further examination of this film see Tony Williams (1998) 'FEKS, *New Babylon*, and Zola', *Excavatio*, 11, 137–42.

4   The one exception to this rule is David for reasons noted above.

5   Despite Romero's citation of Howard Hawks, Orson Welles and Michael Powell as major influences on his work, the Hitchcock association appears more strongly in his films than he actually admits. Romero has admitted that traces of Hitchcock do occur in *Night of the Living Dead* and *Martin* but was

'totally unimpressed' when he saw the director working on *North by Northwest*. See Gagne 1987: 7, 13. Wood notes that *Night of the Living Dead*'s 'debt to *The Birds* goes beyond the obvious resemblances of situation and imagery' (1986: 115). Hitchcock defined the 'MacGuffin' as a mere plot device or gimmick which has no relevance to the director. Romero's zombies and the formally sensationalist aspects of the horror genre involving gore and violence operate in a similar manner. They are less important than Romero's key narrative interests which involve issues of everyday life rather than pure fantasy. See Francois Truffaut (1968) *Hitchcock*. London: Panther, 157–8.

CHAPTER SIX

1   Romero commented that his production team wanted the colour in *Martin* to be 'seedier', resulting in little difference existing between certain scenes set in Braddock and Martin's black-and-white fantasy visions: 'In fact, we had to push the black-and-white sequences further to make them grainier and grittier than the colour ones.' See Yakir 1977: 64.

2   See R. D. Laing (1965) *The Divided Self*. London: Pelican; Laing (1967) *The Politics of Experience and The Bird of Paradise*. London: Pelican; Laing (1971) *Self and Others*. London: Pelican; R. D. Laing and Aaron Esterson (1964) *Sanity, Madness and the Family*. London: Heinemann; Aaron Esterson (1972) *The Leaves of Spring: Schizophrenia, Family and Sacrifice*. London: Pelican; and David Cooper (1971) *The Death of the Family*. London: Penguin.

3   Martin may also be retreating from recognising the full implications of his family situation similar to Daniel Schreber's disavowal of his father's sadistic educational practices by ascribing them to supernatural forces. See here Morton Schatzman (1976) *Soul Murder: Persecution in the Family*. London: Penguin, 81–92. For a defence of the continuing relevance of Laing's work see Tony Williams (1996) *Hearths of Darkness: The Family in the American Horror Film*. Madison, NJ: Fairleigh Dickinson University Press, 283, n.9.

4   Lippe (1979) 'The Horror of Martin', in Robin Wood and Richard Lippe (eds) *American Nightmare: Essays on the Horror Film*. Toronto: Festival of Festivals, p. 90.

CHAPTER SEVEN

1   See Dieter Meindl (1996) *American Fiction and the Metaphysics of the Grotesque*. Columbia: University of Missouri Press, 5: 'The grotesque is thus seen as representing the fragmented American psyche.'

2   See Meindl 1996: 12 for his recognition of grotesque representations in Ellis' novel which he regards as a 'satire of the yuppie mentality'. For confirmation of this feature see the informative interview with director Mary Harron of the 2000 film version: 'The book just had a real sociological analysis that I've never seen anywhere else.' See Emma Forrest (2000) 'Laugh till you die', *The Daily Telegraph*, 1 April.

3   See Brett Easton Ellis (1991) *American Psycho*. New York: Vintage, 308–9. Ellis concludes the description in an appropriate manner listing naturalist-influenced forms of description as well as denying the relationship of the animals to his own perverted sense of values: 'while I sit in the kitchen thinking of ways to torture girls with this animal (unsurprisingly I come up with a lot), making a list that includes, unrelated to the rat, cutting open both breasts and deflating them, along with stringing barbed wire tightly around their heads'. The latter imagery may come from Bateman's forgotten viewing of *Elsa – She-Wolf of the SS*, one of the many videos he has looked at. For a significant examination of *American Psycho*'s relationship to popular horror and Gothic narratives see Philip L. Simpson, *Beyond All Boundaries: Postmodern Narratives of Multiple Murder*, Doctoral Dissertation: Department of English, Southern Illinois University at Carbondale, 125–38. He also quotes Ellis, who states that '*American Psycho* is partly about excess', particularly the capitalist excesses of the Reagan era. Ellis has stated that the novel is not 'a book about violence' but rather 'a satire of American consumerism'. See Tim Lott (1998) 'The Brat Trap', *The Daily Telegraph*, 11 July.

4   See Meindl 1996: 15, where he points out that although 'the grotesque is usually conceived as subverting the natural order ... it can also serve to evoke the nonrational dimension of life as such, a dimension that, in principle, is both alluring and sinister, benign and devouring, and that defines itself against ideas of pattern and order'. He quotes from Wolfgang Kayser's *The Grotesque in Art*

and Literature. Trans. Ulrich Weistein. Gloucester, Mass.: Peter Smith 1968: 37 who emphasises the horror-provoking potential of the grotesque: 'The grotesque world is – and is not – our own world. The ambiguous way in which we are affected by it results from our awareness that the familiar and apparently harmonious world is alienated under the impact of abysmal forces, which break it up and shatter its coherence.' For Mann's comment and its relationship to Edgar Allan Poe's role as a writer of grotesque fiction functioning as 'the archetype of the antibourgeois artist', see Meindl 1996: 26.

5   See also 1996: 79–84 for Meindl's analysis of a figure who is both physically and psychologically associated with death.

6   After commenting upon the use of grotesque imagery in Mark Twain's *The Adventures of Huckleberry Finn* Meindl makes the following important observation, one relevant to both Romero's films and the EC comic tradition he draws upon: 'The grotesque is thus made to serve satire, which relates it to realism. Nineteenth-century realism, which reacted against and superseded romanticism, encouraged a shift of emphasis from concern with the psyche and the past to an orientation toward society and the present. Satire, which utilizes mocking distortion, is not, strictly speaking, realistic but tends rather to ally itself with realism as a society-oriented referential literary mode. In enrolling the services of the grotesque for demonstrating derision and disgust, satire assimilates the grotesque and links it up with realistic ends' (106). See also where Meindl cites the significant interactions between the realist form of narration used by Charlotte Perkins Gilman in 'The Yellow Wallpaper' (106–8) and the grotesque leading towards the following important insight: 'Naturalism is a literary movement on the periphery of realism' (109). See also Robin Wood, *The American Nightmare*, 93; and *Hitchcock's Films Revisited*. New York: Columbia University Press, 1989, 292: 'One of the greatest obstacles to any fruitful theory of genre has been the tendency to treat the genres as discrete ... at best, they represent different strategies for dealing with the same ideological tensions.' This is certainly so where circumstances allow for the creative interaction of authorship and the appropriate cultural and industrial circumstances for its realisation.

7   Meindl 1996: 111–15, 142–5. Meindl also refers to Allbee in Saul Bellow's *The Victim* (New York: New American Library, 1965) as another one of American fiction's 'grotesque death-in-life figures' (177).

8   She makes an astute parallel between capitalism and human slavery here which relates both to Romero's films and contemporary society: 'The reverse side of the dream of democratic luxury shows a mechanical parody of equality, with the individual becoming simply a numerical unit, quantitatively identical to every other worker' (76). The zombies, of course, are quantitative forces.

9   Zola's novel certainly represents consumerism as a form of living dead existence: 'For this section of his enterprise Mouret creates a Darwinian world without illusions, where the big beasts eat the little ones and fraternization is discouraged ... Whereas the image of the store as a "dream palace" relies on its seductive projection of a commodified sexuality, the equally mediated, non-natural jungle behind the counter subsists in the loss of the sexual and social identities current in the world outside.' See Bowlby 1985: 77.

10 Naomi Schor (1978) *Zola's Crowds*. Baltimore: Johns Hopkins University Press, 13–15. She also comments perceptively elsewhere about the dead dominating the living within Zola's fiction due to his belief in animism: 'One of the obvious consequences of this belief is that the dead never really die; they are always with us, about us. Hence the prominent role played by the dead in Zola's fiction: the dead buried in the Aire Saint-Mittre, those "invisible beings" ("etres invisibles") who urge Miette and Silvère to consume their passion ... the dead women whose spectres haunt *La Faute de l'abbé Mouret*, *Le Ventre du Paris*, *Au bonheur des dames*, *Le Rêve* and *Le Docteur Pascal*; the dead men whose cadavers, real or hallucinated, insistently return to separate the lovers in *Thérèse Raquin* and *Germinal*. The invisible crowd of the dead is one of the most active in Zola' (120).

11 For Zola's understanding of the family as the prime mediating group situated between the individual and society see Schor 1978: 136–9.

12 Despite the supposed spirituality of this group, they are also contaminated by consumer practices as anyone encountering their various cunning methods of begging for money will understand. Is this another of Romero's ironic touches? What is the Hare Krishna disciple doing in the mall in the first place?

13 Peter's decision to survive may also reflect Romero's appropriation of Howard Hawks' attitude towards suicide. See Tod McCarthy (1997) *Howard Hawks: The Grey Fox of Hollywood*. New York: Grove Press, 223, where he comments that Hawks regarded suicide 'as the coward's way out of problems, and a simplistic and dramatically expedient way to conclude complicated, high pressure scenarios'. *Dawn of the Dead*'s ending certainly benefits from this as opposed to the original climax contained in screenplay

and novelisation.

14 Sigmund Freud (1984) 'Instincts and Their Vicissitudes', in *On Metapsychology: The Theory of Psychoanalysis. The Pelican Freud Library Volume 11.* London: Penguin, 126.

15 Freud 1984: 130; see also 131–8.

16 This scene is missing from the Dario Argento European cut of *Dawn of the Dead* along with other important scenes such as Fran's realisation of how the mall affects human relationship after the quarrel over the television set. Argento's cut relinquishes Romero's significant use of music library tracks to provide more Goblin soundtrack music, thus making the European version of *Dawn of the Dead* little better than a spectacle of gratuitous violence.

CHAPTER EIGHT

1 See, for example, Pauline Kael (1981) '*Knightriders*', *New Yorker*, 18 May, 147–51; Michael Sragow (1981) '*Knightriders*', *Rolling Stone*, 344, 28 May, 52. For other opinions see Paul R. Gagne 1987: 117–19.

2 See Michael Anderegg (1999) *Orson Welles, Shakespeare, and Popular Culture.* New York: Columbia University Press, 63. See also p. 177 n.15 for his relevant quotation from Adorno's essay 'The Schema of Mass Culture': 'Certainly every finished work of art is already predetermined in some way but art strives to overcome its own oppressive weight as an artefact through the force of its very construction. Mass culture on the other hand simply identifies with the curse of predetermination and joyfully fulfils it.' The present status of contemporary Hollywood cinema certainly demands a re-evaluation of the much maligned Frankfort School despite the previous euphoric celebrations of certain cultural studies critics.

3 Arguing against critical interpretations viewing *Chimes at Midnight* as a lament for the death of Merrie England, Anderegg notes the melancholy nature of the film: 'The several references to the youthful activities of Falstaff and Shallow cannot be taken at face value, and they do not, in any case, add up to anything that might be described as a medieval paradise' (1999: 125). This is also true of the inner and outer worlds depicted in *Knightriders*.

4 Romero also refers to the fact that 'the underbelly in all my movies is the longing for a better world, for a higher plane of existence, for people to get together. I'm still singing these songs.' See Dan Yakir (1981) 'Knight after Knight with George Romero', *American Film*, 6, 43.

5 See Jean Douchet (1996) '*Hatari!*', in Jim Hillier and Peter Wollen (eds) *Howard Hawks: American Artist.* London: British Film Institute, 82, who sees Hawks' film as one 'that bears an extraordinary resemblance to the shooting of a film (with the communal life of its crew, its plan for the next day's work improvised every evening, its idle periods and bursts of effort), perhaps even to a cineaste's life'. For Barry K. Grant, *Knightriders* 'is an unabashed homage to the Hawksian code of professionalism'. See 'Taking Back the *Night of the Living Dead*: George Romero, Feminism, and the Horror Film', in Barry K. Grant (ed.) (1996) *The Dread of Difference: Gender and the Horror Film.* Austin: University of Texas Press, 204.

6 Ed Sikov (1981) '*Knightriders*', *Cineaste*, 11, 3, 33.

7 For the circumstances leading to *Knightriders* see Gagne 1987: 103.

8 See Gagne 1987: 65, where Rubinstein comments about his ruthlessness in slashing the staff and overhead back to a manageable level. Romero was generously attempting to keep as many people with him as possible despite the economic problems involved.

9 Pauline Kael, '*Knightriders*', *New Yorker*, 57, 18 May, 148.

10 See John Hanners and Harry Kloman (1982) '"The McDonaldization of America": An Interview with George A. Romero', *Film Criticism*, 6, 1, 69–81.

CHAPTER NINE

1 See Michael Sragow (1982) 'Stephen King's "*Creepshow*": The Aesthetics of Gross-Out', *Rolling Stone*, 383, 25 November, 48.

2 See Robert M. Stewart (1980) 'George Romero: Spawn of EC', *Monthly Film Bulletin*, 47, 553, 40; Gagne 1987: 124.

3 See Ron Hansen (1982) '*Creepshow*: The Dawn of a Living Horror Comedy', *Esquire*, 97, 76.

4 Sragow emphasises the 'gross-out' effect in *Creepshow* episodes such as 'Father's Day', 'The Crate' and 'They're Creeping Up On You', following King's comments concerning EC's 'gag reflex of revulsion'. He begins his article by noting King's other qualities as a writer: 'Despite King's plodding prose and facile characters, he's managed to concoct plots multilayered enough to sustain the length, and sometimes the scrutiny, a feature film demands. At his best, he puts everyone in touch with the nightmare anxieties of youth' (1982: 48).

5 Tom Milne (1982) '*Creepshow*', *Monthly Film Bulletin*, 49, 261.

6 Hansen quotes King as follows: 'The comic book form allowed us to pare the motivations and characterizations down to a bare minimum and let us just go for scares' (1982: 73).

7 For the role of exaggerated performance style in cinema and the Delsarte influence see James Naremore (1988) *Acting in the Cinema*. Berkeley: University of California Press, 34–67.

8 Despite Romero's stated lack of interest in Hitchcock's films, several works, such as *Night of the Living Dead*, certainly reveal traces of influences such as *The Birds*, as Wood has noted (1986: 115). Although Romero's references in *Creepshow* are more jocular, like his citation of 'Amberson Hall' in 'The Crate', they are not entirely 'extraneous' to the narratives, as Tom Milne believes. See Milne (1982) '*Creepshow*', *Monthly Film Bulletin*, 49, 261. They represent the tongue-in-cheek comedic attitudes displayed by both Hitchcock and Welles in their public appearances, when they gave 'performances' which were designed to mislead spectators as to the real nature of both their lives and art. In 'Something To Tide You Over', the name of Gaylen Ross' character consciously evokes the name of the title character in Hitchcock's *Rebecca* (1941). Like her namesake, she returns from a watery grave to avenge herself on an authoritarian husband.

9 Again, Romero may not be entirely making an in-joke reference to a film by his favourite director. *The Magnificent Ambersons* (1942) deals with a once noble institution facing terminal decline. The same is true of Horlicks University if the activities of two of its prominent faculty are anything to go by.

10 According to Gagne (1987: 138), Romero came up with the idea of making Pratt resemble Howard Hughes.

11 Although Gagne (1987: 147) states the music is sweet jazz from the 1930s era, it is more reminiscent of the previous decade.

CHAPTER TEN

1 Gagne also points out that 'Anubis' was inspired by Richard Matheson's *I Am Legend*, which dealt with the last surviving human in a world taken over by zombie-like vampires.

2 Gagne's synopsis of the original version in his book derives from the second draft, which ran 104 pages as opposed to the original length of 204.

3 See Robin Wood (1985) '80s Hollywood: Dominant Tendencies', *cineACTION!*, 1, 2–5; Andrew Britton (1986) 'Blissing Out: The Politics of Reaganite Entertainment', *Movie*, 31, 31, 1–42.

4 Personal conversation during The Society for Cinema Studies Conference at Pittsburgh, 1 May 1992.

5 Such associations appear in the short documentary following the recently released letterbox version of *Day of the Dead*. When interviewed on screen preparing for his role as Captain Rhodes, Joe Pilato jokes about being the 'good guy' because of the Reagan era's ideological re-evaluation of the military before taking a more serious perspective.

6 See Ethel Spector Person (1980) 'Sexuality as a Mainstay of Identity', *Signs*, 5.4, 527.

CHAPTER ELEVEN

1 According to Kim Newman, Romero was interested in adapting *Mummy's Boys* by British writer Bernard Taylor during this period. See Newman (1990) '*Monkey Shines*', *Monthly Film Bulletin*, 57, 673, 46.

2 For this relationship to Godard's films such as *Weekend*, see Brian Henderson (1970/71) 'Towards a Non-Bourgeois Camera Style', *Film Quarterly*, 24, 2, 2–14.

CHAPTER TWELVE

1 See Kim Newman (1993) '*The Dark Half*', *Sight and Sound*, 3, 11, 40.

2   Andrew Britton (1979) 'The Devil Probably: The Symbolism of Evil', in Robin Wood and Richard Lippe (eds) *The American Nightmare: Essays on the Horror Film*. Toronto: Festival of Festivals, 39, 41.

3   For the complex issues surrounding any definition of *film noir* see, for example, Ginette Vincendeau (1993) 'Noir is Also a French Word: The French Antecedents of Film Noir', in Ian Cameron (ed.) *The Movie Book of Film Noir*. New York: Continuum, 49–58, and the special issue of *Iris* edited by Janice Morgan and Dudley Andrew, 'European Precursors of Film Noir', *Iris*, 21, 1996.

4   The character's surname may refer to Romero's favourite Powell and Pressburger film, *The Tales of Hoffmann* (1951), the title character of which is played by Robert Rounseville.

5   Before the climax Liz reveals her fears about Thad to Pangborn and during the novel's epilogue, Pangborn's thoughts express his rebuttal of Thad's presumed understanding of past events. See Stephen King (1989) *The Dark Half.* New York: Viking, 405, 428.

6   Newman (1993) notes that 'in tidying up King's confusion about where Stark comes from, the film version tends to exonerate Thad by making the villain an "other" rather than a manifestation of the writer's unhealthy impulses'. Liz does articulate this knowledge in the film when she speaks about Thad's continuing awful moods. Thad does affirm this when he replies, 'Even the ugliness is part of me.' But, except for a few isolated instances, the film falls into predictable generic patterns.

7   See Tania Modleski (1988) *The Women Who Knew Too Much: Hitchcock and Feminist Theory*. New York, Macmillan. Again, the sparrows of *The Dark Half* evoke *The Birds* in terms of their external representation of the psychological battle within Thad's own mind.

CONCLUSION

1   Theodor Adorno (1984) 'Loss of Certainty', in Gretel Adorno and Rolf Tiedemann (eds) *Aesthetic Theory*. Trans. C. Lenhardt. London: Routledge & Kegan Paul, 2–3.

2   See also the various *amazon.com* reviews of the film as well as the 'Bruiser' website available on http://www.bruiserthemovie.com.

3   See here Sumiko Higashi (1994) *Cecil B. DeMille and American Culture: The Silent Era*. Berkeley: University of California Press, 89–92, 104. This is a highly significant work relating Zola's studies of commodification and spectacle in works such as *Au Bonheur des Dames* to the post-World War One films of DeMille.

4   'The Amusement Park', *Cinema Spectrum*, Manchester, 1 (1980): 47. I wish to acknowledge the kind permission of its editor, the late Harry Nadler (well-known for his work in organising The Manchester Festival of Fantastic Films), to quote from an article written for this short-lived publication.

5   'What Lies Beneath?' *Senses of Cinema* 15, July-August 2001: http://www.sensesofcinema.com, 4. This article is the preface to Steven Jay Schneider (ed.) (2003) *Freud's Worst Nightmares*. New York: Cambridge University Press.

6   Reynold Humphries, (2002) *The American Horror Film: An Introduction*. Edinburgh: Edinburgh University Press, 113–18.

7   Julia Hallam and Margaret Marshment, (2000) *Realism and Popular Cinema*. Manchester: Manchester University Press, xvi.

8   Both Andrew Britton and Raymond Williams deserve full credit for warning against this movement from its very beginning. Unfortunately, their voices were ignored – at the time. See Andrew Britton (1986) 'The Myth of Postmodernism: The Bourgeois Intelligentsia in the Age of Reagan,' *cineACTION!* 13/14, 3–17; Raymond Williams (1989) *The Politics of Modernism: Against the New Conformists*. London: Verso.

9   See, for example, Steven Jay Schneider (ed.) (2002a) 'Realist Horror Cinema, Part 1', *Postscript* 21.3; Schneider (2002b) '"I guess I'm a pretty sick guy": Reconciling Remorse in *Thérèse Raquin* and *American Psycho*', *Excavatio* 17.1–2: 421–2.

APPENDIX

1   See Nigel Floyd (1988) '*Creepshow 2*', *Monthly Film Bulletin*, 55, 648, 14.

2   Kim Newman (1993) '*Night of the Living Dead*', *Sight and Sound*, 3, 4, 52.

3   For the distribution and financial problems affecting the original version see Gagne 1987: 38–9.

4   See Robin Wood (1997), updated by Rob Edelman, 'George A. Romero', *International Directory of Films and Filmmakers 2. Directors.* Third Edition. Detroit: St. James Press, 839.

5   George A. Romero and Susanna Sparrow (1980) Afterword to *Martin.* New York: Day Books, 210.

6   See Linda Williams, (1996) 'When the Woman Looks', *The Dread of Difference.* Austin: University of Texas Press, 15–34.

FILMOGRAPHY

This filmography only lists the major contributions made to each film. A detailed and meticulous list of credits will be found in Paul R. Gagne's *The Zombies That Ate Pittsburgh: The Films of George A. Romero*.

Night of the Living Dead, 1968

Director: George A. Romero
Producers: Russell Streiner and Karl Hardman
Screenplay: George A. Romero and John A. Russo
Director of Photography: George A. Romero
Film Editor: George A. Romero
Make-up: Hardman Associates, Inc.
Special Effects: Regis Survinski and Tony Pantanello
Music: Stock music from the Capitol Hi-Q music library with additional electronic effects by Karl Hardman
Production Company: The Latent Image, Inc. and Hardman Associates, Inc., Pittsburgh
Distributor: Almi Films
Length: 96 minutes
Cast: Duane Jones (Ben), Judith O'Dea (Barbara), Karl Hardman (Harry Cooper), Russell Streiner (Johnny), Marilyn Eastman (Helen Cooper), Keith Wayne (Tom), Judith Ridley (Judy), Kyra Schon (Karen Cooper), Charles Craig (newscaster), Bill Hinzman (cemetary zombie), George Kosana (Sheriff McClelland), Frank Doak (scientist), Bill 'Chilly Billy' Cardille (field reporter), Vince Survinski (posse gunman), John A. Russo (zombie in house/military aide in Washington, D.C.), George A. Romero (reporter questioning military officials in Washington, D.C.)

There's Always Vanilla (The Affair), 1972

Director: George A. Romero
Producers: Russell W. Streiner and John A. Russo
Assistant Producer: Cramer Riblet
Screenplay: Rudolph J. Ricci
Director of Photography: George A. Romero
Editor: George A. Romero
Make-up: Bonnie Priore
Sound: Gary Streiner

Production Manager: Vince Survinski
Music: Rock music performed by Barefoot in Athens with electronic music by Steve Gorn and additional music by Mikw Marracino orchestrated by Jim Drake
Production Company: The Latent Image
Distributor: Cambist Films
Length: 91 mins
Cast: Ray Laine (Chris), Judith Streiner (Lynn), Johanna Lawrence (Terri), Richard Ricci (Michael), Roger McGovern (Chris's father), Ron Jaye, Bob Wilson, Louise Sahene, Christopher Priore, Robert Trow, Vince Survinski

Jack's Wife (*Hungry Wives; Season of the Witch*), 1973

Director: George A. Romero
Producer: Nancy M. Romero
Executive Producer: Alvin Croft
Screenplay: George A. Romero
Director of Photography: George A. Romero
Editor: George A. Romero
Make-up: Bonnie Priore
Special Effects: Regis Survinski
Production Supervisor: Vince Survinski
Lighting and Additional Photography: Bill Hinzman
Music: Original electronic music by Steve Gorn
Production Company: The Latent Image
Distributor: Jack Harris
Length: 89 mins
Cast: Jan White (Joan), Ray Laine (Gregg), Anne Muffly (Shirley), Joedda McClain (Nikki), Bill Thunhurst (Jack), Esther Lapidus (Sylvia), Virginia Greenwald (Marion), Don Mallinger, Dartl Montogomery, Ken Peters, Bob Trow, Bill Hinzman, George A. Romero ('ass grabber' at party)

The Crazies (*Code Name: Trixie*), 1973

Director: George A. Romero
Producer: Alvin Croft
Screenplay: George A. Romero based on an original script by Paul McCollough
Director of Photography: Bill Hinzman
Editor: George A. Romero
Make-up: Bonnie Priore
Special Effects: Regis Survinski and Tony Pantanello
Production Managers: Bob Rutkowski, H. Cramer Riblett, Vince Survinski
Sound: Rex Gleason, John Stoll, Eric Baca, Michael Gornick
Music: Bruce Roberts
Production Company: A Pittsburgh Films Production (through Latent Image)
Distributor: Cambist Films
Length: 103 mins
Cast: Lane Carroll (Judy), W. G. McMillan (David), Harold Wayne Jones (Clank), Lloyd Hollar (Col. Peckham), Lynn Lowry (Kathy), Richard Liberty (Artie), Richard France (Dr. Watts), Harry Spillman (Major Ryder), Will Disney (Dr. Brookmyre), Edith Bell (Lab Technician), W. L. Thunhurst, Jr (Brubaker), Leland Starkes (Shelby), Bill Hinzman, Vince Survinski

Martin, 1978

Director: George A. Romero
Producer: Richard P. Rubinstein

Screenplay: George A. Romero
Director of Photography: George A. Romero
Editor: George A. Romero
Special Effects and Make-up: Tom Savini
Sound: Tony Buba
Music: Donald Rubinstein
Production Company: Laurel Entertainment
Distributor: Libra Films
Length: 95 mins
Cast: John Amplas (Martin), Lincoln Maazel (Tata Cuda), Christine Forrest (Christina), Elyane Nadeau (Mrs. Santini), Tom Savini (Arthur), Sarah Venable (housewife victim), Fran Middleton (train victim), Al Levitsky (Lewis), George A. Romero (Father Howard), James Roy (deacon), Richard Rubinstein (housewife victim's husband), Albert J. Schmaus, Lilian Schmaus, and Frances Mazzoni (family), Vince Survinski (train porter), Tony Buba, Pasquale Buba and Clayton McKinnon (drug dealers), Regis Survinski and Tony Pantonello (hobos), Harvey Eger and Tom Weber (men in bathroom), Robert Barner and Stephen Fergelic (police)

Dawn of the Dead, 1979

Director: George A. Romero
Producer: Richard P. Rubinstein
Executive Producers: Claudio Argento and Alfredo Cuomo
Screenplay: George A. Romero
Director of Photography: Michael Gornick
Editor: George A. Romero
Script Consultant: Dario Argento
Special Effects and Make-up: Tom Savini
Sound: Tony Buba
Music: The Goblins with Dario Argento; stock library music for American version
Assistant Producer: Donna Siegel
Assistant Director: Christine Forrest
Production Company: Laurel Entertainment
Distributor: United Film Distribution
Length: 126 mins
Cast: David Emge (Stephen), Ken Foree (Peter), Scott Reiniger (Roger), Gaylen Ross (Fran), David Crawford (Dr. Foster), David Early (Mr. Berman), Richard France (scientist), Howard Smith (TV commentator), Daniel Dietrich (Givens), Fred Baker (Commander), Jim Baffico (Wooley), Rod Stouffer (young officer on roof), Jese Del Gre (old priest), Clayton McKinnon and John Rice (officers in project apartment), Ted Bank, Patrick McCloseky, Randy Kovitz, and Joe Pilato (officers at police dock), Pasquale Buba, Tony Buba, 'Butchie', Dave Hawkins, Tom Kapusta, Rudy Ricci, Tom Savini, Marty Schiff, Joe Shelby, Taso Stavrakos, Nick Tallo, and Larry Vaira (motorcycle raiders), Sharon Ceccatti, Pam Chatfield, Jim Christopher, Clayton Hill, Jay Stover (lead zombies), John Harrison (zombie janitor), George A. Romero (TV studio director), Christine Forrest (assistant TV studio director)

Knightriders, 1981

Director: George A. Romero
Producer: Richard P. Rubinstein
Executive Producer: Salah M. Hassanein
Screenplay: George A. Romero
Director of Photography: Michael Gornick
Editors: George A. Romero and Pasquale Buba
Sound: John Butler
Music: Donald Rubinstein

Production Company: Laurel Entertainment
Length: 145 mins
Cast: Ed Harris (Billy Davis), Gary Lahti (Alan), Tom Savini (Morgan), Amy Ingersol (Linet), Patricia Tallman (Julie), Christine Forrest (Angie), Warner Shook (Pippin), Brother Blue (Merlin), Cynthia Adler (Rockie), John Amplas (Whiteface), Don Berry (Bagman), Amanda Davies (Sheila), Martin Ferrero (Bontempi), Ken Foree (Little John), Ken Hixon (Steve), John Hostetter (Tuck), Harold Wayne Jones (Bors), Randy Kovitz (Punch), Michael Moran (Sheriff Cook), Scott Reiniger (Marhalt), Maureen Sadusk (Judy Rawls), Albert Amerson (Indian), Ronald Carrier (Hector), Tim DiLeo (Corncook), David Early (Bleoboris), John Harrison (Pellinore), Marty Schiff (Ban), Taso N. Stavrakis (Ewain), Robert Williams (Kay), Molly McCloskey (Corncook's woman), Judy Barrett, Ian Gallacher, Donald Rubinstein (musician trio), Stephen King (hoagie man), Tabitha King (hoagie man's wife)

Creepshow, 1982

Director: George A. Romero
Producer: Richard P. Rubinstein
Executive Producer: Salah M. Hassenein
Screenplay: Stephen King
Director of Photography: Michael Gornick
Editors: Pasquale Buba ('The Lonesome Death of Jordy Verrill'), Paul Hirsch ('The Crate'), George A. Romero (Prologue, Epilogue, 'Something to Tide You Over'), Michael Spolan ('Father's Day', 'They're Creeping Up On You')
Special Effects Make-up: Tom Savini
Production Design Special Effects: Cletus Anderson
Production Sound Services: Ledol, Inc.
Music: John Harrison with additional stock library music
Assistant Director: Christine Forrest
First Assistant Director: John Harrison
Production Company: Laurel Entertainment
Distributor: Warner Bros.
Length: 122 mins
Cast: Prologue/Epilogue: Tom Atkins (Billy's father), Iva Jean Saraceni (Billy's mother), Joe King (Billy), Marty Schiff (first garbageman), Tom Savini (second garbageman)
'Father's Day': Carrie Nye (Sylvia Grantham), Viveca Lindfors (Aunt Bedelia), Ed Harris (Hank Blaine), Warner Schook (Richard Grantham), Elizabeth Regan (Cass Blaine), Jon Lormer (Nathan Grantham), John Amplas (Dead Nate), Nann Mogg (Mrs. Danvers), Peter Messer (Yarbro)
'The Lonesome Death of Jordy Verill': Stephen King (Jordy Verrill), Bingo O'Malley (Jordy's Dad, bank loan officer, Department of Meteors head doctor)
'Something to Tide You Over': Leslie Nielsen (Richard Vickers), Ted Danson (Harry Wentworth), Gaylen Ross (Becky Vickers)
'The Crate': Hal Holbrook (Henry Northrup), Adrienne Barbeau (Wilma 'Billie' Northrup), Fritz Weaver (Dexter Stanley), Robert Harper (Charlie Gereson), Don Keefer (Mike the janitor), Christine Forrest (Tabitha Raymond), Chuck Aber (Richard Raymond), Cletus Anderson (Host), Kathie Karlovitz (Maid), Darryl Ferruci ('Fluffy')
'They're Creeping Up On You': E. G. Marshall (Upson Pratt), David Early (White)

Day of the Dead, 1985

Director: George A. Romero
Producer: Richard P. Rubinstein
Executive Producer: Salah M. Hassanein
Screenplay: George A. Romero
Director of Photography: Michael Gornick
Editor: Pasquale Buba

Special Effects Make-up: Tom Savini
Art Director: Bruce Miller
Music: John Harrison
First Assistant Director: John Harrison
Production Company: Laurel Entertainment
Distributor: United Film Distribution
Length: 102 mins
Cast: Lori Cardille (Sarah), Terry Alexander (John), Joseph Pilato (Captain Rhodes), Richard Liberty (Dr. Logan), Howard Sherman (Bub), Jarlath Conroy (McDermott), Antone DiLeo (Miguel), G. Howrd Klar (Steele), Ralph Marrero (Rickles), John Amplas (Fisher), Philip G. Kellams (Torrez), Taso N. Stavrakis (Miller), Gregory Nicotero (Johnson)

Tales from the Darkside, 1985–86

'Trick or Treat' (series pilot shot in 1983)
Director: Bob Balaban
Teleplay: George A. Romero
'The Devil's Advocate'
Director: Michael Gornick
Teleplay: George A. Romero
'Baker's Dozen'
Director: John Sutherland
Teleplay: George A. Romero from a story by Scott Edelman
'Circus'
Director: Michael Gornick
Teleplay: George A. Romero from a story by Sidney J. Bounds

Creepshow 2, 1987

Director: Michael Gornick
Screenplay: George A. Romero

Monkey Shines, 1988

Director: George A. Romero
Producer: Charles Evans
Screenplay: George A. Romero based on the novel by Michael Stewart
Director of Photography: James A. Contner
Editor: Pasquale Buba
Music: David Shire
Peoduction Designer: Cletus Anderson
Distributor: Orion
Length: 113 mins
Cast: Jason Beghe (Allan Mann), John Pankow (Geoffrey Fisher), Kate McNeil (Melanie Parker), Joyce Van Patten (Dorothy Mann), Christine Forrest (Maryanne Hodges), Stephen Root (Dean Burbage), Stanley Tucci (Dr. John Wiseman), Janine Turner (Linda Aikman), William Newman (Doc Williams), Tudi Wiggins (Esther Fry), Tom Quinn (Charlie Cunningham), Chuck Baker (ambulance driver), Patricia Tallman (party guest)

Two Evil Eyes, 1988

Directors: George A. Romero and Dario Argento
Screenplay: George A. Romero, Dario Argento and Franco Ferrini
Cast: Adrienne Barbour (Jessica Valdemar), Ramy Zada (Dr. Robert Hoffman), E. G. Marshall (Pike),

Bingo O'Malley (Ernest Valdemar), Nurse (Christine Forrest), Police Officer (Tom Atkins).

Tales from the Darkside: The Movie, 1990

Screenplay: 'Cat from Hell' episode
Director: John Harrison

Night of the Living Dead, 1990

Director: Tom Savini
Producers: John A. Russo and Russ Streiner
Executive Producers: Menahem Golan and George A. Romero
Screenplay: George A. Romero based on the original screenplay of *Night of the Living Dead* by John A. Russo and George A. Romero
Director of Photography: Frank Prinzi
Music: Paul McCollough
Production Company: 21st Century Film Corporation
Distribution: Columbia
Length: 96 mins
Cast: Tony Todd (Ben), Patricia Tallman (Barbara), Tom Towles (Harry), McKee Anderson (Helen), William Butler (Tom), Kate Finneran (Judy Rose), Bill Mosley (Johnny), Heather Mazur (Sarah), Bill 'Chilly Billy' Cardone (TV Interviewer)

The Dark Half, 1993

Director: George A. Romero
Producer: Declan Baldwin
Executive Producer: George A. Romero
Screenplay: George A. Romero based on the novel by Stephen King
Director of Photography: Tony Pierce Roberts
Editor: Pasquale Buba
Music: Christopher Young
Production Designer: Cletus Anderson
Production Company and Distribution: Orion
Length: 122 mins
Cast: Timothy Hutton (Thad Beaumont/George Stark), Amy Madigan (Liz Beaumont), Michael Rooker Alan Pangborn), Julie Harris (Reggie Delesseps), Robert Joy (Fred Clawson), Kent Boradhurt (Mike Donaldson), Beth Grant (Shayla Beaumont), Rytanya Alda (Miriam Cowley), Patrick Brannan (Young Thad Beaumont), Larry John Meyers (Doc Pritchard), Christina Romero (Little Girl), Rohn Thomas (Dr. Alberston), Judy Grafe (Head Nurse), John Machione (Male Nurse), Erik Jensen (Male Student), Tom Mardirosian (Rick Cowley), Glenn Colerider (Homer Gamache), Christine Forrest (Trudi Wiggins), Royal Dano (Digger Holt), Chelsea Field (Anna Pangborn), Sarah Parker (Wendy Beaumont), Elizabeth Parker (William Beaumont)

Bruiser, 2000

Director: George A. Romero
Screenplay: George A. Romero
Cast: Jason Flemying (Henry Creedlow), Leslie Hope (Rosemary Newley), Peter Stormare (Miles Styles), Nina Garbiras (Janine Creedlow), Andrew Tarbet (James Larson), Tom Atkins (Detective McCleary), Jonathan Higgins (Detective Rakowski), Jeff Monahan (Tom Burtram), Marie V. Cruz (Number 9)

BIBLIOGRAPHY

Allen, Tom (1979) 'Knight of the Living Dead', *Village Voice*, 24, 23 April, 44–6.

Anderegg, Michael (1999) *Orson Welles, Shakespeare and Popular Culture*. New York: Columbia University Press.

Bartholemew, David (1978) 'Dawn of the Dead', *Cinéfantastique*, 8, 1, 32.

_____ (1978) 'Martin', *Cinéfantastique*, 8, 1, 16–17.

Beard, Steve (1993) 'No Particular Place to Go', *Sight and Sound*, 3, 4, 30–1.

Blake, Linnie (2002) 'Another One for the Fire: George A. Romero's American Theology of the Flesh', in Xavier Mendik (ed.) *Shocking Cinema of the Seventies*. Hereford, UK: Noir Publishing.

Blanch, Robert J. (1991) 'George Romero's *Knightriders*: A Contemporary Arthurian Romance', *Quondam et Futurus: A Journal of Arthurian Interpretations*, 1, 4, 61–9.

Block, Alex B. (1972) 'Filming *Night of the Living Dead*', *Filmmakers Newsletter*, 5, 3, January, 16–17.

Bowlby, Rachel (1985) *Just Looking: Consumer Culture in Dreiser, Gissing and Zola*. New York: Methuen.

Britton, Andrew (1986) 'Blissing Out: The Politics of Reaganite Entertainment', *Movie*, 31/32, 1–42.

Caputi, Jane (1988) 'Films of the Nuclear Age', *Journal of Popular Film and Television*, 16, 3, 100–7.

Chase, Donald (1979) 'The Cult Movie Comes of Age: An Interview with George A. Romero and Richard P. Rubinstein', *Millimeter*, 7, 10, 200–11.

Chauvin, Jean-Sebastien (2001) 'La trilogie des mortes vivantes', *Cahiers du Cinéma*, 563, 66–8.

Chute, David (1982) 'The Great Frame Robbery', *Film Comment*, 18, 5, 13–17.

Daniels, Les (1971) *Comix: A History of Comic Books in America*. New York: E. P. Dutton.

Davis, Wade (1985) *The Serpent and the Rainbow*. New York: Simon and Schuster.

_____ (1988) *Passage of Darkness: The Ethnobiology of the Haitian Zombie*. Chapel Hill: University of North Carolina Press.

Dillard, R. H. W. (1987) '*Night of the Living Dead*: It's Not Like Just A Wind Passing Through', in Gregory A. Waller (ed.) *American Horrors: Essays on the Modern American Horror Film*. Urbana and Chicago: University of Illinois Press, 14–29.

Dyer, Richard (1997) *White*. London: Routledge.

England Norman (1991) 'George A. Romero'. Available at: http://ww2.gol.com/users/noman/interv1.htm

Fisher, Dennis (1989) 'George Romero vs. Hollywood', *Cinéfantastique*, 19, 36–7.

_____ (1991) *Horror Film Directors, 1931–1990*. Jefferson, North Carolina: McFarland, 635–5.

Flippo, Chet (1978) 'When There's No More Room in Hell, the Dead Will Walk the Earth', *Rolling Stone*, 23 March, 46–9.

Gagne, Paul R. (1987) *The Zombies That Ate Pittsburgh: The Films of George A. Romero*. New York: Dodd, Mead.

Gervasini, Mauro (1998) *Morte in Diretta*. Rome: Edizioni Falsopiano.

Giles James (1989) *Confronting the Horror: The Novels of Nelson Algren*. Ohio: Kent State University Press.

_____ (1995) *The Naturalistic Inner-City Novel in America*. Columbia S.C.: University of South Carolina Press.

Grant, Barry K. (1986) 'Experience and Meaning in Genre Films', *Persistence of Vision*, 3/4, 5–14.

_____ (1992) 'Taking Back the *Night of the Living Dead*: George Romero, Feminism and the Horror Film', *Wide Angle*, 14, 1, 64–76.

Gumpert, Matthew (1993) 'Naturalism as Bakhtinian Grotesque Realism: Mythic Metabolism in Zola and Rabelais', *Excavatio*, 3, 93–8.

Hanners, John and Harry Kloman (1982) '"The McDonaldization of America": An Interview with George A. Romero', *Film Criticism*, 6, 1, 69–81.

Harty, Kevin J. (1991) 'Camelot Twice Removed: Knightriders and the Film Versions of A Connecticut Yankee in King Arthur's Court', in *Cinema Arthuriana: Essays on Arthurian Film*. New York: Garland, 105–20.

Hickenlooper, George (1991) 'George Romero: I Am Legend', in George Hickenlooper (ed.) *Reel Conversations: Candid Conversations with Film's Foremost Directors and Critics*. New York: Citadel, 344–56.

Highashi, Sumiko '*Night of the Living Dead*: A Horror Film About the Horrors of the Vietnam War', in Linda Dittmar and Gene Michaud (eds) *From Hanoi to Hollywood: The Vietnam War in American Film*. New Brunswick, N.J.: Rutgers University Press, 175–88.

_____ (1994) *Cecil B. DeMille and American Culture: The Silent Era*. Berkeley: University of California Press.

Hillier, Jim and Peter Wollen (eds) (1996) *Howard Hawks: American Artist*. London: BFI.

Hoberman, James and Jonathan Rosenbaum (1983) *Midnight Movies*. New York: Harper & Row.

Horne, Philip (1992) 'I Shopped with A Zombie', *Critical Quarterly*, 34, 4, 97–110.

Howard, June (1985) Form and History in American Literary Naturalism. Chapel Hill: University of North Carolina Press.

Inge, M. Thomas (1990) *Comics as Culture*. Jackson, M.I.: University of Mississippi Press.

Kaminsky, Stuart (1975) '*Night of the Living Dead*', *Cinéfantastique*, 4, 1, 20, 23.

Kaplan, Amy (1988) *The Social Construction of American Realism*. Chicago: University of Chicago Press.

Kermode, Mark (1990) 'Twilight's Last Gleaming: George A. Romero', *Monthly Film Bulletin*, February, 56.

Krohn, Bill (2001) 'Itinéraire d'un mouton noir de la contre-culture américaine', *Cahiers du Cinéma*, 563, 70.

Lacy, Norris J. (1989) 'Arthurian Film and The Tyranny of Tradition', *Arthurian Interpretations*, 4, 1, 75–85.

Larcher, Jerome (2001) 'Gare au gore', *Cahiers du Cinéma*, 563, 71.

Larsen, Ernest (1979) 'Hi-Tech Horror', *Jump Cut*, 21, 1, 12, 30.

Lebowitz, Fran, Pat Hackett and Ronnie Cutrone (1973) 'George Romero: From *Night of the Living Dead* to *The Crazies*', *Andy Warhol's Interview*, 3, 30–1, 45.

Leyman, Charles (1993) 'Filming Stephen King's The Dark Half', *Cinéfantastique*, 24, 1, 16–20, 22, 23.

Lippe, Richard (1979) 'The Horror of *Martin*', in Robin Wood and Richard Lippe (eds) *The American Nightmare: Essays on the Horror Film*. Toronto: Festival of Festivals, 87–90.

Lowry, Ed and Louis Black (1979) 'Cinema of Apocalypse', *Take One*, 7, 6, 17–18.

Malausa, Vincent (2001) 'La trilogie du crépuscule', *Cahiers du Cinéma*, 563, 69.

McCollough, Paul (1974) 'A Pittsburgh Horror Story', *Take One*, 4, 6, 8–10.

Meindl, Dieter (1996) *American Fiction and the Metaphysics of the Grotesque*. Columbia: University of Missouri Press.

Michaels, Walter Benn (1987) *The Gold Standard and the Logic of Naturalism: American Literature at the Turn of the Century*. Berkeley: University of California Press.

Milne, Tom (1977–78) 'Communion and Martin', *Sight and Sound*, 47, 1, 55–6.

Mitchell, Lee Clark (1989) *Determined Fictions: American Literary Naturalism*. New York: Columbia University Press.

Nyberg, Amy Kiste (1998) *Seal of Approval: The History of the Comics Code*. Jackson, M.I.: University of Mississippi Press.

Pirie, David (1971) 'New Blood', *Sight and Sound*, 40, 2, 73–5.

Pizer, Donald (ed.) (1995) *The Cambridge Companion to American Realism and Naturalism*. Cambridge: Cambridge University Press.

____ (ed.) (1998) *Documents of American Realism and Naturalism*. Carbondale: Southern Illinois University Press.

Reidelbach, Maria (1991) *Completely Mad: A History of the Comic Book and Magazine*. Boston: Little, Brown.

Romero, George A. with Susanna Sparrow (1977) *Martin*. New York: Stein & Day.

____ (1979) *Dawn of the Dead*. New York: St. Martin's Press.

Rosenbaum, Jonathan (1989) 'Dis moiqui tu manges je te dirai qui tu es', *Cahiers du Cinema* 416 (1989): VI-VII.

Ross, Steven J. (1998) *Working-Class Hollywood: Silent Film and the Shaping of Class in America*. New Jersey: Princeton University Press.

Russo, John (1985) *The Complete Night of the Living Dead Filmbook*. New York: Harmony Books.

Scaperotti, Dan and Paul Gagne (1985) 'Day of the Dead', *Cinéfantastique*, 15, 5, 48–9.

____ (1985) 'Tales from the Darkside', *Cinéfantastique*, 15, 1, 15, 52.

Schor, Naomi (1978) *Zola's Crowds*. Baltimore: The Johns Hopkins University Press.

Scott, Tony (1973) 'Romero: An Interview with the Director of *Night of the Living Dead*', *Cinéfantastique*, 2, 3, 8–15.

Singer, Robert (1997) 'Only the Dead: Urban Mileu in the Contemporary Naturalist Film', *Excavatio*, 9, 194–203.

Seligson, Tom (1981) 'George Romero: Revealing the Monsters Within Us', *Twilight Zone*, August, 12–17.

Shaviro, Steven (1993) *The Cinematic Body*. Minneapolis: University of Minnesota Press.

Spainhower, Mark (1986) 'George Romero', in A. Juno and V. Vale (eds) *Incredibly Strange Films*. San Francisco: Research, 182–5.

Stein, Elliot (1970) '*Night of the Living Dead*', *Sight and Sound*, 39, 2, 105.

Stewart, Michael (1984) *Monkey Shines*. New York: Vintage Books.

Stewart, Robert M. (1980) 'George Romero: Spawn of EC', *Monthly Film Bulletin*, 47, 553, 40.

Strauss, Frederic (1989) 'Les yeux, la bouche', *Cahiers du Cinéma*, 416, 40.

Sundquist, Eric (ed.) (1982) American Realism: New Essays. Baltimore: Johns Hopkins University Press.

Surmacz, Gary Anthony (1975) 'Anatomy of A Horror Film', *Cinéfantastique*, 4, 1, 14–19, 21–2, 24–7.

Szebin, Frederick C. (1988a) 'George Romero: Monkeying with Horror', *Cinéfantastique*, 18, 4, 21, 55.

____ (1988b) 'George Romero's Ella', *Cinéfantastique*, 18, 5, 17, 56.

Taylor, Don (1990) Days of Vision: Working with David Mercer: *Television Drama Then and Now*. London: Methuen.

Vernieri, James (1985) 'A Day with the Dead', *Film Comment*, 21, May–June, 8.

Walcutt, Charles Child (1956) *American Literary Naturalism: A Divided Stream*. Minneapolis: University of Minnesota Press.

Waller, Gregory (1986) *The Living and the Undead: From Stoker's Dracula to Romero's Dawn of the Dead*. Urbana and Chicago: University of Illinois Press.

Wiater, Stanley (1992) 'George A. Romero', in Stanley Wiater (ed.) *Dark Visions: Conversations with Masters of the Horror Film*. New York: Avon, 147–66.

Williams, Raymond (1989) *The Politics of Modernism: Against the New Conformists*. London: Verso.

Williams, Tony (1996) *Hearths of Darkness: The Family in the American Horror Film*. New Jersey: Fairleigh Dickinson University Press.

____ (1997a) *Larry Cohen: Radical Allegories of an American Filmmaker*. Jefferson, North Carolina: McFarland.

____ (1997b) Stephen King, Naturalism, and The Shining', *Excavatio*, 9, 156–65.

____ (2001a) 'Monkey Shines', *cineACTION!*, 53, 30–9.

____ (2001b) 'An Interview with George and Christine Romero', *Quarterly Review of Film and Video*, 18, 4, 397–411.

Witek, Joseph (1989) *Comic Books As History*. Jackson, Mississippi: University of Mississippi Press.

Wood, Robin (1986) *Hollywood From Vietnam to Reagan*. New York: Columbia University Press.

____ (1986) 'The Woman's Nightmare: Masculinity in Day of the Dead', *cineACTION!*, 6, 45–9.

____ (1997) 'George A. Romero', *International Directory of Films and Filmmakers – Directors*. Third Edition. Detroit: St. James's Press, 838–9.

____ (1998) *Sexual Politics and Narrative Cinema*. New York: Columbia University Press.

Yahoo! Chat! (1998) 'George Romero Talks on Yahoo! Chat! Available at: http://geocities.com/Athens/Parthenon/8458/Dead-02.html

Yakir, Dan (1977) 'Morning Becomes Romero', *Film Comment*, 15, 3, 60–5.

____ (1981) 'Knight After Knight with George Romero', *American Film*, 6, 42–5, 69.

INDEX